EMOTIONALLY FOCUSED FAMILY THERAPY

Emotionally Focused Family Therapy is the definitive manual for applying the effectiveness of emotionally focused therapy (EFT) to the complexities of family life.

The book sets out a theoretical framework for mental health professionals to enhance their conceptualization of family dynamics, considering a broad range of presenting problems and family types. The first section applies EFT theory and principles to the practice of family therapy. The second section explicates the process of EFT and examines the interventions associated with the EFT approach to families. In the final section, the authors provide case examples of emotionally focused family therapy (EFFT) practice, with chapters on traumatic loss, stepfamilies, externalizing disorders, and internalizing disorders.

Integrating up-to-date research with clinical transcripts and case examples throughout, *Emotionally Focused Family Therapy* is a must-read for therapists looking to promote the development and renewal of family relationships using the principles of EFT.

James L. Furrow, Ph.D., is co-author of *Becoming an EFT Therapist: The Workbook*, *Emotionally Focused Couple Therapy for Dummies* and co-editor of *The EFT Casebook: New Directions in Couple Treatment*.

Gail Palmer, MSW, RMFT, is Co-Director of the International Centre for Excellence in Emotionally Focused Therapy and Co-Founder of the Ottawa Couple and Family Institute. Gail is co-author of *Becoming an Emotionally Focused Therapist: The Workbook* and leads trainings in EFT internationally.

Susan M. Johnson, Ed.D., is the leading developer of emotionally focused therapy (or EFT). She is a Professor Emeritus of Clinical Psychology at the University of Ottawa, Distinguished Research Professor in the Marital & Family Therapy Program at Alliant University in San Diego, and Director of the International Centre for Excellence in EFT.

George Faller, LMFT, is the President of the New York Center for Emotionally Focused Therapy. He teaches EFT courses at the Ackerman Institute for the Family and is the director of training at the Center for Hope and Renewal in Greenwich, Connecticut.

Lisa Palmer-Olsen, Psy.D., LMFT, is a Certified EFT Trainer and Supervisor for over 15 years and is the co-founder and co-director of the Emotionally Focused Couples Training and Research Institute at Alliant International University, San Diego.

Emotionally Focused Family Therapy offers an important breakthrough in the practice of family therapy. In this wonderfully written book, Furrow, Palmer, Johnson, Faller, and Olsen apply the wisdom and exceptional clinical skills refined over decades in emotionally focused couple therapy to family therapy. Grounded in the same base in attachment and emotion as the couple therapy, Furrow and colleagues astutely and artfully recreate this therapy in a form that addresses the unique sorts of issues that arise and typical problems in focus in family therapy. Filled with rich clinical vignettes, this is the book and treatment manual to consult to learn emotionally focused family therapy, as well as more broadly the use of emotion and attachment in work with families.

> **Jay L. Lebow, Ph.D.,** Senior Scholar and Senior therapist, Family Institute at Northwestern University, and Editor, *Family Process*

Long anticipated, *Emotionally Focused Family Therapy* elegantly details the family version of emotionally focused couples therapy, one of the most popular and well-respected theories in contemporary practice. In addition to clearly outlining the model step-by-step, Johnson and Furrow provide practical guidance for using the approach not only in common situations such as internalizing and externalizing childhood disorders but also with more challenging cases involving trauma and blended families. Without a doubt, this book will be essential reading in the field of family therapy for years to come, transforming how we conceptualize and approach work with children and families.

> **Diane R. Gehart, Ph.D.,** Author, *Mastering Competencies in Family Therapy* and Professor, California State University

EFT revolutionized couple therapy. Now, these groundbreaking pioneers have extended the approach to work with families. This delightfully engaging book is overflowing with enlightening clinical examples and session transcripts that demonstrate the power of emotion in family therapy. It should be required reading for all family therapists.

> **Andrea K. Wittenborn, Ph.D.,** Associate Professor of Human Development and Family Studies and Associate Professor of Psychiatry and Behavioral Medicine, Michigan State University

EMOTIONALLY FOCUSED FAMILY THERAPY

Restoring Connection and Promoting Resilience

James L. Furrow,
Gail Palmer,
Susan M. Johnson,
George Faller, and
Lisa Palmer-Olsen

Routledge
Taylor & Francis Group

NEW YORK AND LONDON

First published 2019
by Routledge
52 Vanderbilt Avenue, New York, NY 10017

and by Routledge
2 Park Square, Milton Park, Abingdon, Oxon, OX14 4RN

Routledge is an imprint of the Taylor & Francis Group, an informa business

© 2019 Taylor & Francis

The right of James L. Furrow, Gail Palmer, Susan M. Johnson, George Faller, and Lisa Palmer-Olsen to be identified as authors of this work has been asserted by them in accordance with sections 77 and 78 of the Copyright, Designs and Patents Act 1988.

Library of Congress Cataloging-in-Publication Data
A catalog record for this title has been requested

ISBN: 978-1-138-94801-3 (hbk)
ISBN: 978-1-138-94802-0 (pbk)
ISBN: 978-1-315-66964-9 (ebk)

Typeset in Sabon
by Wearset Ltd, Boldon, Tyne and Wear

Contents

About the Authors

JAMES L. FURROW is co-author of *Becoming an EFT Therapist: The Workbook*, *Emotionally Focused Couple Therapy for Dummies* and co-editor of *The EFT Casebook: New Directions in Couple Treatment*. James formerly served as the Freed Professor of Marital and Family Therapy and Department Chair, at Fuller Graduate School of Psychology, Pasadena, CA.

GAIL PALMER, MSW, RMFT, has specialized in emotionally focused therapy for the past 30 years. A trainer and supervisor, she gives workshops internationally and is the Director of Education for the International Centre of Emotionally Focused Therapy. Her practice is located in Ottawa and Victoria, Canada.

SUSAN M. JOHNSON, Ed.D., is the leading developer of emotionally focused therapy (or EFT). She is a Professor Emeritus of Clinical Psychology at the University of Ottawa, Distinguished Research Professor in the Marital & Family Therapy Program at Alliant University in San Diego, and Director of the International Centre for Excellence in Emotionally Focused Therapy (ICEEFT). www.drsue johnson.com

GEORGE FALLER, LMFT, is a retired Lieutenant of the NYC Fire Department and the President of the New York Center for Emotionally Focused Therapy. He teaches EFT courses at the Ackerman Institute for the Family and is the director of training at the Center for Hope and Renewal in Greenwich, CT. George is the coauthor of the books: *True Connection* and *Sacred Stress*. www.georgefaller.com

LISA PALMER-OLSEN, Psy.D., LMFT, is a Certified EFT Trainer and co-founder and co-director of the Emotionally Focused Couples Training and Research Institute at Alliant International University. She is founder and clinic director of the Alliant Couple and Family Clinic, in San Diego, CA.

INTRODUCTION

Emotionally focused family therapy (EFFT) actively promotes the development and renewal of attachment bonds in family relationships defined by patterns of emotional distance and distress resulting from enduring conflicts and relational injuries. The EFT therapist seeks to transforms these problematic patterns, which often undermine a family's safety and wellbeing. Following empirically supported practices, parent and child relationships are redefined through new experiences of trust and vulnerability, thereby restoring the flexible connection and responsiveness families need to maintain healthy emotional bonds. These bonds enhance resilience among families facing changing developmental needs and unanticipated demands common to family life.

The practice of EFFT is based on decades of psychotherapy research which has shown that the shared experience of emotion remains a powerful catalyst for growth and therapeutic change. Pioneers in emotionally focused couple therapy (Johnson, 2004) and emotion-focused therapy (Greenberg, 2002) repeatedly demonstrate empirical support for the use of emotion-focused treatments for adult depression, anxiety, and couple distress. Susan Johnson first explored the application of EFT to families in in her book *The Practice of Emotionally Focused Therapy: Creating Connection* (Johnson, 1996). Johnson noted that EFT's couple theory and interventions offered similar promise to distressed family relationships, which was demonstrated in a pilot study testing the effectiveness of EFFT with bulimic adolescents and their parents (Johnson, Maddeaux, & Blouin, 1998). Further elaboration of the approach appears in Johnson's second edition of *Creating Connection* (Johnson, 2004) and *Becoming an Emotionally Focused Therapist: The Workbook* (Johnson et al., 2005).

The clinical process described in this book is based on the fundamental practices of emotionally focused therapy outlined principally in *The Practice of Emotionally Focused Therapy: Creating Connection* (Johnson, 2004), *Becoming an Emotionally Focused Therapist: The*

Workbook (Johnson et al., 2005), and *Attachment Theory in Practice* (Johnson, 2019). Johnson and colleagues highlight three core principles that illustrate the contribution of attachment theory to this relational change model offering promise to both couple and family intervention approaches (Johnson, Lafontaine, & Dalgleish, 2015). These principles are reflected in recent summaries of attachment-based treatment (ABT) practices used in various treatment and educational approaches guiding clinician's work with adolescents and their families (e.g., Kobak, Zajac, Herres, & Krauthamer Ewing, 2015; Steele & Steele, 2018).

- Therapist as an attachment figure and resource for exploration. The therapist's emotional presence is responsive, accessible, and engaged with each person accepting and validating the varied experiences of individual in relational distress. Attachment processes guide the focus and quality of the therapist alliance with couples and families. In EFT the therapist serves as a process consultant that offers a secure base for exploring the underlying experiences and needs that are often disowned or disregarded in moments of relational distress. Kobak and colleagues (2015) highlight the therapist's role in implicitly modeling secure attachment behaviors in ABT treatments. The therapist's attuned ability to track, reflect, and explore relational injuries and empathic failures in family relationships increases individual exploration of self and other at more adaptive emotional levels, which are congruent with the importance of these relationships in their lives. The role of the EFT therapist in EFFT is defined by the core elements of a secure connection: Accessibility, responsiveness, and emotional engagement (Johnson, 2019).
- Attachment and emotion as a catalyst for change. The EFT therapist uses an attachment lens to orient and organize relational processes. Emotion takes precedence as a high-level information system that informs the actions, attributions, and experiences of partners and family members and the connections they seek. The therapist works with these experiences providing a unique resource for regulating emotional experience normalizing and validating the varied experiences of relationships under distress. Attachment theory provides a logical or predictable map for the more extreme emotional responses associated with relational distress. Relational problems seen as reactive patterns "make sense" in an attachment frame where the predictable responses to separation distress result in dysregulated emotional responses (e.g., primal panic).

Kobak and colleagues (2015) point to the principle role of emotional processing and attachment narrative in promoting security in transforming adolescent and parent relationships. The authoring of a "security script" defines the confidence that youth have in parental availability which is established through working through primary emotional experiences. Working through these more vulnerable emotions provides motivation and resource for shifting the family toward a more secure pattern, or "secure cycle". In EFT, emotion is both the target and agent of change (Johnson, 2004) and in EFFT the therapist targets the deeper emotions underlying relational blocks and uses these emotions as motivation and means for restoring confidence in parental availability through enacting a child's attachment-related needs. Johnson (2008, 2019) described these conversations as "Hold me tight" conversations framing the restoration of safety and security found through responsive emotional engagement in couples and families.

• Corrective Emotional Experiences. Attachment theory informs the basis for defining relational repair, recovery, and further growth. Restructuring affection bonds in couple and family relationships is guided by a clear understanding of the relational processes associated with felt security, e.g., accessibility, responsiveness, and emotional engagement. In EFT specific intervention practices focusing on restructuring rigid position through accessing processing and engaging attachment-related emotions and needs result in a shift in individual experience but also a new context that provides a psychological catalyst for growth (Mikulincer & Shaver, 2016) and a resource for resilience (Wiebe & Johnson, 2017).

In ABT treatments reflective dialogue provides the means for attachment-based change where the goal of these conversations is found in the ability of a parent and child to see one another where conversations are more attuned and accurate in their understanding of the child's needs and parental responses (Kobak et al., 2015). The safety and security of parent–child relationships promotes a level of vulnerability where more implicit responses are made explicit and shared relationally. These conversations are characterized by emotional balance and the ability to confront and address differences and changes as parents and children work through messy moments of development being in sync, out of sync, and back in sync (Tronick, 2007). These conversations promote opportunities for family members to "see" and be "seen" in the significance the relationships they hold.

In summary, the process of change in ABFT follows a logical progression. As Kobak and colleagues (2013) suggest, the focus of treatment begins addressing specific situations relevant to attachment and caregiving and attending to the emotions associated with distress in these relationships. The therapist then uses these emotional experiences to foster awareness and understanding of relational injuries and empathic failures that result in relational distress. This prepares the family for new attachment/caregiving interactions where repair is made possible through repairing ruptures and redressing injuries with responsive and accessible caregiving. This is a familiar logic to the EFT therapist whose focus on emotion as the basis for corrective emotional experiences that prime and promote new family patterns that provide a safe and sound basis for human flourishing.

As Johnson (2019) suggests EFT, as an ABT, offers the therapist a well-researched process for harnessing the power of emotions to transform relationships and inspire personal growth. The EFT process is guided by an accessible and responsive therapist who readily responds to the attachment-related dynamics that organize interpersonal and intrapersonal processes. Through assembling and deepening affect, the therapist provides emotional regulation and exploration targeting the emotions underlying self-protective responses. The therapist shifts the family focus from problems to negative interactions including inflexible family positions that result from the loss of emotional balance rooted in these insecure patterns. This sets the stage for the EFT therapist's use of emotion to transform these patterns by deepening a child's vulnerability and promoting parental acceptance and availability to child's unacknowledged and unmet needs. Through choreographed enactments the effective sharing of attachment needs and attuned caregiving responses. These in-session moments provide corrective emotional experiences that enable parents, partners, and child to gain new confidence in the felt security of the family. The attachment process is brought to life in session through a process that enables emotion regulation, exploration, and engagement at the most fundamental level of family life. EFT brings to light and to life the attachment processes that guide love in family relationships and offers families renewed opportunities to repair and renew the affectional ties that are the substance of a secure and loving family.

Purpose

Emotionally Focused Family Therapy: Restoring Connection and Promoting Resilience provides an essential resource to the development and practice of EFFT. The book provides a manual for applying EFT principles to family therapy. EFFT provides a unique framework for the family therapist that is based on empirically established practices used to transform emotional experience and restructure relationship patterns. EFFT focuses on restoring the family as a safe haven and secure base where family members more effectively emotionally respond, and can make repairs with a renewed sense of confidence, cohesion, and belonging. The principle aim of this book is to provide a substantive rationale, practice friendly resource, and reliable guide to EFT practice in family therapy.

About this Book

This book is organized into three sections. In Part I we describe EFT theory and practice applied to family therapy. This review focuses on EFT and its relationship to family systems theory and other attachment-related models of family therapy (Chapter 1). We review contributions from the studies of attachment and emotion regulation to family functioning and implications for EFT treatment (Chapter 2). The EFT process of change is applied to family therapy including a specific focus on the EFT tango meta-framework (Johnson, 2019) used to summarize the core moves in the EFT process (Chapter 3). Throughout this section key differences in the EFT therapist's conceptualization of and intervention with emotional processes in a family environment are clarified.

The second part describes the process of EFFT following the nine steps of the EFT model. Each chapter reviews the process and practices associated with specific steps in the EFT approach to families. Each chapter includes the goals and therapist access points associated with the specific EFT steps. These access points guide the therapist to marks for clinical intervention at each step of the process. The use of EFT interventions typically associated with these steps are described and a case example is used to illustrate the EFT process at work. Chapters in this section include:

- Chapter 4. Steps 1 and 2: EFFT assessment and alliance building review specific steps for managing assessment and alliance building in dyads, triads, and whole family sessions, recognizing the varied nature of family compositions and presenting problems.
- Chapter 5. Steps 3 and 4: Working through relational blocks highlights the specific focus on family relationships where attachment and caregiving responses are disrupted. The chapter describes the therapist's process of working through these blocks in the broader context of the family's negative interaction pattern.
- Chapter 6. Steps 5 and 6: Exploring and engaging family vulnerability turns the treatment focus to a child's unmet attachment-related emotions and needs and working through parental accessibility and responsiveness to these shared concerns. The process includes deeper emotional work targeting the parent and child's view of self and view of other as new possibilities for parental availability and attachment vulnerability are realized.
- Chapter 7. Step 7: Restructuring family positions focuses on the essential enactment used to promote a family's corrective emotional experience. The phases of this enactment are reviewed and illustrated through a family's active engagement of caregiving in response to clear and coherent attachment-related need.
- Chapter 8. Steps 8 and 9: Consolidating security in the family describes the therapist focus on revisiting past problems from new

positions of security and consolidating the meaning these shifts toward connection and support have made to the family's efficacy and identity.

Throughout these chapters common EFT interventions are described and clinical transcripts illustrate how these interventions are applied to families through the steps and stages of the EFFT process. Key EFFT change events are illustrated highlighting the five key moves in the EFT tango process. Special attention is given to the ways that corrective steps in one family relationship often inspire review in other relationships prompting opportunities for working through other relational blocks or enhancing felt security across the family.

The final section provides practical illustrations of EFFT treatment through case examples. Four chapters illustrate EFFT practice with traumatic loss, stepfamilies, externalizing disorders, and internalizing disorders. These chapters demonstrate important EFT principles and practices relevant to the application of EFFT to these clinical presentations. Detailed case examples highlight the therapist's use of EFT interventions in the context of a successful account of EFFT treatment with a specific family.

Throughout the text we use parent, caregivers, and parents interchangeably. We recognize that families form in numerous ways that a single term may exclude. We found it impractical to list or attempt to account for all foreseeable family compositions, so we have opted to use these terms more generically. We also recognize that certain parental terms including mother and father may represent traditional family forms that advance particular cultural conventions related to gender and sexual orientation. Often these terms reflect the cases we have used to illustrate EFFT treatment and are in these instances particular to these family examples. The function of caregiving is essential in formulating an understanding of separation distress in family functioning, and we recognize that the function of caregiving is better defined by the role of attachment figure than by the biological status of that caregiver. We rely primarily on examples of parent and child relationships to illustrate the EFFT treatment process. Clinical examples demonstrate a range of application with families including a range of children from school-age to young adulthood. However, we also suggest that EFFT has promise as a resource to intergenerational relationships as the relationship of attachment needs and caregiving processes remain relevant across the life span.

In our efforts to provide concrete illustrations of EFFT in practice we have relied extensively on clinical examples that represent a broad array of client families who have received EFFT treatment and who have given permission for their material to be used in professional training, presentations, and writing. Some examples include verbatim transcripts and in other examples the case material is a compilation based upon similar case examples. All identifying information has been changed to protect the confidentiality of the families who have generously shared their experiences.

We wish to acknowledge the families who entered our offices with courage and commitment toward a better future together and who generously offered opportunities to learn from their efforts to grow and invest in the lives of those they love. We are truly indebted to our mentors, colleagues, and innovators whose spirited dedication to research and clinical practice informed and guided the development of EFFT practice. Finally, our deepest gratitude and appreciation goes to those families to whom we each belong and the love and grace they have given which has inspired and instilled in us a passion and heart for this work we do.

J.L.F, G.P., S.M.J., G.F., L.P.-O.

References

Greenberg, L. S. (2002). *Emotion-focused therapy: Coaching clients to work through their feelings.* Washington, DC: American Psychological Association.

Johnson, S. M. (1996). *The practice of emotionally focused marital therapy.* New York: Brunner/Mazel.

Johnson, S. M. (2004). *The practice of emotionally focused therapy: Creating connection,* 2nd Ed. New York, NY: Brunner/Routledge.

Johnson, S. M. (2019). *Attachment theory in practice: Emotionally focused therapy with individuals, couples, and families.* New York: Guilford Press.

Johnson, S. M., Bradley, B., Furrow, J., Lee, A., Palmer, G., Tilley, D., & Wooley, S. (2005). *Becoming an emotionally focused couple therapist: The workbook.* New York: Brunner-Routledge.

Johnson, S. M., Lafontaine, M.-F., & Dalgleish, T. L. (2015). Attachment: A guide to a new era of couple interventions. In J. A. Simpson & W. S. Rholes (Eds.), *Attachment theory and research: New directions and emerging themes* (pp. 393–421). New York: Guilford Press.

Johnson, S. M., Maddeaux, C., & Blouin, J. (1998). Emotionally focused family therapy for bulimia: Changing attachment patterns. *Psychotherapy, 25,* 238–247.

Kobak, R., Grassetti, S. N., & Yarger, H. A. (2013). Attachment based treatment for adolescents: Repairing attachment injuries and empathic failures. In K. H. Birsch (Ed.) *Attachment and adolescence.* (pp. 93–111). Stuttgart, Germany: Klett-Cotta Verlag.

Kobak, R., Zajac, K., Herres, J., & Krauthamer Ewing, E. S. (2015). Attachment based treatments for adolescents: The secure cycle as a framework for assessment, treatment and evaluation. *Attachment & Human Development, 17,* 220–239.

Mikulincer, M., & Shaver, P. R. (2016). *Attachment in adulthood: Structure, dynamics, and change,* 2nd Ed. New York: Guilford Press.

Steele, H., & Steele, M. (2018). *Handbook of attachment-based interventions.* New York: Guilford Press.

Tronic, E. (2007). *The neurobehavioral and social-emotional development of infants and children*. New York: W. W. Norton.

Wiebe, S. A., & Johnson, S. M. (2017). Creating relationships that foster resilience in Emotionally Focused Therapy. *Current Opinion in Psychology, 13,* 65–69.

PART I
THEORY AND PRACTICE

ONE

Emotionally Focused Family Therapy

Emotion is at the heart of the relational life of a family. The building blocks of a family are emotional bonds and the confidence one has in the security of these bonds is a resource of resilience for an individual but also for the family as a whole. More than just sentiment, these emotions are a complex signaling system in the family that provides a rapid response system to threats to wellbeing and a resource for signaling meaning and importance. Emotions take precedence in defining what it means to belong, and what it means to be a family. As T. S. Eliot (1970) poignantly suggested, "Home is where one starts from." Home is more than a geographical address, for when we describe being "at home" we are referring to an emotional state, and experience of belonging.

Home is a point of origin, an orientation, and a consistent longing extending from a basic human need for belonging. John Bowlby, the pioneer of attachment theory, recognized this intrinsic need as fundamental to human wellbeing throughout the whole of life. "All of us, from cradle to grave, are happiest when life is organized as a series of excursions, long or short, from the secure base provided by our attachment figure(s)" (Bowlby, 1988, p. 62). However, home and the emotional security it affords, is not guaranteed. Families are faced with navigating the changing demands of developmental transitions, daily life challenges, and unexpected crises each of which require families to find and sustain an emotional balance and coherence that govern what it means to promote both belonging and becoming.

Parents and children gain resilience through their confidence in the connections they share even though over time and development these relationships change. Facing these changes and life's other challenges require families to continuously seek ways to invest and engage in the vital connections that affirm these basic family ties. Families who struggle to maintain these connections or lack opportunity and ability to retain these bonds fall into psychological and relationship distress.

Exploring Emotionally Focused Family Therapy

Emotionally focused family therapy (EFFT) engages the relationship resources families need most in times of disruption and distress. EFFT practices increase the emotional availability of family members and the effectiveness of these relational bonds (Johnson, 2004). Families gain greater "felt security" through corrective emotional experiences. These experiences enable parents and children with greater confidence in the availability of support and strength in the bonds of love that organize a family's sense of connection and resiliency. The process of EFFT enables families to renew and rebuild these affective bonds that promote exploration, encourage growth, and sustain vital relationships across the lifespan.

Susan Johnson first proposed the application of emotionally focused therapy (EFT) to families in in her book *The Practice of Emotionally Focused Therapy: Creating Connection* (Johnson, 1996, 2004). Johnson highlighted the similarity in the EFT approach with couples and families suggesting that the key processes and goals of EFT were identical in principle. The EFT therapist targets the emotional experiences informing problematic interactional patterns that are typically focused on to problematic issues with a child (IP—Identified Person). These problems typically express underlying distress in the attachment dynamics of particular dyadic relationships (e.g., mother and son) but also impact the network of attachment relationships that undergird the wellbeing of the family as a whole (Sroufe & Fleeson, 1988). Rigid behavioral patterns result from negative absorbing emotional states that constrict a family's ability to work together for their shared interest. These patterns are indicative of attachment-related distress typically present when family members lose a sense of safe connection with an attachment figure (Bowlby, 1973). Although most obvious in parent–child relationships these instances of distress are also found between sibling relationships.

EFFT treatment focuses on transforming these negative interaction cycles through engaging the emotional realities underlying these problematic patterns and their role in blocking a family's ability to respond to a child or adolescent's core attachment needs. Johnson (2004) summarized the key shifts that occur in working through a family pattern as including:

- Accessing the unacknowledged feelings underlying interactional positions.
- Reframing the problem in terms of underlying feelings, and interactional patterns.
- Promoting identification with disowned needs and aspects of self and integrating them into relationship interactions.
- Promoting the acceptance of others' experience and new interactional responses.

• Facilitating the expression of needs and wants and creating emotional engagement. (p. 248)

The results of EFFT are seen most clearly in changes in the IP's relationship to his or her family and in new responses that promote more open and flexible interactions characterized by the emotional responsiveness that is the core feature of secure bonding. The family is reorganized to respond to the attachment needs of the IP and heighten caregiving resources.

The EFT therapist takes the role of a process consultant to the family, whose goal is to provide parents and children a safe place to face the challenges and distress they experience in family relationships. Through empathic reflections and validation that the therapist provides an opportunity for families to engage new emotional experiences that transform negative patterns of interaction, typically focused on one family member. The therapist uses emotional experience through empathic reflection, evocative questions, and intensifying interventions to bring forward attachment-related emotions and translate these new experiences into new relationship encounters. As such, change in EFT is less likely to result from new insights and knowledge, or instruction in specific skills or parenting strategies. Instead, the EFT therapist provides a resource for families to together face and respond more effectively to emotional demands, unacknowledged experiences, and unmet attachment needs and find new abilities to solve problems together.

Emotionally Focused Therapy—Overview of Principles and Practices

The practice of EFFT is based upon the principles and interventions used in emotionally focused couple therapy—EFCT. EFCT is supported by three decades of research spanning efficacy trials and process research studies. Reviews of these studies include a meta-analysis (Johnson, Hunsley, Greenberg, & Schindler, 1999) that demonstrated a 70–73 percent recovery rate from relationship distress based on four randomized clinical trials. Other clinical trials have shown EFT to be effective in treating depression, chronic illness, and post-traumatic stress (Weibe & Johnson, 2016). A series of studies demonstrate EFT's effectiveness in resolving attachment injuries including couples facing betrayals of trust and affairs (Halchuk, Makinen, & Johnson, 2010; Makinen & Johnson, 2006; Zuccarini, Johnson, Dagleish, & Makinen, 2013). These researchers demonstrated EFT's successful impact enabling couples to resolve injuries and forgive their partner's offenses. Couples who repaired these injuries demonstrated continued improvement in their relationship satisfaction three years post treatment. Recent findings highlight the ongoing positive effects of EFT on relationship satisfaction following treatment and support for reduction in markers of insecure attachment and gains in secure base behaviors (Wiebe, Johnson, Lafontaine, Burgess Moser, Dalgleish, & Tascam, 2016). EFT process research findings highlight the importance of the depth of emotional experience and the shaping of successful enactments between partners focused on expressing attachment-related emotions and needs (Greenman & Johnson, 2013). Results from these studies highlight the importance of sharing vulnerability in a way that leads to new levels of emotional engagement and evokes empathy and compassion (Burgess Moser, Dalgleish, Johnson, Weibe, & Tasca, 2017; Johnson & Greenberg, 1988; Weibe et al., 2016).

EFT Principles

Five foundational EFT principles underscore the pivotal role of attachment theory in this systemic and experiential approach to couple distress and its treatment. Johnson (2004) used these principles to summarize the integral relationship of emotion to attachment and how the EFT therapist draws on both to transform relational bonds. The following examples illustrates each principle with a couple relationship.

Affectional Bond

First, a couple's intimate relationship is understood as an emotional bond, where each partner has attachment significance. Partners in close relationships provide a level of comfort and security that each rely on in ways that mirror the security a child finds in an attachment relationship with a parent (Hazan & Shaver, 1987). These reciprocal bonds are mutual in their influence in couple therapy where each partner has a shared role in caregiving. However, parent–child bonds are more hierarchical. As parents are the architects of security in the family, they hold a unique role and responsibility for providing care that is not dependent on their child. More than effective communication practice or a positive balance trust and positive experiences, EFT focuses on the many ways romantic partners rely on each other for care and comfort, particularly in a time of need (Johnson, 1986).

Sierra and Steve sought therapy after Sierra's recent miscarriage. Both describe the distance in their relationship as a "deafening silence" that has grown over the years. Sierra found herself frozen in grief over the loss of the pregnancy, and Steve's attempts to reach her in these moments left him feeling alone and ineffective. In her words, "you haven't been there for me for years, why would I now suddenly believe that you really care about me or what this is like for me."

Emotional Precedence

Guided by attachment theory, the EFT therapist recognizes the underlying logic of a couple's distress and the ways that their emotions take control precedence in moments of insecurity. Emotions and their expression organize partners' actions and interactions when attachment needs are at stake. Whether partners react with surface emotions defensively responding to a perceived threat or in moments of safety express deeper vulnerable sentiment, emotions are the signaling system for attachment. The EFT therapist provides a safe relational space fit to explore the emotions that organize the actions and experience of self, other, and their relationship. In EFT, emotion is both the target and the agent of change. The therapist focuses on each partner's emotion as a resource for transforming rigid insecure patterns through active engagement, processing, and sharing of emotion and the attachment messages these emotions hold.

Sierra's cold distance toward Steve defined the protective distance she sought from the pain and loss she knew in her relationship. Her words were sharp with criticism, highlighting how Steve had failed to see what she needed, and appeared indifferent when she confronted him directly. Her critical stance was in its own way a protest to his absence. The intensity and negativity were signals of her underlying pain and fear that he was in fact uncaring. Steve's caution in response, made his attempts to console weak and dispassionate. His fear of losing Sierra fed his tentative efforts to work around her anger in hopes of finding a safer approach. Underlying Steve's caution was his care and his own fear of losing Sierra, taking her anger as a sign of rejection.

Rigid Patterns

The third EFT principle highlights the rigid and patterned behavior found in distressed relationships. Negative emotional states become absorbing and couples sink into predictable patterns that govern and deepen the insecurity in their relationships. Couple distress is mutually determined and reinforced by repeated enactments of reactive response fueled by efforts to shift the relationship toward care and comfort without directly engaging the underlying attachment needs and emotions running behind the scenes. Couples' attempts to cope with this distress only reinforce feelings of fear and futility that intensify the negative state of their relationship.

Steve's caution and Sierra's defensiveness frame the typical positions and actions taken when important or sensitive topics are discussed. The predictable sequence of confrontation and caution has played out over the history of their relationship but its impact on their ability now to connect has left both feeling defeated. Although each can find fault with the other's actions and reactions, the EFT therapist connects each partner's actions and emotions in the interactional sequence driving their distress. This helps partners shift from seeing their partner as the problem to identifying this rigid pattern as the problem.

Attachment Needs

A fourth principle highlights how viewing a couple's reactive pattern through the lens of attachment theory enables the therapist to connect these emotions to each partner's underlying attachment needs. The rigid positions that take hold reflect the primary importance of each partner's need which become distorted through the negativity taking hold in their relationship. The EFT therapist uses these deeper emotions and needs to shift partners from their rigid positions defined by their pattern of distress. As partners are able to engage these emotions, they are better able to see their partner and themselves through a new lens of hope and security.

Steve kept his distance from Sierra's painful criticism. His actions over the years had become a reflex. He withdrew without thinking most of the time and he also lost awareness of his own feelings. Steve was a problem solver and often sought to fix a problem before he had to face Sierra's disappointment and anger. Ultimately, Steve's withdrawal was fed by his fear of failure and Sierra's likely rejection of him. He never shared these fears and found it difficult to allow himself to be vulnerable enough to feel them with the therapist's help. Similarly, Sierra confronted a similar risk letting Steve into her pain and the hurt she endured from someone she loved and still needed. She feared letting go of the protection of her critical anger but also longed for his care and comfort.

Transforming Experience

The final principle highlights the work of emotion to transform a couple's rigid pattern. The blocks to attachment security are worked through accessing, processing, and engaging each partner's underlying emotions and attachment needs. The EFT therapist choreographs and conducts a corrective emotional experience though eliciting and engaging attachment-related emotions and needs in a new context of emotional acceptance, availability, and confidence in the love each partner seeks.

For Steve and Sierra these shifts required Steve to acknowledge his fear of losing Sierra and risk his need for reassurance while also acknowledging his own failings and disengagement. The therapist helps Steve assemble his emotional experience so that he can share vulnerably his deeper feelings and needs with congruence and coherence. Sierra a similar risk in facing her fears of rejections and need for Steve's comfort.

In similar fashion, the therapist provides a secure base to explore her own needs and risk reaching for Steve for comfort. Through the therapist's active and attuned alliance and deliberate direction the couple finds a resource to explore and engage their affectional bond from a new experience of felt security.

EFT Practices

Emotionally focused therapy as a brief systemic approach incorporates an interpersonal focus on negative interaction patterns with an intrapsychic focus on individuals' attachment-related experience. Theoretically, EFT draws on a synthesis of humanistic/experiential and systemic assumptions (e.g., Minuchin & Fishman, 1981; Rogers, 1951) each evident in EFT's dynamic use of emotion to engage partners in new more adaptive relational patterns. From inception, EFT assumed an essential focus on strengthening a couple's emotional ties and that of family members through increased accessibility and responsiveness. EFT treatment follows a nine-step change process which unfolds over three stages of change: Stabilization and De-escalation; Restructuring Interactional Positions; and Consolidation.

Stabilization and De-escalation

In the initial stage the therapist is focused on stabilizing and de-escalation a couple's negative interactional pattern. The presenting complaint often organizes around problem behaviors, negative attributions, and/or relationship injuries. Acknowledging these concerns, the EFT therapist is also attuned to the ways these negative experiences result in a polarizing pattern rooted in the strategies each partner engages to manage their increasing insecurity. In EFT, the therapist alliance provides a secure base for the exploration of each person's experience, honoring individual awareness of intrapsychic and interpersonal dimensions of the couple's distress. The therapist encourages exploration in the present moment, tracking interactional experience and processing immediate responses often indicative of disowned aspects of each individual's personal and relationship experience.

Emotional experience is *assembled* through focusing on the events that trigger a response, basic automatic perceptions made in the moment, felt experience often recalling somatic aspects of feeling, meaning attributed to the experience, and actions taken in response to these emotional cues. The process systematically organizes the negative interactional pattern highlighting the deeper emotional realities that are implicit in the couple's experience. As the sessions unfold, the couple or family and the therapist gain a more explicit understanding and experience of their reactive pattern and the deeper attachment emotions and desires often hidden or protected from the other. These deeper emotions highlight the adaptive intentions and motivations of each person. These attachment dynamics provide the basis for reframing the presenting problem in light of the rigid interactional pattern of distress and emotional disconnection. Through de-escalation couples and families are better able to honor their strengths and unmet longings in their relationship while at the same time working through the negative experiences that threaten their sense of connection.

Throughout this initial stage the therapist is tracking patterns of emotion and action that organize a relationship's most difficult moments. The typical interventions used in Stage 1 focus on building a safe the alliance, accessing emotions, and reframing experience. The therapist uses empathic reflection and validation to create safety and a base for exploring more vulnerable experiences. Emotions are a primary focus of EFT however the therapist is more likely targeting present moment or "here and now" experience rather than labeling feelings. Using evocative questions, empathic conjectures, and heightening of emotional experience each person's position (e.g., withdraw, pursue) is explored at an experiential level and the therapist uses these experiences to move each person toward greater vulnerability. As new experiences are identified that provide new understanding of the couple or family's distress, the therapist reframes perception of a person's actions and experience in terms of the stuck pattern that has taken over their relationship. The therapist may also acknowledge that these new experiences provide insight into the unmet attachment needs experienced in the relationship. A therapist reframes the effect of ongoing relationship conflict.

> When the argument gets to a certain point. It seems to take over, leaving you both fighting from your opposite corners. All alone. When all the while you are both fighting to be seen and heard by the one that ultimately matters.

Johnson (2019) suggests that the key elements of an EFT session can be captured in five basic moves. The "EFT tango" illustrates how the therapist uses emotion to inform, experience, engage, and integrate a deeper understanding and connection between partners and family members. The five moves are:

1. Mirroring Present Process: The first move focuses on the present moment experience of the couple or family. Attention is directed toward the relationship but also individual experiences.
2. Affect Assembly and Deepening: In the second move the therapist works to assemble an individual's emotional experience through accessing and expanding the felt awareness of different emotional states. This includes putting together the whole of a particular experience by focusing on cues to awareness, bodily felt experiences,

meaning, and action tendencies. Through expanding and processing affect deeper emotions are identified and experienced.

3. Choreographing Engaged Encounters: The third move involves sharing these new emotional experiences. An important emphasis is placed on having partners share "from" their experience not simply "about" their experience.

4. Processing the Encounter. In the fourth move the process unfolds as the therapist engages responses from those who were initiating and receiving this shared experience. The therapist provides a safe and validating presence as family members or couples explore the impact of a shared vulnerable experience.

5. Integrating and Validating: The final move in the EFT tango focuses on integrating the meaning of this experience and valuing its impact. This last step focuses on active reflection of these new shared experiences and taking in the ways in which partners and family members see each other and understand themselves relationally.

The tango illustrates well how the EFT therapist works with attachment-related emotion to promote new levels of engagement and through those new levels of shared experience. The stages and steps act as a map for the process, and the tango illustrates how the process itself unfolds.

Restructuring Positions

In Stage 2 the therapist focuses more on shifting the family or couple from the actions that defined and shaped their negative pattern to new positions of vulnerability and connection. In the context of a less reactive relationship, the therapist engages the deeper experiences of client's attachment-related emotions to access the underlying needs that are typically avoided or exploited through defensive interactions characterizing the negative pattern. Through stabilization and de-escalation partners and family members are more aware of these underlying emotional needs and the therapist guides individuals through expressing and exploring these needs in the presence of those they depend on most. Themes related to one's view of self and view of their partner, parent or child are poignantly felt, enabling withdrawing and pursuing partners to clarify the fears that interrupt one's ability to engage effectively in responding to these attachment needs.

In EFT work with couples, processing these fears enables each partner to work through their block to engagement and the therapist invites partners to risk reaching to the other with these newly clarified needs. First through withdrawer re-engagement and then pursuer softening the therapist uses evocative interventions to heighten emotional experiences inviting partners to turn toward one another and enact these primary needs for care and comfort. For families a focus on child vulnerability and disowned attachment needs precedes working through the parent's accepting response to these needs. The primary change event in Stage 2 of EFFT is the repairing of the attachment caregiving interactions between children and parents. Together these change events result in a new bond based on emotional availability seen through a partner's and family member's accessibility, responsiveness, and emotional engagement toward these expressed needs. These shifts occur through corrective emotional experiences that take place in session. Through shifting from negativity to vulnerability and engaging at a deeper emotional level partners and family members create new cycles of positive affect that broaden and build the family and couple's experience of felt security.

Consolidation

After re-establishing this bond of felt security couples and families are better able to confront common problems or issues that trigger disagreement. The therapist guides partners and family member through confronting their differences or difficulties with the strengths they have through a more secure connection. Clients often find that their old pattern may reemerge in moments of distress, however the therapist uses these moments to guide the couple or family toward their new pattern of engagement and empowers them to find greater resilience through reliance on one another.

In this final EFT stage, the therapist invites couples and families to invest in their renewed security through rituals and practices that will signal to one another their shared investment in the closeness they have found. These attachment rituals represent intentional choices the couple or family make to deepen their trust and security found together. Various resources are available for couples and families wanting to further explore the attachment dynamics of their relationships and exercises that further support the changes they have made through the EFT process (e.g., *Emotionally Focused Therapy Workbook: The Two of Us* [Kallos-Lilly & Fitzgerald, 2013]; *Hold Me Tight* [Johnson 2008]; *Hold Me Tight/Let Me Go* [Aiken & Aiken, 2017]).

Differences in EFT Couple and Family Treatment

These foundational principles and practices guide a therapist through the EFT process of change whether working with couples or families. The therapist uses emotion to transform stuck relationship patterns using attachment theory to inform and guide the restructuring of interactions where love, care, and commitment are intrinsic to the purpose of the relationship. Attachment dynamics for parent–child relationships and romantic partners are essentially dyadic and the basic needs experienced in these relationships orient partners, parents, and children toward each other particularly in times of distress. Attachment and caregiving provide the therapist with a predictable map for the emotional dynamics that lead to the wellbeing of couple and family relationships. There are, however, additional considerations required in treating families. Each of these differences is reviewed and implications for treatment are identified.

Parental Responsibility

A distressed family's interactional dynamic shares similar characteristics with partners in couple distress. Problematic patterns between a distant rejecting parent and an angrily protesting adolescent appear to mirror a couple's demand–withdraw pattern. However, the goals of these two types of relationships are fundamentally different. Couples relationships share mutual goals of intimacy and each partner bears equal responsibility for the relationship commitment. Parent–child relationships, while reciprocal, are nonetheless hierarchical, with the responsibility for care resting uniquely upon mothers and fathers. Family therapy models consistently highlight the importance of the parental role in terms of structure (Minuchin, 1974), function (Haley, 1991), and responsibility (Boszormenyi-Nagy & Krasner, 1986).

In attachment terms this responsibility is understood through the parent's caregiving role as the child's attachment figure, her "stronger wiser other." Although the relationships between parents and children possess reciprocal processes including attunement and reflexive communication, a parent's experience of being parented and the attachment narratives that result are an important factor. A parent's attachment history while influential in parent–child interactions, is also independent of these relationships (Kobak, Zajac, Herres, & Krauthamer Ewing, 2015). Therefore, when considering the cycles and patterns in family relationships the EFT therapist recognizes the unique ways in which these problematic patterns reflect attachment processes and strategies that are specific to the parent and child's relationship but also to the parent's history or the adult representations of their caregiving experience. In contrast to couple therapy where the therapist is working with two related systems of romantic attachment, the EFT therapist is aligning the attachment needs of a child with the caregiving responses of a parent.

Developmental Differences

Developmentally, family composition impacts how a therapist works with emotion in the context of relationships. Socio-developmental differences in family relationships inform interpersonal functioning and impact family treatment as a result. The role of cognitive and social development influence differences in family relationships in terms of emotional regulation and attachment functioning (Rutherford, Wallace,

Laurent, & Mayes, 2015). Families face changing developmental tasks and requisite resources vary across the lifespan and demands and roles shift in relationship to developmental achievements and changes in socialization (Carter & McGoldrick, 2005). Assessment of a child's developmental capacities and needs provide direction for the EFT therapist in treating families where these differences matter.

YOUNG CHILDREN

Young children's development abilities and limitations need to be considered. Willis and colleagues (2016) proposed the use of play-based activities in EFFT treatment including children four to six years of age. Modifications in treatment includes specific attention to the use of enactments and emotional engagement with pre-school and school-age children. The therapist may use strategies and objects to help children express their emotions symbolically as well as directly. Accommodating development differences promotes safety and strengthens the therapist alliance with the child and the family overall. Integrating play therapy approaches promotes an environment that supports and integrates emotion into a child's relationships (Schaefer & Drewes, 2011) and improves parental co-regulation of their child's emotional experience.

In EFFT the therapist evaluates a child's capacity to sustain attention, emotional awareness, and ability to interact with more abstract concepts (Willis et al., 2016). Modifications recommended in EFFT with young children include an initial session with parent(s) to identify problem behaviors and their relational context and subsequent sessions with the family and child (IP). This enables the therapist to better assess the developmental capacity of the child independent of the family environment and strengthen the therapist's alliance with the child. The EFT therapist will use a combination of non-directed and semi-directed play in family sessions to promote observation of emotion and the corresponding relational dynamics of the family. Various play therapy strategies enable the therapist to identify and reflect problematic family patterns, as these strategies afford the therapist a more informed position to enhance parental awareness of the attachment-related needs of the child (Wittenborn et al., 2006).

ADOLESCENTS

An adolescent's path to adulthood represents a critical period of change for families as youth define themselves and their relationships through a process of individuation. Families must move toward greater collaboration and exploration as adolescents work out new patterns of peer relationships and balance the need for autonomy along with the need for connection. These developmental shifts involve an increasing distance in relationship to parents that co-occurs with greater investment in peer relationships, which also include moving toward the engagement of pair-bond or sexual mate (Scharf & Mayseless, 2007). Adolescent attachment researchers suggest that shifts in the parental goals of care-giving in adolescents shift toward the youth gaining more autonomy in meeting attachment needs (Kobak & Duemmler, 1994). These changes may be challenging for parents as youth are more likely to de-idealize their parents and increase reliance on their social network for emotional regulation (Allen & Manning, 2007; Steinberg, 2005). Parents need to find a balance between supporting the goals asserted by their adolescent children and balancing the need for exploration and security (Kobak, Sudler, & Sudler, 1991; Kobak, Cole, Ferenz-Gillies, Fleming, & Gamble, 1993). In families with greater insecurity adolescents are vul-nerable to greater psychological distress as they tend to lack of trust in parent's caregiving, greater negative views of self, and limit more auto-nomous actions (Moretti & Holland, 2004).

In EFFT the therapist provides a safe and secure alliance where parents and adolescents are able to face the apparent competition between goals of connection and autonomy. Although research findings continue to affirm the significant attachment role parents play even into young adulthood (Rosenthal & Kobak, 2010), the family's ability to find a balance in these shifting needs of attachment and exploration is challenged when caregiving responses and attachment bids become blocked. The EFT therapist prioritizes the parent's caregiving role and prizes the emotional resources necessary for its effective function. This involves helping parents work through blocks that are triggered by the potential mismatch of these fundamental goals (e.g., autonomy and con-nection). At the same time the therapist invites the adolescent to seek support as the youth explores their emerging needs in the presence of more responsive parental caregiving. Together the parent and adolescent are able to find an emotional balance that supports the mutual goal of the youth's growing autonomy.

ADULT RELATIONSHIPS

Intergenerational relationships in adulthood provide promise for con-tinued growth and healing in families. Relationship concerns between adult children and their parents can be triggered by family transitions (e.g., marriage, divorce, remarriage, elder care) or crises (e.g., chronic illness, job-loss, economic hardship). Although historically some have assumed that adult children reduce their reliance on their parents as attachment figures (e.g., Weiss, 1982), there is growing support for changing yet ongoing importance of these attachment bonds throughout adulthood (Krause & Haverkamp 1996) and their influence on care-giving relationships shared in later life (e.g., Crispi, Schiaffino, & Berman 1997). In adulthood the availability associated with secure attachment is more symbolic or abstract rather than focused on physical proximity (Cicirelli, 1993; Koski & Shaver, 1997). The experience of felt security is more often related to positive memories of parents that are reinforced by ongoing contact, than a present focus on day-to-day interactions. Situations involving a parent's ill health may prompt a "protective" response from adult children, which can be informed by the ongoing adult attachment dynamics in that family. Attachment dynamics provide direction in conceptualizing the availability and attenuation of adult children's support to the parent in ill health, where current demands take place in the context of an adult child's history of caregiving.

An adult child's transition to a parenting role may also trigger challenges in their own parenting including ambivalence and negative expectancies related to their child. Byng-Hall (2002) highlights intergenerational patterns that influence couple and family relationships where attachment insecurity increases the risk of parentification of children. Redressing these intergenerational relationships provides a corrective resource for couple distress and parenting difficulties when a parent's own attachment history results in ambivalence toward the role of parent or partner. Working through insecurity rooted in the history of parents and their adult children as they themselves are parenting enables the family, as whole, to better see the needs of children in the next generation.

The EFT therapist's work with adult children and their parents focuses on present attachment experiences that often reflect past attachment histories. Triggers for relationship distress may result from changes in demands in the current relationships (e.g., caregiving for an ill parent) or indirectly in relationship to distress with one's partner or child in a parental role (e.g., parentification). The focus of assessment and treatment may shift between generational dyads as the therapist identifies problem patterns that organize parental availability and caregiving. Restructuring attachment relationships toward greater security brings new resources that impact future generations through the resources created through felt security.

Generational Influences

The influence of family of origin relationships is often important in understanding a partner's attachment history. The EFT therapist commonly conducts and assessment of each partner's past attachment experience to better acknowledge and understand a partner's secondary attachment strategy (e.g., anxious pursuit, avoidant withdrawal). In EFFT, generational influences are also important to the therapist understanding of parent's caregiving responses. A parent's view of self in parenting is more likely influenced by their history of receiving caregiving than the feedback they receive from their child. This can be seen in the ways a parent enacts behaviors that are consistent with those experienced in the parenting they received as a child, or as a correction to the negative experiences of caregiving they received. Either motivation is organized by their attachment experience in their family of origin and as a result less likely to be attuned to the immediate needs of their child.

The EFT therapist recognizes the primacy of these generational influences and the review of past expectancies that may take place with the parent working through what they did not receive as a child at the same time as they are facing the needs of their child, which may be identical. Understanding parental blocks to caregiving begins with an understanding of each parent's attachment history and its present influence on parenting.

Treatment Process

Differences in family composition and presenting problems require a flexible approach to treatment. The EFT therapist treating a couple primarily works in dyadic sessions that focus on the interaction of one relationship. In EFFT the therapist may work with a combination of relationships, often focusing on specific dyads or triads, following a specific treatment rationale (e.g., EFFT decision guide). Session composition may vary from session to session as the therapist prioritizes attention to the unfolding treatment process and goals. For example, a therapist may meet with a parental dyad following an escalated session where parents became divided over their acting out teen. This session provides parents opportunity to explore their own reactive patterns and the emotional triggers that undermine their ability to support one another in parenting. Shifting between different session formats requires the therapist to remain flexible and maintain clarity regarding the overall treatment process.

Typical EFFT treatment requires a limited number of sessions. Family sessions focus on modifying parent and child interactions that center on family concerns with an identified person. Therefore, treatment is more circumscribed than couple therapy and while couples work may be an aspect of EFFT, shifting the parent–child pattern is the primary treatment objective in EFFT (Johnson, 2004). Unlike couple therapy, the EFT therapist may find that families are able to progress through more than one stage of change in a single treatment session. Shifts in parental openness and accessibility may quickly resolve a child's blocked attachment communication, as a result the family may shift quickly from Stage 1 de-escalation to Stage 2 restructuring parent–child engagement. As a result, family work moves more rapidly through the EFFT stages of change.

EFFT—Advancing the Model

As previously described, EFT has strong empirical support in the effective treatment of couple distress. At present, there is one pilot study evaluating the effectiveness of EFFT with female adolescents being treated for bulimia and their parents (Johnson, Maddeaux, & Blouin, 1998). Findings from this study showed EFFT to be effective in reducing bingeing and vomiting behaviors as well as reductions in adolescent depression and hostility. Results from this study underscore the benefit of adolescents giving voice to their attachment needs, clarifying their relationship expectations, and finding new ways to express a more positive view of self with family members.

A number of studies describe the practice of EFFT with a variety of presenting problems. These include the use of EFFT with childhood mood related disorders (Johnson & Lee, 2000; Stravianopoulos, Faller, & Furrow, 2014); non-suicidal self-injury (Schade, 2013). Other clinical studies include EFFT with families facing marital transitions including divorce (Hirschfield & Wittenborn, 2016; Palmer & Efron, 2007) and stepfamily adjustment (Furrow & Palmer, 2007). EFFT case applications illustrate treatment of young children and explore the incorporation of play therapy strategies essential in assuring EFFT is developmentally responsive and appropriate (Hirschfeld & Wittenborn, 2016; Willis et al., 2016; Wittenborn et al., 2006). These case examples illustrate successful examples of EFFT but do not systematically assess the effectiveness of the treatment. Further research is needed to establish the efficacy of the EFFT approach in family therapy.

EFFT's Distinct Emphases and Assumptions

The continued development of EFFT has emphasized a number of important facets that highlight the model's distinct approach to family related distress. These developments, while inherent in the development of EFT for couples, also require special attention in setting out unique emphases in this family approach. These EFFT distinctives include: Attachment as a resource for resilience; caregiver blocks and family distress; present process focus; and the therapist's role as process consultant.

Attachment and Relational Resilience

Attachment relationships in families are a key resource for family resilience. Most family behaviors, even those that appear problematic, seek to re-establish a connection or correct another's behavior. Attachment theory provides a constructive frame of reference for the positive intention behind what others may experience as problematic action. EFFT is a strength-based perspective that recognizes and validates the positive underlying intent of parents who persist in ineffective caregiving attempts, recognizing how a parent may have a good reason for a level of emotional engagement that furthers a child's distress or problem behavior. Mis-attuned parental actions often result from attempts that over or under respond to the needs of a child. Children, in turn, then act to dismiss or deny their needs for parental support or engage in overly responsible behavior in the face of parental absence. These corresponding actions express a logical and predictable effort to regain balance in a relationship system that is increasingly unstable. Understanding this system and providing means for its correction instils new resources of resilience into a family system through essential relationships.

The attachment system is adaptive and when families are able to retain felt security, they have a resource for resilience that promotes wellbeing personally and socially (Mikulincer & Shaver, 2015). Attachment security promotes prosocial behavior and reduces the need for defensive self-protection thereby freeing resources to promote the wellbeing of others through altruism and compassion for those in need. The demands of family life assume developmental change and environmental challenges and with secure attachment individuals are better able to respond to these demands through the relationships that they rely upon (Sroufe, 2016). These relational resources support resilience in facing adversity and improve the likelihood that families will rebound from difficulty in the direction of growth (Walsh, 2003). As Wiebe and Johnson (2017) observe, promoting secure connections fosters a shared resilience that enables partners to face stress and preserve health through more effective co-regulation of emotion in the context of a committed relationship. EFFT actively promotes family resilience through increasing security in relationships that promote support and growth.

Silvia struggled to support her daughter Alicia (12) following a recent educational evaluation showing further gaps in her academic progress. Alicia's learning difficulties, while identified and supported by school services, were taking their toll on Alicia's self-esteem and social engagement. Silvia often lost her balance emotionally caught between her fears for her daughter's future and the responsibility she held having had similar problems in her own schooling. Through turning to her mother, who continued as an attachment figure in her life, she found support and reassurance through her mother's own experience and caring concern for her daughter and granddaughter. Their relationship gave Silvia greater confidence to engage Alicia and weather the uncertainties of her academic future with a focus on Alicia's needs rather than a mother's fears.

Caregiving Blocks

As a natural system, attachment and caregiving responses are intrinsic to family relationships. Culturally, attachment behaviors that express these manifest systems may vary, yet each exist as a bio-behavioral universal in families. Bowlby (1969, 1988) identified caregiving as a complementary system to a child's attachment system. Distress in parent–child relationships results when children question the availability of parental caregiving and parental reactions over- or under-respond to the negative emotions (e.g., fear, sadness) that accompany this perceived lack of availability (Kobak & Mandelbaum, 2003). As a defensive pattern takes hold, parents and children are more likely to respond with self-protective responses to failed attempts to successfully respond to the child's attachment needs. As this negatively charged pattern unfolds and distress leads to distorted responses children are exposed to anxious and avoidant caregiving that reduces the child's confidence in the parent's accessibility and responsiveness and parents' empathic failures that restrict a parent's flexibility in responding to these negative response (Kobak et al., 2015).

Silvia coped with her fears of her daughter's future and her own culpability in her failures by being vigilant around her daughter's efforts and school performance. She found it difficult to tolerate Alicia's avoidance and lack of effort. Alicia also became more guarded in talking about her feelings at school as her mother often lectured her on Silvia's own experience, often missing the bid for reassurance and comfort Alicia had made. The negative pattern of Syliva's anxious monitoring and Alicia's avoidance dominated their interactions unless both avoided the topic altogether. This only reinforced Silvia's fear that she was failing as a mother and losing contact with her daughter.

Following attachment theory, the EFT therapist conceptualizes rigid patterns that define problematic parent and children interaction in terms of separation distress resulting from blocked attachment and caregiving communication. These negative cycles become absorbing states that precariously shift the emotional balance of family relationships ensnared in escalating patterns of distress (Kobak, Duemmler, Burland, & Youngstrom, 1998). The EFFT process begins with stabilizing these negative patterns and de-escalating the reactive responses through focusing on the deeper emotions underlie the caregiving and attachment ruptures in the family. In EFFT the therapist work through these blocks and the negative emotions that reinforce them. Rather than reframing a block as a failed attempt to care, the EFT therapist moves alongside where the parent is stuck exploring the block and validating or normalizing the parent's effort to respond.

Present Focus

The EFT therapist provides a strong alliance that functions as a secure base for parents and children to explore and engage the "here and now" emotional experiences that drive the distress in the family. These emotional realities provide an important source of meaning and motivation in family relationships. The EFT therapist tracks the emotional pattern or dance that unfolds in session, tracking the emotional experience that organizing family members' actions, just as music orders the moves of a dancer. The therapist's awareness and emotional presence provides a responsive and attuned resource to family members as they experience the disruptive effects of their negative cycle.

Working with these reactive emotional responses, the therapist gains access to the deeper emotions that have been disowned or underlie more defensive responses. Honoring a parent or child's defense with curiosity opens new understanding in facing the fears and hurts that have gone unacknowledged in the family. Families are resourceful when signals are clear. EFFT invites and enables families to communicate more effectively around the needs they have to belong and care for one another. The EFFT process promotes attachment communication through shared vulnerability in families and is the route to greater security through attunement, emotion regulation, and shared experience of accessibility and responsiveness.

Process Consultant

The EFT therapist is a process consultant in session tuning into the experiences of family members as they engage shared experiences of their relational interactions. Rather than teaching or coaching parents in specific strategies or techniques the therapist helps family members make sense of their experience and working through these experiences to engage a new position in the family. In this way the therapist is also choreographing and restructuring positions in the family to engage more secure bonds and effective caregiving. As a process consultant the EFT therapist promotes a collaborative relationship with family members that engages others to move into their experience and through their experience find new meaning and motivation for their relationships with their children and or parents.

EFFT Innovations in Family Therapy

Building on EFT treatment principles and practices the EFFT process offers family therapists an experiential treatment approach focused on emotion and attachment within the family system. As such EFFT offers three innovations in the systemic treatment of families. These include a focus on emotion, separation distress, and corrective emotional experience.

Focus on Emotion

The EFT therapist focuses on the role of emotion in shaping patterns of interaction that define relationship distress in families. Problematic parenting practices are understood in reaction to the disruptive impact of insecurity and the negative emotional cycles that evolve between family members. This differs from programs focused on communication skills and problem solving (Morris, Miklowitz, & Waxmonsky, 2007) or emotion coaching and self-regulation strategies (Gottman, Katz, & Hooven, 1997). The experiential focus of EFFT places emphasis on accessing and working through emotional experience where regulation of emotion is a result of the intervention rather than an intervention in and of itself.

Emotion prioritizes the direction of an EFFT session. The therapist elicits, distills and deepens emotional experience that organizes the problematic interactions in family relationships. These negative experiences provide the gateway for more organized and emotionally regulated experiences that build a basis for greater awareness, deeper understanding, and more effective responding. Working through distress and emotional blocks opens new avenues for more secure interactions where attachment–caregiving relationships are characterized by accessibility, responsiveness, and engagement at an emotional level.

In general, systemic approaches to family therapy focus more on the structures and strategies embedded in family patterns prioritizing the family process over the experience of the individuals (Merkel & Seawright, 1992). The influence of behaviorism and communication theory privileged the actions and interactions of family members with less attention given to the underlying emotional dynamics informing those actions. The role of emotion in family therapy was sufficiently underdeveloped in family system applications by the 1970s (Diamond & Siqueland, 1998; Madden-Derdich, 2002).

Bowen's emphasis on the family emotional system illustrates this tendency. For Bowen a family system maintained an emotional atmosphere that guided and informed the "functioning positions" (Kerr & Bowen, 1988, p. 55) of family members, much like gravitation fields influenced the movements of planets in the solar system. His focus on differentiation (i.e., "The ability to be in emotional contact with others yet still autonomous in one's own emotional function ...", Kerr & Bowen, 1988, p. 145), illustrate the degree to which Bowen's work privileged the function of the system over the person and that it was through the person's ability to objectively process through intellectual functioning that one was able to find freedom toward more autonomous choices.

For Bowen, emotions were recognized as integral to the family system and were prominent in patterns of psychopathology. However, the process of working with emotion was focused on patterns and processes not individual experience and relational engagement. Differentiation understood in terms of attachment is a developmental process that is defined by relationships with other rather than defined by one's separation from others. One's differentiation is then a natural result of a child having a secure bond where one is attuned to, accepted, and encouraged to explore her or his own uniqueness in relationship to a parent (Johnson, 2019).

Salvador Minuchin's theories and techniques focused exclusively on interactional process and the patterns associated with dysfunctional family systems. For Minuchin the therapist role focused on observing family patterns and to "make the how" of those interactions the focus of the process of change. This focus on problematic transactions that were maintained in family systems also illustrates the elevation of the system/process/interaction over individual experience reinforcing what for Minuchin was ultimately more an organizational view of the family. Family dysfunction proved more a lack of boundaries including appropriate levels of separateness, which stands in contrast to the attachment-related assumption that dysfunction and dysregulation are expressions of disconnection. Ironically, as many of Minuchin's techniques (Minuchin & Fishman, 1981) have proven integral to the practice of EFT (Johnson, 2004), Minuchin in a discussion of his work with Susan Johnson reflected: "Ignoring emotion was the greatest mistake we made in family therapy" (Johnson, 2019).

Humanistic and experiential therapists entering the field of family therapy were clearly more prone to value and appeal to individual experience and the emotions that informed. Virginia Satir provided the most salient example of the value of shared emotional experience in promoting growth, self-discovery, and authentic communication (1964). For Satir openness and nurturance were characteristics of a healthy family. "Anything can be talked about—the disappointments, fears, hurts, angers, criticism as the joys and achievements" (Satir, 1972, p. 14). For Kempler (1981) family dysfunction was associated with alienation and restricted emotional communication. He cited families' challenge to express intimacy in a world where no one knows the other at the same time no one knows oneself. He observed how family communication itself became a means to avoid intimacy by avoiding feelings. Carl Whitaker (1975) emphasized the role of individual and shared experience as a resource for recovering caring and compassion in the family. A family's capacity to expand their experience would lead to healing and to growth. Through affective confrontation family members were challenged to examine their feelings before their behaviors (Keith & Whitaker, 1982).

Focus on Separation Distress and Disruption

Historically, a family systems approach conceptualized family patterns in terms of power and control, developing intervention to challenge and disrupt these relationship coalitions (Minuchin & Fishman, 1981). In EFFT the focus is on problematic interactional patterns and the impact they have over time in compromising a family's shared sense of safety and security. EFFT provides the antidote for these relationship disruptions by guiding families toward moments of vulnerable emotional connection. Boundaries and parental authority are addressed with families within the context of re-established security rather than as a basis for connection and safety.

Insecurity in a family system results from separation distress and the problematic behaviors often seen in symptomatic expressions of children are influenced by parent and child attempts to respond to this distress. Human responses to the loss of security follow a predictable sequence. First, the loss of contact with an attachment figure triggers anger and protest over the perceived absence. Without an effective response to these signals, more desperate and controlling responses emerge, all in an attempt to reconnect with the absence. The sequence follows with clinging and controlling behavior followed by a generalized sense of despair (Johnson, 2004). The loss of this attachment connection is traumatizing to the one seeking contact, the degree of this loss is also reflected in the intensity of the related attempts to correct for this loss.

Enacting and Engaging Emotional Experience

Enacting emotion is a hallmark of EFT. Accessing and engaging emotional experience is a primary resource in shifting problematic interactions in families. Emotion provides an adaptive resource that, once accessed and regulated, can be used to promote deeper levels of intimacy and trust in family relationships. Restructuring the emotional bonds of parents and children and partners in families toward patterns of availability and felt security is the bedrock of EFFT.

Enactments promote the relationship between family members as a mechanism for change (Davis & Butler, 2004). Minuchin used enactments to heighten family members' awareness of the roles they had taken in the family in order to shift toward more adaptive positions in the family. In structural family therapy, enactments were used as a technique for boundary making by redirecting lines of communication in the family (Minuchin, 1974). Enactments were focused on the family process as a means of fostering interaction more than the engagement or sharing of relational experience. Enactments can be used for assessment providing illustration of roles and rules in the family and how they may organize interactions.

Summary

In this chapter we have set the stage for exploring the EFT approach to family treatment. EFFT provides therapists with a practical approach to family distress based on empirically informed practices found effective in the treatment of couple distress. In principle, EFT treatment of family follows the same path of transforming change where the critical focus of intervention begins and ends with attachment bonds that provide the family with identity, belonging, and resilient relationships across the life span. Emotion is at the heart of the matter in promoting relationships that are themselves the basis of belonging and becoming.

References

Aiken, N., & Aiken, P. (2017). *The hold me tight let me go program: Facilitators guide*. Ottawa, Canada: International Centre for Excellence in Emotionally Focused Therapy.

Allen, J. P., & Manning, N. (2007). From safety to affect regulation: Attachment from the vantage point of adolescence. *New Directions for Child Development, 117*, 23–39.

Boszormenyi-Nagy, I., & Krasner, B. R. (1986). *Between give and take: A clinical guide to contextual therapy*. New York, NY: Brunner Mazel.

Bowlby, J. (1969). *Attachment and loss: Vol. 1. Attachment*. New York: Basic Books.

Bowlby, J. (1973). *Attachment and loss: Vol. 2. Separation*. New York: Basic Books.

Bowlby, J. (1988). *A secure base*. New York: Basic Books.

Byng-Hall, J. (2002). Relieving parentified children's burdens in families with insecure attachment patterns. *Family Process, 41*, 375–388.

Carter, B. A., & McGoldrick, M. (2010). *The expanded family life cycle: Individual, family and social perspectives*, 4th Ed. New York: Allyn Bacon.

Cicirelli, V. G. (1993). Attachment and obligations and daughters' motives for caregiving behavior and subsequent effect on subjective burden. *Psychology and Aging, 8*, 144–155.

Crispi, E. L., Schiaffino, K., & Berman, W. H. (1997). The contribution of attachment to burden in adult children of institutionalized parents with dementia. *The Gerontologist, 37*, 52–60.

Davis, S. D., & Butler, M. H. (2004). Enacting relationships in marriage and family therapy: A conceptual and operational definition of an enactment. *Journal of Marital and Family Therapy, 30*, 319–333.

Diamond, G., & Siqueland, L. (1998). Emotions, attachment, and the relational reframe: The first session. *Journal of Systemic Therapies, 17*, 36–50.

Efron, D. (2004). The use of emotionally focused family therapy in a children's mental health center. *Journal of Systemic Therapies, 23*, 78–90.

Eliot, T. S. (1970). *T. S. Eliot reading Four Quartets*. New York: Cademon.

Furrow, J., & Palmer, G. (2007). EFFT and blended families: Building bonds from the inside out. *Journal of Systemic Therapies, 26*, 44–58.

Furrow, J. L., Bradley, B., & Johnson, S. M. (2004). Emotion focused family therapy with complex family systems. In V. Bengston, A. Acock, K. Allen, P. Dilworth Anderson, & D. Klien (Eds.) *Sourcebook of family theory and research* (pp. 220–222). Thousand Oaks, CA: Sage.

Gottman, J. M., Katz, L. F., & Hooven, C. (1996). Parental meta-emotion philosophy and the emotional life of families: Theoretical models and preliminary data. *Journal of Family Psychology, 10*, 243–268.

Greenman, P. S., & Johnson, S. M. (2013). Process research on emotionally focused therapy (EFT) for couples: Linking theory to practice. *Family Process*, 52, 46–61.

Haley, J. (1991). *Problem solving therapy, 2nd Ed.* New York: John Wiley.

Hazan, C., & Shaver, P. (1987). Conceptualizing romantic love as an attachment process. *Journal of Personality and Social Psychology*, 52, 511–524.

Hirschfeld, M. R., & Wittenborn, A. K. (2016). Emotionally focused family therapy and play therapy with children whose parents are divorced. *Journal of Divorce and Remarriage*, 57, 133–150.

Johnson, S. (1986). Bonds or bargains: Relationship paradigms and their significance for marital therapy. *Journal of Marital and Family Therapy*, 12, 259–267.

Johnson, S. M. (1996). The practice of emotionally focused therapy: Creating connection. New York: Brunner/Routledge.

Johnson, S. M. (2004). *The practice of emotionally focused therapy: Creating connection, 2nd Ed.* New York: Brunner/Routledge.

Johnson, S. (2008). *Hold me tight: Seven conversations for a lifetime of love.* New York: Little Brown.

Johnson, S. M. (2019). *Attachment theory in practice: Emotionally focused therapy with individuals, couples, and families.* New York: Guilford Press.

Johnson, S. M., & Greenberg, L. S. (1988). Relating process to outcome in marital therapy. *Journal of Marital and Family Therapy*, 14, 175–184.

Johnson, S. M., & Lee, A. (2000). Emotionally focused family therapy: Restructuring attachment. In C. E. Bailey (Ed.), *Children in therapy: Using the family as resource* (pp. 112–136). New York: Guilford Press.

Johnson, S. M., Maddeaux, C., & Blouin, J. (1998). Emotionally focused family therapy for bulimia: Changing attachment patterns. *Psychotherapy*, 25, 238–247.

Johnson, S. M., Hunsley, J., Greenberg L. S., & Schindler, D. (1999). Emotionally focused couples therapy: Status and challenges. *Clinical Psychology Science and Practice*, 6, 67–79.

Johnson, S. M., Bradley, B., Furrow, J., Lee, A., Palmer, G., Tilley, D., & Wooley, S. (2005). *Becoming an emotionally focused couple therapist: The workbook.* New York: Brunner-Routledge.

Kallos-Lilly, V., & Fitzgerald, J. (2014). *An emotionally focused workbook for couples: The two of us.* New York: Routledge.

Keith, D. V., & Whitaker, C. A. (1982). Experiential/symbolic family therapy. In A. M. Horne and M. M. Ohlsen (Eds.), *Family counseling and therapy* (pp. 43–74). Itasca, IL: F.E. Peacock.

Kempler, W. (1981). *Experiential psychotherapy with families.* New York: Brunner/Mazel.

Kerr, M. E., & Bowen, M. (1988). *Family evaluation.* New York: Norton.

Kobak, R., & Duemmler, S. (1994). Attachment and conversation: Toward a discourse analysis of adolescent and adult security. In K. Bartholomew & D. Perlman (Eds.), *Attachment processes in adulthood* (pp. 121–150). London, PA: Jessica Kingsley.

Kobak, R., & Mandelbaum, T. (2003). Caring for the caregiver: An attachment approach to assessment and treatment of child problems. In S. M. Johnson and V. E. Whiffen (Eds.), *Attachment processes in couple and family therapy* (pp. 144–164). New York: Guilford Press.

Kobak, R. R., Sudler, N., & Gamble, W. (1991). Attachment and depressive symptoms during adolescence: A developmental pathways analysis. *Development and Psychopathology, 3*, 461–474.

Kobak, R., Duemmler, S., Burland, A., & Youngstrom, E. (1998). Attachment and negative absorption states: Implications for treating distressed families. *Journal of Systemic Therapies, 17*, 80–92.

Kobak, R., Zajac, K., Herres, J., & Krauthamer Ewing, E. S. (2015). Attachment based treatments for adolescents: The secure cycle as a framework for assessment, treatment and evaluation. *Attachment & Human Development, 17*, 220–239.

Kobak, R. R., Cole, H. E., Ferenz-Gillies, R., Fleming, W. S., & Gamble, W. (1993). Attachment and emotion regulation during mother–teen problem solving: A control theory analysis. *Child Development, 64*, 231–245.

Kosiki, L. R., & Shaver, P. R. (1997). Attachment and relationship satisfaction across the lifespan. In R. J. Sternberg & M. Hojjat (Eds.), *Satisfaction in close relationships* (pp. 26–55). New York: Guilford Press.

Krause, A. M., & Haverkamp, B. E. (1996). Attachment in adult child–older parent relationships: Research, theory, and practice. *Journal of Counseling & Development, 75*, 83–92.

Madden-Derdich, D. A. (2002). The role of emotions in marriage and family therapy. *Marriage and Family Review, 34*, 165–179.

Makinen, J. A., & Johnson, S. M. (2006). Resolving attachment injuries in couples using emotionally focused therapy: Steps toward forgiveness and reconciliation. *Journal of Consulting and Clinical Psychology, 74*, 1055–1064.

Merkel, W. T., & Seawright, H. R. (1992). Why families are not like swamps, solar systems or thermostats: Some limits of systems theory applied to family therapy. *Contemporary Family Therapy, 14*, 33–50.

Minuchin, S. (1974). *Families and family therapy.* Cambridge, MA: Harvard University Press.

Minuchin, S., & Fishman, H. C. (1981). *Family therapy techniques.* Cambridge, MA: Harvard University Press.

Mikulincer, M., & Shaver, P. R. (2015). Boosting attachment security in adulthood. In J. Simpson & W. S. Rholes (Eds.), *Attachment theory and research* (pp. 124–144). New York: Guilford Press.

Moretti, M. M., & Holland, R. (2003). The journey of adolescence: Transitions in self within the context of attachment relationships. In S. M. Johnson and V. Whiffen (Eds.), *Attachment processes in couple and family therapy* (pp. 234–257). New York: Guilford Press.

Morris, C. D., Miklowitz, D. J., & Waxmonsky, J. A. (2007). Family-focused treatment for bipolar disorder in adults and youth. *Journal of Clinical Psychology, 63*, 433–445.

Palmer, G., & Efron, D. (2007). Emotionally focused family therapy: Developing the model. *Journal of Systemic Therapies, 26*, 17–24.

Rogers, C. (1951). *Client-centered therapy.* Boston, MA: Houghton-Mifflin.

Rosenthal, N. L., & Kobak, R. (2010). Assessing adolescents' attachment hierarchies: Differences across developmental periods and associations with individual adaptation. *Journal of Research on Adolescence, 20*, 678–706.

Rutherford, H. J., Wallace, N. S., Laurent, H. K., & Mayes, L. C. (2015). Emotion regulation in parenthood. *Developmental Review, 36*, 1–14.

Satir, V. M. (1964). *Conjoint family therapy*. Palo Alto, CA: Science and Behavior Books.

Satir, V. M. (1972). *Peoplemaking*. Palo Alto: Science and Behavior Books.

Schade, L. C. (2013). Non-suicidal self-injury (NSSI): A case for using emotionally focused family therapy. *Contemporary Family Therapy, 35*, 568–582.

Scharf, M., & Mayseless, O. (2007). Putting eggs in more than one basket: A new look at developmental processes of attachment in adolescence. *New Directions for Child and Adolescent Development, 117*, 1–22.

Schaefer, C. E., & Drewes, A. A. (2011). The therapeutic powers of play and play therapy. In C. E. Schaefer (Ed.), *Foundations of play therapy* (2nd ed., pp. 15–25). Hoboken, NJ: Wiley.

Sroufe, L. A. (2016). The place of attachment in development. In J. Cassidy and P. Shaver (Eds.) *Handbook on Attachment*, 3rd Ed. (pp. 997–1011). New York: Guilford Press.

Sroufe, L. A., & Fleeson, J. (1988). The coherence of family relationships. In R. A. Hinde & J. Stevenson-Hinde (Eds.), *Relationships within families: Mutual influences* (pp. 27–47). Oxford: Oxford University Press.

Stavrianopoulos, K., Faller, G., & Furrow, J. L. (2014). Emotionally focused family therapy: Facilitating change within a family system. *Journal of Couple & Relationship Therapy, 13*, 25–43.

Steinberg, L. (2005). *Adolescence*. New York: McGraw-Hill.

Walsh, F. (2003). Family resilience: A framework for clinical practice. *Family Process, 42*, 1–18.

Weibe, S. A., & Johnson, S. M. (2017). Creating relationships that foster resilience in emotionally focused therapy. *Current Opinion in Psychology, 13*, 65–69.

Weibe, S. A., Johnson, S. M., Lafontaine, M., Burgess Moser, M., Dalgleish, T. L., & Tasca, G. A. (2016). Two-year follow-up outcomes in emotionally focused couple therapy: An investigation of relationship satisfaction and attachment trajectories. *Journal of Marital and Family Therapy, 43*, 227–244.

Weiss, R. S. (1982). Attachment in adult life. In C. M. Parkes and J. Stevenson-Hinde (Eds.), *The place of attachment in human behavior* (pp. 171–184). New York: Basic Books.

Whitaker, C. A. (1975). Psychotherapy of the absurd: With a special emphasis on the psychotherapy of aggression. *Family Process, 14*, 1–16.

Willis, A. B., Haslam, D. R., & Bermudez, J. M. (2016). Harnessing the power of play in emotionally focused family therapy with preschool children. *Journal of Marital and Family Therapy, 42*, 673–687.

Wittenborn, A., Faber, A. J., Harvey, A. M., & Thomas, V. K. (2006). Emotionally focused family therapy and play therapy techniques. *The American Journal of Family Therapy, 34*, 333–342.

Zuccarini, D., Johnson, S. M., Dalgleish, T. L., & Makinen, J. A. (2013). Forgiveness and reconciliation in emotionally focused therapy for couples: The client change process and therapist interventions. *Journal of Marital and Family Therapy, 39*, 148–162.

TWO

Families and Emotion— Sharing the Language of Attachment

In the broadest sense, the field of family therapy had its origin in a simple shift in treatment focus. In family therapy the starting point for conceptualization of psychopathology and its treatment shifted its focus toward patterns of interaction in families rather than individual issues (Nichols & Schwartz, 2007). The advent of family therapy took place in the context of a broader discussion of the science of cybernetics and self-regulating systems. General systems theory (Bertalanffy, 1968) sought a broader conceptualization of the more mechanistic metaphors of cybernetics, emphasizing instead a more universal orientation toward living systems. As numerous theories of family therapy spawned from this initial shift, increasing attention was given to the power of the system over and against the influence of the individual, creating a false dichotomy of sorts (Nichols, 1987). John Bowlby, not commonly listed in the panoply of family therapy pioneers, represents an alternate legacy that followed a similar shift from the individual to relationship within the context of family life.

In this chapter we explore the relationship of Bowlby's attachment theory and core principles from family systems theory focusing on their relationship to the practice of EFFT. Then we examine Bowlby's own ideas about family treatment and recent developments in attachment-oriented family therapy and their related contributions to EFFT. A review of the core tenets of attachment theory is provided and their role in shaping EFFT practice is identified. Finally, we conclude with a brief review of the role of emotion in EFFT practice as we work to restore resilience through strengthening the affectional bonds of families.

Attachment and Family Systems Theories

Family systems theory proved central to development of a majority of family therapy theories in their approach to treatment. Bowlby's development of attachment theory drew upon related influences including general systems and control theories (Marvin & Britner, 2008). In fact, attachment is a systemic theory focusing as it does on the power of

29

feedback loops of emotional messages and responses between intimates and the impact of such loops on individual functioning (Johnson & Best, 2003; Marvin, 2003). An EFFT theory of family assessment and treatment follows several systemic principles outlining the relationship of symptoms to the structure of family interactions and the predictable processes that keep these interactions in place.

Attachment theory and family systems theory intersect in the following ways.

Interdependence. In both theories, families are seen as a system that is composed of individual persons and patterns of communication between them. The family, as a whole, is different from the simple sum of these parts, nor is one able to reduce an understanding of the family to just the individual patterns between the parts. Although one can understand the dynamics of a unique dyad (e.g., mother–child) in the family, to understand the functioning of a family one must also consider the broader function of the family as a whole. Both attachment theory and family systems theory recognize the integration of interpersonal and intrapsychic influences in shaping the individual and corporate experience of being a family. Traditionally, a family systems approach may emphasize triadic interactions over dyadic ones exclusively, but both assume that relationships in a family system represent more than the specific relationships between individuals. In EFFT the therapist recognizes that while shifts in individual dyads may unlock insecure patterns of responding, the positive emotions and felt security from this change will impact other relationships in the family and the general family experience.

Circular Causality. Linear assumptions of simple cause and effect are challenged in systems and attachment theories. Rather than being determined in one direction (e.g., parent to the child), the process of influence in a family system is organized by reciprocally determining circular patterns. The process of establishing and maintenance of attachment security requires an ongoing feedback system based on an attachment figures availability in a time of need. Feedback loops are intrinsic to interpersonal systems and inform behaviors of individuals impact and influence the actions of others and shape change and stability within a system (Watzlawick, Bavelas, & Jackson, 1967, 2011). The EFT therapist recognizes the negative emotional states that define maladaptive patterns in the family are co-created and mutually reinforced by family members unilateral attempts to resolve threats and distress within the family. This most often occurs without awareness or acknowledgment that the problematic actions of an over-involved parents or a withdrawn child are best understood as part of a stable pattern of negative interactions between parent and child.

Dysfunction. The presence of symptoms in family, while often attributed to the behavior and function of one member, is better understood within the context of the family as a relational system. Maladaptive behaviors have their own logic when seen and experienced in the context of overly diffuse or rigid boundaries which heighten threats of rejection and abandonment. Dysfunctional interactional patterns block family members' ability to access and process the information necessary to retain an emotional balance individually and relationally (Johnson & Best, 2003). This shift from problem to pattern need not imply blame or responsibility to the family for an individual's disorder and maladaptation. The EFT therapist identifies the problematic patterns and the maladaptive responses that result, reframing the focus on the problem to the patterns that prime these negative responses. Viewing these negative interactions as blocked attachment communication also increases understanding for the function of symptoms in the family system.

Adaptive Systems. Family processes are principally adaptive responses to changing demands and needs within the family system. Both attachment theory and family systems adopt a non-pathologizing understanding of family behavior. Both theories recognize the role of homeostatic processes which seek to retain balance in the system and organize behaviors accordingly.

Bowlby (1973) proposed a developmental pathway model that emphasized that this trajectory was influenced by early experience and later inputs that continue to influence developmental outcomes. The adaptive function of the attachment system is to shape secure connection across development and the skills and behavioral systems that promote wellbeing and survival. EFFT concentrates on the adaptive resources of attachment-related emotions and uses these emotions to prompt the natural systems that guide caregiving and attachment responding in family relationships.

In working with a family, the EFT therapist moves the focus of a parent and adolescent conflict to the impact of the self-protective responses that disrupt more adaptive emotional responses. For example, a therapist would reflect an adolescent's frustrations as his pleas to be heard by a parent are ignored. Joining his protest, the therapist validates the impenetrable wall of indifference that has grown between them and explores what it's like to be left outside of the support he seeks. As themes of rejection and the hurt along with a slowly shifting sadness in his voice develop, the therapist heightens his sadness as a signal of the son's emerging need but also the importance of the parent's support. The deeper emotion of sadness begins to prime the parent's concern and interest given the vulnerability experienced in this moment. The therapist also works through blocks in the caregiving responses of parents and partners, while also accessing the attachment-related experiences of those in need of care or support. Through these resources and corrective experiences, the EFT therapist assists the family in correcting their responses and finding new resources that get them back on a developmental pathway toward exploration and growth.

There is significant common ground in family systems theory and attachment theory. Both share the influence of Bertalanffy (1968) and his recognition of the function and attributes of living systems. These theories share an understanding of the nature of the individual in the context of relationship and the complex relationships of causality in treatment of individual and relationship dysfunction. Together family systems and attachment theory underscore the adaptive nature of change in development and the role the family plays in promoting adaptation and thriving.

Attachment and Family Therapy

John Bowlby (1979) envisioned the contribution of attachment theory to the maturing field of family therapy that was limited back then to a focus on communication patterns, behavioral interactions, and multi-generational structures. In fact, he wrote one of the earliest family therapy papers (1949) and espoused the acknowledgment of the vulnerability and pain, such as fear and aloneness, underlying negative behavior in children and adolescents. For Bowlby family therapy provided a context where families could discuss their experiences of the family that were seldom discussed if even noticed, providing a safe context to explore the implicit realities often disrupting the natural ability of the family to adapt to new demands and change.

Bowlby (1979) saw in family interviews an opportunity to explore the defensive processes that governed family interactions. Too often, he reasoned, "there are strong pressures toward forgetting, distorting, repressing, and falsifying, exonerating one party and then blaming another" (p. 177). Therefore, family therapy provided a focus on the experiences that family members seldom discussed, at least in a manner that they were clear about their experiences and their own responses in the moment. Bowlby's assumption was that the family therapist would provide a secure base where individual members could explore a here and now experience to arrive at a personal understanding of themselves and others. This exploration would focus on the reality of everyday life experiences, especially those where patterns of connection and disconnection were involved. The therapist would also be listening for typical responses over each individual's relationship history, especially where working models of self and other were represented. Specific attention was given to relational responses specific to separation and how clients responded to this stressor. Following Bowlby's suggestions regarding family assessment and treatment three themes emerge:

1. A focus on the here and now interactional experiences of family life.
2. A focus on predictable or patterned responses that are indicative of working models of relationship.
3. A focus on separation-related distress and the primacy of love and care in the face of uncertainty.

For Bowlby (1979) this need for care was intrinsic to human nature.

> I regard the desire to be loved and cared for as being an integral
> part of human nature throughout adult life as well as earlier and
> that expression of such desires is to be expected in every grown-up,
> especially in times of sickness or calamity.
>
> (p. 184)

John Byng-Hall (1999), a contemporary of Bowlby, elaborated further
on the application of attachment theory to family therapy. He reasoned
that the dyadic focus of attachment theory was a limiting factor in the
integration of attachment theory more readily into mainstream family
therapy models. In response, Byng-Hall proposed a "secure family base"
to represent the network of attachment relationships that are held
within a family and one in which individual family members are
responsive to and responsible for its maintenance (Byng-Hall, 1995).
Collaboration among caregivers remained a crucial factor in the development of this attachment network, where there was a common awareness of the importance and necessity of protecting attachment
relationships. The boundaries and nature of these caregiving alliances
vary in composition by family and by culture, but the universal expectation remains one of caring for others when in need. Family conflict,
parentification, abuse, and competition for care may lead to power- or
distance-related conflicts in the family disrupting the secure family base.

Attachment Approaches to Family Therapy

Recent developments in attachment research and its implications for
family functioning have supported the development of attachment-
related approaches to family therapy. Two family therapy approaches,
related to EFFT, are reviewed. Each illustrate the application of attachment theory to family intervention. Principles and practices similar to
EFFT are identified and key differences in these approaches are
addressed.

Attachment Focused Family Therapy/Dyadic Developmental Psychotherapy (DDP)

Psychologist Daniel Hughes developed Dyadic Developmental Psychotherapy (2004, 2007) based on his clinical treatment of children and
youth who suffered abuse and neglect and were often in adoptive and
foster placements. These children suffered from severe forms of psychological distress including a fragmented sense of self and disorganized
attachment as a result of complex traumatic experiences. Hughes (2004)
proposed DDP with the goal of providing children a secure attachment

relationship through the therapist, who could support the child in accessing disowned aspects of self, expand a range of affective experience, and increase their capacity to reflect on and integrate new understandings of self and others. Although DDP does not meet criteria as an evidence-based treatment, the published findings do suggest that it is promising (Hughes, Golding, & Hudson, 2018).

In attachment-focused family therapy (AFFT), Hughes (2007) broadened his DPP approach to general family treatment following the same principles and practices he found successful in treating children in the DDP model. In AFFT, the therapist uses playfulness, acceptance, curiosity, and empathy (PACE) to foster a strong alliance with the child that provides a platform for affective-reflective dialogue, which is the core process involved in AFFT (Hughes, 2011). The AFFT approach fosters attachment security as a resource to promote affect regulation and reflective functioning, helping children and caregivers make meaning of their experience through affectively attuned relationships. Together these processes promote the accurate awareness, sharing, and responding of a child's experience and a coordinated and engaged parental response.

Overall, Hughes' work with young children highlights the essential role of the therapist as a resource for co-regulation of emotion and the development of meaning. The interpersonal regulation of emotion promotes the development of a child's internal regulation, including inner self-awareness. Hughes' work in AFFT demonstrates how a therapist matches non-verbal cues of a child following the ways in which positive parenting responses match the child's expressions in rhythm, beat, intensity, duration, and shape. AFFT underscores the ways in which a parent's more regulated affective state is "absorbed" by the child and used as a means for ordering the child's inner world and giving meaning to the child's experience. Affective attunement is essential to AFFT, where intersubjective experience between parents and children provides inner awareness through relationships that are in synchrony, where intentions are shared, affect is matched, and attention and awareness is directed toward the same experience (Hughes, 2007). In AFFT, attachment and intersubjectivity co-inform the mechanism of therapeutic change and promote developmental growth.

Attachment Based Family Therapy

Attachment-based family therapy (ABFT) offers clinicians a family-based, empirically supported treatment, focused on rebuilding and restoring caregiver and child relationships following attachment-related ruptures in parenting. Guy Diamond and Gary Diamond (Diamond, Diamond, & Levy, 2014) formalized and evaluated the efficacy of ABFT efficacy through a series of clinical trials treating depressed and suicidal adolescents (Diamond, Russon, & Levy, 2016). The primary goals of

ABFT are to renew a child's confidence in the availability of their caregiver and to promote more responsive parenting. Through fostering corrective attachment experiences, the ABFT therapist increases affect regulation in the family and better communication in the family characterized by greater perspective taking and more effective collaborative problem solving. As a result, parents and children increase their capacity for affect regulation, conflict resolution, and family cohesion that remain important buffers against suicidal thinking, depression, and youth risk behaviors.

Five treatment tasks organize ABFT through defining the goals and directing steps to resolve the family's presenting concern. The first task (Relational Reframe) focuses on the reduction of criticism and hostility in the family by shifting intentions to rebuilding relationships rather than managing behaviors. The reframe draws attention toward relational needs and solutions that already exist within the family. In the second task (Adolescent Alliance), the therapist meets with the adolescent to understand and explore the attachment ruptures and their impact on the care and support the child has received. The third task (Caregiver Alliance) invites parents exclusively to focus on the pressures and distress experienced in caregiving, prompting attention and concern for their child's need. Parental investment in responding to these needs is heightened, emphasizing more effective parenting strategies and including parent emotion coaching. These previous tasks prepare youth and caregiver to address the attachment rupture in the fourth task (Repairing Attachment). Caregivers and child directly address core relationship failures, and parents are encouraged to respond to the adolescent's grievances with empathy and openness. Parent acknowledgments and apologies are encouraged. In the final task (Promoting Autonomy) the focus shifts to promoting the adolescent's sense of competency and self-esteem. The therapist invites parents to challenge and support their child's growth in self-responsibility and taking steps toward greater autonomy. Specific attention is given to increasing parental awareness of the connection between adolescent mood-related problems and parent and child attachment ruptures related to the child's need for love and support.

Contributions and Considerations for EFFT Practice

As attachment-based interventions, these approaches share a common goal of correcting the attachment and caregiving experiences of parents and the children who depend on them. These models guide the conceptualization of child problems and family distress using attachment theory as a principle resource. Each approach provides unique contributions to an attachment-informed family therapy and insights for the EFT therapist working with families.

Similarities with EFFT

EFFT and AFFT share a similar focus on attachment-related emotion as a resource for promoting change in increasing felt security in families. Dan Hughes' work with children provides a remarkable demonstration of the power of affective-reflective dialogue through attention to attunement and attachment-related affect states. Similar to EFFT, AFFT sessions focus on processing emotion in "here and now" interactions, where poignant emotional experiences are the focus of attention, regulation, and understanding. In their work with emotions both models rely on the therapist's attunement to present experience and their awareness of attachment emotion to guide children and parents into new experiences. In these moments the therapist conjectures aloud about these concrete emotional experiences, often giving voice to the expression of attachment-related emotion and needs. The therapist in AFFT and EFFT works to establish moments of affective resonance that provide a source of new understanding about self and other.

Both models emphasize the therapist's alliance as essential to accessing and expanding emotions. The therapist's role as an attachment figure is pivotal in dyadic regulation of emotion and meaning construction for children. Hughes (2007) promotes an open and curious stance (PACE) in interacting with children and families as a resource for exploration and engagement, which mirrors the EFFT emphasis on the therapist's curious, genuine, and empathic stance. The therapist in each model frames the problematic behaviors and negative emotions in the context of insecure attachment experiences and creates opportunities for the family to repair these connections.

Conceptually EFFT and ABFT (Diamond et al., 2013) share several common assumptions regarding family treatment and attachment processes. Both ABFT and EFT recognize that a central task in adolescence requires accessing and negotiating autonomy in family relationships. This is a coordinated effort between parents and requires a balance in relatedness and autonomy (Allen, 2008). Each approach offers parents and adolescents relationally based resources for navigating the need for support and safety in a stage of developmental exploration and shaping of adult identity (Johnson, 2019). Specifically, ABFT incorporates EFT focus and practices that promote the sharing of vulnerable emotions related to attachment experiences. In Task 4 of ABFT the therapist leads a family into more vulnerable conversation regarding core attachment themes where the sharing of emotional experiences related to key attachment experiences is pivotal to treatment change. EFFT and ABFT promote the use of attachment-related emotions to organize corrective experiences between caregivers and youth.

ABFT and EFT focus on shifting the family's focus from the presenting problem to the relational distress that is associated with these symptoms. Both models reframe negative interactions in the context of blocked attachment communication and actively provide a process for correcting these relationships interactionally. Using this frame, the therapists in ABFT and EFFT heighten parents' caregiving intentions and awareness to a child's unmet attachment needs and vulnerabilities. Both approaches follow a specific process for resolving these blocks through modifying attachment-related communication and contact in the family.

Differences with EFFT

Although each of these attachment-based interventions share a common overarching goal and many related practices, key differences are evident in the practice of EFFT. These differences highlight EFFT's emphasis on working with emotion and relationships in the moment. EFFT's experiential focus uses the accessing and sharing of attachment-related emotions to promote more secure interaction and this occurs through active engagement of those emotions and relationships in the moment. Two primary differences between these models and EFFT are best seen in EFFT's systemic focus and its approach to experiential focus.

Systemic Focus. AFFT and EFFT share a similar focus on accessing and processing attachment-related emotion as a core feature of transforming insecurity. EFFT, however, emphasizes the systemic or relational impacts of insecurity and similar to ABFT, targets systemic patterns that emerge from insecure family processes and the ways these patterns interrupt attachment processes. Three differences result from this systemic emphasis.

First, in EFFT attachment insecurity is engaged at a self and a system level. AFFT retains a stronger child focus, relying more heavily on the therapist's relationship with the child to promote new experiences of security that are used as a basis for involving a more responsive parent. EFFT emphasizes multiple attachment processes in the family system and the ways in which family distress and felt insecurity at a systemic level can organize more than one dyad and the child's individual experience.

Second, EFFT focuses on actively working through parental blocks to engagement and these blocks are seen as interacting with a child's own blocks to care-seeking. AFFT focuses on guiding parents around issues that block their availability so that parents can respond with greater accessibility and responsiveness. Systematically coaching parents in more secure responses is a critical element in the AFFT change process.

Finally, EFFT relies on enactments of shared emotional experience to move parent and child relationships toward greater security. The therapist works with parents and children together to track and engage moments of attunement, mis-attunement, and repair. The primary focus on attunement in AFFT is used more broadly and more dynamically with family relationships, where the EFT therapist is focused on specific interactions in session that capture parents' and children's successful and unsuccessful attempts at mutual regulation of attachment-related affect and needs.

Experiential Focus. EFFT and ABFT target relationship blocks and attachment ruptures as a focus for intervention. Thematically both approaches follow a similar trajectory: Shifting focus from the problem to the relationship, accessing child attachment experiences and needs, promoting parental responsiveness, and engaging repair through reparative enactments. Whereas EFFT and AFFT share a similar approach to accessing, processing, and engaging emotion, EFFT and ABFT approaches differ in their use of emotion to transform relationships experientially. This difference is apparent in three ways.

First, the task-focus of ABFT orders sessions focused on person-specific alliance goals (e.g., adolescent or parental alliance) where in EFFT the focus of a session is guided by the relational process of the family. Both ABFT and EFFT use family, parent, and individual sessions, however these sessions are more flexibly determined in EFFT based on the process of treatment and unique needs of a family. Apart from the initial sessions, the EFT therapist dynamically engages the development and strengthening of parent and child alliances through actively processing the child's and parents' experience in session. This process focus underscores the stronger experiential and relational emphasis found in EFFT sessions.

Second, the EFT therapist as a function of this experiential and relational emphasis will use enactments throughout the process rather than organize around a specific enactment session. In EFFT, enactments are used as a resource to resolve relational blocks and engage deeper levels of felt security and in that way EFFT and ABFT share a common goal. However, in EFT enactments serve a number of functions including assessing family members' responses to direct conversation, intensifying present experiences including sharing a newly felt experience, engaging a stuck position such as a relational block; or using enactment for turning deeper emotional experiences into new relational connections (Tilley & Palmer, 2013). Enactments are essential in identifying relational blocks and working through those blocks. For example, the EFT therapist may ask a father to share a caring response to his daughter only to find that the daughter rebuffs her father's comfort. The therapist uses this enactment of the relational block unfolding in session as an entry point to working through the experience of the child's defensive block to caregiving. Emotional processing and engagement are critical to effective use of enactments through the EFFT process of change.

A final difference in EFFT and ABFT centers on how each approach works with emotions. Although both ABFT and EFFT promote access to vulnerable emotion and support parents empathically responding to the attachment needs of their children, ABFT relies on the use of emotion coaching to assist parents in increasing their parenting skills, specifically around emotion. In ABFT the therapist serves as a coach to parents in practicing various emotion skills including: Validation, acceptance of negative emotion, and negotiation and compromise. In EFFT the therapist uses emotion as a catalyst for awareness, understanding, and action. The EFT therapist helps parents and children assemble their emotional experience and through a secure relational context explore and connect to a parent's caregiving intentions and a child's attachment-related needs. In EFFT the crucible for transforming the relational blocks of family distress exists in the heart of a parent's and child's ability to communicate at an emotional level about the needs and care that matter most.

The similarities in these approaches underscore the influence of attachment theory as a powerful resource for transforming relational bonds in families. Broadly these approaches work toward a similar goal using attachment theory as a guide. The differences noted highlight EFT's approach to emotion as a target and agent of change in relationships, and the active use of attachment processes in the present moment to promote family bonds that promote growth and strengthen resilience.

Attachment Theory and Emotionally Focused Therapy

Emotionally focused family therapy assumes the primacy of attachment relationships in the conceptualization and treatment of maladaptive family patterns. In development of EFT, Johnson (1986) drew attention to attachment theory as a resource for understanding couple relationships, highlighting the difference between approaching relationship problems as bonds to be repaired instead of bargains to be negotiated. EFT sought to advance a focus on intimacy and love rather than the conflict and communication, both long standing emphases in couple therapy at the time. Through the development of EFT Johnson continued to advance the role of attachment theory in conceptualizing EFT treatment as evident in her second edition of *The Practice of Emotionally Focused Therapy* (Johnson, 2004), *Attachment Processes in Couple and Family Therapy* (Johnson & Whiffen, 2003), *Love Sense* (Johnson, 2012), and her most recent overview of EFT practice (Johnson, 2019). The practice of EFT is then perhaps best understood as a clinical application of attachment theory whether one is working with an individual, couple or family. In previous works, Johnson (e.g., 2004, 2019) has outlined core tenets of attachment theory and their relevance to EFT practice. Here we review a series of these core assumptions and their relevance to an EFT approach to family therapy.

1. Attachment is a Fundamental Motivating Factor in Human Relationships

Human flourishing presumes an individual has others who one can rely upon for safety and security. This longing for a "felt sense" of connection is fundamental in prioritizing human goals and needs. This basic motivational system animates and organizes relational interactions across the lifespan as the need for social contact particularly in moments of uncertainty or threatened wellbeing. These basic human instincts are themselves universal phenomenon though their expression may vary by particular culture (Mesman, IJzendoorn, & Sagi-Schwartz, 2016). Attachment provides an adaptive model to understand the core motivations that shape human behavior.

Attachment, then, as a relational motivation system, can be used to explain the intricacies of family interactions. A parent's caring response to a child's nonverbal cues of pain and discomfort illustrates how the intrinsic logic of attachment bids link to caregiving responses. When these normal or expected actions are present a child's need is addressed and over a series of these interactions a child learns something of value about his social world and his place in it. A child cries, a parent responds, this is expected. Conversely, when this system is disrupted, and the expectancies of a child are not met distress results, which sets in motion a negative reinforcing pattern that sends a contrary message about one's wellbeing and value. A similar, though more mutual, pattern of caregiving also informs a couple's relationship (Feeney & Collins, 2001). These reciprocal systems govern the network of attachment resources that make up a family system (Sroufe, 1988) and provide the family therapist with a relational framework for understanding individual distress and psychopathology within the context of a family system (Cowan & Cowan, 2005). In EFFT the therapist understands the motivations of parents and children based on the intrinsic motivations of care-seeking and caregiving. The EFT therapist attunes to these underlying motivations that inform an individual's behaviors and organize more secure or insecure relational patterns.

2. Constructive Dependence and Autonomy are Mutually Informing and Reinforcing, but not Mutually Exclusive

Individual wellbeing is premised upon the ability to engage and sustain mutually beneficial relationships. The development of personhood whether organized around assumptions of individuation, autonomy or differentiation all presume a relational context. Attachment theory implies a "dependency paradox" where an individual's ability to sustain an effective reliance on a trusted other is associated with greater autonomy (Feeney, 2007). When a child or adult has another that he or she can effective rely on they have in this relationship a source of strength and resilience (Johnson, 2019). Secure attachment, founded in a felt sense of confidence in the availability of another, is associated with increased identity coherence and positivity (Mikulincer, 1998). Therefore, secure attachment relationships provide a basis for belonging through which individuals explore and become whole.

Bowlby (1975) suggested that proximity seeking is essentially an adaptive response, not one that often results in a loss of self or emotional fusion. One's attachment bonds are specific to a particular person, an attachment figure. As affectional ties they may be shared with a parent, sibling, friend, romantic partner or spiritual figure (e.g., God). Bowlby recognized that the attachment system was primary in infancy and early childhood and lessened in activation over development. Nevertheless, the need for these bonds is durable over time and present throughout one's life. As affectional ties, the activation, maintenance, and disruption of these bonds are characterized by emotional experience, particularly evident when threatened or repaired (Bowlby, 1979). Through secure attachment individuals are more effective in close relationships and better able to express their needs and respond to those of others. Through more attuned and congruent interactions attachment security promotes resilience through buffering stress and supporting positive forms of coping.

For family therapists, attachment theory offers a model of interdependence rooted in behavioral systems that provide security, buffer fear, and promote exploration. As a goal-oriented and goal-correcting system, attachment offers therapists a map for the motivations and meanings that order affective experiences in a family system that provides essential resources for safety and security but also for growth and development. Bowlby illustrates this balance in his description of parenting:

> A central feature of my concept of parenting [is] the provision by both parents of a secure base from which a child or an adolescent can make sorties into the outside world and to which he can return knowing for sure he will be welcomed when he gets there, nourished physically and emotionally, comforted if distressed, reassured if frightened. In essence this role is one of being available and ready to respond when called upon to encourage and perhaps assist, but to intervene only when clearly necessary.
>
> (Bowlby, 1988, p. 11)

In order to maintain this balance, parents and children must have attuned communication regarding the signaling of attachment-related emotions and needs. The EFFT process of change enables families to find their *emotional balance* as they are navigating the changing needs and new demands faced across the lifespan. Through assembling and engaging emotional experiences the therapist guides parents and children and couples toward more vulnerable emotions that promote clear and direct information about caregiving and care-seeking within the family.

3. Felt Security is a Primary Goal of the Attachment System

The experience of felt security provides a resource of protection, support, and growth. As a psychological state, felt security is a safety cue, one that signals the suspension of proximity seeking in the face of a threat or a need for support. Over time the successful experience of seeking protection, gaining comfort, and security increases an individual's perceived confidence in the availability of others and consequently the ability to regulate emotion and effectively engage in close relationships. The impact of felt security broadens and builds with this confidence as does one's sense of being loved and valued, as noted specifically in romantic attachment (Mikulincer & Shaver, 2015). The presence of felt security is evident in two essential attributes of secure attachment: Safe Haven and Secure Base.

SAFE HAVEN

Attachment figures offer a source of comfort and reassurance in a time of need. Access to a responsive attachment figure in times of distress provides a "safe haven" that provides relief and a sense of wellbeing in uncertainty. Further, the repeated experiences of safety and assurance of this responsive parent or partner provides a buffer against everyday demands and uncertainty in life (Mikulincer, Florian, & Weller, 1993). Ultimately this provision of safety is contingent on the availability of one's attachment figure and the confidence one has that this person will effectively respond to the need for safety from emotional or physical distress.

SECURE BASE

Attachment figures provide a resource for supporting exploration and development through their support and availability if needed. In this way a child or adult experiences confidence in the availability and responsiveness of another who is there when needed. This confidence frees the explorer to attend to interests and activities with the freedom that they have a solid base standing behind them when needed. The presence of security promotes greater engagement and understanding of oneself and one's actions (Fonagy & Target, 1997) and greater awareness and openness to one's own world (Mikulincer, 1997).

For the family, felt security remains a general goal and Bowlby specifically identified "availability" as the "set goal" of the attachment system. Perceived availability means one believes that a line of communication is open to the attachment figure; that the attachment figure is within physical reach; and the attachment figure will respond to a signal of need (Ainsworth, Blehar, Waters, & Wall, 1978). Therefore, the belief and confidence in a caregiver's availability is based on experience. This cognitive belief is a representation of an experienced reality of the ready presence of another to be available if and when needed. In addition, the experience of felt security is an interactional reality and one that is based on reciprocal responses to needs and concerns that are relationally specific, where everyday actions of the attachment figure matter (Kobak & Madsen, 2008).

Through the process of EFFT the therapist promotes a predictable and stable environment characterized by a therapeutic alliance that is accessible, responsive, and emotionally engaged. The EFT therapist represents a type of attachment figure that enables partners, parents, and children to explore their experience of the family and take new risks of vulnerability together. The treatment alliance provides a safe haven for individuals caught in the storms of family distress and a secure base to promote exploration of new experiences found in the deeper emotions related to their family's affectional bonds. The therapist provides the family with new opportunities to explore and expand their understanding of their views of others and help each person learn to see their own attachment-related responses and needs as valid and attainable.

4. Emotional Availability and Engagement are Necessary for Sustained Bonds of Trust

A parent's availability and responsiveness to her child's emotional cues are pivotal to the development of felt security and vital relationship bonds. The active attunement to emotion is central to attachment communication and necessary in differentiating motivation and meaning inherent in maintaining access and response to key relationship bonds. Consequently, the blocking of emotion or absence of responsive action in poignant moments of personal vulnerability are fundamentally disruptive. Bowlby (1980) noted the role of "defensive exclusion" in families where certain emotional responses and communication was excluded. The "still face paradigm" demonstrates the negative effects of a parent's withdrawal from interaction with an infant or young child (Tronick, Als, Adamson, Wise, & Brazelton, 1975). The loss of the parent's expected emotional engagement and availability to the child's attempts to correct a loss of connection poignantly demonstrate the key role of engagement and availability in primary relationships.

Relational blocks between parents and child are less dramatic than the shift that occurs in the still face paradigm. A parent who chronically dismisses his child's complaints and protests, labeling these behaviors as "too sensitive" and "not important," creates a relational block that negatively impacts the child's trust in the parent, his own value in his parent's eyes, or both.

The absence of parental engagement or even the acknowledgment of a loss of connection in a parent–child interaction impacts the felt security experienced in that relationship. The child's emotional responses are a distress signal associated with separation distress and the failure of the system to correct for these signals impacts the child and his relationship to the parent.

The EFT therapist follows a family's interactional process through the emotional signals they use to navigate their needs, looking for relational blocks. The therapist's alliance functions as a pivotal resource in supporting the regulation and validation of the varied and often competing experiences of family members. Through the availability of the therapist and the family's emotional engagement, new emotions and experiences are explored as family members make sense of their actions and experiences at moments of distress. For example, the EFT therapist focuses on the interactions where a parent disregards their child's emotional signal and explores the underlying experience of both child and parent in these moments. Fears related to the child's perceived lack of importance and value are acknowledged, as well as the parent's parallel feelings of shame and incompetence, that somehow he is failing the child. The therapist's goal is not simply to acknowledge or understand these deeper attachment-related emotions but to also share these experiences and shape a greater sense of trust between family members.

5. Isolation and Loss are Traumatizing Experiences

The experience of loss, separation, and deprivation are essential to an understanding of attachment. For Bowlby, these negative impacts proved pivotal in the formation of a child's development and on an individual's ability to address life's other challenges. Without confidence in another's availability, children and adults are more vulnerable to chronic fear in response to perceived threats (Bowlby, 1973). As such, attachment theory provides the therapist with an orientation to the significance and impact of actions that result in emotional hurt, rejection, and abandonment. The pre-eminence of loss and isolation underscore the basic reactions that predominate relationship interactions particularly when attachment needs are at stake and in turn normalize the efforts children and adults take to cope with these encompassing traumatic experiences.

Family patterns of insecurity promote more extreme vigilant and protective responses between family members. These more extreme responses are consistent with fears of loss and separation from those who are sought to provide connection and care. In EFFT the therapist reframes the more extreme behaviors parents and children use in distress to the underlying fears of loss, isolation, and desperation. These fears also provide important information regarding the significance of these relationships and how what is feared is also often what is most needed. The EFT therapist enables children and parents to access and engage these fears and the needs which they signal.

6. Predictable Patterns of Separation Distress

The process of family interactions follow an in sync, out of sync, and back in sync pattern. No parent and child relationship is perfectly attuned, there is an inherent "messiness" in the process of development especially in the experience of self and self-regulation (Tronic, 2007, p. 11). The attachment system is a guidance system that through feedback provides correction for the mismatches that normally occur in parent-child interaction. The failure to gain comfort or contact from an attachment figure results in predictable patterns of distress (e.g., increased anger and anxiety, which then coincide with predictable negative interactional responses including: Angry protest, clinging demands, depressive withdrawal, and despair (Bowlby, 1979). A child's so called "over sensitivity" may also be a signal for correction that going unheeded results in escalation of negative emotion.

These negative responses trigger more defensive parental behaviors creating and reinforcing a relational block between parent and child. As these blocks and the negative emotions that accompany them escalate, parents, partners, and children are all less able to maintain their emotional balance and less likely to connect with one another, especially at an attachment level (Kobak, Duemmler, Burland, & Youngstrom, 1998). The isolation and loss of connection from these attachment resources is traumatizing and compounds feelings of helplessness, fear, and despair (Mikulincer, Shaver, & Pereg, 2003). The EFT therapist follows the emotional process as cues to a child's underlying needs and a parent's caring response are often masked by protective response to the separation distress organizing their interactions. The greater the threat to the relationship and to each person's wellbeing the more extreme distress responses become, including critical attacks or defensive withdrawal.

7. Rigid Positions Most Often Reflect Underlying Strategies

The predictable pattern of a parent's persistent withdrawal from a child's contemptuous complaints and the escalation of defensive negativity that results as this interaction plays out highlight rigid interactional positions driven by an increasing field of negative emotion. Patterns of family distress reflect the underlying positions or strategies parents and children use to cope with the lack of emotional balance and regulation in a relationship of attachment significance. These interactional positions become evident in the predictable actions and repetitive emotional sequences that follow times when families confront attachment-related needs. A child comes to expect that his needs do not matter and that his parent's indifference is predictable. Similarly, the parent anticipates the child negative behavior and has a ready response related to the negativity regardless of the nature of the child's concern. These interactions become both practiced and predictable. As a family struggles to resolve these concerns family members draw upon increasingly ineffective strategies, giving rise to greater insecurity rooted in the relational blocks to caregiving and attachment communication.

In a more secure family interaction parents and children rely on primary attachment and caregiving responses that result in effective support and care in moments of distress and concern. A primary attachment strategy describes a parent's active engagement and deliberate response to a child's need for care, protection, or support. These interactions promote felt security and provide an emotional balance where family members gain confidence in the responsiveness of others and their own value and importance. When family interactions are defined by unsuccessful attempts marked by a lack of availability or support, individuals are more likely to draw on secondary attachment strategies to cope with distress through de-activating or hyper-activating the attachment system using varying degrees of avoidance and anxious responding (Fraley & Waller, 1998).

In a more insecure interactions these secondary strategies form the basis for the complementary rigid positions found among parents, partners, and children in patterns of insecurity. In romantic attachments, partner positions are often described by of pursuit (anxious or hyperactivating strategy) and withdrawal (avoidant or deactivating strategy). These secondary attachment strategies form the basis of the common demand withdraw pattern found in distress couple relationships. Secondary attachment strategies in parent and child interaction are also informed by anxious and avoidant responses serving a similar attempt to redress the breakdown in attachment communication. The goal of a parent and child relationship is different than that of romantic partners, therefore the positions associated with parents and children are better framed by the action tendencies associated with caregiving and care-seeking. Focusing on the actions associated with these underlying strategies a parent's rigid position may be over-responsive (anxious) or under-responsive (avoidant) and the child strategy may be described by actions that intensify (anxious) or minimize (avoidant) attachment-related cues.

HYPERACTIVATING

The more anxious strategy focuses on engaging an attachment figure who is not available or supportive. Responses are hyperactivated and often include actions that are common in distressed relationships and may include: Demanding or domineering responses, critical pursuit, and anxious clinging behaviors. The demanding quality of these actions underscore the preoccupied focus on the attachment figure and often desperate but unsuccessful attempts to address attachment-related injuries and fears. Individuals who identify with more anxious strategies are more likely to have more negative views of their own worth and be prone to self-doubt (Mikulincer & Shaver, 2015). Reactive responses shaped by this more negative view of self, increase the likelihood of greater negative emotion through critical complaints, intense emotional exchanges, and emotionally intrusive actions focused on another.

DE-ACTIVATING

The more avoidant strategy emphasizes actions and efforts to de-activate the attachment system. Individual actions seeking to avoid or distance from attachment signals include dismissing and suppressing emotional cues and responses. This strategy includes instrumental attempts to address and correct problems without engaging the emotional aspects of the problem. Physical and relational distance may be used to cope with the impact and heightened emotional intensity, particularly in the face of another's hyperactivating responses. A primary goal of the avoidant strategy prioritizes self-reliance while maintaining relational distance and de-emphasizing the importance of relational needs and intimate concerns (Mikulincer & Shaver, 2016). These strategies undermine an individual's ability to deal effectively with negative experiences through avoidance of vulnerability and compromises one's ability to effectively regulate negative emotions.

MIXED

A third strategy involves a mix of avoidance and anxious responses to attachment communication. This attachment style is described as fearful avoidant in adult attachment relationships (Bartholomew & Horowitz, 1991) and disorganized attachment for individual child-focused assessments (Main & Hesse, 1990). Individuals may find it difficult to determine whether to anxiously pursue or avoidantly withdraw and as a result embody a more chaotic or disorganized style (Simpson & Rholes, 2002). Traumatic experiences often are precursors with this strategy, where the source of one's attachment support is also a source of threat or pain. These competing experiences contribute to the lack of coherence and consistency in this strategy and impact in attachment and caregiving interactions. Caught between both the tendency for dismissing and distancing from others and the desire for others' love and support, often a fearful avoidant strategy is accompanied with an underlying sense of regret (Mikulincer & Shaver, 2016).

These strategies can be described as "habitual forms of engagement" (Sroufe, 2016) underscoring their practiced and routine use interpersonally.

In family life these secondary attachment strategies impact the effectiveness of partners and parents to provide meaningfully secure responses to the attachment bids of others. More anxious responses in adult relationships results in caregiving that is out of sync with a partner's needs and in more extreme ways controlling or emotionally intrusive. Similarly, more avoidant strategies inhibit effective caregiving resulting in more insensitive and insufficient emotional connections. Moreover, parental caregiving reflects similar difficulties when secondary attachment strategies govern parent and child interactions. Parental insecurity can disrupt parents' ability to effectively regulate their emotions in interactions with their children (Mikulincer & Florian, 1998), which in turn also limits a parent's ability to repair relational ruptures through forgiveness, compassion, and empathy (Jones, Cassidy, & Shaver, 2015).

The EFT therapist, through tracking the actions embedded in problematic interaction patterns, brings light to the predictable underlying attachment strategies that organize individual and relationship experiences particularly in moments of distress. There is a recognition that these patterns inhibit the effectiveness of a family to support and care for one another in times of significant need. These secondary strategies represent the family's best attempts to cope and manage family distress, as such they also point to the underlying motivations these family members have for something different than the negative patterns that disrupt the family's emotional balance.

8. Working Models of Self and Other

Over time attachment experiences provide a mental model of self and other in one's relational world. These mental representations based on attachment histories serve important roles in emotion regulation, intimate relationships, exploration, and caregiving. Bowlby (1973, 1980) proposed the concept of an "internal working model" to describe how these mental representations offer unique procedural scripts that shape and order expectation regarding interactions with self and others. Individuals with secure attachment are more likely to see their relational world as responsive and available for support, and at the same time seeing themselves as worthy of love and valued. These models provide predictions of others' actions and one's own in response, so these models carry forward a view of self and a view of other that guides and shapes interactions without and within the family.

These models primarily inform the expectancies one has about being loved and counting on others. Two primary questions summarize these implicit attachment-related concerns: "Can I count on you," and "Am I worthy of your love?" The predictions one carries into attachment relationships shape the expectations, automatic perceptual biases, episodic memories, beliefs and attitudes, and one's procedural knowledge informing close relationships (Collins & Read, 1994). Bowlby (1980) recognized that these models were subject to review through the lifespan as other attachment relationships provide a basis for reflecting and revisiting the meaning of past attachment experiences. In addition to parent–child relationships the influence of peer attachments, romantic relationships/marriage, and psychotherapy provide cogent sources to review the expectations informed by one's attachment history.

These emotionally loaded "hot" models are a primary focus in EFT's approach to modifying attachment orientations. EFT seeks change in couples' relationships through accessing and regulating attachment needs and fears; shaping new ways partners engage attachment-related needs, priming newly revised working models, highlighting availability of one's partner, and clarification of views of self as vulnerable, but competent and effective in their relationship to others (Johnson, Lafontaine, & Dalgleish, 2015). In the same way the EFFT approach focuses on accessing attachment-related needs and their related emotions and promoting responsively attuned caregiving responses to remove the blocks to felt security that defined distressed family relationships.

The EFT therapist focuses on accessing and delineating the deeper emotions associated with attachment longings and needs. These experiences are used through attuned attachment-focused interactions to make explicit the expectancies parents and children engage in the context of insecurity. These internal models serve to forecast what is expected from the other as well as how one sees himself or herself. The father who reacts harshly to his son's aloof indifference may hold in mind a rejecting view of his child and his own shame in failing to be the father he intends. Similarly, the son shields himself from his father's distant anger fearing his own rejection and confirming that his father should not be trusted.

9. Caregiving

The innate motivational system of caregiving prioritizes a parent's focus on her/his child's wellbeing whether that is confronting a threat of harm or supporting an opportunity for growth and development. As a complementary system to attachment, the caregiving response works in synchrony with attachment-related needs (George & Solomon, 2008). Bowlby (1980) suggested that a parent's protective responses provided a safe haven and Ainsworth (1991) identified similar ways caregiving contributed to a secure base, promoting exploration and growth. As an innate system, the signals for caregiving are cued in circumstances of danger or threat and when there are opportunities for growth. Caregiving behaviors include taking active interest in another's problems and supporting or acknowledging successful efforts in coping with these difficulties. Expressions of love and affection giving instrumental support and providing direction and advice are also common to caregiving (Collins, Ford, Guichard, Kane, & Feeney, 2010). Caregiving behaviors characterize the care, support, and protection given to the young by parents and comfort, security, and care shared in adult attachment relationships. We expect to see a parent soothing a distressed child just as we also do the caring response of two adults in love. Caregiving is an expected response in the context of relationships of attachment importance.

As a response system, effective caregiving is marked by empathic concern and a sensitivity to the other's signals of distress or need for support. A parent's accurate reading of these cues promotes responses that are characterized by generous intentions, validation of concerns and needs, respect for beliefs, attitudes, and helping the person feel cared for, understood, and loved (Reis, 2014). Effective caregiving also contributes to a generalized awareness of felt security and an increase in coping ability as a result (Collins et al., 2010). Reciprocally, caregivers in turn benefit from greater positive affect through self-efficacy, moral affirmation, and stronger relational ties through their actions promoting others' wellbeing.

In EFFT, the therapist promotes more effective caregiving responses through aligning with parental caregiving intentions and working through blocks to accessibility, responsiveness, and emotional engagement in the parent's interaction with the child. The EFT will deepen attachment-related affect to prime parental motivations of care and concern. A parent who hears her child's hurt and fears of abandonment shared with the therapist is more likely to be aware of their caregiving intentions in response to these emotional cues. The therapist, using evocative interventions, would deepen the parent's awareness of their child's attachment cues and the parent's underlying emotional response. A parent might say in response to an evocative question:

> I hear her fears and I want to comfort and reassure her [caregiving motivation and attuned awareness] but I don't think she wants that from me at least like she used to. She keeps me at a distance in these moments [relational block].

The therapist slows the family interaction and makes space for the emotional cues of attachment and caregiving, which are inherent in the parent and child's relational struggle.

10. Emotional Balance and Regulation in Caregiving

Effective caregiving requires emotional regulation on the part of the caregiver. In parenting, caregiving responses are informed by the parental expectations, values, and how the parents view the child (Solomon & George, 1996). Flexibility in a parent's representational model or view of their child enables more effective awareness and differentiation of the care-seeking goals of the child and the parent's ability to effectively respond. Consider the mother who pauses to consider the demanding tone of her adolescent daughter as not dismissive of her mother's efforts but perhaps a less regulated signal of the daughter's need to assert her interest. This mother's flexibility reflects her ability to see her daughter and her relational world, including its emotional terrain.

Flexibility and emotional balance are negatively impacted by defensive processes that block parental attunement, understanding, and responsive action. Defensive caregiving is more than a deficit in parenting skills, rather it reflects a loss of attunement and empathic failure. Parents may abdicate their caregiving role altogether, through failing to respond or failing to protect. Other negative caregiving responses may also result from dysregulated caregiving when the caregiver is overwhelmed by fear or a loss of confidence in an ability to respond. Parental shame may block a caregiver's ability to attune and attend to the attachment communication, creating a self-reinforcing cycle that amplifies distress for the parent that in turn impacts the family as a whole.

The EFFT process promotes emotion regulation and emotion generation for parents blocked in their caregiving responses because of the negative patterns of insecurity. The EFT therapist's alliance with parents provides emotional ballast to ground the parents' experience in the present moment and through assembling affective experiences, the therapist assists the parent in accessing and processing caregiving intentions and attunement to their child's attachment-related needs. Evocative interventions are essential in focusing parental awareness of the parents' own vulnerability, through access to their own fears the parent is better able to attune to her child. For example, a therapist uses an evocative question to explore a mother's experience just hearing her daughter express her fear of rejection

DAUGHTER: *(looking away in tears)* I just don't know if she cares like she used to, you know after all my mistakes, I am not the daughter I once was. The daughter I used to be, the one she really wanted me to be.

THERAPIST: This is so hard to hear, to see the pain in her face as she says she might not be the daughter you really want. What happens for you as you hear your daughter's pain?

The therapist primes the parent's caregiving awareness by focusing the daughter's attachment-related emotions.

MOTHER: It breaks my heart that she feels like I don't want her. She will always be my daughter.

The therapist validates the mother's care and provides a resource for the mother to explore her own heartbreak and pain as it resonates with the pain of her daughter. As parents access their deeper emotions, they are better able to review the values, expectations, and representational models they have of self (parent) and of other (child) (Solomon & George, 1996). The therapist promotes greater flexibility in the parent's view of their child through increasing awareness and delineation of that parent's goals for the child (e.g., parental intentions) and supporting the ability of that parent to effectively respond. Increased parental emotional regulation results in more accurate attunement to their child's needs and a greater range of emotional responses enables parents to more effectively respond to the specific emotions and needs of their child.

The EFT therapist may also draw upon the caregiving alliance shared between two parents to promote caregiving. A couple's parenting alliance represents the attachment bond they share as a couple or their romantic attachment and their explicit alliance as caregivers. Kobak and Mandelbaum (2003) suggest that "cooperative caregiving alliance" includes a mutual investment and shared responsibility for each partner's role as a caregiver and open communications and feedback in their individual efforts to raise their child. These qualities often follow from parents with more secure attachments as couples, as they are more likely to be more accessible, responsive, and emotionally engaged in their relationship and their parenting.

Partners and parents can lose their emotional balance in caregiving roles. Ineffective caregiving alliances result from a number of sources (Kobak & Mandelbaum, 2003). First, parental disagreements and differences in parenting beliefs and histories can prove emotionally threatening given the importance of the parenting role. Second, a parent's insecurity in the parenting role may inhibit that parent's ability to effectively attune to the child's experience and needs. A couple's more anxious alliance can disrupt their attention to the unique needs of their child, particularly if the child's problems are difficult to understand or have negative impact on the parents. A third source is the couple's relationship itself. Patterns of insecurity in the couple relationship may organize around parental concerns and the couple's insecure patterns of pursuit and withdrawal. These patterns can in turn unbalance a partner's parental involvement and interest in the child and replicate the couple's pattern of avoidance and anxious responding into the parents' responses as caregivers.

Parents who are well adjusted as a couple offer children a sense of "emotional security" and as a couple in distress the child is vulnerable to maladjustment (Davies & Cummings, 1994). Children may react to their parents' relational strife through disengaging or emotionally distancing from family interactions, or reactively engaging their parents in a way to diffuse or de-escalate the couple's conflict. Children may also seek to stabilize their parents' relationship distress through direct involvement in the couple's relationship or balancing the family through adopting a more "parentified" role (Byng-Hall, 2008; Crittenden, 2008;

Dallos & Vetere, 2012). Children in family environments with parental discord seek to regain balance through proactive efforts to manage parental distress and the negative effects of their conflict on the family. The quality of this caregiver alliance is a key influence in a family's overall emotional climate and a potential source of risk to parenting practice (Morris, Silk, Steinberg, Myers, & Robinson, 2007).

In EFFT the therapist conceptualizes these reactive patterns following the unique attachment-related goals of the distressed relationships. The multi-level nature of family interaction requires the therapist to identify the layers of insecurity in the family, which may involve parent and child as well aa couple-related distress. EFFT provides a process of change that enables a therapist to work through the relational blocks of insecurity in any of these three levels: parent–child, parental alliance, or at the couple level. Through engaging the family distress the therapist is able to better assess and prioritize the focus of each session and the significance of the attachment-related blocks and their impact on family functioning. These tenets of attachment theory offer the therapist a conceptual framework for understanding and modifying family relationships through the affectional bonds they share.

EFFT and Working with Families and Emotion

In EFFT emotion is central in transforming a family's insecure pattern to positive cycles of security. A common goal of an EFT session involves seeking change through how a client(s) engages and expresses her or his emotional experience (Johnson, 2019). EFT interventions facilitate the therapist's ability to access, expand, understand, and engage emotional experience in a process that promotes emotional regulation. Through more regulated states the therapist leads the family through reversing reactive mutually reinforcing interactional patterns, and revisiting negative expectancies and representations of self and other that block effective caregiving and attachment communication. Through corrective emotional experiences, families shift to more secure interactional patterns. In this final section we explore the role of attachment and emotion regulation as critical developmental influences that shape the relational processes that point families toward adjustment and growth or dysfunction and distress.

Emotion Regulation

Emotion regulation describes the ability to influence emotion and its expression (Gross, 1998). The process of regulating emotion includes being able to access and respond to a range of emotions, identify and modify an emotional experience, and form meaning through these experiences. The development of this capacity is a complex skill that is learned and evolves over one's lifetime. Regulation of emotion involves an individual's ability to impact the process of generating an emotional response given that this process is also influenced by the individual's awareness, goals, and strategies (Gross & Thompson, 2007). These strategies or regulatory processes range from avoiding situations to avoiding emotional experience, changing situations to redirect emotional experiences, shifting attention to redirect one's experience, shifting the meaning of an experience, and modulating emotional experience through changing behaviors or physiological responses to emotion. The process of employing these strategies which involves both explicit and implicit responses to influence the occurrence, intensity, and expression of emotion is the essence of emotional regulation (Morris et al., 2007).

There remains wide acceptance that emotion regulation serves a principle role in the etiology and maintenance of psychopathology. Suppression, rumination, and avoidance, all strategies of emotional control, are associated with a range of psychological disorders, especially problems of anxiety and depression, while more adaptive strategies such as acceptance (leading to reduced experiential avoidance) and cognitive reappraisal are not (Mennin & Farach, 2007; Aldao, Nolen-Hoeksema, & Schweiser, 2010). Difficulties in a child's ability regulate his emotions are related to greater risk for behavior problems later in life (Cicchetti, Ackerman, & Izard, 1995; Silk, Steinberg, & Morris, 2003) and psychopathology more generally (Gross & Jazaireri, 2014).

Families and Emotion Regulation

Families play an important role in the development of children's emotional regulation. A child's capacity to regulate emotional experience is influenced by what they observe from family interaction, what parents and caregivers do directly through parenting practices, and the quality of family relationships including the emotional climate of the home (Morris et al., 2007). These influences have direct effects and indirect effects. A parent's dismissive response to a child's fearful elicitation for support has a direct impact on the child's ability to regulate that fear; whereas more indirect influences may be seen in a child who avoids household interactions that include excessive and hostile parental conflict. This background anger has a negative impact on the family's emotional climate, similar to the ways that ratings of expressed emotion (Leff & Vaughn, 1985) that have been used to assess the deleterious effects of hostility, criticism, and emotional over-involvement in family communications. Increasing attention is being given to the family's role in providing a context that influences individual capacities (e.g., emotional regulation) through understanding the family as an "emotion system", where attachment plays a critical role (Henry, Morris, & Harrist, 2015).

Attachment relationships play a critical role in the co-regulation of emotional experience in childhood and form the basis for the development of the self-regulation of emotion. Parents play a crucial role in shaping emotion regulation. Through co-regulation, a parent offers a child resources for regulating his or her own physiological, behavioral, and emotional responses (Sroufe, 2016). These acts of mutual regulation and their resulting experience provide stepping stones to the development of the child's ability for self-regulation (Kopp, 1982). The absence of parental presence and lack of these regulatory resources may result in loss of the child's regulatory abilities (Calkins & Leerkes, 2011). The role of mutual regulation also presents a common challenge for parents that is to maintain their own regulated state in the face of caring for their distressed or dysregulated child and at the same time seeking to help the child regulate his or her own experience (Rutherford, Wallace, Heidemarie, & Mayes, 2015). While greater attention has been given to parental role in shaping emotion regulation in the early stages of childhood, developmental changes in adolescence and young adulthood continue to influence this capacity (Steinberg, 2005; Steinberg & Morris, 2001).

Attachment theory provides insight into the rewards and consequences of felt security in family interactions that assume the availability of mutual regulation. The confidence in a caregiver's availability provides a resource for resilience and a foundation for social adjustment and psychological wellbeing (Mikulincer & Shaver, 2016). Parents who are more secure are more likely to be open to expressing their emotions and communicating their feelings without distortions and communicate with others more clearly and accurately. Securely attached parents and children are more likely to find and maintain their emotional balance, together. Family members are less easily triggered by the other and are better able to tolerate ambiguity in interactions as they have a felt awareness that distress is manageable and one is not alone. Felt security enables individuals to reflect on their emotional experience and put order to it, in effect regulating that emotional experience. Their emotional balance renders secure individuals less likely to deny, distort or exaggerate their emotional experiences (Shaver & Mikulincer, 2007). This resource enables parents to be receptive to their own emotions and those of their children, express and communicate those emotions, and use them as a guide to effective action.

In contrast, more insecure individuals are more vulnerable to distorting negative experiences (through suppression or repetitive activation of negation emotion as a consequence of their secondary attachment responses). When these insecure strategies come into play in moments that anticipate a child's mutual regulation with their parent, distortions in attachment communications easily result. Overall, these secondary strategies compromise an adult's abilities to identify, describe, and explore emotional experience (Mikulincer & Shaver, 2019). These dyadic influences define the reciprocal function of emotional regulation, where a parent's regulatory responses influence a child's emotional regulation and a child's responses impact a parent's regulation (Rutherford et al., 2015). Therefore, more secure interactions promote adaptive cycles characterized by effective emotional regulation including more effective emotional communication, and insecurity results in maladaptive patterns subject to greater emotional dysregulation.

Negative Patterns of Family Distress

The impact of maladaptive patterns of dysregulated affect in family relationships increases the likelihood that the emotional climate itself will become organized by negative affect. Patterns of negative affect increase the likelihood of triangulation in a family system as a result of the insecurity experienced in the family, particularly in families that include a distressed couple relationship (Byng-Hall, 2008; Crittenden, 2008; Dallos & Vetere, 2012). Insecure family systems either amplify or suppress negative emotions resulting in a greater likelihood that distorted emotional responses will cascade into reactive sequences that result in a runaway escalation of hostility or shutdown of communication and loss of contact.

Family relationships, similar to couple relationships, face a common risk of falling into absorbing negative affect states (e.g., Gottman, 1994). Insecure processes in family interactions increase the likelihood that negative emotions (e.g., fear, anger) lose their corrective influence as parental responsiveness and accessibility is reduced by more anxious or avoidant responses (Kobak et al., 1998). Over time the loss of parental availability drives separation distress and the resulting efforts to correct for these deficits and corresponding negative emotions erode confidence in the family's ability to effectively respond and family members increasingly rely on self-protective strategies to cope with the impact of a negative family climate. Attachment communication in the family becomes distorted as different members respond to negativity and distress through strategies that seek to manage rather than resolve the attachment-related distress driving the felt insecurity

Family patterns provide templates for emotional realities in the distressed family. Following interaction patterns enables the therapist to access and explore these realities that bring regulation and engagement to the emotional experiences that naturally signal individual needs and responses in the family. Tracking positive interactions in secure family relationships demonstrates a similar function of emotion. A child who turns with joy toward her mother when receiving an excellent mark on a school assignment and is met with her mother's attuned and perhaps exaggerated response experiences a capitalization (Gable, Gonzaga, & Strachmen, 2006) of that experience and a confirmation of importance not because of the excellent mark, rather as a result of being met emotionally in a moment that mattered. Thus, the engagement of positive affect states broadens abilities, enhances perspectives, and promotes resilience and wellbeing (Fredrickson, 2001). Negative affect states also serve important survival functions by narrowing attention and prompting actions to avoid danger. Together the ability to sustain and maintain a positive balance over time enables flourishing (Fredrickson & Losada, 2005).

EFFT focuses on shifting the relational blocks that persist when family interactions are defined by negative emotional states. These negative affect states emerge from ineffective attempts to read and respond to attachment-related need in the family system. Rigid patterns of interaction illustrate the predictable emotional realities organizing actions, understanding, and experience. The EFT therapist uses these emotional realities as a guide and a resource for creating corrective experiences that shift the emotional balance toward a self-sustaining, self-reinforcing pattern of relational growth and flourishing. Emotions are EFT's target and the agent of change (Johnson, 2004).

Summary

This chapter reviews the theoretical background for the EFFT process of change. Attachment theory provides a resource for human and relationship functioning that elaborates aspects of individual development and functioning that are consistent with family systems theory. Reviews of two prominent models exploring the use of attachment theory and family therapy emphasize new formulations in family treatment that privilege the intrapersonal and interpersonal systems within a family. The core attachment-related tenets were explored emphasizing the application of EFFT, and emotion regulation was highlighted as one of the core processes that leads to new experiences through the process of EFFT treatment. The following chapter illustrates the core assumptions of EFFT and the steps to practice.

References

Ainsworth, M. D. S. (1991). Attachment and other affectional bonds across the life cycle. In C. M. Parkes & J. Stevenson-Hinde (Eds.), *Attachment across the life cycle* (pp. 33–51). New York: Routledge.

Ainsworth, M. D. S., Blehar, M. C., Waters, E., & Wall, S. (1978). *Patterns of attachment: A psychological study of the strange situation.* Oxford: Lawrence Erlbaum.

Aldao, A., Nolen-Hoeksema, S., & Schweizer, S. (2010). Emotion-regulation strategies across psychopathology: A meta-analytic review. *Clinical Psychology Review, 30,* 217–237.

Allen, J. A. (2008). The attachment system in adolescence. In J. Cassidy & P. R. Shaver (Eds.), *Handbook of attachment theory research, and clinical applications* (2nd Ed., pp. 419–435). New York: Guilford Press.

Bartholomew, K., & Horowitz, L. M. (1991). Attachment styles among young adults: A test of a four-category model. *Journal of Personality and Social Psychology*, 61, 226.

Bertalanffy, L. (1968). *General system theory*. New York: Braziller.

Bowlby, J. (1949). The study and reduction of group tensions in the family. *Human Relations*, 2(2), 123–128.

Bowlby, J. (1973). *Attachment and loss: Vol. 2. Separation*. New York: Basic Books.

Bowlby, J. (1975). Attachment theory, separation anxiety, and mourning. *American Handbook of Psychiatry*, 6, 292–309.

Bowlby, J. (1979). *The making and breaking of affective bonds*. London: Tavistock Publications.

Bowlby, J. (1980). *Attachment and loss: Vol. 3. Loss, sadness and depression*. New York: Basic Books.

Bowlby, J. (1988). *A secure base*. New York: Basic Books.

Byng-Hall, J. (1995). Creating a secure family base: Some implications of attachment theory for family therapy. *Family Process*, 34, 45–58.

Byng-Hall, J. (1999). Family couple therapy: Toward greater security. In J. Cassidy & P. R. Shaver (Eds.), *Handbook of attachment: Theory, research, and clinical applications* (pp. 625–645). New York: Guilford Press.

Byng-Hall, J. (2008). The significance of children fulfilling parental roles: Implications for family therapy. *Journal of Family Therapy*, 30, 147–162.

Calkins, S. D., & Leerkes, E. M. (2011). Early attachment processes and the development of emotional self-regulation. In K. D. Vohs & R. F. Baumeister (Ed.), *Handbook of self-regulation: Research, theory, and applications* (2nd ed., pp. 355–373). New York: Guilford Press.

Cicchetti, D., Ackerman, B. P., & Izard, C. E. (1995). Emotions and emotion regulation in developmental psychopathology. *Development and Psychopathology*, 7, 1–10.

Collins, N. L., & Read, S. J. (1994). Cognitive representations of attachment: The structure and function of working models. In K. Bartholomew & D. Perlman (Eds.), *Advances in personal relationships: Attachment processes in adulthood* (Vol. 5, pp. 53–92). London: Jessica Kingsley.

Collins, N. L., Ford, M. B., Guichard, A. C., Kane, H. S., & Feeney, B. C. (2010). Responding to need in intimate relationships: Social support and caregiving processes in couples. In M. Mikulincer & P. R. Shaver (Eds.), *Prosocial motives, emotions, and behavior: The better angels of our nature* (pp. 367–389). Washington, DC: American Psychological Association.

Cowan, C., P., & Cowan, P. A. (2005). Two central roles for couple relationships: Breaking negative intergenerational patterns and enhancing children's adaptation. *Sexual and Relationship Therapy*, 20, 275–288.

Crittenden, P. M. (2008). Why do inadequate parents do what they do? In O. Mayseless (Ed.), *Parenting representations* (pp. 388–433). Cambridge: Cambridge University Press.

Davies, P. T., & Cummings, E. M. (1994). Marital conflict and child adjustment: An emotional security hypothesis. *Psychological Bulletin*, 116, 387–411.

Dallos, R., & Vetere, A. (2012). Systems theory, family attachments and processes of triangulation: Does the concept of triangulation offer a useful bridge? *Journal of Family Therapy*, 34, 117–137.

Diamond, G. S., Diamond, G. M., & Levy, S. A. (2014). *Attachment-based family therapy for depressed adolescents*. Washington, DC: American Psychological Association.

Diamond, G., Russon, J., & Levy, S. (2016). Attachment-based family therapy: A review of the empirical support. *Family Process, 55*(3), 595–610.

Feeney, B. C. (2007). The dependency paradox in close relationships: Accepting dependence promotes independence. *Journal of Personality and Social Psychology, 92*(2), 268.

Feeney, B. C., & Collins, N. L. (2001). Predictors of caregiving in adult intimate relationships: An attachment theoretical perspective. *Journal of Personality and Social Psychology, 80*, 972–994.

Fonagy, P., & Target, M. (1997). Attachment and reflective function: Their role in self-organization. *Development and Psychopathology, 9*, 679–700.

Fraley, R. C., & Waller, N. G. (1998). Adult attachment patterns: A test of the typological model. In J. A. Simpson & W. S. Rholes (Eds.), *Attachment theory and close relationships* (pp. 77–114). New York: Guilford Press.

Fredrickson, B. L. (2001). The role of positive emotions in positive psychology: The broaden-and-build theory of positive emotions. *American Psychologist, 56*, 218–226.

Fredrickson, B. L., & Losada, M. F. (2005). Positive affect and the complex dynamics of human flourishing. *American Psychologist, 60*, 678–686.

Gable, S. L., Gonzaga, G. C., & Strachman, A. (2006). Will you be there for me when things go right? Supportive responses to positive event disclosures. *Journal of Personality and Social Psychology, 91*, 904–917.

George, C., & Solomon, J. (2008). The caregiving system: A behavioral systems approach to parenting. In J. Cassidy & P. R. Shaver (Eds.), *Handbook of attachment: Theory, research, and clinical applications* (2nd Ed.) (pp. 833–856). New York: Guilford Press.

Gottman, J. M. (1994). *What predicts divorce? The relationship between marital processes and marital outcomes*. Hillsdale, NJ: Lawrence Erlbaum.

Gross, J. J. (1998). The emerging field of emotion regulation: An integrative review. *Review of General Psychology, 2*, 271.

Gross, J. J., & Jazaieri, H. (2014). Emotion, emotion regulation, and psychopathology: An affective science perspective. *Clinical Psychological Science, 2*, 387–401.

Gross, J. J., & Thompson, R. A. (2007). Emotion regulation: Conceptual foundations. In J. J. Gross (Ed.), *Handbook of emotion regulation* (pp. 3–24). New York: Guilford Press.

Henry, C. S., Morris, A., & Harrist, A. W. (2015). Family resilience: Moving into the third wave. *Family Relations, 64*, 22–43.

Hughes, D. (2004). An attachment-based treatment of maltreated children and young people. *Attachment & Human Development, 6*, 263–278.

Hughes, D. A. (2007). *Attachment-focused family therapy*. New York: W. W. Norton.

Hughes, D. A. (2011). *Attachment-focused family therapy: The workbook*. New York: W. W. Norton.

Hughes, D., Golding, K. S., & Hudson, J. (2015). Dyadic developmental psychotherapy (DDP): The development of the theory, practice and research base. *Adoption & Fostering, 39*, 356–365.

Johnson, S. M. (2004). *The practice of emotionally focused therapy: Creating connection*, 2nd Ed. New York: Brunner/Routledge.

Johnson, S. (2008). *Hold me tight: Seven conversations for a lifetime of love.* New York: Little Brown.

Johnson, S. M. (2019). *Attachment theory in practice: Emotionally focused therapy with individuals, couples, and families.* New York: Guilford Press.

Johnson, S. M., & Best, M. (2003). A systemic approach to restructuring adult attachment: The EFT model of couples therapy. In P. Eerdman & T. Caffery (Eds.), *Attachment and family systems: Conceptual, empirical, and therapeutic relatedness* (pp. 165–189). New York: Brunner Routledge.

Johnson, S. M., & Whiffen, V. E. (Eds.). (2003). *Attachment processes in couple and family therapy.* New York: Guilford Press.

Johnson, S. M., Lafontaine, M.-F., & Dalgleish, T. L. (2015). Attachment: A guide to a new era of couple interventions. In J. A. Simpson & W. S. Rholes (Eds.), *Attachment theory and research: New directions and emerging themes* (pp. 393–421). New York: Guilford Press.

Jones, J. D., Cassidy, J., & Shaver, P. R. (2015). Parents' self-reported attachment styles: A review of links with parenting behaviors, emotions, and cognitions. *Personality and Social Psychology Review, 19*, 44–76.

Kobak, R., & Madsen, S. (2008). Disruptions in attachment bonds: Implications for theory, research, and clinical intervention. In J. Cassidy & P. R. Shaver (Eds.), *Handbook of attachment: Theory, research, and clinical applications* (pp. 23–47). New York: Guilford Press.

Kobak, R., & Mandelbaum, T. (2003). Caring for the caregiver: An attachment approach to assessment and treatment of child problems. In S. M. Johnson and V. E. Whiffen (Eds.), *Attachment processes in couple and family therapy* (pp. 144–164). New York: Guilford Press.

Kobak, R., Duemmler, S., Burland, A., & Youngstrom, E. (1998). Attachment and negative absorption states: Implications for treating distressed families. *Journal of Systemic Therapies, 17*, 80–92.

Kopp, C. B. (1982). Antecedents of self-regulation: A developmental perspective. *Developmental Psychology, 18*, 199–214.

Leff, J., & Vaughn, C. (1985). *Expressed emotion in families.* New York: Guilford Press.

Main, M., & Hesse, E. (1990). Parents' unresolved traumatic experiences are related to infant disorganized attachment status: Is frightened and/or frightening parental behavior the linking mechanism? In M. T. Greenberg, D. Cicchetti, & E. M. Cummings (Eds.), *The John D. and Catherine T. MacArthur Foundation series on mental health and development. Attachment in the preschool years: Theory, research, and intervention* (pp. 161–182). Chicago, IL: University of Chicago Press.

Marvin, R. S. (2003). Implications of attachment research for the field of family therapy. In P. Eerdman & T. Caffery (Eds.), *Attachment and family systems: Conceptual, empirical, and therapeutic relatedness* (pp. 3–27). New York: Brunner Routledge.

Marvin, R. S., & Britner, P. A. (2008). Normative development: The ontogeny of attachment. In J. Cassidy & P. R. Shaver (Eds.), *Handbook of Attachment*, 2nd Ed. (pp 269–294). New York: Guilford Press.

Mennin, D., & Farach, F. (2007). Emotion and evolving treatments for adult psychopathology. *Clinical Psychology: Science and Practice, 14*, 329–352.

Mesman, J., Van Ijzendoorn, M. H., & Sagi-Schwartz, A. (2016). Cross-cultural patterns of attachment. *The handbook of attachment: Theory, research, and clinical applications* (pp. 852–877). New York: Guilford Press.

Mikulincer, M. (1997). Adult attachment style and information processing: Individual differences in curiosity and cognitive closure. *Journal of Personality and Social Psychology, 72*, 1217–1230.

Mikulincer, M. (1998). Adult attachment style and affect regulation: Strategic variations in self-appraisals. *Journal of Personality and Social Psychology, 75*, 420–435.

Mikulincer, M., & Florian, V. (1998). The relationship between adult attachment styles and emotional and cognitive reactions to stressful events. In J. A. Simpson & W. S. Rholes (Eds.), *Attachment theory and close relationships* (pp. 143–165). New York: Guilford Press.

Mikulincer, M., & Shaver, P. R. (2015). Boosting attachment security in adulthood: The "broaden-and-build" effects of security-enhancing mental representations and interpersonal contexts. In J. A. Simpson & W. S. Rholes (Eds.), *Attachment theory and research: New directions and emerging themes* (pp. 124–144). New York: Guilford Press Press.

Mikulincer, M., & Shaver, P. R. (2016). *Attachment in adulthood*, 2nd Ed. New York: Guilford Press.

Mikulincer, M., & Shaver, P. R. (2019). Attachment orientation and emotion regulation. *Current Opinion in Psychology, 25*, 6–10.

Mikulincer, M., Florian, V., & Weller, A. (1993). Attachment styles, coping strategies, and posttraumatic psychological distress: The impact of the Gulf War in Israel. *Journal of Personality and Social Psychology, 64*, 817–826.

Mikulincer, M., Shaver, P. R., & Pereg, D. (2003). Attachment theory and affect regulation: The dynamics, development, and cognitive consequences of attachment-related strategies. *Motivation and Emotion, 27*, 77–102.

Morris, A. S., Silk, J. S., Steinberg, L., Myers, S. S., & Robinson, L. R. (2007). The role of the family context in the development of emotion regulation. *Social Development, 16*, 361–388.

Nichols, M. P. (1987). *The self in the system.* New York: Brunner/Mazel.

Nichols, M. P., & Schwartz, R. C. (1998). *Family therapy: Concepts and methods*, 4th Edn. Boston: Allyn & Bacon.

Reis, H. T. (2014). Responsiveness: Affective interdependence in close relationships. In M. Mikulincer & P. R. Shaver (Eds.), *The Herzliya series on personality and social psychology. Mechanisms of social connection: From brain to group* (pp. 255–271). Washington, DC: American Psychological Association.

Rutherford, H. J. V., Wallace, N. S., Heidemarie, K. L., & Mayes, L. C. (2015). Emotion regulation in parenthood. *Developmental Review, 1*, 1–14.

Shaver, P. R., & Mikulincer, M. (2007). Adult attachment strategies and the regulation of emotion. In J. J. Gross (Ed.), *Handbook of emotion regulation* (pp. 446–465). New York: Guilford Press.

Silk, J. S., Steinberg, L., & Morris, A. S. (2003). Adolescents' emotion regulation in daily life: Links to depressive symptoms and problem behavior. *Child Development, 74*, 1869–1880.

Simpson, J. A., & Rholes, W. S. (2002). Fearful-avoidance, disorganization, and multiple working models: Some directions for future theory and research. *Attachment & Human Development, 4*, 223–229.

Solomon, J., & George, C. (1996). Defining the caregiving system: Toward a theory of caregiving. *Infant Mental Health Journal: Official Publication of The World Association for Infant Mental Health, 17,* 183–197.

Sroufe, L. A. (1988). The role of infant–caregiver attachment in development. In J. Belsky & T. Nezworski (Eds.), *Clinical implications of attachment* (pp. 18–38). Hillsdale, NJ: Erlbaum.

Sroufe, L. A. (2016). The place of attachment in development. In J. Cassidy and P. Shaver (Eds.), *Handbook on attachment*, 3rd Ed. (pp. 997–1011). New York: Guilford Press.

Steinberg, L. (2005). Cognitive and affective development in adolescence. *Trends in Cognitive Science, 9,* 69–74.

Steinberg, L., & Morris, A. S. (2001). Adolescent development. *Annual Review of Psychology, 52,* 83–110.

Tilley, D., & Palmer, G. (2013). Enactments in emotionally focused couple therapy: Shaping moments of contact and change. *Journal of Marital and Family Therapy, 39,* 299–313.

Tronick, E. (2007). The neurobehavioral and social-emotional development of infants and children. New York: W. W. Norton.

Tronick, E., Als, H., Adamson, L., Wise, S., & Brazelton, T. B. (1978). The infant's response to entrapment between contradictory messages in face-to-face interaction. *Journal of the American Academy of Child Psychiatry, 17,* 1–13.

Watzlawick, P., Bavelas, J. B., & Jackson, D. D. (1967, 2011). *Pragmatics of human communication: A study of interactional patterns, pathologies and paradoxes.* New York: Norton.

THREE

Exploring the EFFT
Process of Change

Emotionally focused family therapy follows a process of change that is principally informed by the EFT treatment approach to couple treatment. The three stages of change are identical as the therapist focuses first on the de-escalation of negative patterns that organize distress in the family before leading a process of restructuring interactions between parents and children. Treatment concludes with a focus on consolidation of the family changes made in treatment and promoting new commitments to new-found patterns of security and positive affect. In this chapter, we provide an overview of the EFFT process of change with an emphasis on the processes that guide the therapist in restoring security and confidence in the family connections they share. Special attention is given to unique attributes of family work defined by working with the hierarchical and reciprocal dynamics organizing parent and child relationships. A case example is used to illustrate the progression of a family through EFFT treatment.

The sources of family distress are varied and the patterns that organize this are influenced by the composition and emotional dynamics of the family. The EFFT focus on de-escalation privileges the role of negative absorbing states and their influence in sustaining distress through the rigid positions parents and children take in response. These problematic patterns are composed of dyadic and triadic interactions typically organized by separation distress in a parent–child relationship, even though multiple family members may also be impacted by the experience of these negative interactions.

The EFT therapist offers a significant resource of support and security to families knocked off balance by these negative patterns. The therapist acknowledges the level of distress in a family and provides a source of support and felt security. Through accessing and processing the family members' emotional experience associated with these fixed patterns, a family is better able to face the blocks that inhibit and interrupt their ability to reach and respond to specific attachment-related needs. Through restructuring interaction patterns, family members engage and experience more productive ways to express and respond to the injuries and needs that typify loss of connection in parent and child relationships. New patterns of emotional accessibility and responsiveness increase a family's ability to engage and encourage felt security in response to changing developmental needs of a maturing family.

In EFFT, we focus on blocks to attachment and caregiving and how children, parents, and partners become stuck in patterns that fuel insecurity and reactive emotional responses. As a result, the process of treatment and a family's participation will vary by those most involved in these negative patterns. More complex than a couple relationship, EFFT uses a decision framework for determining how to organize treatment sessions including those who are invited to each session. We introduce the decision framework in this chapter and provide clinical examples throughout the following chapters to illustrate the principles used to organize treatment. This chapter concludes with a summary of the "EFT tango" and its application to EFFT treatment. The tango illustration provides a parsimonious description of the typical session-to-session process of EFT which is the hallmark of the therapist's work with attachment relationships and the emotions that shape them.

Case Example

Sandra and Darlene sought family therapy with their only child, Erin (19). Erin lived with her moms and was pregnant and in her second trimester. Family tension and conflict centered on concerns regarding the birth of Erin's baby. Sandra was Erin's birth mother and Darlene joined Sandra in raising Erin. Darlene often served as the buffer in Erin and Sandra's conflictual relationship, however in recent years their arguments had diminished yet the two remained distant. This conflict pattern reignited after Erin gave birth to her son. Sandra returned to being critical and overbearing toward Erin, who would withdraw from Sandra's constant complaints and advice. Darlene and Sandra also fought over the best way to approach Erin and her new baby. The conflict escalated to the point Erin threatened to move out and restrict Sandra from seeing her grandson.

EFFT Stages of Change

The stages of EFT provide a summary of the unfolding processes of transforming patterns of insecurity in couple and family relationships. In viewing an EFFT session, the observer would find the therapist tracking and reflecting interactional sequences and the emotional experiences that accompany these reactive moves and through these moments creating new opportunities for making new connections at intrapsychic and interpersonal levels. The process Johnson (2004) delineated for transforming couple relationships through accessing, processing, and restructuring attachment bonds provides a useful framework for organizing

EFFT Process of Change

Stage 1 De-escalation	Stage 2 Restructuring
Step 1: Forming an alliance and family assessment.	Step 5: Accessing and deepening a child's disowned aspects of self and attachment needs.
Step 2: Identifying negative interaction patterns that maintain insecure attachment.	Step 6: Fostering acceptance of a child's new experience and attachment-related needs.
Step 3: Accessing underlying emotions informing interactional positions / relational blocks.	Step 7: Restructuring family interactions focusing on sharing attachment needs and supportive caregiving responses.
Step 4: Redefining the problem in light of relational blocks and negative interaction patterns.	**Stage 3 Consolidation**
	Step 8: Exploring new solutions to past problems from more secure positions.
	Step 9: Consolidating new positions and strengthening positive patterns.

Figure 3.1 EFFT Process of Change.

EFT work with families. The EFFT Process of Change and the accompanying therapeutic steps are listed in Figure 3.1 and an annotated summary is found in Appendix 1.

Stage 1—Stabilizing and De-escalating Family Distress

The goal for the initial stage of EFFT is the stabilization of family distress through the de-escalation of negative interactional patterns. The EFT therapist establishes a treatment alliance with the family members involved in treatment. This alliance is informed by the goals of the family with specific attention given to parental concern. As a source of security to individual family members, the therapeutic alliance supports family exploration of new solutions and alternative interactions from those that currently organize a family's attempt to change. The EFT therapist's genuine and empathic interest establishes a working alliance with those family members involved in treatment. Engaging family member with emotional attunement, relational responsiveness, and accessibility to the primary interests of those involved in the family's struggle furthers the safety and emotional security of the therapeutic alliance.

As the therapist validates each member's various perceptions and experiences, she highlights the family's corporate strengths (Johnson, Maddeaux, & Blouin, 1998). The family's need for security, protection, and support are all critical aspects of family wellbeing and restoring a family's functional balance begins with acknowledging the strengths and vulnerabilities found in their relationships. Assessment of the presenting problem may include separate sessions with parents, siblings, and the child who is the focus of the family's concern. When possible, an initial family session is conducted with all family members relevant to the presenting compliant. These family sessions provide a unique opportunity to assess the family's interaction patterns and overall emotional climate.

Throughout these sessions the therapist is tracking and organizing an understanding of the family through their actions associated with the presenting problem. Following principles of Family Systems (e.g., Bertlanffy, 1968; Minuchin & Fishman, 1981), the therapist explores the everyday actions of family members and how their actions are organized around a problem. Family problems result in distance and distress, often focused on a particular relationship or child. Specific attention is given to tracking interaction patterns and the negative emotions resulting from attempts to address the problem behaviors defining the family distress, and priority in treatment is given to the most distressed dyad, often a key source of the insecurity driving the family's distress.

Attachment theory provides a useful lens of understanding the emotional dynamics of a family. Negative emotional states result from heightened insecurity in the family and the individual typically responds through secondary attachment and caregiving strategies that block the accessibility and responsiveness of attachment figures within the family. These blocked attempts to share needs and provide support foster negative absorbing states that are characterized by emotional states of fear, loss, and anger (Johnson et al., 1998). Children may struggle with feeling unloved or unimportant as their expressed needs for comfort and reassurance are often blocked by fears of rejection or further injury. Similarly, parents may lose confidence in their role and its effectiveness further compounded by parental shame. The effect of these negative interactions furthers the negativity experienced by the family and increases a corporate sense of hopelessness and greater despair (Diamond & Siqueland, 1998). The family's inability to respond to these increasing and intensifying negative emotions leaves family relationships vulnerable to these patterns.

At an emotional level the family experience can reflect a futility and hopelessness that change is unlikely. Often the enduring negative experiences breed deeper fears in the family about the loss of connection and eventual abandonment. Children may struggle with feeling unloved or unimportant as needs for comfort and reassurance are often blocked by fears of rejection or further injury. Similarly, parents may feel increasingly ineffective often failing their own expectations and struggling to respond in the face of their own shame. Parents may over-respond with anxious control, withdraw with critical rejection, or seeming indifference in efforts to cope with their own negative view of themselves.

The safety provided by the therapist's alliance enables family members more readily to access and explore the emotions and actions that define blocks to bonds of caring and connection within the family. The focus on the negative emotions that disrupt parent–child interactions leads to the discovery of more adaptive emotions and related needs that the family's distress is obscuring. Reactive parental concern often betrays an underlying fear or worry for a child's wellbeing. The process of the therapist reflecting surface and underlying emotions along with validating their function lessens the reactive parental and child responses and slows painful reactive interactions. Thereby increasing opportunities for the therapist to explore the impact of these reactive responses and the experiences each family member has as a result. A parent's anxious control, once understood, makes space for that parent to attune to his underlying fears and regrets. Through this experience the therapist heightens the felt concern of the parent and the implicit care that drives his or her heartfelt concern. Similarly, the exploration of a child's defended withdrawal gives attention to the confusion and isolation a child feels in the family. The impact of this isolation is seen in the child's sadness as she shares what it is like for her to feel alone and unwanted at school and at home.

The therapeutic process focuses on reflecting the family's emotions and validating each individual's present experience. As parents and children are better able to attend to these experiences, family members are more likely to access and express the underlying emotions associated attachment needs and parental intentions. The therapist prioritizes the role of emotion in organizing the family's experience and views working through emotional experience as the most powerful resource for promoting change in family patterns of distress (Johnson et al., 1998). In general, EFT assumes that access to and the experience of more adaptive emotions promotes corrective emotional experiences and that these experiences support the family's ability to sustain more regulated and vulnerable emotional communication (Davila, Karney, & Bradbury, 1999; Johnson, 2009).

As the therapist emphasizes the actions and emotions that compose these patterns more attention is given to the role these patterns play in defining specific experiences within the family. Defensive and maladaptive responses are made sense of in the context of a pattern or cycle that takes hold in moments of distress. As a result, parents and children experience blocks in their ability to reach and respond to relevant needs. The therapist reflects and reframes the intensity and importance of these blocks as an attachment struggle where attempts to engage attachment-related needs are met with ineffective and insufficient responses or initiative (Palmer & Efron, 2007). This active focus and validation of these negative patterns enables families to shift their understanding of the problem to an experience that they share rather than just the problem of one person. Families begin to find greater agency as they recognize these patterns and recognize their potential to undermine the ability of the family to respond to needs and expectations.

Similarly, the therapist reframes a parent's frustrated anxious concern as attempt to provide support and care when it matters. Rather than reappraising the parent's action as a matter of intent, the therapist will access the underlying fear and felt concern associated with their frustration, thereby giving demonstration of that parent's concern in session. Whether reframing problems as patterns or recasting parental efforts to control as intentions to care, the EFT therapist is working from the underlying emotions made clear in accessing and processing a parent or child's primary emotion. A parent's ability to see more clearly their own desires and intentions and to witness the unspoken fears and concerns of their children promotes greater openness toward their child and a desire to explore the relationship differently.

De-escalation in EFFT involves assessment processes that outline and increase a family's awareness of the negative interactional patterns that generate distance and insecurity. This requires a safe and secure treatment alliance with all relevant family members that enables the therapist to evoke attachment-related emotions that are implicit in these negative interactions. Through the security of the therapist alliance, parents and children are able to explore the emotions that underlie these patterns and are better able to recognize the attachment-related emotions and the needs being blocked by these relationship patterns.

As a result of de-escalation, the family moves toward less reactivity and more responsiveness once the presenting problem is better understood in the context of these negative cycles. In turn, parents respond with greater openness to their child's vulnerability given their new understanding of their child's need and children become less reactive after seeing more clearly their parent's caregiving intent and experiencing less of their parent's reactivity. A parent's motivation to change may be only "good enough" at this point, recognizing that some parents will struggle to trust the child's experience (Diamond, Diamond, & Levy, 2014) and in EFFT the therapist will continue to support parental openness before asking a child to risk and engage the parents with her or his attachment longings and needs (Palmer & Efron, 2007). Through this initial stage families possess a greater sense of safety and stability, resulting in fewer escalated interactions and greater empathy toward others in the family.

Case Example—Stage 1

Erin (19) reluctantly attended the first family therapy session at Darlene's request. Erin's partner declined to attend the session that focused on Sandra and Darlene's concern about their involvement with their grandson. In the family session the therapist made space for Erin and her mothers to each share their experience of the family including the recent conflicts. Sandra shared that she felt misunderstood in her attempts to offer Erin advice at which Erin reacted with contempt at her mother's statement and Darlene jumped in to shift the discussion to the anticipation the family shared in the upcoming birth. The therapist followed the family's experience in this moment and other related conflicts that captured the same reactive processes in the family.

Tracking the unfolding conflict, the therapist reflected the varied family members' experience and the ways they became stuck in a negative pattern. Sandra's efforts to provide direction and advice were dismissed and ignored by Erin. Sandra responded with anger and more aggressive questions challenging Erin's experience and competence as a mother. Underlying her persistent and aggressive manner Sandra hoped that Erin would know she cared and allow her back into her life as a support and caring mother. Erin in turn, would withdraw emotionally or physically from the confrontation, not allowing the conversation to continue. Erin acknowledged her hurt and the longstanding belief that she was a disappointment to Sandra. Darlene explored her own role as peace keeper, often focusing on avoiding conflict or lightening the impact of Sandra and Erin's bitter exchanges. Darlene shared her own fears that as the non-birth parent she had less of a role in Erin's life and the family as a whole. The therapist validated the positions and experiences of each family member, highlighting the relational block between Sandra and Erin and the ways that the reactive pattern hijacked their relationship leaving them both with desperate means to stop the pain they each felt as a mother and daughter.

Through Stage 1 the family members were better able to see their pattern and the more vulnerable emotions underlying the defensive actions that defined their cycle. Darlene was able to see more clearly how her role often kept the peace but did not help either of those she loved address the pain she also felt between them. Through the therapist alliance and an increasing safety in the sessions, Sandra shared about her own struggle as a new mother. "When I had Erin, I had no one. My mother was gone, my sisters thought I was crazy. I had no one to turn to." Sandra shared the pain of isolation she felt as a mother in a same sex relationship and how hard it was to have a moment of such joy mixed with so much pain at a family level. The therapist framed how Sandra's own fears of loneliness and pain fed a desperate need to protect Erin from the same. Sandra acknowledged that her "over the top" advice and questioning came often in moments of her own fear and expressed sorrow that what she wanted most was to protect her daughter. Erin expressed relief that Sandra could see her actions as extreme and invasive and was moved by Sandra's stories of fear and pain as a mother not being what others wanted or expected.

The couple recognized their own pattern that was triggered in parenting Erin. In a separate parent session Sandra acknowledged how she blamed Darlene for not "standing up" to Erin when Erin withdrew or was threatening. This triggered Sandra's feeling of being alone and unwanted as a mother. Darlene was afraid that if she joined Sandra, they would both lose Erin. Darlene's fear of being less important and less needed by Erin was a surprise to Sandra, who had assumed that given how easily Darlene and Erin interacted that they truly had a special bond. The therapist framed the couple's reactive pattern of fear, focusing on how the family and couple cycles left everyone afraid that they did not belong, when that was what they sought most. The couple's more vulnerable conversation opened new possibilities in their caregiving alliance. Darlene asked Sandra to include her more in the discussions with Erin and asked if they could be a team for Erin and the new baby. Sandra was able to talk about how responsible she felt toward Erin, and that she felt like a failure that Erin was pregnant at 19 and unmarried. She expressed her fear that her daughter did not need her or even love her, which exacerbated her need for Darlene's loyalty. When Darlene saw Sandra's fear, she stated "we are both afraid." The therapist validated and normalized their fears as the cost of being a mom and invited both of them to help each other with their fears. This new awareness helped the couple strategize about how they could be "Team Grand-mom."

Erin requested a separate session with her partner Steve. He had refused to be part of the initial family session because he wanted strict boundaries with Erin's intrusive mothers and felt protective of Erin given the negative impact on Erin's confidence as a new mother. The therapist created space for Erin to explore her own experience of the transition to parenthood and what she needed from others. Erin readily expressed her anger over Sandra's self-absorbed approach and never feeling like she could meet her expectations, which opened Erin to the hurt she felt at her mothers' disappointment, especially Sandra who did not want to be a grandmother. Erin identified that she longed for her mothers' confidence and acceptance: "I want my moms to be proud of me, not to question me, but to believe in me." At this juncture, Sandra and Diane were aware of the fears that drive their reactive patterns with Erin and as a couple, where Erin was able to name her hurt and unmet needs. The parents' openness and engagement together with the daughter's more engaged response evinced the family's de-escalation and stabilization.

Stage 2—Restructuring Attachment in Family Interactions

In Stage 2 of EFFT the therapist shifts toward engaging family members in positive patterns best characterized by felt security and responsive caregiving. The goal of Stage 2 is to realign parent and child relationships so that attachment needs and caregiving responses are effectively engaged. This shift necessitates a system level change, reorganizing family around the processes of care-seeking (attachment system) and caregiving (caregiving system). Whereas Stage 1 emphasizes the broader overlapping impact of attachment-related distress at play in the family, in Stage 2 the focus narrows to address specific dyads and triads where the blocks to attachment and caregiving are most prominent. Attachment-related emotions are deepened as parents and children more effectively communicate in a more attuned and responsive manner.

Parents must move to new positions defined by greater accessibility, responsiveness, and emotional engagement to successfully respond to their child's attachment-related emotions and needs made explicit in Stage 2. Children are better able to reach to their parents with greater clarity and confidence in sharing their attachment-related needs. The combination of these new positions removes the relational blocks to the attachment and caregiving cycle and provides or restores a basis for a generative pattern of security for the family as a whole. These shifts occur though the access and assembly of attachment-related emotions and actions through the EFFT process.

Restructuring attachment bonds begins by focusing on engaging the attachment-related emotions and needs associated with the child's blocked attachment responses. Here the focus is on deepening the experience and expression of the child's concerns and needs that are typically identified initially as informing the rigid patterns identified in Stage 1. This requires the therapist's exploration and engagement of unformulated or disowned attachment-related emotions and needs (Johnson et al., 1998). Processing a child's distrust and fear of their parents' emerging care and openness is a constant focus as these fears are often the child's blocks in reaching for their attachment needs to be met (Bowlby, 1988). Consequently, the therapist actively addresses these fears with children and parents alike, increasing a focus on the underlying longings of children and the often unexpressed and at times unexpected vulnerability of parents in response. This process enables parents and children to move toward greater effectiveness in expressing and responding to the vulnerable emotions common to parent, child, and family relationships (Johnson, 2004).

The therapist maintains a parallel focus on parental acceptance of the child's emerging vulnerability, which is essential to further confidence in the child's exploration of her underlying experience and unmet attachment needs. Deepening child vulnerability primes parental caregiving and paradoxically may surface parental blocks that interrupt a parent's ability to attend to a child's hurt, fears, or needs. Accessing these blocks in session provides the therapist with an experiential opportunity to attune and attend to her or his own experience to work through this blocked response. Parental fears and insecurities are acknowledged and parental motivations regarding caregiving are explored through these blocks. Many parents recoil in moments focused on their child's hurt and fears and parental shame blocks their attunement to the child's needs. The EFT therapist enables the parent to identify their shame but not organize around the parent's negative view of self. Instead these moments provide new opportunities to attune their underlying emotions as a resource for responding to their child. The process promotes confidence and supports a parent's ability to respond in that moment. Working through these blocks and heightening parental accessibility and responsiveness improves the clarity of caregiving signals to the child.

The culmination of Stage 2 involves the enactment of the child's attachment-related needs and the parent's accessible and engaged response. The therapist provides direction through choreographing how the parent and child might enact responses that lead to a more secure interaction. The enactment represents a risk of the child to reach toward his parent with hope and emerging confidence that the engaged parent will effectively respond. A child's needs are often specific to a particular experience of a situation where there has been need for comfort or support. These needs may include a need for safety: "It is scary when you yell. It seems like you are always mad and threaten me. I do try and do my homework but you don't believe me." Others may emphasize a need for security and consistency: "I need to know you are there for me. I don't know if you are going to pick me up when you say you will." "Who is going to come and watch my game? Who is going to show up for me?" Or a plea for reassurance of a child's importance or significance "I need to know I am important to you," "You love Susan more than me," "I suck at everything," "No problem, don't worry about me" (Kobak, Rosenthal, Zajac, & Madsen, 2007). New family responses tend to reflect clearer definitions of self, more assertive boundary definitions, and more explicit expectations of the relationships desired in the family (Johnson, 2004). The essence of the change event focuses on the child's attachment bid and the parent's attuned caregiving response.

Case Example—Stage 2

In the following family session, the therapist framed Sandra and Darlene's openness to understanding Erin's experience and being more responsive to her needs in the family. Erin listened cautiously as the therapist summarized the negative pattern, highlighting the isolation, hurt, and fear that it brought to the family. The therapist asked Sandra and Darlene if they were curious about how their grown-up daughter Erin needed their help at this stage of her life and the parents responded emphasizing their desire to understand and help if they could. Erin remained reluctant to engage them directly and instead focused on the birth of her son. The therapist redirected her focus to what Erin's experience was like as young woman and new mother. Erin responded sharing her suppressed anger at not being seen and valued. As she wept, she questioned if they knew what it was like to feel like you were born to "make a statement" not to just be a child. Did they really want to know what it was like to be a young girl with two moms? Sandra's voice dropped to match her daughter's sadness, "I do want to know, sweetheart. You are right I don't know." Erin's sadness and loneliness was felt as she recounted memories of a specific time when friends asked "where is your dad?" Turning to Sandra, Erin shared, "You said, it's their problem they're homophobic! And I just felt so alone in that moment." Darlene and Sandra held space for Erin's sadness and fear. As the therapist processed this moment with Erin, Erin turned to Sandra in tears, "I am so scared I am hurting you." Sandra took Erin's hand and spoke calmly about the relief she felt having this conversation and that she understood how hard this must have been and her efforts to try to be some kind of "super mom" had gotten in the way. "I am so sorry, the last thing I wanted was for you to be hurt." Sandra reached to hug Erin and Darlene joined the embrace. As this moment unfolded the therapist led the women in reflecting on this experience where the anger and fear were now replaced with comfort and caring. Erin replied, "I am going to need a lot of this."

The EFT therapist maintains a clear focus on the underlying emotions that motivate caregiving and effective attachment communication. In this example the parents' openness to their daughter's hurt and needs sets the stage for a vulnerable conversation about her relationship to her birth mother, and her experience of not feeling seen or heard. Her mothers responded with comfort and reassurance first to her immediate experience and then engaging the daughter's past fears and hurts. The therapist supports the parents' attuned and accessible response as the child shares her need to be seen and reassured. The new experiences created through these enactments provide a source for deepening the impact of the corrective emotional responses. The therapist highlights and emphasizes the positive emotions often evident in these poignant moments and other family members involved in the session are also invited to respond to these shifts in the family.

The impact of shift in one of these parental–child attachment blocks may expose other insecurities in other family relationships. The resolution of the presenting problem may shift focus to unresolved conflicts in another parent–child relationship or continued distress in the couple's caregiving alliance. For example, the openness and vulnerability found in Erin and Sandra's relationship may impact the expectations that Darlene has to revisit blocks in her relationship with Sandra. The EFT therapist frames the steps the family has taken to increase security in the family as a resource for addressing other blocked relationships in the family. The Stage 2 restructuring process then shifts to a new dyad or triad where the process of accessing vulnerability, promoting acceptance, and enacting attachment bids and caregiving responses becomes the focus.

Stage 3—Consolidating Secure Bonds

The final stage of EFFT promotes consolidation of the new patterns of security achieved by the family in the preceding stages. The family is better able to engage discussions together and make intentional steps toward enhancing the felt security experienced by the family in working through the previous blocks to emotional engagement and effective caregiving (Johnson, Bradley, Furrow, Lee, Palmer, Tilley, & Woolley, 2005). Confidence is restored in the bonds of safety and security and family members are able to express their concerns and cares directly and are able to articulate the importance of these changes to oneself and the family as a whole.

Case Example—Stage 3

In the family's final session all three women were joined by Erin's partner Steve and the grandson. The therapist joined the family in celebrating the new arrival and this opportunity to share a conversation about the growth the family had achieved through their work together. The family referred to a recent example of how they had returned to their old pattern but found a way forward. After Erin had moved out, Sandra offered to fix up her new apartment and Erin found herself struggling with accepting this support. Instead she stated what she needed from Sandra and that she felt some of the work was hers to do on her own. Sandra reported that she did not feel rejected but with Darlene discussed how helpful it was that Erin would let them know what she needed from them. Sandra and Darlene were also explicit in their support of Steve and shared their appreciation for all he was doing to be a good dad to his son. At the end of the session, Erin captured the pride she felt and gratitude for what she had gained, "I know we are lucky because my son not only has a grandmother, he has Team Grand-Mom." Sandra and Darlene glowed with happiness and joy knowing that even in a complex and changing family everyone had a place to belong.

The effect of greater security in the family is associated with greater openness and responsiveness in family relationships as the effects of these changes "broaden and build" felt security in interactions that promote positive emotions, relief from distress, and greater emotional security (Mikulincer & Shaver, 2016). Families are more flexible in responding to developmental demands and are more effective in problem solving (Johnson et al., 1998). Finally, the therapist guides the family to new ways of seeing and understanding what it means to be a family. This may include helping the family engage new rituals of connection that enhance opportunities to share in more vulnerable sharing, greater positive affect, and appreciation for their stronger ties as a family (Stavrianopoulos, Faller, & Furrow, 2014).

EFFT Assessment and Decisions in Treatment

The composition of a family therapy session is often determined by those who are most relevant to the presenting problem. Over time family therapists have differed in determining who "should be present" to conduct family treatment. In EFFT our focus in organizing sessions depends on a number of factors. Figure 3.2 illustrates the different types of sessions that compose EFFT assessment and treatment.

Typically, the therapist initiates the EFFT process with a family assessment session where relevant family members are invited to attend. Relevance is determined by those involved in the household and those most influenced by the presenting complaint. Subsequent sessions include a parent session focused on parenting and attachment history and assessment of the couple's relationship satisfaction and parental alliance in two-parent households. The therapist also conducts a sibling-focused session and when needed a separate IP-focused session. The process of assessment is focused on developing a working alliance with the family as a whole, strengthening parental commitment to the family session, identifying family strengths, and exploring possible contraindications for family treatment.

Alternatively, a parent-focused session may be necessary to secure the parent's interest and commitment to family treatment. The initial session provides the EFT therapist an opportunity to process parental concerns and enhance their interest and commitment to a family-oriented treatment for a specific child-related problem and inform expectations particularly when parental concerns are such that family therapy blames the parents at the expense of addressing a child's problem. Parental sessions provide an orientation to family treatment and support for the goal alliance with the parent through informing the expectations and experiences parents bring to a family treatment approach.

Similarly, the EFFT treatment process may vary depending on the family, including the use of different treatment modalities: Family sessions, couple sessions, sibling sessions, and individual sessions. The therapist determines participation based on factors related to who should attend treatment and factors related to how the treatment process should be conducted (see Figure 3.2).

EFFT Decision Framework

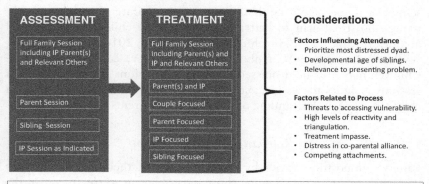

The structure of EFFT sessions may vary by factors related to the composition of a family, their presenting problem, and the evolving process of treatment.

Figure 3.2 EFFT Decision Framework.

EFFT Decision Framework

Most Distressed Relationship

The EFFT process prioritizes the areas of greatest relationship distress in the family. This is often most evident in one parent and child relationship. Conceptualizing family distress as separation distress, the EFT therapist focuses on blocks to the attachment and caregiving system in the family. These blocks are most evident at the dyadic level (e.g., parent and child) or triadic level (e.g., two parents and child), however the influence of this relationship distress can impact the family as a whole. The emotional dynamics and composition of the family inform the EFT therapist who determines the focus of sessions and which family members should be involved.

Family participation is important in the assessment of family dynamics during the early stage of stabilization. Although the most distressed dyad provides a key focus in treatment, the involvement of other family members supplies a valuable resource of security in the family and a support to the family's efforts to resolve the blocks that impact the family as a whole. When possible family members relevant to the focus of treatment are encouraged to participate in support and involvement in the resolution of the family's distress.

Developmental Level

The EFT therapist evaluates the development age and maturity of a child in treatment in organizing the treatment process. Young children are often a resource to family assessment but are less able to contribute to treatment if it is focused on the needs of a family member at a more advanced age.

When the presenting problem is focused on a younger child (e.g., preschool or school age), the therapist may incorporate play therapy techniques into treatment to better approximate the child's developmental abilities (Efron, 2004; Hirschfeld & Wittenborn, 2016; Willis, Haslam, & Bermudez, 2016; Wittenborn, Faber, Harvey, & Thomas, 2006). Children may also be dismissed from family sessions when the focus of sessions includes topics (e.g., sexuality) that may be inappropriate for a child's level of understanding or a concern for parents.

Relevance to the Problem

Family composition varies by household and a therapist collaborates with the family on determining those most relevant to treatment. In the initial stages of assessment participation by a broader family group is helpful in gaining perspective on the problem and in identifying family strengths. As treatment progresses the EFT therapist is more exclusively focused on the interactional dynamics associated with the presenting problem and its impact on emotional security. Excusing family members from treatment provides greater focus on the patterns specific to the family's complaint and greater access to emotional dynamics present in session when that pattern is the focus.

Shifts made in one presenting problem may evolve to another family relationship where blocks to caregiving and attachment are present. Consequently, the therapist may reorganize the process of treatment around this block that new experiences of parental security uncovered. The EFFT process is flexible and provides the therapist with a map for the process of resolving these blocks and an attachment lens to prioritize which relationships are most relevant to engaging this process of change.

The EFT therapist may also consider factors influencing the process of treatment in organizing the composition of a family session. These factors principally focus on the ability of the therapist to provide a safe and secure alliance with family members as they explore and overcome blocks to caregiving and attachment in specific relationships. Shifting the focus of treatment onto specific relationships offers the therapist a resource for increasing the felt security needed in deepening emotional experience and accessing underlying needs. Further, it also intensifies the focus on the specific attachment dynamics in a given relationship. The common reasons a therapist may focus on a specific dyad or triad include: Highly reactive and disruptive patterns, limited engagement, alliance ruptures, co-parental alliance distress, and competing attachments.

Disrupting a Rigid Reactive Pattern

A child's over-involvement in a parental or marital subsystem is widely recognized as a factor in problematic family functioning. Whether a child is anxiously enmeshed into the marital system or actively engaged in pitting parents against one another, these patterns lock into place emotional dynamics that blur boundaries and undermine executive functioning within the family (Minuchin & Fishman, 1981). The therapist shifts the focus to dyadic work to better isolate the patterns of insecurity unique to specific dyads. Sessions may be designed to focus on the parental alliance or couple relations with two parents, or sessions with one parent and a child may be used to promote attention to the unique emotional processes organizing these problematic positions. The dyadic focus also enables the therapist more opportunity to strengthen the therapeutic alliance with specific family members while also being more responsive to the concerns and unmet needs often obscured by the family's reactive coping attempts.

Limited Engagement

Patterns in a family can result in one parent or child less engaged in family interactions and when met with unsuccessful attempts by the therapist to engage this family member the therapist may alter the composition of the family session. Shifting the composition of a family session or shifting between sibling and parent sessions creates different dynamics that shift focus and attention to the disengagement, as well as provide a more secure context to explore the parent or child's dis-engagement.

A parent's reluctance to engage in exploration of her or his experience may result from a fear that showing vulnerability in their role will reduce their authority in the child's eyes. A child might avoid sharing his experience out of fear that being vulnerable will be met with future risks of insult or injury. The EFFT explores the possibility that this guarded reluctance is more than avoidance, rather a concern for safety that is better met by shifting the composition of conjoint sessions to maximize opportunity for a disengaged family member to share his or her experience.

Treatment Impasse

Therapist efforts to balance the interests and experience of parents and children can result in misunderstandings and loss of confidence in the treatment alliance. The therapist may switch to an individual session or dyadic session to focus on treatment impasses including increased resistance or disengagement in session. These blocks may represent a perceived conflict in the goals of treatment between parents seeking behavior change and an adolescent seeking greater autonomy. The use of a parent-focused session enables the therapist to address parental concerns with the treatment process and provides opportunities to inform parents regarding developmental needs and parenting practices.

When efforts to work through a block in the therapist alliance with a given family member remain unsuccessful, the therapist may shift attention to these blocks through an individual session. An individual session with a child provides opportunity to strengthen the therapist's understanding and alliance particularly when that child is the focus of the family's problem.

Co-parental Alliance

The processing of parental blocks to caregiving may expose couple conflict related to parenting. Negative emotions associated with differences dividing parents increases reactivity in parent–child relationships, particularly as a child is exposed to these negative interactions. Couple sessions focused on the couple's shared belief and practices regarding parenting enables the EFT therapist to focus on blocks to caregiving that are informed by the couple's relationship distress. These sessions provide additional support to partners as they seek to resolve these differences and reduce the likelihood of triangulation with children and the secondary emotional distress that children experience in relationship to inter-parental conflict for which the child sees herself as the cause.

EFFT treatment may conclude with a referral for couple therapy when the couple distress is the predominant source of distress in the family. Presenting problems focused on child behavior prototypically resolve quickly when the primary source of family distress is relationship dysfunction in the couple's relationship. A couple's frequent unresolved conflict can expose children to enduring negative emotion and heighten a child's anxiety about family stability. Isolation of a couple's distress and referral for couple therapy reduces the child's distress and the need for family treatment abates.

Competing Attachments

Stepfamily relationships often require attention to differences in the family based on the bases of the relationship. Biological ties commonly take precedence in parent–child alliances, particularly in the early stages of stepfamily development (Papernow, 1993). The priority of these biological ties may inform competing interest in attachment relationships particularly between the remarried couple and the stepparent and stepchild relationship. Complex insecure patterns in stepfamilies can be simplified by sessions organized around privileging the biological parent and child relationship separately from the stepparenting relationship. Couple sessions focused on the remarried partners prove important to de-escalating the tensions that often organize around the formation of new attachments in the presence of existing connections that new partners experience as a competing interest or in other cases threatening, to find a desired role in the family.

Dyadic sessions with biological parents and children also provide opportunities to process loyalty conflicts and unresolved loss from parental death or divorces. The pressure to "move on" or embrace the new formation of a stepfamily may block a family's ability to honor and make meaning of the losses from the previous family. Sessions honoring the uniqueness of the different family ties and their evolving and changing meaning provide the EFT therapist resources for working through emotional blocks that are specific to the unique needs a child may have with their biological parent in a stepfamily.

In-Session Process—The EFT Tango

The typical EFFT session follows a familiar sequence of EFT-related interventions, which Johnson (2019) titled "the EFT tango". The tango consists of five particular moves a therapist makes that organize and guide the process of change from session to session. The tango provides a meta-framework that orients the therapist to the "here and now" work of emotion that is critical in restructuring family attachment relationships. Five specific moves compose the tango and each of these moves works together to engage emotion to transform relationship interactions. The five moves are briefly described, with a case example summarizing the shifts that occur as the therapist moves through this process with a mother and son.

Mirroring Present Process

The EFT therapist tracks and reflects a family's experience as it unfolds in session. Following the shifts in verbal and non-verbal expression the therapist empathically attunes to the varied experience of family members as they engage the therapist and one another in making sense of what is happening and has happened in the family. Through attuning to the present process, the therapist helps the family explore the intrapersonal and interpersonal aspects of their shared experience. The focus of the therapist is tuned into the unfolding sequence of action and emotion playing out as family members navigate a shared story and experience of their relationships as a family. This is most clearly seen in the blocks to caregiving and care-seeking that organize the family's pattern and their efforts to manage its impact.

> James sighs and picks up his cell phone turning away from his mother's frustration and complaints about his failing grades and motivation. Her voice intensifies as James becomes more resolute in demonstrating his indifference. Exasperated by this common dynamic James' mother complains that therapy is having little to no discernible impact and time is running out. James glances at the therapist's reaction then returns to his phone, signaling to all his intention to keep his distance.

Acknowledging the familiar dynamic, the therapist validates the mother's concern and communicates understanding for her escalating frustration at her son's seeming disengagement. Using the present process, the therapist retraces this typical interpersonal sequence, highlighting the mother's frustration and anger and the son's resignation in the face of her disappointment. Shifting focus to the present moment promotes opportunity for the family and the therapist to work from the same unfolding emotional experience. The therapist acknowledges the mother's frustration and irritation at not being able to reach her son when it matters and also observes the son's weariness and distance when it would appear that he is solely a problem and disappointment in his mother's eyes.

Affect Assembly and Deepening

As the session unfolds the EFT therapist centers in on the elements of emotion that begin to emerge, often putting these pieces of experience together into a more coherent and congruent whole. Through accessing and processing these experiences family members often deepen their awareness and understanding of these felt experiences and their import-ance to the self and other.

> Tears form as James' mother expounds on her fears that he is failing his potential and that her frustration gets the best of her. She acknowledges that her anger is driving James away even as she des-perately seeks to provide support. The therapist reflects her emerg-ing pain at not being able to help her son, who she holds hope for fiercely. Her shoulders sink at this recognition and her voice softens as she admits that her hope gets lost in these moments, especially for James. "I am angry, and contemptuous at times. Nothing seems to get through, except maybe that I am mad at him. That is not what I want." The therapist reframes her pain as a sign of her care and her desire to be a support, which gets lost in her anger, frustra-tion, and fear when James pulls away.

Following back to James' initial response, the therapist validates his shift away from the conversation. The topic and tone have become all too familiar, almost all that seems of concern to his mother, and that in those moments he reaches for a survival strategy that makes sense. He doesn't leave the room but distances from his mother's frustrations, complaints, and disappointment. The therapist reflects how her hope feels too much like pressure that leads to no escape, no hope.

THERAPIST: (*focusing on present process*) It's like your sigh seems to say it all.
JAMES: (*speaking disdainfully*) Yeah, she just doesn't get it.
THERAPIST: Those things that you are facing at school, and life?
JAMES: (*looking down*) Basically, she has no idea.

Therapist responds to his downcast expression as a cue to an underlying emotion and with a softened voice, the therapist prompts the sadness appearing in his face.

THERAPIST: (*softly*) And that leaves you all the more alone in all this I would guess?
JAMES: Exactly! (*emphatically, not letting on to his pain*)

Choreographing Engaged Encounters

The EFT therapist uses these newly found experiences to engage family members in structured interactions where these new experiences once shared become a new way of engagement and interaction. More vulnerable expressions of emotion are used to engage new ways of relating between family members who more typically avoided these experiences rather than used them as opportunities for understanding and connection.

The therapist explores with James whether his mother truly understands how difficult he finds these conversations, and how this leaves him caught between either fighting or shutting down and both leave him feeling alone. Then the therapist asks: "What would you want her to know about this dark place you find yourself in, this lonely place?" James hesitates, unsure about the question and the suggestion he could talk to his mother about the struggle he feels. The therapist choreographs with James a new opportunity to engage his mother and invites him into exploring this, even if only experientially.

Following James' willingness to consider the conversation, the therapist asks James to tell her about his uncertainty, and this struggle he knows all too well. James, still looking down, begins to share: "I don't like it. I don't think you understand. It's harder than you think and when you talk to me about it all, it just feels worse." The therapist affirms James sharing and asks: "Can you tell her about being on your own with all this?" James responds: "Yeah, I feel that way sometimes. Like this is not going to go well. Best to just try to deal with it, by myself."

Processing the Encounter

Following these moments of engagement, the EFT therapist explores and integrates the experience with those involved. This creates space for those engaged and those receiving these new experiences to begin to make sense of these encounters and what impact sharing these experiences has on how one sees themselves or a particular relationship.

Building on James' last thought the therapist acknowledges his effort to help his mother see his side of these conversations and how that leaves him in a place where he is alone and feeling worse about himself and his situation. The therapist also makes space for the mother to respond by focusing on her experience of hearing her son and the caution with which he shares his side of things. "It's helpful, better than the silence." James' mother speaks slowly and with caution not wanting to close the opportunity that has opened.

> I don't want him to be alone and I hate how these conversations drive a wedge of silence between us, so this is much better. I don't

want him to feel alone in that and the last thing I want is to make it all worse.

The therapist acknowledges the mother's care and effort to see James' experience and to recognize the distance that results from their conversations. James' mother returns to her fear about his academic work and the therapist acknowledges these fears and at the same time highlights her expressed concern and care.

THERAPIST: Your response to James in this moment showed your care. You heard his uncertainty and that mattered to you. You also know his academics matter, but in this moment, you are also seeing a different side. The part of him that is looking for support and for help. That sounds new and something you long to provide.

The therapist frames the mother and son's efforts to respond as a small step but one where it is clear that they are taking different steps together.

Integrating and Validating

The final move in this process focuses on the experience of what has just been encountered and the new understandings that these experiences produce. New insights and connections between family members are supported and emphasis is given to the ways in which one's new-found experience provides new possibilities for further engagement. Through the process of sharing these encounters, one can find new insight and awareness of self and family members.

The therapist replays for James and his mother what just unfolded in the session, highlighting the ways that what matters most between them so easily gets lost in the pressures they both feel and also the fears and concerns that they seldom share. Through the process of slowing down their interaction and finding space for James' experience of mounting rejection and his mother's heartfelt concern opens new opportunities for the mother to see her son more clearly and to better understand his own pressure to perform, but also his need for his mother's support and confidence. The therapist refocuses on the ways these moments can quickly escalate, where pressure and failure seem inevitable, and how in this moment they can each see a bit more clearly that listening to these emotions and what is going on behind the scenes actually helps them move toward facing these challenges together. Validation of the son's concern, even at an early stage of treatment, creates greater acceptance and understanding of his needs for support in exploration. Acknowledging the mother's intention and care reinforce her awareness and underscore how in this moment her ability to respond in an accessible way opens the door for a different conversation, that still takes to heart her concern for her son.

Summary

The EFFT process of change follows the same map used in EFT treatment of couples and individuals. Special attention is given to the unique role of parents and the complementary dynamics of the attachment and caregiving systems found in families. The EFT therapist's use of evocative and process interventions guides family members toward shifting their attention to a particular problem in the family to the relational processes and patterns that complicate the family's ability to resolve a problem or address need for change in family relationships. The therapist guides the family toward the underlying emotions that inform the relational blocks that are disrupting effective attachment and caregiving responses. The EFT tango describes the primary shifts the therapist makes in processing and sharing emotional experience and through the stages of EFFT the therapist transforms relational patterns through connecting attuned caregiving responses to attachment-related emotions and needs. The process of EFFT offers the family a secure base to explore new experiences of past problems through facing these challenges together. The EFFT decision framework provides the therapist with a reliable guide to organizing the complexity of family treatment with flexibility and a clear attachment rationale. This chapter summarizes EFFT in three stages of change and the chapters in the following section explore EFFT practice in the specific steps that define the EFFT process of change.

References

Bertlanffy, L. (1968). *General systems theory.* New York: George Braziller.
Bowlby, J. (1988) *A secure base.* New York: Basic Books.
Davila, J., Karney, B. R., & Bradbury, T. N. (1999). Attachment change processes in the early years of marriage. *Journal of Personality and Social Psychology, 76,* 783–802.
Diamond, G., & Siqueland, L. (1998). Emotions, attachment, and the relational reframe: The first session. *Journal of Systemic Therapies, 17,* 36–50.
Diamond, G. Diamond, G., & Levy, (2014). Attachment based family therapy for depressed adolescents.
Efron, D. (2004). The use of emotionally focused family therapy in a children's mental health center. *Journal of Systemic Therapies, 23,* 78–90.
Hirschfeld, M. R., & Wittenborn, A. K. (2016). Emotionally focused family therapy and play therapy with children whose parents are divorced. *Journal of Divorce and Remarriage, 57,* 133–150.
Johnson, S. M. (2004). *The practice of emotionally focused therapy: Creating connection,* 2nd Ed. New York: Brunner Routledge.
Johnson, S. M. (2009). Attachment theory and emotionally focused therapy for individuals and couples. In J. H. Obegi & E. Berant (Eds.) *Attachment theory and research in clinical work with adults* (pp. 410–433). New York: Guilford Press.

Johnson, S. M. (2019). *Attachment theory in practice: Emotionally focused therapy with individuals, couples, and families*. New York: Guilford Press.

Johnson, S. M., Maddeaux, C., & Blouin, J. (1998). Emotionally focused family therapy for bulimia: Changing attachment patterns. *Psychotherapy*, *25*, 238–247.

Johnson, S. M., Bradley, B., Furrow, J. L., Lee, A., Palmer, G., Tilley, D., & Woolley, S. (2005). *Becoming an emotionally focused therapist: The workbook*. New York: Routledge.

Kobak, R., Rosenthal, N. L., Zajac, K., & Madsen, S. D. (2007). Adolescent attachment hierarchies and the search for an adult pair-bond. *New Directions for Child and Adolescent Development*, *2007*(117), 57–72.

Mikulincer, M., & Shaver, P. R. (2016). *Attachment in adulthood*, 2nd Ed. New York: Guilford Press.

Minuchin, S., & Fishman, H. C. (1981). *Family therapy techniques*. Cambridge, MA: Harvard University.

Palmer, G., & Efron, D. (2007). Emotionally focused family therapy: Developing the model. *Journal of Systemic Therapies*, *26*, 17–24.

Papernow, P. L. (1993). *Becoming a stepfamily: Patterns of development in remarried families*. San Francisco, CA: Jossey-Bass.

Stavrianopoulos, K., Faller, G., & Furrow, J. L. (2014). Emotionally focused family therapy: Facilitating change within a family system. *Journal of Couple & Relationship Therapy*, *13*, 25–43.

Willis, A. B., Haslam, D. R., & Bermudez, J. M. (2016). Harnessing the power of play in emotionally focused family therapy with preschool children. *Journal of Marital and Family Therapy*, *42*, 673–687.

Wittenborn, A., Faber, A. J., Harvey, A. M., & Thomas, V. K. (2006). Emotionally focused family therapy and play therapy techniques. *The American Journal of Family Therapy*, *34*, 333–342.

PART II
FOLLOWING THE STAGES AND STEPS

FOUR

Alliance and Assessment of Family Patterns

Step 1. Forming an alliance and family assessment.
Step 2. Identifying negative interaction patterns that maintain insecure attachment.

Throughout the initial stage of EFFT the therapist establishes a working alliance that provides a source of security and safety for family treatment. This alliance is foundational to the therapist's goal of stabilizing the family and de-escalating their patterns of distress. The initial steps of EFFT promote a shared understanding and define goals with those involved in treatment. This requires a systematic assessment of the problematic interactions in the family and a clear focus on the family's relational blocks associated with the presenting problem. The therapist's attention to the treatment alliance is active and ongoing throughout the EFFT process, as configurations of those involved in treatment may vary from session to session. Similarly, ongoing assessment is required through the various shifts that occur as specific relational blocks resolve, and others emerge.

In this chapter we address the initial steps of the EFFT process and the therapist's practice that guide alliance formation and assessment of the family's presenting problem and negative interaction pattern. We review a multilevel approach to assessment than guides the initial sessions of family treatment. Case examples illustrate the use of the EFFT decision framework and interventions used to direct treatment and organize relational patterns contributing to family distress.

Alliance and Assessment Goals

Four goals guide the initials steps of EFFT. First, the therapist actively assures that family members are seen and their perspectives on the family recognized. Focus is given to individual perspectives on family concerns and the family strengths also evident in session. The therapist observes interactions and intentions expressed to reflect the strengths that are often missing in the initial conversations about the family's

89

problem. A second goal involves joining with each family member and validating their understanding of the problem and its origin. The therapist gives attention and acknowledgment to each family member's understanding of the problem and how the individuals and family as a whole make sense of the problem. The therapist listens to the family's story of the problem with an ear toward themes of insecurity including loss, rejection, abandonment, or relational injuries.

The EFFT assessment includes a third goal focusing on safety and establishing a direction for treatment. The EFT therapist evaluates the readiness of the family for conjoint treatment and secures parental investment for family-focused work. Although assessment is the primary focus of the initial EFFT sessions, ongoing assessment or family relationship dynamics guide the organization of treatment including the use of individual, dyadic, and family sessions. The fourth goal emphasizes the therapist's role in identifying the interactional patterns associated with the family's presenting problem. Through sequencing and organizing interactions associated with the presenting problem the therapist tracks the unfolding interactional patterns that occur in times of felt distress and insecurity. EFFT places an explicit focus on these relational patterns, making them understandable and predictable. This is a necessary step toward reframing the family's understanding of the problem and promoting hope in finding repair as a family.

Access Points

Three access points guide the therapist's interventions in these initial EFFT sessions. The EFT therapist uses the initial sessions to establish an alliance with family members and to assess the fit of the presenting problem to EFFT treatment. This includes working with parents and the family to focus on relational patterns and goals.

1. Facilitating a Family Conversation

First a therapist focuses on facilitating a family conversation about the presenting concern. The therapist convenes this conversation as a basis for joining each family member in their experience of the family and their unique experience of the presenting problem. The process gives light to dominant descriptions used to define the problem and uncovers alternative experiences and concerns often masked by the family's distress. These may include other less obvious or indirect means of coping within the family (e.g., withdrawal, escape). Bowlby (1979) highlighted one inherent value of family therapy, which is simply providing a family an opportunity to talk about what the family does not talk about, even though they share these experiences together. Throughout the EFFT process the therapist makes explicit the implicit emotional realities of family members embedded in negative interaction patterns. Typically the therapist will also find underlying experiences or emotions that are also resources of resilience within the family's attachment and caregiving systems.

2. Securing Parental Investment

The second access point focuses on securing parental investment in the family treatment process. Child-focused complaints are common in referrals for treatment and the therapist's ability to establish a caregiver's consent and investment in a family-based treatment process is critical to establishing a working alliance for the whole family. The parent's concern and focus on a specific child problem must be balanced with the therapist's appeal to focus treatment at a relationship level. Both levels are necessary in treatment planning and determining the appropriate resources needed for successful relational intervention, and EFFT provides a resource for directly impacting the moderating role of attachment insecurity in psychopathology (Ein-Dor & Doron, 2015), and support for the ways in which attachment insecurity is mutually linked to psychopathology in adolescence (e.g., Kobak et al., 2015).

Some parents react to the suggestion of conjoint treatment as an indication of blame or a trigger for a personal reaction of shame. The therapist's efforts to inform parents of the purpose of treatment and a rationale that is consistent with their problem focus is essential to establishing a working alliance. A parent session may be necessary to establish goals for conjoint treatment and assuage parental concerns regarding misattribution of the problem. Reframing the presenting problem in attachment terms is common in attachment-related family approaches (e.g., Byng-Hall, 1995; Dallos, 2006; Diamond, Diamond, & Levy, 2014; Hughes, 2007). In EFFT the alliance and processing family interactions precedes the reframe as a rationale for treatment. The EFT therapist offers EFFT as a resource for supporting parents and families to work more effectively together to resolve the problem and strengthen their resources as a family as a result.

3. Tracking Patterns Related to the Presenting Problem

The third access point marks the therapist's intervention, focusing on tracking interactions and reflecting the family's experience of the problem. The therapist leads the family in a discussion of specific experiences that organize relationship blocks that typically inform the family's presenting problem. Concurrently, the therapist conducts a safety assessment including the family's readiness for conjoint treatment. Through this initial family interview the therapist begins to formulate with the family an understanding of their presenting problem organized around the interactional sequences that drive relational distress within the family system.

Therapist Practices and Interventions

Johnson (2004) outlined key practices organizing the therapist's focus in working with families in the beginning stage of EFFT. These practices reflect the core elements of in establishing a working alliance with the family and focusing direction for treatment. EFFT follows the EFT interventions found effective in promoting a working alliance and tracking relationship patterns in couple therapy. Core interventions include: Empathic reflection, validation, evocative responding, and tracking relationship interactions.

Joining through a Family's Story

The therapist invites family members to share their experiences offering common and contrasting points of view regarding the presenting problem. The family discussion provides the therapist with opportunities to align with the different experiences and normalize ways in which families seldom have one understanding of the same problem. Gathering details on family experiences also creates opportunities to identify family values and strengths that are associated with the family's efforts to address these concerns and endure their consequences. Focusing on specific insights and experiences enables the therapist to join with the individual experiences and highlight the different ways family members seek to resolve the family problem and the strengths that are associated with these individual efforts. Broadening a family's conversation, the therapist explores the influences of family values, history, and cultural background as the deeper meanings of a family's concern often reflect a broader context including parent's family of origin and cultural similarities and differences within the family.

Peter and June sought treatment for discipline problems they were having with their 10-year-old son Jay (Jaeyoung). The couple expressed pride in their differences as an inter-racial couple, yet these differences led to challenges in parenting Jay. As the therapist gathered the different perspectives on the problem, Peter and June fought often over Peter's mother's involvement in discipline of Jay. Eunjoo, Peter's mother, recently joined their household after her husband's death in Korea. June struggled with Peter's ability to maintain clear boundaries between the generations in the household, and Peter was challenged to support June and honor his mother's interests. Peter remained focused on Jay's behavior and the lack of consistent support and discipline, which infuriated June who felt Peter was unwilling to support her as Jay's mother, instead deferring to his mother. The EFT therapist joins both parent's understanding of the problem and the way that these differences become a threat to their alliance as parents and as a couple.

Building Alliances within the Family

Through the process of defining the focus of treatment and the family's understanding of the presenting problem, the therapist explores and clarifies the goals for each family member and the family as a whole. The therapist's goal is to establish a connection with each person in the family that communicates acceptance and promotes safety. This requires attention to developmental and situational factors that influence the openness family members have in sharing about their experience in the family. The therapist's ability to communicate an accessible and responsive stance to the differing needs in a family system increases the confidence that family members have in the clinical process and the therapist's ability to lead the family into areas that they often avoid or fear. A clear rationale for conjoint family treatment provides the family with focus and direction, particularly when the individual interests of a parents and child appear to compete.

The EFT therapist explores June and Peter's conflict and recent arguments that spilled over into interactions with Jay. Both parents were concerned that their inability to resolve their parenting difference was negatively impacting Jay and this was also affecting his school performance. The therapist acknowledged and validated the parents' differences, while also joining their common concern for Jay. Treatment goals for the family included family sessions with Jay focused on his experience at school and at home, and a couple session to further explore the struggles that were dividing June and Peter as a caregiving team.

Assessing Availability in the Family

Following an attachment frame the therapist assesses the availability of caregivers to respond to the attachment cues and needs of others. Often the initial session provides an first impression of the family's level of defensiveness and reactivity. The felt security of a family is reflected in the degree to which family members are able to turn to one another for support, and whether those bids are met with accessibility, responsiveness, and emotional engagement. The assessment of caregiving availability includes parent and child relationships as well as couple relationships. Although these attachment dynamics are specific to a particular dyad (e.g., mother and son vs. adult romantic partners) their influence in the family's overall availability is shared. For example, a child may withhold her need for comfort from parents who are caught in an insecure cycle of couple distress. The lack of availability in one relationship spills over into another.

Blocks to effective caregiving may include the generational influence of a caregiver's own attachment history. In co-parenting relationships exploring the attachment history of each partner provides important context for the expectations partners have regarding availability in their romantic relationship. Similarly, assessing a parent's childhood experience of caregiving offers insight into the orientation a parent may bring to their caregiving role. The assessment of availability through exploring attachment histories of caregivers guides the therapist to the resources and challenges that parents and partners confront when facing discord in family relationships.

June complained of being "sidelined" in her parenting role by Peter's deference to his mother, however her frustrations were also driven by her own fears as a mother. The therapist explored June's frustrations as she shared her ongoing battle as a parent between the models she had of her own father and mother who were together equally emotionally intrusive and physically unavailable. She felt "off balance" as a parent and often criticized by Peter's mother through indirect actions and comments that eroded her own confidence to navigate Jay's problems. She felt she was failing at what mattered most in her life and Peter was not able to see her struggle.

Attuning to the Emotional Climate

The absorbing influence of negative emotions can spread through a family's experience even if particular members are not directly involved. Tuning into the emotional tone of the family the therapist acknowledges and organizes the secondary impact of these negative interactions and the ways reactive emotions result in reactive strategies and impact the family's ability to promote regulation of negative emotions (Morris, Silk, Steinberg, Myers, & Robinson, 2007). The contagious effect of negative emotion reduces the flexibility and openness within the family to respond to the increasing negativity and increasing insecurity within the family system.

The family session with Jay, June, and Peter was tense as both parents tried to manage Jay's behavior in session. Together they would glance at each other with expressions that appeared to signal frustration, disgust, and desperation. Each parent offered suggestions to Jay and as their efforts increased Jay became less responsive. As the tension increased and Jay's behavior escalated, Peter excused himself to retrieve Jay's game unit from the car and June glared her disapproval as he left the room.

Tracking Negative Patterns

Throughout the initial sessions the therapist follows the unfolding actions and emotions associated with the family's experience of the presenting problem. The therapist tracks the negative behaviors and emotions that organize repetitive interaction patterns that shapes the family's emotional climate. In session, the therapist asks family members to revisit a recent stuck conversation or interaction that characterizes the typical troubles family members face. Through tracking the escalation, the therapist punctuates the reactive chain of negative actions that define the predictable protective responses that family members use to cope with an increasingly polarized interaction.

Once Peter returned the therapist asked if the family would be willing to have a conversation about what it's like in "moments like these." The therapist sought the parental support to shift focus to the present moment and their struggle to work together. The therapist invited Jay and his parents to each come up with a word that describes these moments and using these reflections the therapist asked the family to explore moments where tension rises in the family. Tracking the family's responses, the therapist began to follow the actions of the different family members and explored their experiences along the way. The therapist shifted the focus to a recent situation that escalated at home following a fight over schoolwork. The therapist reflected and validated the different experiences of each family member and their responses to a situation that in Jay's words just "felt really bad."

EFT Interventions

The therapist relies on the following intervention in alliance formation and assessment of family discord and distress. A focus on empathic responsiveness includes therapist responses that promote a family member's sense of being seen, heard, and understood, which is critical to maintaining a strong alliance in family treatment.

Reflection

The use of empathic reflection centers on accessing and processing emotional experience in family relationships. This includes reflections that focus on the content of what individuals share through the process of talking together about their relationships. Reflections may also focus on someone's experience in the moment, where the therapist uses a reflection to draw attention to an interaction or experience taking place in the session. Active use of reflection makes space for individuals being seen and heard within the family and increases the family's awareness of their unique and shared experiences.

Example:
The therapist responds to a distraught father after criticizing his daughter for her disrespect and apathy.

THERAPIST: So you see your daughter turn away and not respond, and your anger builds. "How can she ignore me like that and not see how bad her situation is?" This seems like the only way you can get through to her.

THERAPIST: And I see you turned away. There is nothing to be said to his anger that would not make things worse. What else is there to say? (*therapist noting daughter's withdrawal*)

The therapist follows a sequence of interactions between the daughter and father summarizing this sequence in a series of statements that illustrate how the father and daughter's reactions and response create a predictable sequence or interaction pattern. The therapist tracks these interactional patterns highlighting the behavioral and emotional responses of each of those involved, summarizing the ways in which these patterns reflect the family's efforts to connect.

Validation

Validating comments promote acceptance of different family members' experiences suggesting that in a given situation one's response is understandable. Validation legitimates an individual's perception or emotional experience as simply that person's response in a particular circumstance of moment. An impactful validation statement also informs the therapist about the client's experience, often at a deeper or more profound level. The use of validation strengthens the therapist alliance with family members and provides a resource for regulating distress in escalating moments between family members.

Example:
THERAPIST: (*to father*) This is unbearable when you can't seem to reach your child, she is your daughter and you care deeply about her especially when you see the warning signs. Her ignoring you, this feels like life and death, you need to protect her anyway you know how.
THERAPIST: (*to daughter*) And when you see your Dad so mad at you, that doesn't feel safe to you, so you go away, stay away to weather the storm. It makes sense that you question his care, when it seems like he doesn't see you or believe you.

Evocative Questions and Statements

Throughout EFFT, evocative questions and statements prompt exploration of an individual's experience through engaging moments where that person's experience is unclear or uncertain. The use of these evocative statements slows the family conversations and enables the therapist and the family to begin to access and expand the emotion-related experiences associated with the negative patterns that govern family relationships. As the therapist is getting to know the family in this early stage, use of evocative questions is offered in a tentative manner.

Example:
Therapist invites a mother's response as she witnesses father's escalating anger as her daughter shuts down emotionally and withdraws.

THERAPIST: (to mother) What do you say to yourself in these moments as you see the pain and distance in your husband and daughter's relationship driving them apart?

Here the therapist focuses on the mother's perception of this difficult moment in the family relationship. The therapist could also more directly ask the mother about her feelings in this moment by asking a focusing related question: "What is it like in these moments when the distance in their relationship almost pushes you out of the picture, because when they are in this place no one is looking to you. That must be so difficult?" The therapist's use of evocative statements and questions directs the attention of the family to the relational realities of their negative interactional patterns and opens opportunities for different family members to be seen and heard in response. This change of focus is essential for accessing the emotions that inform the meaning and actions playing out in a family's negative pattern.

Reframing

The Stage 1 goal of de-escalation requires a shift in how a family understands their presenting problem. Through this initial stage the therapist is working with family members to reframe the problem in terms of negative interactional patterns that are held in place by relational blocks. As the therapist tracks and reflects the actions and experiences of the family's interactional pattern a tentative reframe is used to highlight this pattern. In the initial EFFT sessions reframing is used in summarizing and making explicit the possibility of a problem-related pattern in family relationships.

Example:
THERAPIST: It sounds like this is something you all know well, these moments when the family gets caught and everyone is frustrated and feels powerless to change the situation. Dad, your efforts to advise and correct your daughter's situation are ignored or dismissed and this is where your anger takes hold trying to get through her wall of indifference. Yet for you Tina, this wall is there to protect you, you don't feel safe in these moments because dad doesn't get it. He doesn't see you. And mum you are on the sidelines watching this all take place, frozen at times wondering how you can make things better without seeming to take sides. This can play out anytime and for a lot of different reasons, but it feels like the same pattern each time.

Throughout this early treatment stage these summaries are repeated as the patterns are made explicit to the family. Slowing the pace of escalation in a pattern can be difficult, but the therapist's use of empathic reflection and validation highlights the experiences of family members in these negative states and begins to shift the focus of sessions toward how a family faces their concerns rather than an exclusive focus on the problems. In the following section we focus more explicitly on the process of alliance building and assessment that the forms the basis for identifying negative patterns in a family's presenting problem.

Alliance and Assessment

The EFFT process begins with a conjoint family session and follow-up sessions with parents, siblings, or with a single child. Our preference is to meet with the family first to assess the family conversations about the presenting problem and to initiate the process of building alliances with family members who may prove important in the treatment process. The focus of the initial family session is framed as an assessment session where the therapist can learn more about the presenting problem and its impact on the resources and relationships within the family. All family members who are impacted or involved in the presenting problem are invited to the initial session given the focus on informing a general understanding of the challenges that the family are facing. Follow-up assessment sessions are then conducted with parent(s) or caregivers and siblings to explore further the resources and demands the family is encountering within specific family subsystems. For some parents, the request for a conjoint family session is resisted or refused. In this case, the therapist may meet with parents for a preliminary session to focus on developing an alliance through acknowledging the particular parental concerns, and secure parental commitment to a family focused approach.

Initial Family Session

In the family session the therapist solicits the experience of all family members present to ascertain the various experiences in the family and their relationship to the presenting problem. This session provides the therapist a first look at the relational blocks including the negative experiences that color the interactions of a family in distress. Directed questions promote opportunities for all family members present to share about their experience of the family. The therapist may ask: "Can you tell me what it is like to be you in this family? What one word would you use that describes your family? I would like to hear from each of you." This enables the therapist to gain different perspectives on the family and at the same time provides an opportunity to affirm the value of each person's contribution and understanding of the family. As each person tells their story of the family, the therapist observes how the story is being told, how the members are interacting with each other, the strength of the emotional connection and how emotions generally are expressed in the family unit.

These questions are difficult for families in active distress. The focus of the session can shift very quickly to the problem child, with one parent, or both parents and even other children, strongly blaming one family member. This demonstrates the power of the negative pattern to influence upon the family process and limit the family's ability to engage more neutral or positive interactions. The therapist engages this negative escalation by reflecting and validating the urgent concerns of family members, while also acknowledging the ways these concerns dominate the experience of the family. The therapist might ask evocative questions or responses including:

What is that like for you, when that happens? What do you end up doing or telling yourself when you see this happening? I can see this is really hard for you and I can hear the urgency in your voice as you talk about this. What's happening on the inside, as you see this happening to your son?

The therapist also actively redirects blame and criticism to maintain safety in the family session.

The EFT therapist avoids potential alliance ruptures by empathically attuning to each family member and their understanding and experience in the family. The therapist's active presence and accessible, responsive leadership of the session interrupts the negative escalation so that the family can quickly overcome a difficult conversation. Actively guiding the process assists the therapist to introduce alternative perspectives and other voices that may otherwise go unheard. Ensuring that all members are able to speak and express their own perspective in the safety of the therapy room is a crucial first step in the family work and by doing this the therapist is assessing how open, accessible or reactive and rigid the system is to these interventions. The session concludes with the therapist's summary of her understanding of the family and the concerns that bring them to treatment. The therapist explains the process of assessment and future family sessions are scheduled as indicated by the goals of treatment. The therapist promotes openness to feedback from family members and their ongoing concerns and suggests that family members communicate their concerns through the parents or directly to the therapist.

Parent Assessment Session

A separate session with parents is important to strengthen support for the caregiving system, assess the caregiving alliance, and establish common treatment goals. These sessions focus explicitly on the caregivers' concerns, often surfacing their frustration and struggles in the parenting role. The therapist provides a strong base of support acknowledging these concerns, including parents' uncertainties about family treatment and the therapist's understanding of the presenting problem. For some parents the suggestion of family treatment triggers feelings of shame and reactions to therapist validation of a child's complaint can leave parents distrusting of the therapist's support for their role. In other cases, the exploration of child vulnerability in relationship to family difficulties may escalate parental protection or defensiveness. Securing the parents' commitment to conjoint treatment and a focus on vulnerability promotes goal alliance. Establishing clear support and alignment between treatment and the parents' caregiving goals provides a prognostic indicator for family treatment.

Parent sessions focus on four areas that inform family treatment. First the therapist establishes a working alliance with the parents in support of conjoint treatment. This includes revisiting parental concerns regarding the presenting problem and questions raised in the family session. Second the therapist focuses on assessing parental availability and the demands and resources impacting the parenting role. The therapist explores concerns identified in the family session and the parents' understanding of their role in relationship to these problems and how they see the problem in relationship to the child and their own parenting. A third area examines their view of self as parents and their view of their child includes the parents' attachment history and the role their history of parenting plays in their own experience as a parent. A fourth area is relevant when families have more than one parent or caregiver involved in childrearing. Assessment of the co-parental alliance focuses on the level of agreement and shared support parents bring to their parenting. The therapist seeks to distinguish the degree to which either support or disruptive conflict may result from the couple relationship and when reactive differences are more a function of difference in parental roles, expectations, and practices.

Parental Alliance

Promoting a parent's investment in conjoint family treatment begins with honoring the parent's efforts to correct the problems they are facing in the family. The therapist normalizes the challenges parents face and the demands they have endured in their efforts to promote a better situation for the family. Acknowledging the parents' courage and willingness to take steps to better their child and family's future, the therapist recognizes the unique role of the parent as an irreplaceable resource and that the therapy focus will build on the importance of their influence in the child's life and future. Predicting moments in parent sessions where the therapist may appear to side with a child's experience is discussed, emphasizing the therapist's goal of promoting openness and understanding from each person involved. By predicting these moments, the therapist creates an opportunity to anticipate parental concerns and fears regarding their influence and responsibility for the presenting problem.

Providing opportunities to understand reactive and problematic behavior requires making space to acknowledge these reactive responses and through more open and safe interactions in the session. The therapist's role gives light to the multiple experiences in the family while acknowledging the important roles parents play in raising their child. Acknowledging and understanding reactive emotions sets the stage for moving deeper into the more vulnerable needs that often go unexpressed in negative patterns. The therapist may refer to different parenting styles (e.g., authoritarian, authoritative, permissive [Baumrind, 1978]) as a way to frame how these emotional dynamics can undermine effective parentings. More than a focus on parent practices, EFFT places emphasis on maintaining an emotional balance in parenting and the ways in which that is achieved through a more responsive relationship between parents and children rather than an exclusive focus on parenting strategies.

Parental Availability

The exclusive focus on parenting in this session enables the therapist to better explore the availability of parents to others in the family including the identified patient. The therapist assesses the parents' ability to attend and read cues from their child and how curious and open they are to alternative understandings of their child's behavior. The parents' ability to communicate thoughts and feelings and the question of whether they have developmentally appropriate expectations of their children and how able are they to communicate emotion, including their use of tone, body gestures, facial expressions is considered. Finally, evaluating a parental flexibility in problem solving provides insight into the degree a parent is able to balance expectations and acknowledge their own failures in parenting (Kobak & Mandelbaum, 2003).

Parents are more likely to speak candidly about their frustrations with the IP and their efforts to resolve the problems described in the family session. The therapist joins the parents' best efforts to respond to the child and recognizes the parental efforts in the context of caregiving. Processing these parental concerns also provides the therapist with opportunities to expand the parents' awareness and sensitivity to child's needs and concerns. Tentative reflections based on the family session can be used to focus on the child's emotions and experience and the therapist validates the child's experience and its impact on parents. For example, a therapist recalls a child's defensive rejection of parental reassurance, which occurred in the initial family session. Identifying with a parent's sense of rejection, the therapist also frames the child's action as a self-protective response coming from the child's fear that he is unwanted. The therapist emphasizes the goal of working through these insecure moments which are currently blocking the parent's efforts to care and support a child.

Assessment of parental availability also includes personal and relational factors that impact a parent's emotional presence. Kobak and Mandelbaum (2003) suggest three factors that may impact a parent's availability based on intrapersonal, interpersonal, and situational stressors. Individually, psychological distress including mood-related disorder may reduce parental attention and awareness to a child's emotional needs. Interpersonally, a parent's hostility or rejection can result in an attachment rupture or injury that deems the parent unreliable for safe support and care. Finally, stressful life events including poverty, unemployment, and chronic illness may distract parents and increase distress in the family system making parental availability less consistent. Each of these factors also impacts the emotional climate of the family, placing an additional emotional load on a system that is prone to greater emotional reactivity and less capable to co-regulate stressful emotions effectively (Morris et al., 2007).

Parental responsibilities for discipline and boundary setting are acknowledged and affirmed. The therapist also invites parents to consider ways that current strategies have become less effective as a result of the deterioration of caring and trust in the parent–child relationship. Parents are asked to recount times which have been successful in managing boundaries and setting expectations as well as other times when past strategies have failed. The therapist's assessment focuses on parent behaviors that are over- or under-responsive to a child's needs, particularly in the context of negative or reactive interactions.

Parental actions often express an underlying intent to care for the child but are distorted through parents' own efforts to respond to negative expectations of the child or themselves as a parent. Reframing all parental actions as caring behavior is premature at this point without greater understanding of the underlying emotions associated with specific parental behaviors. However, it is sufficient simply to recognize the general motivation behind parental behavior and to reflect upon parental efforts to better their child's life. Moreover, not all parental actions reflect this intention toward care and the therapist must assess the parents' response as these actions may reflect the parents' own negative view of the child or themselves. When appropriate, highlighting and reflecting the parents' good intention makes space for building a stronger therapeutic alliance.

Parent Attachment History

The therapist's assessment and exploration of a parent's attachment history often unfolds throughout treatment. The processing of parental blocks to availability often reveals negative views of self or a child that are rooted in the parent's childhood experience of being parented. As such the therapist's assessment of attachment history provides a preliminary understanding of themes that inform the parents' experience of their role given what they have known through their childhood. The therapist frames the attachment history questions as a resource for better understanding the family and their experiences that each parent brings to the parenting role.

A therapist may ask a parent to share about their experience as a child when they were the same age as the identified child, focusing on who they turned to for care and support and what they learned from those experiences. Further the therapist may question whether the parent faced similar challenges as a child and how they responded when facing those difficulties.

Caregiving Alliance

Parent sessions enable the assessment of the co-parenting alliance and couple relationship for two-parent families. Although the quality of a couple's relationship and their shared cooperation in parenting often are related, the therapist should assess for a couple's caregiving alliance as distinct from their adjustment as romantic partners. Kobak and Mandelbaum (2003) identity two essential elements of a functioning caregiving alliance. First, each partner shares responsibility for the parenting of the child. Second, each partner respects the contribution their partner makes as a parent. Shared responsibility and respect characterize the caregiving alliance and parental sessions provide the therapist with insight into the role parenting plays in the couple's relationship.

Couples with problematic caregiving alliances are more likely to encounter distress in parenting. Discussions of parenting issues often become the source of conflict and personal attack. Differences in parenting approaches are judged as problematic, polarizing partners' attempts to coordinate care. In return, parents may sabotage the other's efforts at parenting, undermining the couple's confidence in working together in support of the child. Parenting issues trigger couple discord which in turn heightens the vulnerability of the couple to greater distress in shared efforts at parenting. Alternatively, other couples may join together against a child through scapegoating the child's negative behavior. These partners ally together against their child and fail in providing emotional availability to the child.

Similarly, relationship distress independent of parenting also impacts the emotional climate of a family. A couple's chronic conflict undermines the emotional security a child may find in their family (Cummings & Davies, 1996) and that conflict may also erode the support each partner has for the other. The effects of this distress are compounded when partners cope with their relational distress by taking complementary approaches to parenting, where one partner is overinvolved in the child's life and the other is under-involved in parenting. When parenting and partner conflicts collide, children are particularly vulnerable.

when parent–child caregiving alliance, and adult attachment relationships become distressed and undermine the adult's confidence as a caregiver and partner in an adult attachment relationship, distress can escalate in an exponential fashion and fundamentally jeopardize the caregiver's capacity for remaining available to the child.

(Kobak & Mandelbaum, 2003, p. 155)

Sibling Assessment

Following the parent session, a final assessment session is arranged with the identified child and siblings. The purpose of the session is to strengthen the therapist alliance with each child and to assess for safety and readiness for conjoint family treatment. The session provides children an opportunity to share their concerns or questions about family treatment and enable the therapist to deepen trust and understanding of the children's family experience. The therapist gains further detail on how the children respond to the reactive patterns identified in the family and parent sessions.

Sibling sessions create a space for children to express their family experiences without parental input and evaluation. Often children provide unique perspectives that yield insight into unspoken family history or experience. The therapist explores how children see their family when they are connecting, fighting, repairing, negotiating, caring and responding. The therapist may ask if the family shares feelings openly or if the family has rules about feelings like anger or sadness.

The sibling session expands the focus on the presenting problem to a broader understanding of the family and the therapist reinforces the unique voice children have in their family and the role they can play in making their family stronger. Assessing the siblings' views of parents, self and each other reveals additional strengths and blocks in the overall family's ability to respond. Can members in this family turn to another for support? If they cannot turn to their parents can they turn to another sibling or are they alone? Painting a picture of how the siblings experience life in this family provides great detail of the family's dynamics and provides the therapist an opportunity to highlight parental caring intentions often running behind what frequently comes across in controlling or absent ways.

Self-Report Assessment Resources

Numerous measures have been developed to assess attachment-related behaviors and experiences. Johnson (2019) identifies two self-report measures that have clinical utility for the EFT therapist working with families. The Inventory of Parent and Peer Attachment (IPPA; Armsden & Greenberg, 1987) provides an assessment of an adolescent's report of peer and family relationships focusing on themes of communication, alienation, and trust. Findings examining the constructs used in the

IPPA suggest that adolescent ratings of communication associated with measures of attachment anxiety and alienation scores are related to attachment anxiety and avoidance (Brennen, Clarke, & Shaver, 1998).

The McMaster model provides a resource relevant to the assessment of parental confidence in attachment relationships (Dickstein, 1999). The Family Assessment Device (FAD) developed by Epstein, Baldwin, and Bishop (1983) provides an assessment of general family functioning that has proposed clinical cut-off scores. The measure is composed of seven individual scales that provide family ratings on: Affective Responsiveness, Affective Involvement, Behavioral Control, Problem Solving, Roles, Communication and General Family Functioning. Johnson (2019) notes the measures of affective functioning are of specific interest in assessing EFFT treatment impact.

Contraindications and Confidentiality

EFFT treatment is not appropriate for families where there is a significant risk and ongoing threats of violence or abusive behavior. The receptivity and openness of the parent to the therapist is critical as a strong therapeutic alliance with parents and children is needed for the therapist to effectively join and work experientially with family relationships. Expression and vulnerability are essential to the treatment process and use of EFFT with violent or abusive families may put individuals at further risk (Johnson & Lee, 2000). Family situations involving untreated substance-related or other mental health disorders require additional assessment to determine whether the appropriate level of care is in place to support family treatment. Disengaged parents or actively hostile caregivers also could prevent family work as parents are not motivated to improve their contact between members. The EFT therapist is continuously monitoring safety throughout treatment as the expression of vulnerability and emotional risk-taking in the family requires that all family members feel safe in taking these steps and confident that they are not opening themselves to severe reprisal or punishment.

Therapists using EFFT should follow their ethical and legal standards regarding confidentiality when a treatment process involves a combination of individual and conjoint sessions. At a minimum the therapist should notify participating family members prior to treatment of the therapist's policies and practice regarding confidentiality and informed consent when different modalities are involved. Family members should be informed of the potential use of individual, couple, and family sessions in EFFT treatment and the ways the therapist will maintain continuity between sessions, which may or may not involve the same family members. Clients should also be reminded of these practices prior to sessions where the presence or absence of family members may impact expectations regarding confidentiality and privacy.

EFFT Decision Framework and Treatment Planning

Following the assessment process, the therapist organizes treatment sessions to maximize focus on the most distressed relationships in the family. In the initial stage focused on de-escalation the therapist will privilege sessions with family members most impacted by the family distress. The therapist is guided by the EFFT Decision Framework (Figure 3.2) to modify session composition typically varying between dyadic, triadic, and family sessions. As treatment progresses, the therapist may use dyadic or triadic sessions to intensify focus on specific attachment dynamics and promote safety through honoring the intimate concerns and uniqueness of a particular relationship. For example, the therapist may invite a parent session to explore conflict associated with the caregiving alliance or a session between a biological parent and her daughter in a stepfamily.

Following the EFFT Decision Framework the therapist may use dyadic or triadic sessions with parents and the identified patient as a means to increase safety, narrow treatment focus, and to deepen individual experiences without the influence of other family members. In situations where safety is a concern, the EFT therapist needs to assess whether one parent can assure that the children are protected. If necessary, the therapist may need to contract specifically with that parent so that actions will be taken to ensure safety. Conjoint family treatment may be delayed until necessary resources are in place to assure child wellbeing and safety concerns.

Excluding younger, vulnerable siblings from whole-family sessions when the content is not developmentally suitable ensures safety for these family members and establishes appropriate boundaries for the family unit. Family structure and history may influence the composition of family treatment. Special attention is given to biological and step differences in stepfamilies. As these families are often in transition and dealing with loss, the bond between biological parent and children needs to be focused on and strengthened before children can be asked to relate to new family members that were not of their choosing. Combining the biological family sessions alongside couple sessions is often the optimum treatment plan for these families.

Tracking Family Patterns

Through the assessment process the therapist has to strengthen her alliance with the family, and following from the family, parent, and sibling sessions the therapist organizes the treatment process to focus on the negative patterns dominating the family. This final goal moves the focus of sessions from assessment to treatment through the identification and processing of negative patterns associated with the presenting problem. The therapist's goal is to help the family articulate an understanding of the predictable sequences that drive distress and uncertainty in the family.

Commonly, the EFT therapist when treating a couple focuses on a single negative interaction organized around partners' rigid positions. These positions are typically described as pursuit or withdraw and represent the secondary attachment strategies each partner uses to respond to relationship insecurity. In EFFT the patterns are more complex and involve more than one attachment relationship. The impact of family distress is felt across the family system even though its source may be primarily located in one relationship. The therapist tracks the interactions of the family in session as members recount specific moments where the family distress took hold. The goal of mapping a family's interactional sequences is to make explicit the predictable actions that family members make in times of negative emotion and insecurity.

Consider Laura and Tom who sought family treatment after their son Dylan's therapist recommend family therapy in support of Dylan's individual treatment for depression and social difficulties. Following the assessment sessions, the therapist convened a family session involving Dylan, Laura, Tom, and Dylan's two sisters Aimee and Angel. The session focused on a recent argument between Dylan and Laura after Laura asked Dylan to pick up his things in preparation for a party the family was having for Aimee and her friends. Laura went out of her way to approach Dylan with support. Dylan reacted defensively, lashing out against his mother's efforts to help. Aimee in turn burst into tears and Angel bitterly complained about how Dylan always seems to ruin the good moments that many families enjoy. Dylan threw his belongings at his sister's feet and left to lock himself in his room. Laura chided Angel for her attitude and tried to comfort Aimee, and Angel left for her room. Tom entered the room to find Laura and Aimee in tears and music blaring from Dylan's room. Exasperated by the chaos and emotional display Tom incredulously remarked "What the hell happened here?" Laura reacted and lashed out at Tom suggesting if he were around to help more things like this wouldn't happen. Aimee cried harder and Laura turned her focus back to Aimee and Tom in disgust left the room to admonish Dylan for not being helpful to the family. Tom and Dylan's conversation concluded in distant silence after Dylan said the family would be better without him.

In what might otherwise be a typical family conflict, the therapist sees clearly the fractious power of insecurity to undermine a family's ability to connect and work together. As negativity impacts the family environment, family members lose flexibility and the resources to regulate escalating negative affect diminish. Tom's defensive critical position reflects his parenting frustration in not being able to coach Dylan to better behavior and his resistance to Laura's overly sensitive approach to Dylan. Laura often feels alone in parenting situations as the strain of dealing with Dylan's difficulties has fallen on her. Long arguments between Tom and Laura have left each feeling greater distance and less support as a couple. Aimee is sensitive to the family tension and often expresses the hurt she feels when others fight and argue, and Angel is increasingly frustrated by the family's organization around Dylan, believing that Dylan often manipulates her mother and disrespects her father.

In EFFT the therapist begins by helping the family see the bigger picture of their distress through the interactional sequences that reflect the deeper emotions that organize the experience and actions of the family. In this initial stage of treatment, processing the family experience and organizing interactions makes the family distress understandable and the actions of others more predictable. The therapist tracks the specific interactions reflecting and validating each member's experience as the negative pattern plays out between them. Focusing on individual's experience and underlying emotions the therapist provides a secure base for the family to begin to explore the insecurity driving their distress. Different experiences of the same interactions are honored as the therapist identifies and connects to the potential blocks in attachment-seeking and caregiving behaviors. Through the session the family members are able to be seen and heard and the protective strategies used in distress are named enabling the family to begin to face a prototypical moment of distress differently.

Case Example

This case example illustrates the initial steps used in EFFT treatment of a family with an adult daughter recently diagnosed with a mood-related disorder. The EFFT process is described through the assessment of the family using examples from their initial session.

Background

The Kingston family requested family therapy due to problems they were having with their youngest daughter, Laura (22), who was recently diagnosed with depression. Kaitlyn (25) lived on her own with her boyfriend but agreed to participate in family therapy. Laura had joined her parents Shirley and Les at the family owned business, where Kaitlyn had also worked until she took leave for a medical disability. The family bonded around the family business but otherwise shared limited leisure time together.

Parent Session

At intake the intensity of the parents' frustration and concern for safety resulted in scheduling a parent session prior to the initial family session. Shirley and Les expressed their frustration with Laura's sullen and withdrawn behavior and their concerns over the level of financial support they provided including employment and housing. They resented her lack of appreciation for their generous efforts and struggled with Laura's angry outbursts when confronted with these realities. Laura recently ended a long-term relationship and following the break-up she was more belligerent, spending most of her time in her room, and missing time at work. Les and Shirley saw Laura as "lazy" and "difficult," and were seldom able to have a conversation with her that did not deteriorate into hostility and accusation.

The parents were sobered by Laura's depression diagnosis and felt overwhelmed at trying to help their daughter. The therapist supported the parents, emphasizing their vital role in Laura's struggle and encouraged the parents' availability through accessibility, responsiveness, and emotional engagement. In session the therapist mapped out how being stuck in a negative pattern with their daughter reinforced negative experiences for them as parents and left Laura estranged from receiving the comfort and support she needed at this critical point in her life. It was a new perspective for both Les and Shirley as they had thought that Laura just needed to be stronger and move on with her life. By empathizing with the parents and framing their intentional efforts to help their daughter, both parents left the session being more open to learning how to better reach Laura.

Sibling Session

Following the parent session, the therapist invited Laura and Kaitlyn to a session to discuss their experience of the family. The therapist formed an alliance with the daughters and solicited their impressions of the family. Both agreed that the family organized around conflicts between Les and Laura. Laura also fought with her mother who would "hit and run," making critical remarks about Laura and then withdrawing. Their father, on the other hand, was more confrontational and would escalate a disagreement into a literal "screaming match." Kaitlyn avoided family conflicts by keeping her distance and detaching emotionally. She felt closer to her mother and Laura shared that her closest ties were with her father even though they fought frequently. Laura saw herself as the problem child in the family and this was underscored following a recent physical altercation between the daughters on a family vacation. In session the daughters recounted their ongoing conflict regarding the parental attention Kaitlyn received concerning her medical problems. Laura shared openly about her hurt and loneliness directly to Kaitlyn who accepted and acknowledged her sister's pain. Both girls felt closer as a result and Laura started to see Kaitlyn as an ally in the family. The therapist reinforced the importance of their reliance on one another as sisters. Both sisters acknowledged how they often felt isolated and alone in the family and were surprised to hear that neither one felt like they were "good enough" in their parent's eyes.

Family Session

The goal of the initial family session is to promote openness and understanding as each family member has an opportunity to voice their concerns and perspectives on the family. The previous sessions with parents and siblings found that both parents shared a negative view of Laura, but each responded differently. Shirley responded with critical avoidance and Les with critical control through direct confrontation. Neither parent had a positive connection with Laura and Kaitlyn was emotionally distant from all family members.

The therapist maintains a focus on processing interactional patterns, through reflecting and validating underlying emotions and promoting positive interaction. This segment illustrates the first three moves of the EFT tango, and how this process provides direction at the very beginning of a family session. Excerpts from this initial family session illustrate how the therapist integrates the previous assessment sessions into a family conversation about the current patterns of distress and conflict.

The family session began with the therapist summarizing highlights from the parent and sibling sessions. The therapist noted the parents' intention to be better listeners to their daughters and reinforced their desire to support what they each needed. The daughters' efforts to reconcile difference was noted as a sign the family was already working to make positive changes in their relationships. The therapist invited the family to comment on their communication and conversations over the past week.

KAITLYN: I don't think I can comment because I haven't been around.
THERAPIST: Right, but I am wondering how you are feeling, maybe what you have been observing about the three of them.
KAITLYN: I feel good. I feel better about the way things are going. I think it is on the up.
MOTHER: It's getting better, it's getting better for Laura and I and Kaitlyn and I.
THERAPIST: Ok, so what do you think is better?
MOTHER: For me, I have been working on being patient and just giving them more space.
THERAPIST: So, you are conscious and mindful of giving them more space, is that what you are saying? Yeah, you're trying and Laura, how do you feel about that?
LAURA: I don't want to diminish her efforts but if she thinks she is making an effort. I don't notice a difference, and I don't mean that in a negative way
THERAPIST: You're just not seeing a difference. Right, would that be something you would be waiting for from your Mom? Wanting her to be more patient with you?

LAURA: (shrugs) I don't really find her to be impatient.

THERAPIST: I guess you wouldn't necessarily notice that she is being more patient because that wasn't a problem for you. (therapist paces with Laura's caution in giving an opinion in the family)

LAURA: Yeah, right! (rolling her eyes)

THERAPIST: (to Mom) But this is something you are aware of—you're trying to do and you're trying to do that because ...

MOTHER: I am just being accepting of Laura's pace to get on with the next phase of life

THERAPIST: Oh, ok, you want to be accepting of where she is

THERAPIST: So how about for you Dad, how are you experiencing things?

FATHER: I think my communication with the girls is back to where it was prior to everything kind of coming to a head. I am probably being a bit more aggressive then Shirley is. If Laura feels like she is moving forward, I am trying to encourage her, trying to keep up with her and asking has there been any progress? You know things like that.

THERAPIST: And you are wanting to know what is happening with Laura? It sounds like it is really important that you know what is happening with her that it leads you to kind of pushing or prodding?

FATHER: Prodding I would say, trying not to make a big deal about it, but I put out a general question and she has been very supportive and responding and saying, "I did this yesterday, Dad."

THERAPIST: So, she has been open to you?

FATHER: I believe she has. Some things haven't changed much. She has a tendency not to do much and then can freak out.

THERAPIST: Right! So if you see Laura not doing much, there is something about that's a trigger for you?

FATHER: Yeah, I get a bit pushy and she just ignores me or puts me off in some way.

THERAPIST: Sure that makes sense, we all want to be able to reach our kids, no matter how old they are, we want to know we can talk to them, that they will hear us, and when we can't or when that doesn't seem to make a difference that is alarming

FATHER: Yeah and I guess that is when I kind of lose it.

The therapist turns the conversation to Laura who continues to offer limited one-word responses. Her tentative and restrictive responses are a contrast to her father's energy and effort. The therapist acknowledges Laura's more quiet presence in the family and a possible need to "test the waters" of her parents' new efforts. The therapist joins the father's anxious concern as Laura remains hesitant and guarded in session. The therapist mirrors his present experience and begins to assemble his affective experience.

THERAPIST: So, you are aware of trying not to get so big, so reactive. Even right now. You are really focused to be responsive like we discussed in our last session.

FATHER: I have been aware of this and I am trying to change both at home and at work—I am a very active person

THERAPIST: And when you are anxious or concerned, your voice might get louder, you might get more expressive, you might sometimes get in someone's face. And you are very aware of that Les, you are wanting to do something different with your family

LES: Well it has come to a head not only with Laura, but Kaitlyn has more or less said that to me that I can be very intimidating with my voice with how I act and Laura would say "you push me, Dad," with my words, with my face and even with Shirley too. So now I step back and she said to me "just cut it" and "don't crowd me."

THERAPIST: She has asked for more space and you are reflecting on yourself and pulling yourself back a bit. How you come across in this family?

FATHER: And I am doing that with Laura and have pulled back given that has been going on. I am really trying here.

THERAPIST: I hear you, this is really important, you want your kids to be able to talk to you, and actually Laura did, when she said "you push me, Dad."

FATHER: But I need her to talk to me, and it seems to me that I am not sure what would happen if I didn't push, maybe she would just sit there, get more depressed, I have got to get her moving, breaking up with a boyfriend is not the end of the world.

THERAPIST: Right, seeing her so sad and heartbroken is hard for a dad to see?

FATHER: I want to fix it, get her to think of other things.

THERAPIST: (softly) Right, seeing her pain, is alarming, right? So painful to see our kids struggle. And for you it is automatic, you want to fix, you try harder, get bigger, anything to try and get her moving.

FATHER: (exiting) She has a lot of potential, in the office, she is the one everyone goes to if they want answers. (father's caregiving intent is mixed with his anxious fears about her future)

THERAPIST: Yeah, she is a talented young lady but right now, things are really difficult for her, and when you see her not moving or getting more and more depressed, it pushes you into action mode, which then you Laura, get quieter and quieter, because it's hard to have your dad prodding you, and crowding you

FATHER: I just don't want anything to happen to her.

THERAPIST: Yep, that is the hardest, right? Something bad happening to your daughter? As a dad you want to protect her and when you can't reach her, you just feel like she is just going downhill. (therapist reinforces caregiving intention)

FATHER: It terrifies me, and (*getting louder*) it makes me angry. Her boyfriend shouldn't have this kind of power over her.

THERAPIST: Right, this where it gets difficult and it's the fear, that fear, we all have as parents, that fear is underneath the prodding. (*father responds in agreement as therapist validates his fear*) So, I am wondering if Laura knows this, can you tell her, that when you see her in her room, alone and not doing anything, that's what scares you? That's what's behind all the anger?

FATHER: (*softly, looking at Laura*) Yeah, it does scare me, I am your dad, I don't want anything bad to happen to you, but I guess yelling and pelting you with questions, isn't the way to help you.

The session continued focusing on Laura's response to her father's beginning steps toward openness and transparency with her. This allowed Laura to express more directly her sadness and despair about her boyfriend's abandonment of her and the parents were able to hear Laura's pain without minimizing it or prematurely solving it. Future sessions focused on Laura's relationship with her mother, which on the surface looked less problematic but held more insecurity for Laura in terms of how lovable she was in her mother's eyes. Laura's emotional work with her parents helped lay the framework for Kaitlyn to be more vulnerable emotionally, specifically her shame around consuming so much of her family's attention, her low self-worth and her fear regarding her future. Generally, the parents learned how to empathically attune to their children and each other. Together they found a new way to reach each other without the polarizing actions of attack and avoid.

Summary

A family's exploration of its own struggles begins with the foundational support of a therapist's alliance forming a source of security that family members can rely on as they work together against the problem they face. In EFFT, the initial steps orient the family toward a responsive and accessible therapist who seeks to acknowledge and understand the various experiences that family members share in relationship to their presenting problem. The therapist also gathers information on the family's experience through their interactions as a family, parents, siblings, or as a single child. This multi-layer assessment guides the therapist toward a stronger alliance with each person and an understanding of differences that exist as a function of the roles and responsibilities in the family. The therapist's assessment also considers the caregiving alliance shared by couples and the ways in which distress may ripple across relationships, fueling a generalized distress in the whole family. Though the process of assessment the therapist establishes her role as a process consultant making observations and providing support to the family as it finds voice for the negative emotions and distress that fuel patterns of insecurity. The therapist tracks the experience of the family at times where these negative experiences are most acute and begins to unfold a relational understanding of the predictable patterns that disrupt the family's efforts to care and connect.

EFFT Process Points

The following process points highlight the therapist's essential role in forming an alliance and assessing the family.

1. The therapist solicits different family members' accounts of their experience of the family and the presenting problem. Empathic reflection and validation show support for each person's experience in the family and build toward the therapist's alliance with the family as a whole.
2. The therapist focuses on securing the parents' investment in the treatment process through setting specific goals for treatment, aligning parental concerns for their child, and affirming the parents' unique role in the family.
3. The therapist highlights family strengths and individual efforts to face the problem and past experiences that demonstrate the family's resilience and investments and efforts to cope with the current challenge.
4. The therapist promotes safety through soliciting individual family perspectives and conducting assessments across the different subsystems of the family.
5. The therapist places emphasis on the different family members' experiences of the presenting problem. Attention is given to the family's process associated with the problem as the therapist begins to track the interaction pattern and reactive positions found in the family's attempts to cope with the presenting problem.

References

Armsden, G. C., & Greenberg, M. T. (1987). The inventory of parent and peer attachment: Individual differences and their relationship to psychological well-being in adolescence. *Journal of Youth and Adolescence, 16*, 427–454.

Baumrind, D. (1978). Parental disciplinary patterns and social competence in children. *Youth and Society, 9*, 239–276.

Bowlby, J. (1979). *The making and breaking of affectional bonds*. London: Tavistock Publishers Ltd.

Brennan, K. A., Clark, C. L., & Shaver, P. R. (1998). Self-report measurement of adult attachment: An integrative overview. In J. A. Simpson & W. S. Rholes (Eds.), *Attachment theory and close relationships* (pp. 46–76). New York: Guilford Press.

Byng-Hall, J. (1995). Creating a secure family base: Some implications of attachment theory for family therapy. *Family Process, 34,* 45–58.

Cummings, E. M., & Davies, P. (1996). Emotional security as a regulatory process in normal development and the development of psychopathology. *Development and Psychopathology, 8,* 123–129.

Dallos, R. (2006). *Attachment narrative therapy.* Maidenhead: McGraw-Hill Education.

Diamond, G. S., Diamond, G. M., & Levy, S. A. (2014). *Attachment-based family therapy for depressed adolescents.* Washington, DC: American Psychological Association.

Dickstein, S. (1999). Confidence in protection: A developmental psychopathology. *Journal of Family Psychology, 13,* 484–487.

Ein-Dor, T., & Doron, G. (2015). Attachment and psychopathology. In J. A. Simpson & W. S. Rholes (Eds.), *Attachment theory and research: New directions and emerging themes* (pp. 346–373). New York: Guilford Press.

Epstein, N. B., Baldwin, L. M., & Bishop, D. S. (1983). The McMaster family assessment device. *Journal of Marital and Family Therapy, 9,* 171–180.

Hughes, D. A. (2007). *Attachment-focused family therapy.* New York: Norton.

Johnson, S. M. (2004). *The practice of emotionally focused therapy: Creating connection.* 2nd Ed. New York: Routledge.

Johnson, S. M. (2019). *Attachment theory in practice: Emotionally focused therapy with individuals, couples, and families.* New York: Guilford Press.

Johnson, S. M., & Lee, A. C. (2000). Emotionally focused family therapy: Restructuring attachment. In C. E. Bailey (Ed.), *Children in therapy: Using the family as a resource* (pp. 112–136). New York: Norton.

Kobak, R., & Mandelbaum, T. (2003). Caring for the caregiver: An attachment approach to assessment and treatment of child problems. In S. M. Johnson and V. E. Whiffen (Eds.), *Attachment Processes in Couple and Family Therapy* (pp. 144–164). New York: Guilford Press.

Morris, A. S., Silk, J. S., Steinberg, L., Myers, S. S., & Robinson, L. R. (2007). The role of family context in emotion regulation. *Social Development, 16,* 361–388.

FIVE

Working Through Relationship Blocks

Step 3. Accessing underlying emotions informing family interactional positions/relational blocks.
Step 4. Redefining the problem in light of relational blocks and negative patterns.

The process of transforming negative interaction patterns in families requires a level of emotional safety between the therapist and family members that fosters a growing everyday awareness of these patterns. Emotion provides the EFFT to transform family experience, meaning, and action. Emotion is a target and agent of change in EFT (Johnson 2004) and provides an essential focus of the therapist work with maladaptive relationship patterns. The therapist leads the family toward stabilization and de-escalation of reactive patterns through accessing, processing, and sharing new emotional experience. Through assembling and engaging emotion, family members are able to identify the relational blocks that are at the heart of the family's negative cycle and begin to explore the deeper emotions that shape the attachment processes between family members.

This chapter reviews the EFFT steps used to move a family toward stabilization and de-escalation. De-escalation is the first change event in EFFT treatment. We examine how relational blocks disrupt the family's attachment and caregiving process and describe the therapist's use of EFT interventions to access and explore these relational blocks. Case examples illustrate two prototypical relational blocks and their role in fueling negative interactional patterns. EFFT practices for working through blocks are highlighted including EFT interventions used to access and engage underlying emotions often associated with blocked attachment needs and caregiving intentions. A case example illustrates the use of these interventions at this stage of the EFFT process.

Goals for Steps 3 and 4 in EFFT

Two goals mark the therapist focus in Steps 3 and 4 of the EFFT process. First the therapist expands the focus from tracking the family's negative interaction pattern to now include deeper emotions associated with an individual's experience of the pattern. In Steps 3 and 4, sessions concentrate on eliciting and expanding family members' underlying emotions and making use of these new experiences to increase awareness of attachment-related emotions and corresponding needs. Through acknowledging and exploring the family's relational blocks the therapist is better able to attune and access the good reasons for not responding in the family at a more vulnerable and responsive level of engagement. Increasing vulnerability in the family requires the safety of the therapist alliance with family members and greater focus on mirroring the present process and assembling affect in family interactions occurring during the clinical session. These are two of the initial steps in the EFT tango process (Johnson, 2019).

The second goal related to Steps 3 and 4 includes the reframing of the family's problem and shifting the family's focus to the disruptive influence of the family's negative pattern and the relational blocks it represents. Through accessing and processing family members' emotional experiences the family is better able to experience the positive intention of parental caregiving and the negative consequence of the relational blocks. The cycle first traced in the beginning of Stage 1 is now made more explicit with specific attention given to the deeper emotional experiences that give the family more hope and reason for overcoming this pattern. Now that there is greater attention focused on adaptive emotions, the family climate begins to shift in the direction of more responsive interactions and away from the constricting impact of negative emotions and self-protective strategies. This enhances the family's ability to explore and understand the blocks that disrupt attachment and caregiving responses.

Access Points

Four key access points organize the therapist's interventions with the family as the treatment moves through stabilization and de-escalation. The EFT therapist explores the relational blocks driving the family's relational distress through the accessing and assembling underlying emotions associated with these patterns. Parental exploration invites greater openness in revisiting the presenting problem in light of these relational blocks.

1. Exploring Relational Blocks

First, when family members begin to recognize the key relationship blocks disrupting effective attachment communication and promoting insecurity in family interactions, the therapist focuses on exploring their experience around these blocks. This informs the family's awareness of the pattern and the emotional realities that shape and inform its function. These relational blocks are tied to the core needs often unexpressed in the family.

2. Accessing and Assembling Underlying Emotions

Second, in processing these patterns and the self-protective responses family members engage, the therapist accesses and assembles deeper emotions that underlie these blocks. Family members are invited to explore and share the impact of these relational blocks on their experience within the family. Family conversations become more organized and less reactive as greater safety leads to greater vulnerability.

3. Clarifying Caregiving Intentions

Third, as attachment-related emotions and needs are made explicit the therapist focuses on clarifying caregiving intentions in response to these needs. Through the shared experience of vulnerability, a focus is also given to the unmet attachment needs across the family and particularly associated with the relational blocks.

4. Promoting Parental Openess

The fourth access point is the parental shift toward greater openness and intentional engagement toward their child. Here the therapist heightens and frames the parent's shifting interest and motivation to respond to their child. Parents share their intentions to revisit their approach to their child, particularly as it relates to the relational block between them. The therapist reinforces these new parental responses even if at this point it would be premature to have the parent reach with their intention as they do not yet have a full understanding or an invitation from their child to respond.

Relational Blocks and Family Patterns

In Steps 3 and 4 the therapist shifts the sessions' focus to specific relational blocks that are a key factor in driving the family's negative interaction pattern. The family's negative interaction patterns are shaped by specific relationship blocks, most clearly seen in dyadic relationships (e.g., parent to child; parent to parent, or partner to partner). In this section we focus specifically on these relational blocks and how the therapist works with these blocks to de-escalate the family's reactive pattern.

In EFFT the therapist conceptualizes the family problem through the lens of attachment where blocked attachment communication results in separation distress. Family responses to this distress result in reactive strategies to overcome and cope with unsuccessful attempts to resolve attachment needs. This reactivity is evident in the increasing negativity and amplifying effects of individual behaviors that organize specific relational blocks rooted in failing attempt to share needs for contact, comfort, and support and receive effective response to these needs from attachment figures in the family. The spreading negativity colors family interactions and individual efforts to regulate emotional experiences are constricted as patterns of insecurity in the family become mutually reinforcing.

In Steps 3 and 4 the treatment narrows to focus on specific relational blocks that fuel the reactive family pattern. These blocks feed insecurity through eroding a child's confidence in a caregiver's ability to respond effectively to the child's attachment-related concerns. In turn, a child's attachment-related communication is distorted through more self-protective strategies in responding to these needs. We refer to this mutually occurring and mutually reinforcing disruption in attachment and caregiving as a relational block. These relational blocks, while dyadic, also impact the larger family system through related negative interactions that reduce the family's flexibility in responding to the broader needs of the family. The inability to establish a family-wide secure base is rooted in the separation distress of specific attachment relationships.

Family Insecurity and Emotional Gridlock

A family as a dynamic system is governed by relational networks and feedback processes. Attachment theory points to the role of control processes in governing relationship interactions signaling the need for safety and support between those who are capable to respond (Bowlby, 1969, 1980). Relational patterns in families are organized by networks of attachment relationships that orient children and parents to responding to intrapersonal, interpersonal, and environmental demands. Emotions provide a signaling system for monitoring and responding to these demands and the ability to effectively regulate these emotion signals and promote effective communication results in a felt security that defines the network of relationships providing an emergent sense of wellbeing and source of flourishing (Mikulincer & Shaver, 2015).

However, when this system is blocked, the impact is felt in specific relationships and the family as a whole. Attachment relationships are guided by the expectation that support is available in specific relationships (e.g., parent to child, romantic partners) and when these attachment figures are not available and responsive, secondary attachment strategies are employed that seek to amplify or de-activate the signals related to these attachment needs. As the system fails and negative emotions take precedence the specific relationship and those also in the broader family system are impacted by the separation related distress and the spreading negative emotional contagion. For example, distress between a father and son envelopes distress in the couple's relationship as mother and father argue over effective ways to respond to their son's acting-out behavior. The couple's distress adds to the negativity experienced in the family environment, increasing the demands on the sibling relationships, with the daughter blaming her brother for ruining the family. As a dynamic system the negative emotions in the family become an absorbing state that results in emotional gridlock and increasing negative responses.

In Steps 1 and 2 the therapist joins the family system and provides safety and a secure base to explore the negative emotions associated with the broader problem patterns in the family. The therapist uses the negative patterns to access and deepen the emotional experience of family members. This shifts attention away from problem behaviors and toward specific relational blocks that trigger distressed emotions and disruptive actions. In Steps 3 and 4 the therapist narrows their focus to specific interactions, most often where the pain and distress in the family are most poignant. The most distressed dyad is the focal source of the attachment-related distress in the family. As treatment progresses these relational blocks provide key points of intervention and are the aim of restoring effective attachment and caregiving responses.

Throughout the EFFT process the therapist attends to moment-to-moment experience and uses the emotions that emerge through family members' shared experience. The therapist primarily relies on conjoint sessions focused on specific relationship blocks and working through these blocks to increase caregiving availability and greater awareness of a child's attachment needs. Conjoint couple sessions are used to address relational blocks in the couple relationship and caregiving alliance. These sessions are integral to balancing the need to work within specific dyads in the family and at the same time account for their influence upon the family system as a whole. Individual sessions may be used to strengthen the therapist alliance with a particular family member or address safety concerns within the family. Differentiating the appropriate level of care for a couple relationship is strategic to resolving the negative patterns in the family.

Identifying Relationships Blocks

Relational blocks are a central focus of Steps 3 and 4. These blocks represent key sources of insecurity that reinforce negative patterns within the family as member seek to cope with the disruption in these essential relationships. For example, the negative pattern is seen in how a family interacts together when all are aware that a mother and son are locked in a persistent conflict. Their rigid conflictual interaction is the relational block. Figure 5.1 illustrates the impact of these relational blocks on parent–child interactions and the different potential responses

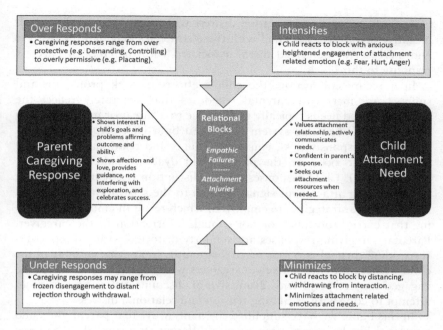

Figure 5.1 Relational Blocks in Caregiving and Attachment Responses.

a parent and child might take in response to one of these blocks. These interactional blocks are evident in moments of distress, crisis, and need where attachment communication is necessary and/or expected. This figure is adapted from Kobak and colleagues' "secure cycle" (Kobak, Zajac, Herres, & Krauthamer Ewing, 2015).

In EFFT the mutual influence of parent and child distress forms the basis of the relation block concept. The block in the center of the diagram illustrates the disruption of key attachment and caregiving functions in the family. The mutual regulation of emotion and a caregiver's response to attachment needs are challenged by distortions in the ability to attune to emotional signals and attachment-related needs with empathy and accurate responses. The arrows toward the center indicate the parent and child's typical response to attachment and caregiving needs when felt security organizes family interactions. The blocks and arrows pointing toward the relational block illustrate the secondary attachment and caregiving responses to a specific relational block. Parents and children use different strategies to respond to a blocked attachment relationship.

Negative patterns of family distress are rooted in relational distress to the attachment and caregiving system. These blocks reflect disruption in a parent's ability to actively and accurately attune and respond to a child's attachment-related needs. Attachment communication and caregiving responses are distorted by anxious and avoidant strategies to manage the increasing separation distress when this system is disrupted. Negative emotions associated with these strategies heighten the distress and increase the perceived threat associated with the child or parent's response to this block.

In a secure connection, the child's efforts to seek protection and support are met with parental responses that accurately reflect the child's initiated needs typically in response to a threat or need related to exploration. When this system is blocked by a lack of parental availability and responsiveness, empathic failures and relational injuries are more likely to occur in the parent–child dyad (Kobak, Grassetti, & Yarger, 2013). Child responses to this disruption result in maximizing or minimizing attachment signals related to the separation distress and self-protective strategies are employed, which result in emotional signaling that carries too much or not enough information to the caregiver. Parental caregiving responses are similarly distorted with parents overresponding through anxious reactive attempts to appease or control the child's reactions. Alternatively, caregivers who are overwhelmed or disengaged may respond with dismissive or disconnected responses as an attempt to cope with escalating tension and relational distress.

In this figure we have simplified the many ways that parent and child relational blocks occur, often mixing different strategies of responding to emphasize that these relationship blocks are informed by both parent and child strategies and the inability of the system to regain its emotional balance through effective attachment communication. Insecurity processes in the family possess emergent emotional properties that organize the family interactions around negative affect states evident in negative family patterns.

Relational blocks result from poor affect regulation where the lack of emotional balance triggers oversensitivity to attachment cues. Generally, these blocks emerge in key moments of importance (e.g., a child's need for support or protection), when an attachment bid triggers further dysregulation, which in turn blocks vulnerability and access to another's underlying needs. As this interaction proceeds there is greater likelihood for mis-attunement and ineffectual caregiving responses. Parent availability is diminished as parental responses increasingly lack accessibility, responsiveness, and emotional engagement. This results in greater distress through greater negative emotion and more compromised emotion regulation.

Although at certain levels of distress a parent may shift toward greater availability, children may reject their parent's corrected response and react against this repair, further contributing to the dysregulation in the family. These predictable responses organized by the caregiver's over- and under-regulated signals arise from the heightened emotional states or shutdown that complicate attuned emotional communication between caregiver and child. As these interactions become characteristic of parent–child interactions, family members find themselves in a rigid position of emotional isolation unable to navigate the distress together, and the corresponding emotional resources of the family become blocked by rigid patterns characterized by anxious coercive demand and shutdown withdrawal (Kobak, Duemmler, Burland, & Youngstrom, 1998).

Case Examples of Relational Blocks

Two case examples contrast differences between relational blocks that include over-responsive versus under-responsive caregiving and illustrate the negative family patterns that result. The first case example describes a distant and rejecting father who assumes primary parenting responsibility following a divorce and abdication from parenting by the other biological parent. The relational block is reinforced by the harsh rejecting approach of the father combined with the resistant acting-out behavior of his adolescent daughter. The second case describes a family caught between the father's over-responsive block with his more avoidant son and a complicating relational block between the parents.

Case 1: Family Background

Pasha, age 19, was admitted to a community shelter because she could no longer live at home with her father, Karim, and her two older brothers. Karim worked as a commercial pilot and was absent from home for extended periods of time. Karim stated he could no longer manage his daughter as she did not follow his rules and he was unable to provide adequate supervision due to his work travel commitments. Pasha stayed out late, often consumed drugs with her friends and was not working or going to school. Three years ago, Pasha's parents divorced after her mother left the country to live with a new partner. The couple's divorce had been a shock to Karim as he had thought that his wife was content and that they had both accepted their familial roles and worked well as a team. Following the divorce Pasha spent much of her time alone, often crying in her room. Karim's work schedule kept him away from home and he hired domestic help to manage care for the household. The father issued strict household rules and his primary interactions with Pasha revolved around her compliance with these rules and school performance.

Negative Interaction Pattern

Pasha became involved in drug use through her brothers who visited the home when their father was away. She found relief from her painful lonely life through the party culture and substance use. When Karim discovered her drug use, he punished her by taking her cell phone and restricting her activities and Pasha protested her father's discipline as her brothers' drug use and destructive behaviors were ignored. Karim remained calm but stern stating that there was nothing to discuss, to which Pasha reacted more fiercely. Karim, in a harsh and rejecting tone said, "You are going to be no good and live on the street. You are a disgrace and a dishonor to our family!" Her father's disapproval was unbearable and she began to spend more time away from home and became truant at school. Finally, after a night out partying, she met her father returning home from his latest work trip. The father exploded saying, "Pack your bags! You are no longer welcome in my home."

The shelter offered individual and family treatment for Pasha. She remained distant and dismissive regarding her own goals for treatment and was primarily concerned with whether she would ever be allowed home again. Karim would periodically contact the shelter, demanding that the staff discipline his daughter for breaking rules, and efforts to involve him in family therapy failed as Karim failed to keep the scheduled appointment. Over time the therapist's efforts to initiate family treatment were successful as an alliance was established with Karim through aligning with his parental fears about his daughter and the urgent efforts he had taken to change the direction of her life. Karim felt powerless and alone in his parenting given his lack of parental involvement and as a single parent he now relied on others who encouraged him to respond with discipline and consequences. He feared appearing "soft" and weakening the consequences his daughter needed to change. In conjoint sessions he began to understand his daughter's loneliness and her fear that she was now on her own having lost her mother and now her father.

Relational Block

The father's fears for his daughter and shame over his feelings of inadequacy as a parent resulted in his inflexible approach to consequences and emotional distance. He saw his use of authority as a means to "fix" Pasha's poor choices, protect her from negative peer influences, and stop her dangerous behaviors. Underlying his outward harsh parenting stance was a desperate fear that he would fail in his efforts to save his daughter, and feeling powerless to escape the escalating shame and failure he felt as her father. The family's negative cycle of Karim's over-responding through rejection and control escalated Pasha's defensive withdrawal and isolation. Karim's authoritarian stance and his consistent absence from the family kept Pasha from turning toward her father in her pain and isolation. In turn Karim's fear for his daughter and lack of confidence in parenting drove his harsh and unrelenting parenting. He felt he had already failed in his relationship with his adult sons and he was desperate to save his daughter with what little influence he felt he had.

In this example the father's authoritarian and controlling response served to reinforce his daughter's dismissive and rejecting position.

The father and daughter's relational block hardened the defenses each held to the vulnerability of their role in the family.

Case 2: Family Background

Rich is a self-made, extremely intelligent, successful entrepreneur. His son Elliot, 15 years old, is a poor student who struggles with ADHD and acting-out behaviors such as lying, truancy, and angry outbursts. Elliot spends lots of time on video games and surfing video channels. Rich is constantly dissatisfied with Elliot's work ethic and performance. Moreover, Rich relies on criticism of Elliot's mistakes as a resource to motivate Elliot and responds with advice or punishment for his bad behaviors. As a child, Rich's parents were very strict, focusing on following the rules, which Rich now understands as necessary to his professional success. Sharon, Elliot's mother, resents Rich's negative approach to Elliot. Over the years Rich's dogmatic routine has worn down Sharon's resistance. She is scared her son is heading down the wrong road in life and she is constantly searching for small victories to celebrate in order to build him up. Sharon blames much of Elliot's bad behaviors and low self-esteem on Rich's negativity and unrelenting approach and she has grown deeply resentful of Elliot's continued struggles. Sharon protects herself by being the peace-making parent and the distant wife. She often withholds her love and affection for Rich in protest, hoping this will motivate him to treat Elliot better. The couple fights often over their differences in parenting. The combination of Rich's angry criticism and Sarah's placating withdrawal mirrors the distress and mistrust found in the couple and family relationships as a whole.

Negative Interaction Pattern

The family described their negative pattern in recounting a recent argument that ensued when Sharon was unsuccessful in setting limits regarding Elliot's homework and video gaming. Rich began the family session with his typical authoritarian style.

> We need to stop coddling our 15-year-old son, who seems to think we are overly harsh, out of date, and unrealistic. All the while, he gets whatever he wants and there is only one of us willing to hold the line.

Elliot reacted with contempt: "Like yelling at me, calling me names, taking and breaking my phone, that's not harsh, right!" Sarah jumped into the conversation attempting to control the runaway tension between the two. Sarah anxious and tearfully recalled how she had allowed Elliot time away from homework to play video games and after a set time she then asked him to return to his school work. Elliot exploded in response which triggered the family's negative pattern.

ELLIOT: Stop being such a nag, I told you I'll get to it when I'm ready. I'm sick of you always watching what I do, leave me alone.

SHARON: Calm down. We agreed and if you don't keep your word then there will be consequences. I don't want to take away your phone but if you act disrespectful then it's your fault.

ELLIOT: Right it's always my fault. Nothing to do with living in a house with strict parents who live in the 1900s. Wake up Mom and try living in this century.

Rich overhead the argument and rushed into the room to intervene.

> We are too strict? You get away with murder, you little spoiled brat. Your mother makes you food and gives you time to relax and instead of responding with gratitude you give her attitude. You cause dissention whenever you open your mouth. How about shutting up and doing what you are told.

Elliot responded "Screw you dad, why don't you stay out of it." Outraged, Rich rushes up to Elliot and rips the phone out of Elliot's hand, screaming "you lost your phone for a week. Go to your room and think about how your consistent bad actions are destroying this family." Sharon reacts trying to calm the situation. "Elliot, you are not destroying this family. Dad is just frustrated and doesn't mean it." Elliot rejects her consolation, saying: "Screw you both, I wish I lived in another family. You believe I'm bad well I think you both suck as parents." Elliot leaves the house to go to a friend's home.

Sharon reacts to Rich with sarcasm. "Great job! Why can't you just stay out of this! All you do is make everything worse. You agreed last time to say nothing when we argue. Can't you see how your dislike for him is crushing his spirit?" Crying, she turns to walk away. Rich, now yelling says:

> How dare you blame me for this fiasco. He is so disrespectful because you enable it. We'd never speak to our parents the way he does. Sticking up for him all the time only makes it worse. You are right I'm negative all the time because our son is a disaster. Now we are fighting again because of him. He is destroying our family.

When Sarah reached the door to their bedroom she said coldly: "I can't stand being around you. It is pathetic that you are an adult who acts like a baby. How is Elliot ever going to figure this out when his father is such a bad role model?" She slams the door. Now alone in the hallway, Rich grabs his head with both hands and cries "I can't take this anymore. I'm sick of you picking him and blaming me. If I'm so bad, then maybe you both should just move on without me." Rich walks away and when he reaches his office slams the door.

Relational Blocks

This episode captures a polarizing family pattern characterized by high levels of expressed emotion evident in the family's emotional over-involvement, hostility, and criticism. The conflict cascades toward distance and isolation in all three relationships. The conflict pattern includes anxious attack and defensive withdrawal across both parent–child and couple dyads. Focusing on the relational block in the father and son relationship, the father's negative view of his son and controlling behaviors escalate in response to the son's defiant protest and withdrawal. The mother also adopts a more anxious position in the family interaction, responding by her vigilant efforts to keep the peace even if that at time means she has to placate others' concerns at the expense of her own.

Working with Relational Blocks

The process of working with relational blocks in Steps 3 and 4 includes accessing and assembling the emotional experiences that underlie the secondary attachment strategies that form these blocks. Through processing these relational blocks, the therapist redefines the family's problem in terms of the family's negative pattern, emphasizing the role of these relational blocks in driving this pattern. As family members access and explore the deeper emotions underlying the relational blocks this provides new understanding and motivation for change as the parental intentions of caregiving and attachment-related emotions and needs are clarified. We now review the EFT interventions used in working with relational blocks and revisit the five moves of the EFT tango in Stage 1.

EFT Interventions

The EFT interventions used primarily in Steps 3 and 4 focus on eliciting and exploring emotions. In shifting more focus to relational blocks, the therapist concentrates on interactions occurring in session that reflect the blocks that parents and children experience in the family. These experiences enable the therapist opportunities to elicit, explore, and engage new emotional experiences. These experiences promote greater vulnerability and access to the attachment-related emotions associated with a child's needs and a parent's caregiving responses. The therapist may also focus on the partners' caregiving alliance and relational blocks that are present in the couple's relationship. EFT interventions commonly used to process these emotional blocks emphasize the generation and regulation of deeper emotional experiences.

Tracking and Reflecting Interaction

The process-oriented focus of EFT emphasizes the use of present experience as a source for accessing and expanding emotional experience. Family interactions are a rich resource for eliciting experiences associated with the family's negative pattern and discussions of these difficult family moments illustrate the role of emotion in organizing the rigid positions of family members. In Step 3, greater focus is given to the most distressed dyadic interactions in the family, as these points of painful distress often indicate the family's primary relational block. The therapist reflects family members experience as the family recounts relevant events related to the presenting problem and tracks the unfolding sequence of actions, attributions, and emotions found in those moments. Through tracking these moments, the family patterns typically emerge in session.

Example:

THERAPIST TO MOTHER: So, the door slams shut and again you are on the outside again.

MOTHER: Yes, again. It's terrible to be shut out like that. (*tearful*) To have your child lock you out.

THERAPIST: And you are feeling that now? The tears in your eyes ... are about this feeling?

MOTHER: It's so hard to stand there. Knowing I have no way in ... nothing I can do to make this better.

THERAPIST: (*turning to the son*) And in those moments, it's like you need to get some space, to get away. You are not looking for her to make it better?

SON: Right. She doesn't get that. It's about her—what she needs me to be.

The therapist tracks a poignant moment in a family's negative pattern, where the actions of the mother and son illustrate their efforts to navigate a threatening moment in their relationship. The therapist follows the sequence of actions and reflects the experience of mother and son as they recount this painful interaction.

Evocative Reflections and Questions

This EFT intervention promotes accessing and expanding a family member's emotional experience, a technique often used to focus on an experience in the moment it is happening (Johnson, 2004). The use of questions and reflections about experience are often more effective at eliciting experience rather than direct questions about feelings. In response to a specific action or comment, the therapist follows with a statement or question inviting the family member to further explore their experience. As the therapist tracks a family's interaction, evocative questions may be used to prompt a present-moment experience.

Example:
THERAPIST: What happens for you when you are standing at the door, shut out, not able to make this better?
THERAPIST: After you shut the door and you are sitting in your room, the only place you can go to get away? What is that like for you?
THERAPIST: So, the door shuts you feel again left on the outside. This is where it really gets hard. Where you feel so lost as a parent, as his mother, yes?

Empathic Conjecture

Often in Step 3 the therapist is asking a family member to take one more step into her experience in a moment of emerging emotion. Empathic conjectures build off the recognition of a person's present experience followed immediately by inference of a deeper often attachment-related experience. These attachment inferences often point to the parent's caregiving intentions and the needs a child may be experiencing but finds difficult to name to themselves or to others in the family. Effective conjectures are based on the therapist's empathic ability to stand in the shoes of a family member and conjecture in an attachment-informed perspective about his experience. As conjectures, the therapist makes them in a tentative manner, inviting family members to correct an inference that fails to resonate with that person's experience.

Example:
THERAPIST: So, when you say that you are not what she needs you to be, I may be off here, but it sounds hard in these moments to even begin to think she would really want to see you as you are? Like it would be actually, ok to be you?
SON: Yeah, I guess. No one is happy with me in this house.
THERAPIST: And that's tough, because this is your home. Where you should belong, a place where you feel like you are wanted, and you matter for just being you. Is it something like that?
SON: Nobody sees anything good about me, I don't belong.

Empathic conjectures in Step 3 promote awareness of underlying attachment and caregiving responses. The therapist uses her understanding of separation distress and secondary attachment strategies to conjecture about the underlying importance of a particular experience. For example, the therapist may say to a parent reacting to a rejecting response from their child:

This is what you have come to expect, that you reach out and she rejects your offer. It's like a part of you says why try, let her learn for herself, but then there is this other part that sees her vulnerability, how this could really hurt her, and you feel deep in your heart how much you care for her, how important she is, yes?

Validation

Therapist validation is important in Step 3 as family members access and express new emotional experiences, particularly when those emotions create new levels of vulnerability. Through acknowledging and normalizing these experiences individuals are more entitled to these emotions and are better able to be present to their experience (Johnson, 2004). Validation also makes more room in a family for different experiences of the same event. Through validation emotions can be understood and acknowledged as a legitimate experience. This is particularly important in families where different experiences are threatening to the expectation that everyone will share the same understanding or experience in a family. Validation makes more room for emotional exploration through honoring and appreciating individual experience as a resource for connection and felt security in the family.

Example:
THERAPIST: Right, it makes sense that you would question if your family really chooses you, wants you, cares about you. Especially when you get the message you need to be somebody different.
THERAPIST: Of course, any parent would feel at a loss in that moment. Like they have somehow failed as a parent, having your child lock you out.

Validation of parental efforts and child mistrust is important to managing new steps parents may take as they gain a greater understanding of their child's experience. Recognizing positive intention and effort is necessary in also acknowledging a child's mistrust at new parental effort. Parents' actions may be out of sync with the child's need and working through a relational block involves parents and children working together against the impasse that has defined their relationship. Validation assures that the therapist acknowledges and understands the predictable differences that divide family members and normalizes how each may have their own experience of the same situation.

Heightening

As focus shifts to exploring and expanding emotional experience the therapist uses heightening to bring attention and focus to family members' underlying emotions. The therapist uses a combination of responses to promote a fuller engagement of experience. These moments emphasize the significance of a given experience through a vivid engagement of emotion (Johnson, 2004). The therapist may repeat a client's words or an image that helps crystalize and focus a present emotion. Varying the tone and pace in reflecting this emotion also can intensify and deepen that experience.

Example:
THERAPIST TO SON: Sometimes you say to yourself. "I am not what they want. I don't really belong to this family." I am on my own. Alone.
SON: Sometimes. (*looks away, downcast*)
THERAPIST: Right and that's really hard being that alone. It's hard to shake, hard to get away from that feeling. That feeling that's here right now?
SON: Yeah, I hate it. (*pauses to wipe a tear*) No one really cares.
THERAPIST: That's what's so painful. It's tough enough at school, and then to come home and feel even more alone, to say no one cares, no one sees what I am going through, if they did they would see that I am hurting.

Heightening paces with a family member's emerging experience, walking deeper into that experience, and inviting one into more of that experience. Evocative responding and empathic conjecture focus on emotional experience but it is through heightening that the therapist intensifies making explicit core emotional experience (Johnson, 2004). Non-verbal cues point to emerging emotional experience and slowing an interaction to focus on that cue makes space for that emotion. The therapist uses an empathic conjecture to access that experience and heightening to deepen the experience and reflection on that emotion. These emotion-focused interventions are important in Step 3 as the therapist shifts the focus to the emotional realities underlying the rigid positions that form relational blocks.

Reframing the Problem

A key objective in Step 4 is the family shifting to see the presenting problem and resulting distress in the context of their negative interaction pattern and the relational blocks that inform it. The reactive responses that define a negative interaction cycle are organized around family members' defensive self-protective responses. Through Step 3 the therapist expands a family's experience of these negative patterns through accessing the underlying experiences that are also part of these reactive interactions. Shifting focus to these deeper emotions the family has more access to the vulnerable emotions that inform more secure attachment communication.

Reframing, used throughout Stage 1, frames the family distress in the context of rigid patterns that interrupt the family's ability to effectively cope and resolve specific challenges. Through tracking specific inter- actions and experiences the therapist organizes these responses into a summary that highlights the actions and emotions organized around the relational block. Through this summary the therapist expands the focus to the impact of the cycle on the family as a whole. The use of reframing shifts the focus on to the family's relationship patterns and how they interfere and disrupt the family's ability to respond effectively to dis- tress. These summaries often follow the processing of deeper emotional experiences and provide a context for these experiences to be seen and understood in terms of failed attachment and caregiving attempts.

Example:

THERAPIST: (*to mother and son*) It is at this point you can really see where this pattern leaves you. Both frustrated and hurting for different reasons. Jon your mom worries that there is a problem, and she goes to you, and all you hear is her disappointment and concern. You put up roadblocks to get some space and slow her down. And mom you see him backing up and this only confirms your fears that he is blocking the help he needs. The cycle is full force when the yelling starts and door slamming. It's hard because there is no place in this moment for talking for finding a way to be heard or to care in a way that works. The cycle has won again.

FATHER: (*resisting*) But there is also the school problems and failing grades. That's an issue for Jon. He needs to face his responsibilities.

THERAPIST: Yes, the concerns are real. You see the consequences if Jon's situation doesn't change. And I wonder if we pause a second here, we might also see that when this cycle takes hold, the yelling and door slamming take over, and all this negativity fills the house. There is no homework getting done, no support happening. That's how the cycle wins. Make sense?

FATHER: Well, I get that, but I don't think we can excuse responsibility.

THERAPIST: Right, there is only one person who can handle the home- work and school situation and you and your wife are here to help. To come alongside Jon, right? So, what happens for you in these moments when this negative pattern has taken over?

In this example the father challenges the shift to focusing on the family conflict. The therapist validates the father's concerns and acknowledges the importance of his caregiving concern (e.g., responsibility). At the same time the therapist focuses on the impact of the negative family climate and its role in disrupting the parent's best efforts to support Jon. In this way the therapist reframes the father's concern in terms of his caregiving intent.

Relational Blocks and Parental Openness

In EFFT the therapist gives specific attention to the relational blocks that form in attachment and caregiving interactions. As an experiential approach the therapist works with the emotional experiences that inform and result from these blocks to initiate a process of transforming these blocks and re-establishing secure connections in the family. Safety and security in the therapy process are paramount in working with reactive family processes. The therapist's working alliance with individual family members and assessment of safety guide the use of conjoint and individual sessions in family treatment. The EFFT decision framework illustrates the possible choices a therapist may make in shifting the composition of a particular treatment session. The assessment of parental responsiveness and reactivity is central to determining the readiness for conjoint sessions, where relational blocks are the focus and three conditions direct the therapist's use of individual or conjoint sessions in response. These include: Parental openness with mis-attunement, parental ambivalence and defensiveness, and parental defensiveness and hostility.

Parental Openness with Mis-attunement

Parents are supportive and engaged in efforts to respond to the child, but they have difficultly attuning to the experience and needs of their child. Parental responses may be dismissive of the child's negative emotions or minimizing of his attachment-related concerns. Conjoint sessions focusing on parental awareness and responsiveness to the child's experience promote opportunities for parents to increase attention to the child. If parents shift away from their engaged position and withdraw support or react against their child's need the therapist shifts their focus to the second condition: Parental ambivalence and defensiveness.

Parental Ambivalence and Defensiveness

The second condition, parental ambivalence and defensiveness, is more likely when parents react to the mistrust and angry protest of their child. Reactive parental responses are normalized and parental intentions are validated. The therapist validates the child's negative responses to a lack of parental availability. Tracking this interaction, the therapist slows the reactive moment and makes space for parents to better see themselves and their child through the underlying emotions that accompany these reactive strategies. A parent's fear that their child's anger is a sign of disrespect for the parent provides a source for acknowledging the importance of caregiving to the parent and the fear that they somehow in these moments are less able to be a resource to their child. Concurrently, the therapist's accessing and processing of the child's protest points to the fear that the child's efforts to be more autonomous are not valued by the parent. The child's fear blocks their bid for reassurance from the parent, and their anger is the result of their guarded response to the parent's defensiveness. The therapist's alliance provides a resource for the parent and child to access the deeper emotions and work through this moment. When a parent or child escalate their defensive responses and protest with hostility or complete withdrawal, the therapist should consider the family's readiness for working through a relational block in a conjoint session. We consider this situation an unsafe condition particularly in interactions that risk furthering injury.

Parental Defensiveness and Hostility

Safety and readiness are primary concerns for the therapist when processing a relational block. Heightened levels of expressed emotion (e.g., emotional over-involvement, hostility, and criticism) provide the therapist with markers for determining the readiness for conjoint sessions at this stage of EFFT. Following the EFFT decision model the therapist may use separate parent sessions and individual child-focused sessions to work through the heightened levels of defensiveness and reactivity. In situations where the parent or child's reactive response erupts in a conjoint session, the therapist must address the injury unfolding in the moment. In EFT, the therapist "catches the bullet" in reactive couple exchanges and this intervention is relevant in working with families (Johnson, 2004).

In reactive moments where defensiveness and hostile response occur in response to vulnerability the therapist must intervene to address the threat and negative impact of these negative responses to a vulnerable risk. The therapist acknowledges the vulnerable experience shared and shows support and care for the risk taken. This is essential when a child's vulnerable risk is rejected. For example, as a daughter becomes tearful in expressing how alone she feels and her mother reacts harshly saying: "Your loneliness is your own doing. You need to take responsibility for how badly you treat others, especially in your family!" The therapist quickly responds,

Ok, yes, I can see this is where it gets tough. (*turning to daughter*) Your tears seem to bring out your mom's anger and I'm not sure what's happening for her, but I am guessing that her anger makes it hard for her to see your tears. I know you are taking a risk here telling us just how hard this loneliness is for you, especially in moments like this, yes? It would be for anyone, right? [Shifting focus to mother]. So, I am wondering if we can take a breath now and try to understand this moment, because it is hard to see her tears and hear her talk this way about her loneliness. I wonder if it's so hard to see her pain, when you so often see her pushing you and others away, it's like you want her to see what she is doing, especially when you see her hurting, yes?

The therapist acknowledges and validates the child's vulnerability and the parent's rejecting response and at the same time acknowledges the parent's defensive response conjecturing about the possible caring intention of her response.

EFFT and the Process of Stage 1

After a review of the EFFT steps in Stage 1 and the EFT interventions used to build an alliance, track family patterns, and work with relational blocks, this final section provides an overview of the EFFT process in Stage 1. First, we review the EFT tango meta-framework (Johnson, 2019) as a summary for the process of EFT across Stage 1 of EFFT. Then we conclude with a case example to illustrate this process at work.

EFT Tango and Stage 1

We recognize that the EFT therapist does not organize sessions following the steps in a strict linear fashion, rather the therapist flexibly follows the EFFT model of change as it unfolds through building an alliance, identifying patterns, accessing underlying emotions, and redefining problems as patterns. In this section we highlight the use of the EFT tango framework in illustrating an EFFT session.

Mirroring Present Process

In Stage 1 the therapist engages the family's reactive process related to the presenting problem. Through tracking the family interactions around their presenting concern, the therapist organizes the predictable sequences that result in deepening levels of negativity and relational distress. At the same time the therapist reflects the experience of various family members in the midst of this rigid pattern. Through mirroring the present process, the therapist focuses specifically on the actions, perceptions, and feelings associated with this unfolding pattern. EFT interventions focused on alliance building and tracking interactions are necessary to engage a family in exploring their typical experiences. The therapist uses present-moment experiences that result when the family's negative pattern is triggered in session.

Affect Assembly and Deepening

Focusing on these present-moment experiences the therapist elicits and expands the emotional experiences associated with these negative family interactions. Using affect assembly and deepening of emotion the therapist shifts to using these present moments to mine emotional experience focusing on the deeper more adaptive emotions related to attachment and caregiving. The therapist leads family members through reactive defensive positions to more adaptive and vulnerable experiences. Evocative EFT interventions are frequently used to increase attention and deepen each family member's experience and understanding of the underlying emotion/attachment drama at play in their conflicts and distance. These interventions include evocative responding, empathic conjecture, and heightening. Therapist's reflection and validation of present experiences enables family members to purposefully explore emerging emotional experiences that often underlie the self-protective actions found in family cycles and relational blocks.

Choreographing Engaged Encounters

As the therapist guides the family to access and assemble their emotional experience the therapist leads family members to share with others these experiences from a more regulated and organized state. These enactments may involve the sharing of present experiences to increase ownership and awareness of the negative impact of the family's reactive pattern. More often these engaged encounters focus on an individual family member's deeper emotional experience and understanding. The therapist works to actively support and entitle family members to these experiences and to engage those experiences in session through sharing with others. The therapist uses evocative intervention to keep a focus on the more vulnerable emotions being experienced and then shared. The use of enactments to engage these emotional experiences are typical of the focus of Step 3 in the EFFT process of change.

Processing the Encounter

The therapist follows the impact of sharing this emotional encounter with other family members. In Stage 1 the sharing of vulnerable emotions may result in inviting others to accept and join in that vulnerability or react against the vulnerability. For example, a parent may contact their sadness in response to realizing the negative impact of harsh parenting strategies on the child and family. The father's sadness while vulnerable and congruent is not trusted by his children who suffered under his wrath. His softer emotional stance is a trigger for their mistrust and lack of confidence in the authenticity of his emotion. The therapist uses reflection and validation to help family members make sense of these new encounters. Reframing harsh or rejecting responses may also be necessary when another family member is triggered by an expression of vulnerability. The therapist monitors the alliance to support family members in being able to stay present and organize a response to this encounter.

Integrating and Validating

In Stage 1 the therapist's overarching goals are stabilization and de-escalation of the family's reactive cycle. These cycles are composed of relational blocks that interrupt attachment communication and effective caregiving responses. Throughout Stage 1 the therapist is incrementally helping the family shift their focus from a specific child-related problem to the patterns of interaction that either exacerbate the symptomatic behaviors or are themselves the actual distress in the family. This final move in the tango process promotes the creation of meaning and felt understanding in response to the assembly and sharing of emotion. Processing interventions including validation, reflection, and reframing provide family members resources for exploring and making sense of the emotional experience of the family. The therapist promotes coherence and shared understanding through focusing on present experience and the ways that coping with separation distress can lead typical families into disconnection at personal and relational levels.

Case Example—Stage 1

The following Stage 1 example provides an overview of the process of treatment illustrating how Steps 3 and 4 focus on working through a primary relational block found between a mother and her son. A summary of treatment reviews the progress the family has made through Stage 1 and excerpts from a treatment session are used to demonstrate the shifts that occur as a family faces a specific relational block together. The session includes the son, mother, and father.

Family Background

Carl (16) was referred to treatment by his school therapist after showing a marked decrease in school performance and attendance. He was failing the majority of classes and this was a dramatic change for the otherwise successful student. Carl lived at home with his sister Angela (13) and parents Sarah and George. Angela was diagnosed with a developmental disorder and while living at home attends a specialized school program. The primary parenting responsibilities fell on Sarah as George's work required him to travel several days a week. Sarah was diagnosed with a chronic illness five years ago and has been successful in managing her symptoms, though at times they can be debilitating. At the onset of her illness she relied heavily on Carl for Angela's care and general family support as George was not available.

Both Sarah and George escaped from difficult family situations, marrying at 16 and 18 years of age. They each wanted a better life for their family and especially for Carl, given the limitations of Angela's condition.

The patterns of abuse in the family began shortly after Sarah's declining health. Frequent fights erupted between Carl and his parents as he resisted the family pressure to take responsibility for caring for his mother and sister given his father's absence. After intervention from protective services, Sarah received more support and help with parenting skills and George changed jobs enabling him to be more present to the family. The abuse abated but the emotional struggles in the family continued. Carl's school struggles triggered Sarah's fear which she managed by vigilantly monitoring Carl's efforts and time, all the while cautious to avoid the previous patterns of abuse.

Negative Interaction Pattern

Sarah found it difficult to get Carl's attention and concern regarding his school work. She relied on family dinner conversations to question Carl about his future and his priorities at school. These one-way conversations were tense as Sarah restrained her frustration with Carl's insolence and passivity. As Carl fended off her increasingly anxious appeals for engagement, Sarah demanded: "Talk to me! I can't help you if you won't talk to me." George remained silent, not sure what to do to keep the situation from exploding. Sarah, feeling even more alone, reacted to the silence at the table, firing a series of increasingly anxious comments pleading for a response from Carl who had now left the dinner table. In tears Sarah followed Carl saying: "I am so sorry. I need to talk to you! What can I do to change?" Sarah's tears frightened Carl and he needed to get away from her as all he felt was shame for how his mother was feeling. He locked his bedroom door and screamed, "Leave me alone." Sarah's entreats became more desperate; her voice dropped and she began to whimper. Carl became enraged as now he felt totally responsible for his mother's depleted emotional state. He screamed in rage "LEAVE ME ALONE!" George then intervened, pulling his wife away from the door and yelling at Carl to quit attacking Sarah. Carl collapsed on his bed, saying to himself, "I hate her, I hate my life, I get blamed for everything." Sarah and George would retreat into separate places in the house and in time Sarah would try to reconnect with Carl, only to repeat the cycle of her initiation and his rejection. The negativity and powerlessness the family felt to change this pattern increased with each iteration.

Relational Block

In spite of Sarah's good intention and multiple efforts to educate herself, she would fall into the same negative anxious interaction with her son. Her own negative models of self (I am a bad mother) and negative model of others (there is no one there for me), blocked her ability to clearly see her son and what he needed. She was driven by an internal need to gain access to Carl, to receive reassurance that she was a good parent, and that her son needed her. Carl felt the pressure of his mother's anxiety, which just drove him further away and feeling alone, frustrated, and demoralized. George felt pulled by his desire to protect both his wife and his son and would intervene only in crisis moments, when their interaction was out of control. He felt helpless in knowing how to soothe and comfort his wife and had his own blocks to caregiving which he dealt with through avoidance. He felt his best bet was to support his wife and that action combined with his own inaction regarding his son, left Carl alone, feeling bad about himself and his family.

Assessment and Alliance Building

The initial family session followed two individual sessions with Carl focused on his personal struggles. Carl was withdrawn and somewhat depressed. He reported having no friends at school, and no idea what he wanted to do in life. Carl was careful and cautious in response to the therapist's question, talking slowly and editing his words. He became more animated talking about his family situation and how he "hated" his parents and wanted to leave home as quickly as possible. Carl tired of his family conflicts, "All we ever do is fight," and resented his mother's intrusion "She just can't leave me alone." Carl rejected the suggestion of family sessions, lacking confidence that any session with his family would go well. Carl recalled how he had at times had to resort to physically pushing his parents away in order to get them to back away. The therapist acknowledged how hard this would be for Carl as he was all alone and unprotected in his family, and Carl became visibly sad. The therapist wondered if in spite of how hard it has been for him, as it would be for anyone in his shoes, if he also still loved his parents and wanted something different in the future. Carl agreed, and the therapist suggested combining individual sessions with family treatment. The therapist ensured that Carl would be safe in the conversations with his family and with this reassurance conjoint family sessions commenced.

During the parents' assessment session, Sarah dominated the conversation, talking quickly and rapidly as she recounted the ways that Carl was failing at school and spending most of daytime hours locked in his bedroom. While the therapist slowed her down, stating how much she wanted to hear Sarah's story, Sarah related how much she had done to try to help her son, including hiring tutors to help with his schoolwork, making many trips to the school to intervene with teachers on Carl's behalf, and enrolling him in various extracurricular activities.

In exploring Sarah's frustration and anger, related to these behaviours, Sarah stated she resented having a "fully able-bodied son" at home who refused to engage in any of the ways she tried to help him and who also refused to help her with household tasks. She related how hard it had been for her to be off work and couldn't understand how Carl not only did not go to school, but also did not help her with her own disability. George jumped in at this juncture, supporting his wife, saying that he expected his son to "be the man around the house" when he was away and expressed his dismay at Carl for squandering all of his advantages that he worked so hard to provide. The therapist reflected and validated each parent's experience, as she began to clarify each parent's position in the family pattern.

George and Sarah affirmed their commitment to a strong caregiving alliance but George's physical absence and his anxious support for Sarah indicated ongoing assessment of the caregiving alliance was necessary. Both agreed they were on the "same team" when it came to providing discipline to their son although both felt helpless in knowing how to best support him. George felt called to be the "United Nations" between Sarah and Carl when things escalated, and he tried to mediate their fights when he was home. The therapist assessed the risk of potential physical and verbal aggression in the family and Sarah disclosed her previous abuse episodes with Carl and the protective services interventions as a result. The therapist validated Sarah's strength and courage in facing these issues through individual treatment and Sarah acknowledged her residual shame and guilt over how her abusive actions impacted Carl. George on the other hand, dismissed this concern as "being a long time ago" and that everyone was in a very different place now and Carl now had all the advantages that he never had as a kid. The therapist reflected George's efforts to make things better between Carl and Sarah, then George chuckled, "There I am again, being the United Nations!" Both parents laughed and shared a moment of light connection.

The parent session concluded focusing on each parent's attachment history. Sarah describer her parents as "master manipulators" and she currently had no contact with either of them. Her fear was that Carl would make a similar cut off from her, and she acted in ways to do anything to prevent losing her relationship with Carl as a result. George stated that he had been on his own from a very young age, as his mother was busy looking after his younger siblings and he described his father as absent. He left home at age 16 years of age and learned to look after himself, beginning full-time work at a very young age. The parent session concluded identifying a shared goal for treatment that would include assisting each parent in developing a stronger relationship with Carl beyond the current discipline practices they found ineffective. Sarah and George acknowledged that they needed to find a better way to communicate to the son they both loved. The therapist amplified this positive parental intent, reinforcing how much they wanted to be there for Carl, validating and normalizing how hard it is when a parent is not able to reach a child, especially when they see him struggling. Naming the parents' openness and intention highlighted their commitment to the alliance and provided the therapist an opportunity to reinforce the hope that as parents they would be able to offer their son a better start to adulthood than they themselves had had.

Initial Family Session

Carl began the family session complaining that he felt "stressed" at home and sought solace alone in his room playing his guitar. The therapist followed his complaint asking the family what happened when Carl retreated to his room, shifting the focus to the family's interaction pattern in a moment of stress. Sarah shared that she would follow Carl in these moments and demand that he come out of his room and talk. The therapist, focusing on Sarah's experience, asked her what she says to herself in those moments. "Three things. First, he doesn't want to be with me. Second, I must have done something wrong, and third, I need to fix it." Carl responded saying he felt "suffocated" at those moments and that he believed that all this was more about her getting what she wanted than what he needed from her. Sarah went on to explain how these situations would escalate as she would plead with Carl to talk, with her voice signaling her increasing distress. Carl, hearing her fast pace and increasing pitch, would move away in silence or react by swearing at her to leave him be. George intervened at this point admonishing his son for swearing and telling both his wife and his son to go their separate ways.

Once the therapist had a better sense of the relational blocks, she engaged the family's more distressed dyad through asking about the times that Carl refused to respond or reacted with attack. Sarah identified how much she needed to fix things with Carl. Carl's negative emotions meant to Sarah that he was "shunning" her, that Carl didn't want to be with her, and that she has failed as a mom. She owned that when he was younger "I hit him and that was wrong, and it was ugly" and then follow quickly with, "but that was a long time ago and I think he should shake it off." The therapist focused Sarah on this moment of regret and acknowledged her strength in speaking about this difficult time. The following illustrates a Step 3 interaction focused on accessing and assembling underlying emotions.

THERAPIST: So, let's go slow and take this a step at a time, because you guys are hurting here, you're hurting, I hear that, and we are jumping into the deep end. I want to make sure all of us can swim together, we're going to swim around in that slowly boiling (*father's image*) kind of place that all of you are acknowledging that is happening. (*therapist turns directly to Sarah*) What I hear you are saying right now is: "I do know what I did. I do know for all the reasons." Like your own mental health.

MOTHER: And my upbringing.

THERAPIST: Yes, and your upbringing made you vulnerable and resulted in you, (*pointing to Carl*) (*softly*) hurting this precious little guy. (*Sarah nods, looking down*)

THERAPIST: And when you think about that now?

MOTHER: I feel sick to my stomach.

THERAPIST: It makes me sick to my stomach, it touches a deep place, and makes you really, really sad. (*pause*) Is that the right word? (*therapist reflects the pain that flashes across her face*)

MOTHER: I can't even describe the way it makes me feel because I know the pain of growing up like that.

THERAPIST: Right. You know how bad this all feels.

MOTHER: But I think to myself thank God I caught it in time before it became a regular thing.

THERAPIST: Right, there was a part of you that was observing you, and that was able to pull you back. But there is also this pain that rises up in you when you think of the hurt he endured. (*therapist refocuses Sarah on her underlying pain*)

MOTHER: I didn't ever want to do that, ever. (*reaching over to touch Carl*)

THERAPIST: So, as you touch him right now and you stroke his shoulder, what are you saying? (*therapist reflects the non-verbal process*)

MOTHER: I always want to touch him, I always want to be close to him.

THERAPIST: What are you saying to him about what happened? (*therapist directs Sarah to the present moment*)

MOTHER: (*tearfully looking at Carl*) I am so sorry.

THERAPIST: You're saying I am sorry. I know what I did. (*therapist reinforces parental intent, deepening parental responsiveness, through using proxy voice*)

MOTHER: (*sinking into shame*) And I hate myself for it all.

THERAPIST: It's so hard for me, because it makes "me hate me," yes? (*Sarah nods finding it hard to come up with words.*)

THERAPIST: But what you are saying right now takes a tremendous amount of courage, and I see your husband right beside you, he has his arm around you. (*therapist reinforces caregiving support*)

MOTHER: (*sobbing*) George knows what I went through growing up.

THERAPIST: Right he is supporting you right now. (*therapist refocuses on the present moment*)

MOTHER: I shouldn't do this.

THERAPIST: Its ok, its ok, its ok (*therapist reassures and validates Sarah*)

MOTHER: (*looking at Carl*) But I love him more than anything.

THERAPIST: Yes, I understand, as a Mom I know that too.

MOTHER: (*becoming agitated*) He is a fantastic person and I have done this to him. (*sobbing*)

THERAPIST: (*moving closer and leaning in*) Ok we need to go slow here. Let's go slow with this, all right? Because you are showing a tremendous amount of courage here. And this is one big, big step. You're saying to Carl "I hurt you and I am sorry for the hurt and the pain you endured." He was young, alone, and he was scared. (*therapist validates Sarah's courage and heightens her caregiving regret*)

MOTHER: I can't imagine seeing that monster, but I can, that's the thing.

THERAPIST: That's what makes it even harder, right? Yes, but you want him to know that you see his pain, right? This takes so much courage and strength Sarah. You are showing incredible strength here to say this out loud, to say this out loud to Carl sitting beside you now.

MOTHER: (*pulling back*) And when he gets angry at me?

THERAPIST: (*lifts hand, pausing Sarah*) ok, let's just ... (*Sarah interjects*) Stay in the moment.

THERAPIST: Yes, let's stay in this moment because you are doing such a great job. (*pauses as mother nods*) We are just going to breathe through this one. (*therapist slows the conversation, regulating mom through slow intentional breathing*) You are actually touching the place that is so painful, the place you don't want to go to and actually is part of the panic that drives your tone of voice, your rapid words, your efforts to connect with Carl when he pulls away.

MOTHER: Yes, I just want to keep calm and fix it.

THERAPIST: Right, make it better. But right now, you are just saying, you know that you hurt him, you know that you hurt him?

MOTHER: I do (*looking at Carl*) I do know how hard it is and how hard it is to forgive me for it.

THERAPIST: Let's just take this slow. You are saying, "I see you Carl, I see you as a little guy." You were telling me downstairs about him growing up and dad you were talking about when you used to carry this guy around in your arms, and (*looking at Carl*) he was a little guy. (*therapist evokes the image of Carl as a young vulnerable boy*)

MOTHER: Man, you were a cute kid!

THERAPIST: And you were remembering these times, right, and you are here today as a family talking about being a family, and letting that Carl today, and the cute kid of yesterday, know that you see his pain today. (*therapist turns toward Carl*) Your mom is sharing right now what is in her heart. What is it like for you says she knows that she hurt you (*coming alongside Carl*) what's that like for you to hear that, right now?

CARL: I can't really describe the feeling because it makes me feel relieved and sad at the same time. I don't know how to describe it.

THERAPIST: That's pretty beautiful what you just said, makes me feel relieved and it makes me feel sad. It's a relief on one hand that your mom can see you and what happened to you, is that the relief part?

CARL: Relief, yeah.

THERAPIST: And what's the sad part?

CARL: Seeing her like that.

MOTHER: I can take it Carl. (*mom anxiously interrupts*)

THERAPIST: It's ok, that he cares about you, and what makes him feel sad is that you are sad. Yes? But you are also saying to your son. (*therapist gestures sitting upright with open arms*) "I am the mom, I can take it, I have lived many more years then you Carl and I have navigated lots of things in my life and I have both feet on the ground here, and I am ok," is that what you are saying?

MOTHER: Yes, I can handle this, I can handle my emotion, a lot better now. Better than when I was 16 (*turns toward Carl*) and you are 16, and it's hard to process everything on your own at 16 and it is difficult being 16 without having all this emotional trauma on top of everything else. (*Sarah speaks in a solid regulated tone*)

THERAPIST: Sarah, you are seeing Carl right now. This is so different than your typical pattern of you pressing him and Carl pulling away or attacking. This pattern makes it hard because it moves so fast and there is so much emotion. But we are slowing this down and you are both talking in a different way. Carl is being very clear about his emotions.

MOTHER: And that is taking some of that panic away.

THERAPIST: Talking this way is turning down the panic. You are able to look at this panic? (*Sarah nods*) You looked at it, you went into it, you felt the pain underneath that panic and you actually did something about it. (*Sarah says "Yeah" in an understated tone*) You were able to say to Carl: "I know I hurt you, I know I caused you pain," but you are also saying you know that Carl has his own experience, his own pain and that is different. That's something you want to see and understand, yes?

Session Summary

The therapist began the session focused on the family's negative interaction pattern associated with the family's concern for Carl's future. The therapist concentrated on the relational block between Sarah and her son. Although George also plays a mediator role in this reactive pattern, the therapist narrows attention to the more distressed dyad as a poignant source of family pain. The therapist accessed the mother's experience through creating safety and space for her to explore her underlying emotions in the present moment. Overcome by an anxious panic Sarah found Carl's withdrawal triggered profound feelings of shame and regret for the "monster" she had been toward him. Sarah reacted to these painful feelings by trying to fix Carl and dismissing or minimizing the painful impact of her abusive actions toward him. Sarah's self-protective responses left Carl feeling responsible and alone in the pain he endured. He believed his pain was invisible to his mother and he stopped trusting his mother could be there for him, all she was focused on was her needs. The session illustrates how the therapist demonstrates and enacts greater parental openness and engagement by processing through a relational block. This, however, does not accomplish a relational repair, the processing of the mother's anxious block to caregiving only begins to shift how caregiving is experienced between this mother and son.

The therapist follows the five moves of the EFT tango. First, the therapist focuses on "mirroring the present process" and engaging Sarah in exploring her experience on her side of the relational block with Carl. As her experience is explored and engaged the therapist slows the process to concentrate on Sarah's underlying emotions as they emerge in sharing about her experience of Carl closing off and refusing her care. The therapist shifts to "affect assembly and deepening" Sarah's experience through focusing on the experience of feeling "shunned" by Carl. When Sarah began to touch the pain of her shame, she would immediately dismiss and minimize her experience, and shift the focus to Carl. The therapist refocused and redirected her back to her pain by also validating and shoring up her positive caregiving intent in order to provide her with a stronger position to face her shame without becoming overwhelmed by it. By holding Sarah in this experience, the therapist promoted Sarah's ability to focus on this part of herself she didn't want to see. This was "the monster" that had hurt her child and the monster she knew from her own abuse as a child.

Through the support and presence of the therapist and awareness of her husband's support, Sarah engaged her regret and expressed more tenderly her concern for Carl. This "engaged encounter" happened more spontaneously and the therapist worked through this enactment by heightening the caregiving themes in Sarah's response, shifting her focus from shame to guilt and grief. Sarah was able to begin repair with her son through expressing her regret and sorrow to him directly. The therapist shifted to "processing the encounter" with Carl who was able to share his relief and his sadness. Sarah was available to be responsive to Carl's sadness, which was a different response than the anxious panic he had come to expect. Through "integrating and validating" the therapist solidifies the differences experienced in this family conversation. Sarah was able to see that her panic in the cycle was connected to her shame, and the success of having a more responsive conversation with Carl which he in turn reciprocated.

Summary

In Stage 1 the therapist redefines the family's presenting problem in the context of negative patterns of distress that extend from relational blocks in caregiving and attachment. In Steps 3 and 4, the processing of relational blocks, the therapist engages new levels of vulnerability associated with disconnections in attachment and caregiving. Through accessing and processing these underlying emotions new encounters are possible between these blocked relationships, promoting greater openness and exploration of the family's attachment-related distress. The therapist's focus on negative patterns and relationship blocks enables parents and child to see the impact of separation distress and the resulting negative emotion on the ability of the family to respond effectively to the core needs of family members.

EFFT Process Points

The following process points highlight the essential role of alliance formation and assessment in this initial phase of EFFT.

1. Identifying the family's negative interaction enables the therapist to narrow the focus of treatment on blocked patterns of attachment and caregiving.
2. The therapist explores relational blocks and the emotions underlying the unsuccessful family attempts to overcome these difficulties. Negative emotions and symptomatic behaviors are seen in light of possible separation distress resulting from disrupted attachment and caregiving processes.
3. The therapist follows the steps of the EFT tango in engaging relational blocks, including accessing and engaging underlying emotions associated with the rigid positions in these relational blocks. The therapist's exploration of underlying emotions facilitates more adaptive responses between family members and a de-escalation of more reactive interactions.
4. A parent's positive parental intent is highlighted and validated to foster greater parental openness and prime parental emotions associated with caregiving. The therapist elicits the child's deeper emotions underlying self-protective responses to relational blocks.
5. Family distress is reduced through the identification of predictable patterns of emotional distress and access to more vulnerable emotions that promote more effective attachment and caregiving responses.

References

Bowlby, J. (1969). *Attachment and loss: Vol 1. Attachment.* New York: Basic Books.
Bowlby, J. (1980). *Attachment and loss: Vol 3. Loss.* New York: Basic Books.
Johnson, S. M. (2004). *The practice of emotionally focused therapy: Creating connection*, 2nd Ed. New York: Brunner/Routledge.
Johnson, S. M. (2019). *Attachment theory in practice: Emotionally focused therapy with individuals, couples, and families.* New York: Guilford Press.
Kobak, R., Grassetti, S. N., & Yarger, H. A. (2013). Attachment based treatment for adolescents: Repairing attachment injuries and empathic failures. In K. H. Birsch (Ed.), *Attachment and adolescence* (pp. 93–111). Stuttgart: Klett-Cotta Verlag.
Kobak, R., Duemmler, S., Burland, A., & Youngstrom, E. (1998). Attachment and negative absorption states: Implications for treating distressed families. *Journal of Systemic Therapies, 17*, 80–92.
Kobak, R., Zajac, K., Herres, J., & Krauthamer Ewing, E. S. (2015). Attachment based treatments for adolescents: The secure cycle as a framework for assessment, treatment and evaluation. *Attachment & Human Development, 17*, 220–239.
Mikulincer, M., & Shaver, P. R. (2015). Boosting attachment security in adulthood: The "broaden-and-build" effects of security-enhancing mental representations and interpersonal contexts. In J. A. Simpson & W. S. Rholes (Eds.), *Attachment theory and research: New directions and emerging themes* (pp. 124–144). New York: Guilford Press.

SIX

Engaging Family Vulnerability

Step 5. Accessing and deepening a child's disowned aspects of self and attachment needs.
Step 6. Fostering acceptance of a child's new experience and attachment-related needs.

In the EFFT process of change, family stabilization and de-escalation represent a threshold to new opportunities for the family's repair and growth. Through Stage 1 family members are more aware of the predicable conflict patterns that dominate the family in distress and greater attention is focused on specific relational blocks that interrupt a family's ability to sustain felt security and emotional balance. Parental openness and awareness of the underlying emotions informing the relational block prepares the family for Stage 2 of the EFFT process.

In this chapter we review EFFT practices that facilitate exploration of a child's attachment-related emotions and needs. Stage 2 processes focused on promoting parental acceptance and engagement are illustrated using case examples where empathic failures and relational injuries disrupted attachment and caregiving processes. This chapter also highlights the use of EFT interventions that support a family taking new steps of vulnerability and acceptance.

Goals for Steps 5 and 6

In EFFT the principle aim of Stage 2 is to promote positive bonding experiences between parents and children through engaging child vulnerability and parental availability. Four goals guide a therapist's focus through Steps 5 and 6 that are essential to the restructuring of attachment and caregiving bonds. First, a child's unacknowledged attachment-related needs are identified including the child's view of self and view of others (e.g., caregiver). The child's anxiety and anger associated with the relational block are explored and the more vulnerable emotions related to the child's unexpressed needs are made explicit.

A second and related goal is that a child's models of self and other (e.g., parent) are named and redefined in the presence of greater parental availability. For example, a child who questions whether she matters in her parent's world is now able to name her fears and longing for her parents' interest and attention. Her ability to claim this experience and to share this with a parent, enables her to move into a deeper expression of feeling unwanted and fearful of rejection. Through these experiences the child is better able to name her need for care and reassurance. The child's increased confidence in parental availability is fostered by a parent's acceptance of the child's new experience and the child's own efforts to share more vulnerably with this parent. Later in Step 7, the focus will shift to an enactment where she will actively share her need to her parent and with the parent's available response the daughter not only receives support but is also more likely to see herself as worthy of this need (view of self) and seeing her parents as more available to her most vulnerable concern (view of other). The therapist work in Steps 5 and 6 is crucial for preparing for this coming corrective experience.

A third goal involves the active expression of parental acceptance of the child's vulnerable expressions. Parental engagement and attunement to the child are essential in promoting a shift in the child's experience of parental availability. For example, the therapist encourages a parent to express their support and interest in the child's new experience of being unseen and longing for reassurance of her importance. The therapist works with the parent to make the signals of their acceptance clear, coherent, and emotionally accessible.

The final goal anticipates the ways in which a child's new experiences of vulnerability may trigger the parents' own negative views of the child or themselves. Therefore, the fourth goal involves working through ongoing or returning parental blocks to acceptance. These blocks may include revisiting the parental blocks named in Step 3 and exploring their impact through the parents' view of their child and view of themselves as parents. These relational blocks may also reflect the parents' own struggles with their attachment history and unresolved needs from their past experience. This goal requires increasing support for the parents' efforts and needs in their role as an attachment figure through shoring up their presence as the child's stronger, wiser other.

Access Points

Therapist access points for intervention in Steps 5 and 6 prioritize accessing a child's attachment-related emotions and needs and promoting parental support to the child's new experience. In session, the EFFT process follows the EFT tango framework more explicitly with greater attention to affect assembly and deepening, engaging new encounters of more vulnerable experience, and processing the impact of these deeper emotional moments. Four access points highlight specific shifts the therapist makes in working through previously blocked attachment and caregiving responses.

1. Accessing a Child's Underlying Emotions Associated with Relational Blocks

The therapist elicits a child's experience of the relational block identified in Stage 1. Specifically, the therapist monitors the present process for verbal and nonverbal cues associated with a child's emotional responses when responding to parental openness in the context of past parental blocks. The child's new experience may reflect residual anger and hurt related to past empathic failures or attachment-related injuries that have negatively impacted the child's confidence in parental openness. The therapist engages affect assembly and deepening to further explore and name the child's previously unacknowledged emotions, thereby giving voice to the child's pain and fear. The therapist also validates the child's usual response to these feeling and the actions that result (i.e., the child's response to the relational block). For example, the therapist may follow a daughter's contemptuous response to her father's efforts to offer care and reassurance, the therapist engages with the intensity of her reaction as an access point to her fear of his rejection.

2. Working through a Child's View of Self and View of Parent

Through accessing and exploring deeper emotions, themes related to a child's view of self and view of their parent are evident. Typically, the most intense and dramatic emotions experienced in Stage 2 are related to these particular themes. The therapist validates these emotions and promotes the child's entitlement to these fears and the longing they represent. Working through these experiences the therapist assembles the child's experience which typically leads to identification of attachment needs. Naming these needs may occur in the earlier steps of Stage 1 but when the focus is on deepening emotions in Stage 2 these needs have a poignant felt sense. The therapist's presence validating these emerging needs honors their importance and invites the child to take a new position in relationship to their parents. This work prepares the child for the process of enacting these needs in Step 7.

At the same time focusing on the child's experience may also include fears and hurt related to harsh parental treatment and rejection. Children may be reluctant to name from a more vulnerable position the fears they experience that result from a negative view of their parent. The therapist uses validation, reflection, and empathic conjecture to enable to youth to name and express the impact of the injuries resulting from harsh parental treatment. These ruptures in relationship leave children uncertain about positive parental intention and efforts to correct for the past. Therefore, children have difficulty taking in care from more available family members. Naming and evoking the fears and hurt associated with a child's mistrust and need for safety provide the therapist a foundation for gradually shifting toward identifying the needs specific to the relational injury. Typically, a child's more vulnerable emotions prime a parent's softer caring responses and regret, but for other parents these moments of vulnerability can appear blaming and trigger a defensive response. The therapist uses her alliance with parents to understand their struggle and also redirect their defensive responses by catching the bullet. Individual sessions with parents may be necessitate further processing of the parent's own injuries and work toward their availability to the child's complaint. Parental goals and support may require additional support to sustain the Stage 2 process.

3. Promoting Acceptance and Revisiting Parental Blocks

Although parental blocks to availability have been identified and explored in Stage 1, the process of exploring a child's vulnerability may trigger these blocks in Stage 2. An essential role for the therapist is validating and acknowledging the parents' struggle to accept the child's vulnerable sharing of attachment-related affect and needs. It is important to recognize that a parent's block is in response to the child's vulnerability and attachment needs, which may be different from the self-protective responses that triggered parental blocks in Stage 1. Parents may freeze in fearful response not knowing how to respond to their child's clear signals of fear, hurt, and sadness associated with the child's experience of the relational block. Parental fears of incompetence may block parental attunement and empathy in response to a child's experience and needs. Similarly, parental shame results in dismissive parental responses, as parents seek to save face through minimizing the concerns being raised by the child. Parents may lack confidence in being available to respond effectively to the child's need.

The therapist's support and validation of parental struggles enables a parent to regain their emotional balance and focus on their underlying experience. Accessing a parent's vulnerability enables the parent to better attune to their child's experience when focused on the parent's caregiving intention. For example, when a mother freezes in response to her son's hurt and angry protest reacting to her absence, the therapist validates the parental fear and expands attention to the parental intention to care. The therapist uses an empathic conjecture to hold the mother's fear and honor her intention.

It's so hard to hear his anger. You freeze in these moments not knowing how to respond, especially when you know he is looking to you and you know how you respond really matters. It's like you know he really matters to you and that this moment really matters, you're just not sure how to get that across, especially given his anger. So, when you listen to that part that of you that really cares, that comes from your heart, that says this really matters because he is your son. What would it say?

The therapist processes a parent's block by validating his or her secondary response and focusing on the underlying caregiving intention that is also in play at these moments. In working through moments of a parent's own vulnerability the therapist gives attention to the parental fears and hurts, however, does not enact those emotions to the child. This would confuse the parent's caregiving responsibility and for some children invite further parentification. Instead the therapist offers her alliance as a secure base and safe haven to the parent and offers support in facing the emotions blocking the parent's caregiving. Working through these blocks provides the parent an important resource for attuning to the child. The parent's own vulnerability promotes empathic understanding for the child's experience and when the parent is able to regulate their own emotional experience they can use this awareness and experience to be more emotionally present to their child. If a parent is not able to work through their block with the child present, the therapist would recommend a parent session to work with this block without the child present.

4. Increasing Confidence in Parental Responsiveness

A fourth access point is strengthening parents' confidence in their resourcefulness to their child, especially at an emotional level. The example above illustrates how the therapist provides a parent with support that enables the parent to regain her emotional balance and respond with empathy and attunement to her son's concerns. Kobak and Mandelbaum (2003) assert that changes in a family, particularly those facing separation distress, are most often tied to an increase in a caregiver's confidence through the support of another adult. The authors also note how the therapist can ally with the parent in an alliance for the child. The therapist highlights the significance of the child's importance to the parent, invites the parent to see more clearly the child's concern, and actively explores ways the parent can respond more effectively in that moment.

In two-parent families the therapist may enlist the support of the other parent in these moments focusing on their support for their partner. Together the caregiving alliance can provide empathy and support for the struggling parent and promote greater attunement and empathy toward the child through the support of the other partner. If, however, the other parent is triggered by their partner's parental block and responds with a critical or rejecting response, the therapist will redirect attention to the therapist alliance with the struggling parent and revisit the couple's blocked caregiving alliance in a separate couple session.

Exploring Child Vulnerability and Promoting Parental Acceptance

In this section we review the therapist's focus on deepening a child's associated attachment-related emotions that have been blocked in interactions with their parent. As the family makes the transition to Stage 2 the therapist underscores the parents' openness to exploring new parental responses to the relational issues that have blocked effective attachment and caregiving interactions. This sets the stage for the therapist to concentrate on assembling and deepening a child's deeper emotions and attachment-related needs. As the child's vulnerability becomes the focus of the EFFT process the therapist promotes the parents' acceptance and engagement of the child's newly expressed experiences and articulated needs. In this section we follow the therapist's role in working through relational blocks in Steps 5 and 6, including a review of the interventions commonly used in Stage 2. Two case examples illustrate how the therapist approaches relational blocks based on empathic failures and attachment injuries.

Transition to Stage 2

The shift to the second stage of EFFT follows clear demonstration of the de-escalation of the family's negative pattern. This occurs through identifying and processing the relational blocks that disrupt specific family relationships and compromise the family's flexibility to respond to needs effectively. Underlying these blocks are deeper emotions that more clearly capture the caregiving intentions of parents and their awareness of the emotional impact of these blocks for children. Consequently, parents demonstrate openness and interest in their approach particularly related to the child's underlying needs. Therefore, parental openness and de-escalation mark the shift from EFFT Stage 1 to Stage 2.

The process of emotional change seldom follows a linear progression, instead parents and children will take risks to engage greater vulnerability only to find others in the family are not able to respond at that same level. The therapist paces the family's steps toward deeper engagement guided by attunement to the emerging confidence that children have in the therapist's support and parent's increasing availability. Thus, parental openness is critical in the therapist's shift to the child's attachment emotions and needs in Step 5 and the therapist's facilitation of parent's availability to their child's deepened vulnerability and related needs. In EFFT, Steps 5 and 6 work in tandem to prepare parent and child to re-engage the attachment and caregiving positions that have been previously blocked in the family. This requires engaging and exchanging deeper emotional experiences that result in interpersonal and intrapersonal change.

Stage 2 sessions promote deeper access to the emotions that bring clarity to attachment needs and caregiving responses. Similar to EFT treatment with couples, family members are asked to shift to new positions of vulnerability and responsiveness through engaging these attachment-related emotions and needs. Johnson (2019) notes two key differences in family and couple sessions in Stage 2. First, the attachment dynamics between parents and child are less mutual than is experienced in a romantic relationship. The EFFT therapist actively promotes the parent's role as the "stronger wiser other" and initiator of safety and security in family relationships. Rather than focusing on shifting mutually related position of withdrawers and pursuers, the EFFT therapist is focused on moving children toward vulnerability and promoting parental availability and responsiveness to new expressions of a child's attachment-related emotions and needs. Johnson also suggests that the emotional intensity in Stage 2 work with families is often less than EFT Stage 2 work with romantic partners. This second difference indicates the importance of the therapist's ability to attune and match the level of intensity expressed by children and adolescents balancing evocative strategies with cognitive reflections to best approximate a youth's capacity and tolerance for processing emotion.

Families in Stage 2 are less prone to reactive escalations of their negative patterns. Through greater parental openness and increased emotional security in the family, the therapist is better able to access the attachment-related emotions and needs previously distorted through the child's secondary responses to separation distress. Clear attachment messages are difficult to discern in patterns of family distress including threatening, aggressive, and risk-related behaviors (Moretti & Craig, 2013). The therapist acknowledges the desperate ways family members sought to manage damaging escalations and their painful outcomes. Through framing and normalizing the child's unmet attachment need the therapist invites opportunities for the youth to share the underlying experiences of hurt, fear, and sadness often resulting from the impact of these negative patterns. Often the therapist is returning to the child's more vulnerable emotions named in Step 3, now deepening a child's experience through focusing on their view of self and view of other, typically the child's parent.

Promoting Parental Openness

Family sessions in Stage 2 emphasize parental caregiving intentions and the parent's openness to greater parental availability. The therapist explores themes of the parent's caregiving intention and desire to move away from the relational blocks that have plagued previous parent and child interactions. Acknowledging and validating these intentions, frames the parent's position and readiness to respond to learning more from their child's experience first alluded to in Stage 1. The therapist may comment on a parent's curiosity or concern in not knowing or understanding their child's experience. In the following example the therapist uses an empathic conjecture to validate and frame a father's increasing empathic concern for his son.

THERAPIST: (*reflection and reframe*) Your concern for your son has been obvious from the beginning and the conflicts you have had with his behaviors have gotten the best of you.

FATHER: I am seeing that more clearly now. Things kept getting worse, the harder I tried to make them better. I hate what this was doing to both of us.

THERAPIST: (*reflection, empathic conjecture*) Yes, and it has been painful for both of you in different ways. It makes a difference that you can see that, right? It seems like for months you were sounding the alarm, trying to get his attention, to change his way, because danger was ahead, which is all you could see. And now another part of you is saying, "I want to protect him. He's my son, that matters. It's not just the danger I see, but he's my son, and I want to be there in the way that he needs. I don't want him to leave him alone in this."

The therapist validates the parent's caregiving intention and refocuses the father on attuning not just to the fears he has about his son's actions but also on his son's need to be seen and understood. For some parents, the present concern of their child's behavior may trigger the parent's more defensive position. In this case, the therapist validates and acknowledges the parent's intents while also working though that parent's more defensive stance. This increases the child's confidence in parental openness because they have experienced the parent's shift in session. Even in this conjecture the therapist is framing the needs for protection (attachment) and the needs for support (exploration). Increasing and honoring parental awareness of the balance of attachment and autonomy needs increases the safety and promotes exploration of the child's needs (Moretti & Obsuth, 2009). Through adolescence the process of working through the competing goals of connection and autonomy is the pathway toward maintaining ongoing felt security (Allen, 2008).

Shifting Focus to Child Vulnerability

Whether through promoting parental openness or joining a youth's protest in response to parental caregiving, the therapist mirrors the present process and uses evocative interventions to elicit the child's attachment-related emotions. The therapist validates the child's defensive position communicating understanding for the role of self-protective actions in response to parental empathic failures and injuries. The use of evocative strategies promotes greater awareness of the child's attachment emotions and needs, making these feelings more explicit and felt in session (Kobak, Duemmler, Burland, & Youngstrom, 1998). In EFT these evocative strategies include: Empathic conjecture, heightening, and evocative responding. As noted by Johnson (2019) the use of reflection and validation provide cognitive reflections for aiding children in organizing their experience.

Following the example above, the therapist elicits the son's experience of his father's more engaged response.

FATHER: (*responding to the therapist's conjecture*) That's right. I don't think that's come across. I don't think he really believes I care ... about more than the trouble he has caused. It's like I am just one more person against him, rather than someone on his side. That's hard to see ...

THERAPIST: (*empathic conjecture*) Not the father you want to be, not the father you have in your heart.

FATHER: Exactly.

THERAPIST TO SON: (*evocative response*) What's it like to hear your father say, that at a heart level, he can see how he has missed seeing you?

SON: (*defensive*) It's kind of of late ...

THERAPIST: Hard to believe this would make a difference now.

SON: I guess. It's like he's just saying what you are saying, anyway.

THERAPIST: (*reflecting and empathic conjecture*) It hard to trust when he is just following my words. It's like part of you is saying "how can I trust he really could see me after all that has happened," but I wonder if there is part that still hopes maybe somehow he could understand better, and see what this is has been like for you? Really see with his heart?

SON: I guess.

THERAPIST: (*validation, evocative question*) It makes good sense that it would be hard to believe your dad would show up now, especially in this way. You'd have to let down your guard a bit and that's when you have gotten hurt in the past. But right now, when you see your dad sitting here, saying he doesn't get it, doesn't see what it's been like for you, you hear his sadness about leaving you alone in this.... What's it like to hear him say he wants to know what this has been like for you?

SON: It's hard. Not sure I know ... I feel like I let him down too.

THERAPIST: (*validation, reframe, evocative question*) Sure. This hasn't gone the way you wanted either. You and your dad. Right? It's like this struggle you get caught in has created all this distance. Made it hard to talk about what really matters ... like how hard all this has been for you?

As this sequence unfolds the therapist stays focused on the son's emerging vulnerability. The therapist uses evocative interventions to heighten the son's struggle and lonely feelings, helping him to put words to this experience. Reflecting and validating these emerging experiences the child is better able to contact the hurt and rejection he has felt.

SON: (*downcast*) It's like looking in a mirror and nothing is there. It's just nothing. Nobody cares, they don't see you. No one wants you because you are a problem, too many mistakes.

THERAPIST: (*reflecting, validation, enactment*) As you say that, I see the pain in your face. Anyone would feel alone, invisible, unwanted.... Do you think you could tell your Dad about how bad it is to feel unwanted?

The therapist helps the son crystalize the attachment-related themes and underlying emotions that result from the isolation he experienced in the negative cycles that erupted when he acted out. The pain of that isolation is made present and understood in the presence of a father who has affirmed his intention to be available to his son. The therapist uses an enactment to invite the son to share his experience with his father and begin a gradual process of reworking this father and son's relational block. This process requires the father's response and acceptance of the son's underlying experience.

Promoting Parental Acceptance

In EFFT processing parental acceptance of a child's vulnerability requires parents to shift toward a more accessible and responsive caregiving approach. If parental openness is a prerequisite to the therapist's focus on deepening a child's vulnerability, parental acceptance of that vulnerability is the essential result required to facilitate new relational bonds between parents and child, which is the goal of Step 7. Although the attachment-related emotions often prime more attuned caregiving responses from parents, the poignancy of a child's fears or hurt may also trigger parental blocks to acceptance. In Step 6 we focus exclusively on the parent's block, acknowledging its function and exploring the deeper emotions that prove resourceful in restoring a more attuned and available caregiving response.

The therapist uses evocative and processing intervention to promote and clarify a parent's caregiving responses to a child's sharing of their underlying experiences and attachment-related needs. Evocative responses and empathic conjecture are helpful in guiding a parent toward the most poignant attachment-related theme shared by their child. For example, a therapist may ask a parent about the impact of hearing their daughter's felt rejection. "As you hear this now, and even feel the fear that your daughter shared in speaking about these times she felt rejected and dismissed, what happens when you hear her fear, right now?"

In Step 6 the therapist focuses on expanding and organizing the parent's response to this moment. Through the therapist's alliance or caregiving alliance with another caregiver the therapist supports the exploration of the parent's own vulnerability in his or her caregiving role. The parent's vulnerability provides a resource for attuning to their child by actively responding to the emotional cues in the moment. This, however, is distinctly different in using EFT with couples where mutual accessibility, responsiveness, and engagement are sought. The focus of parent vulnerability is on strengthening the parent's acceptance and caregiving response.

Processing interventions expand parental awareness and acceptance. The therapist uses validation and reframing to focus parents on the attachment themes and emotions shared by their child. For example, the therapist acknowledges a parent's disappointment focusing on the regret she feels in response to her daughter's fear.

> You see her fear and inside there is your own fear. It makes sense when you see her pull away 'Will she trust me again?' In the past this leads you to do anything to win her back, yet at the same time if we listen to your fear right now, it is also a sign of how much you care and how much concern you have for her because, she really matters to you.

The therapist is actively working alongside the parent to make sense of her vulnerability as a caregiver and to find her confidence as a stronger wiser other. The therapist may also encourage the parent to turn to their partner in this moment for support regarding this fear. As parental acceptance and support is acknowledged, the therapist invites the parent to share directly with the child if the parent has not already spontaneously turned to their child.

Processing Parental Blocks to Acceptance

A child's shift toward a more vulnerable position in Step 5 may also trigger a parental block to acceptance. These blocks may result from parental insecurity rooted in the parent's fear or shame. These parental blocks focus more on the internal struggles parents find in the parental role than the interactional blocks explored in Step 3. As a result, individual parent sessions may be beneficial to work through a parent's negative view of self and its distortion of the parent's attunement and availability. Conjoint parent sessions are also helpful in strengthening the caregiving alliance and working through a parental block.

Parental Fear and Inadequacy

A child's attachment-related emotions and needs may trigger parental insecurity as a father may doubt his ability to respond effectively to his daughter's needs or a mother fears the return of the painful pattern if she makes a mistake. A parent's negative view-of-self fuels fears that the parent will not have the knowledge or ability to respond to needs of their child. These blocks are reinforced by the self-protective strategies a parent may use to cope with these fears. Rather than turning to other adults who could offer support and assistance, these parents lose their emotional balance and anxiously over-respond or dismiss their child's need.

In EFFT the therapist focuses on the present moment as these blocks occur and engages the parent in working through their fear. The therapist provides a secure base for the parent to explore his or her concerns and to organize their emotional experience as a resource for attuning to the child's need. Through accessing, processing, and sharing this fear with the therapist or working together with another adult, the parent is better able to return with confidence to a position of responding to the child. Parental confidence increases as the therapist and parent work together to respond effectively to the child's vulnerability.

Parental Shame

MOTHER: I failed. I know I pushed too her hard and now she is just afraid of me. I just wanted her to respect me, instead she hates me.

THERAPIST: Your daughter's fear is a hard message for you. It so hard to hear that she struggles this way and you say I failed her. She doesn't want me in these moments. Right?

MOTHER: (escalated) Yes there's nothing I can do to get her back.

THERAPIST: And you can get lost in these moments feeling like you have lost your daughter. It is so overwhelming, frightening. Can we take a breath right here? To stay in this moment. It makes sense that when you hear her fear you panic and go to that place you easily feel unwanted and ineffective as a mother. But if we stay here in this moment, I see you here in session, wanting to show up for her wanting to send a different message to her. Is that right?

MOTHER: Yes, but I don't think she wants to hear from me.

THERAPIST: Right that's the fear that takes over here. So could we hold that fear together for a minute here. I wonder if we were to tune into that part of you, that sees your daughter alone and afraid. That says I do care, I'm here. I'm your mom. What would you say to her fear?

The therapist provides the parent resources to acknowledge the trigger for her shame and to regain her emotional balance by acknowledging her reactive response and staying present. The therapist normalizes the mother's fear and shame and its function, then refocuses the parent on her daughter's fear. The therapist organizes around the mother's underlying fear as a resource for her attunement to her daughter and returns the focus of the session to the daughter. Helping the mother work with her fear to stay responsive to her daughter the therapist enables the mother to use her emotion differently. Pervasive parental blocks may require individual sessions focusing on parental fear and shame. The focus of these sessions serves the purpose of promoting a parent's regulation of feelings of distress in their parenting role and working through negative views of self and the ways these experiences hijack the parent's ability to remain present and attend to the emotional needs of their child.

EFT Interventions in Steps 5 and 6

Throughout Stage 2 sessions, attachment-related emotions and caregiving intentions are made explicit through exploring the emotional experiences underlying the family's relational blocks. Accessing and expanding these deeper experiences clarifies the attachment-related needs that implicitly inform a child's self-protective responses to ineffective or harmful caregiving responses. The therapist's use of empathic reflection, validation, and monitoring the alliance is essential as the family risks sharing more vulnerable experiences associated with injuries and failed attachment responses.

The therapist's alliance with caregivers is important to sustaining parental openness as blocks are explored and the negative impacts of a caregiver's empathic failure or injuries are exposed. Incrementally, exploration of a child's attachment emotions and needs occurs in the context of actively working through parental acceptance. These new attachment encounters restore confidence in parental availability that is necessary for the enactment of a child's attachment needs in Step 7. EFT interventions that promote emotional experiencing are essential in promoting child and parental awareness and processing of view of self and view of parent/child. Deeper emotions are engaged through enactments between children and parents to foster concrete responses of parental availability and acceptance.

Evocative Interventions

The therapist invites family members to focus on their emerging experience as greater safety in the therapy process promotes greater exploration through the use of evocative interventions. These include evocative responding, heightening, and empathic conjecture.

Evocative statements and questions are combined with therapist's reflections and validation of present experiences. Evocative questions accentuate experience in the present moment. Evocative responses provide invitations to explore and expand a family member's experience that is evolving through a deeper understanding of the actions and intentions that are behind the relational blocks that have defined specific family interactions. Evocative questions prompt greater awareness and understanding of another's felt experience as family members are more directly exposed to the emotional realities underlying family distress and distance. These emerging experiences are deepened through intensifying these experiences using heightening.

Heightening includes therapist statements and empathic reflections that capture the essence of a present felt experience and use these responses to intensify and focus attention on the emotion. The therapist draws on family members' words or images to best capture a felt experience and will slow the pace and soften the tone of a reflection to communicate the feeling state embodied in these words and experience. Repetition of attachment-related themes can also be heightened underscoring the attachment significance of an experience of interaction. "You don't want to leave him alone, on his own in this desperate place. Everything inside of you says, that's not ok. I don't want to leave him alone."

Empathic conjectures encourage clients to explore and engage the leading edge or emerging emotional experience. Following an attachment understanding the therapist tentatively offers conjectures about attachment or caregiving related responses. The therapist guides the client through forecasting potential responses or experience that is emerging in the present moment of the session.

> It is almost like part of you says, don't trust this, don't trust their care, but I wonder if there is another part here that really hopes this could be real, this part of you that really hopes that they do love you?

Processing Interventions

In Stage 2 new experiences are a key focus of EFFT sessions and processing interventions enable family members to reflect and make sense of this new understanding and acceptance. Just as empathic reflection communicates the therapist's emotional accessibility and responsiveness to the impact of shared vulnerability, a therapist's reflections also provide a means to pace with a client's unfolding experience, adding a level of intentionality in the therapist's attunement to the present moment. For example, a therapist may slow a parent's more reactive response using reflection, "Let me make sure I understand what you are saying here, it's frustrating to hear that your efforts to show you care, don't seem to matter." The reflection promotes greater attention to the parent's more defensive response in an understanding manner.

Validation provides the therapist with a response that promotes acceptance of experience, both for oneself but also for another family member. In Stage 2, there is greater focus on underlying emotions consequently validation is essential in honoring the unique experience of family members and encouraging a sense of entitlement to this, often unexpressed or unacknowledged, experience. Validation can be used to normalize experience, recognizing the emotions in families are common even if not always shared. The use of validation can help family members "save face" in moments that otherwise may appear shameful and serve as a resource for self-compassion, recognizing these experiences are universal. For example, a therapist might respond to a parent's shame by saying,

> These are the hard moments as a parent, when you see so clearly what you wanted to do, but what came out was actually what you were trying to avoid. Getting it right as a parent is like trying to hit a moving target. We often miss."

The therapist uses reframing in Stage 2 in several ways. First a therapist may reframe a present experience in the context of the relational block or negative family pattern. This reorients the family to relational realities, which can distort family efforts to influence and communicate. For example, the therapist invites a mother to also see her daughter's anger as a desperate attempt to break through their relational block. "It's discouraging to hear her anger again especially after all the progress you have made, and this is where the cycle can take hold of both of you through her anger and your fear." More often reframes, in Stage 2, focus on attachment-related themes, where underlying emotions are reframed in terms of attachment. For example, a therapist reframes the anger of a daughter's protest,

> You hear her anger and in the past that has been her way of keeping you at a distance, but right now her anger is about you not seeing her, when it really matters, when she needs to matter to you.

In EFFT attachment reframes also include family-of-origin relationships for parents. The therapist may frame a parent's present experience in terms of her past experience of receiving care in her family of origin. "You hear your daughter's loneliness, and part of you aches to see her pain, but also this pain is also a pain you have known, when you were a young child, and you were all alone as well."

Processing interventions promote meaning making from new experiences. New understandings and new emotional experiences work together to promote new relationship encounters, which are at the heart of EFFT change events. Throughout Stage 2 the therapist uses enactments to engage the sharing of new emotional experience and facilitate the active exchange of a child's attachment-related emotions and a parent's caregiving responses. In EFT, an enactment is a directive to turn toward another in session, at both an emotional as well as relational level. Through Stage 2 the parent and child are working toward more attuned attachment communication and more effective caregiving responses.

Case Examples

The following two case examples illustrate the EFT therapist using evocative and processing interventions in working through the child's experience of a relational block One example focuses on a child's block as a result of a parent's empathic failure and the other case illustrates how the therapist supports a family confronting a specific relational injury. Each example highlights the EFT process using the five moves of the EFT tango.

Case Example—Working through Empathic Failures

The following example illustrates the therapist working through a parent and grandparent's empathic failure which blocks the youth's ability to share his struggles and failure. The case example demonstrates the therapist's focus on the child's vulnerability and processing parental acceptance through the five moves in the EFT tango (Johnson, 2019). The session highlights the shifts that occur as a child's deeper attachment-related emotions associated are accessed, explored, and engaged. This then enables two of his primary attachment figures to work through their own blocks to availability and begin to promote greater emotional balance in the family.

Jack is a bright, highly intelligent, 17-year-old boy, who has not attended high school for the past three years. He lives with his mother, Sonya, and father, Greg, as their only child. Sonya is a professional educator and Greg has been unemployed for several years. Sonya and Greg separated recently following years of unresolved estrangement. Jack's grandfather Sid lived close by while he was not involved in issues related to Jack's schooling or his parent's failing marriage, Jack spent much of his time when away from home with his grandfather. Jack's school absence was a constant focus for his parents who worked with school staff to plan Jack's return to formal education. Greg protested these efforts arguing that Jack's chronic stress and panic attacks were a result of the school environment and he encouraged Jack to develop interests outside of academics. Sonya, felt she had little influence in Jack's life, and failed repeatedly to motivate him to return to school. The family was referred to family therapy after several behavioral interventions did not succeed in bringing Jack back to school. Treatment focused on conjoint sessions with Jack and his mother. Greg refused to participate in family sessions. Sonya's shame and felt inadequacy as a mother often paralyzed her efforts to engage Jack, instead she coped with these insecurities by investing extensive time in her career and leaving Jack to his own interests, often mostly alone.

Through Stage 1 of EFFT Sonya began to re-engage with Jack more intentionally. This included asking him about his dreams and also his fears. Jack began to demonstrate more initiative in his school-related work and worries he had about his father's future. Family conversations regarding success and failure often triggered the family's negative pattern. Sonya's anxious efforts to re-engage Jack in school felt like pressure to Jack who would retreat to his room or to his grandfather's apartment. Sonya would try harder to reassure Jack of his potential and past successes and apologize for not being able to do more to help Jack return to school. Eventually the topic of Jack's schooling would be dropped, until the school contacted the family and the pattern would return again. In the following session Jack, Sonya, and Sid are present to discuss a recent plan to return to school and Sonya's positive approach again triggers the relational block with her son. Key moments from the session are highlighted emphasizing the unfolding EFT process in Stage 2 using the EFT tango.

Mirroring the Present Process

The therapist shifts the focus from the discussion of the proposed plan for Jack's return to school after Sonya expresses her hope and confidence that Jack will succeed. Sonya's anxious fears color her positive comments about Jack's potential for success. Jack withdraws from the conversation and the therapist turns her attention to Jack.

THERAPIST: So right now, Jack what's it like for you to hear your mother say, "I am proud of you?" what happens for you? I notice you (*squirms in his chair*)

JACK: I don't like compliments.

THERAPIST: Can you help me with that? What happens to you when she says she is proud?

JACK: It makes me uncomfortable.... Because I don't feel like I really deserve it.

THERAPIST: You don't deserve it?

JACK: I am not doing anything that's special, so when people say I am proud of you or you are good at that ... it's just whatever.

THERAPIST: Ok, so you don't take it seriously?

JACK: I just don't take the praise. It's not a big deal.

THERAPIST: So, you say something like: "I don't deserve that. I don't deserve this. What have I done isn't that special, you're just saying that?" Almost like it's not real, they're just trying to make you feel good?

JACK: Yeah like people are just saying that because they're being nice. Like Grandpa is always saying "You're so bright", and I really don't see how he can say that?"
GRANDFATHER: Yes, but we need to acknowledge who we are.
JACK: Well, I still don't believe those things Grandpa. I don't believe that I am any of those things you all say, because if I were those things I wouldn't be in this kind of mess. (*sighs*)
GRANDFATHER: That's what you always say.
JACK: (*defensive*) It's what I always say because it's what I believe.
THERAPIST: Right, right, there is no way that you can take praise or let in how good someone might see you, because right now the reality is, the way you see yourself is ...
JACK: Six or seven years of constant failure.

Affect Assembly and Deepening

The focus of the session shifts to Jack challenging the family tendency to promote a positive message at the same time as ignoring the negative. For Jack the negative is the pain and fear he feels in response to his failure to make academic progress. Jack's mother and grandfather's confidence in Jack's abilities only heightens his shame at failing the family, which is amplified with the unspoken disdain for his father who has similarly failed at gainful employment. In the following excerpt, the therapist acknowledges Jack's frustration and focuses on the emerging sadness and disappointment that the family seldom sees because Jack more often withdraws in these moments. Parental openness is critical to the safety necessary to deepen Jack's engagement of his underlying sadness, shame, and fear.

THERAPIST: (*in a softer tone and leaning toward Jack*) And that's really hard. That's a lot of failure.
JACK: I haven't done anything worthwhile in a long time. This should have been my first year of university and I am not there. I probably have two more years of high school, so all of this praise, all this "I am so good at this and you're so gifted in that" that makes no sense. (*frustrated and fighting back tears*)
THERAPIST: You can't really believe that your mom is proud of you. Instead you say: "I am a failure, in my eyes I am a failure, I am not doing what I should be doing. I have failed."
JACK: Yeah. (*looking down*)
THERAPIST: And when you try and say something about how you feel about where you are right here, right today.
JACK: (*looking at mother and grandfather*) I can accept those are your feelings and I am glad that you feel that way about me, but I don't really believe it.
THERAPIST: (*proxy voice*) It's like you are saying: "But I can't believe it. No, it's really, really hard for me to even begin to take that in." Right?

JACK: Yeah, I am glad Mom you are proud of me and you Grandpa think I have so many gifts, but it doesn't mean anything to me. I am a failure, always a disappointment.

THERAPIST: So that's how you feel ... in your mother's eyes, your grandfather's eyes ... your father's eyes ... you feel like a failure. And you feel this alone because for the past several years you have had to stuff your feelings down, that's what you have been doing for over six years.

JACK: My anger is stuffed down and the feeling of failure is there too. I don't want to let these people down. I don't want to let them down by being a failure and saying I am a failure because, look at what this does to them right now, as I am talking about it. (*mother in tears*)

THERAPIST: Right, right, you're taking a big chance here right now saying this is how I end up feeling. I can't take your praise in because inside I feel like a failure.

JACK: I feel like I am holding it together. Like the story of the kid with his finger in the dike and holding back the flood.

THERAPIST: You're holding it all together, it's all up to you to hold back this flood, and if you open up here, then ... (*therapist heightens Jack's felt experience using client's words and images*)

JACK: It'll all let go, my emotions, my failure. I am terrified of what that will happen. I will go under ... it's too much.

THERAPIST: I am terrified of.... It will drown me. (*reflecting catastrophic fear*)

JACK: It will drown me, it will drown you, I worry more about the people around me, I don't care about me.

THERAPIST: You are afraid of drowning your mom, letting her down she might get overwhelmed by your feelings. She might not be able to handle that. (*therapist heightens fear associated with Jack's fear related to parental availability—loss of confidence*)

JACK: Right, I am the last person, that I care about. (*negative view of self*)

THERAPIST: (*softly*) And that's hard because right now we are talking about you.

JACK: And that's what I hate to do.

Choreographing Engaged Encounters

Jack's negative view of self and sense of failure are made explicit. The focal awareness of his felt insecurity is evident as he struggles to acknowledge his own grief and fear and at the same time protect others from these negative feelings. The therapist uses his deepened emotional experience to share these emotions with his mother and grandfather. The therapist guides Jack through sharing what he would otherwise keep silent, holding his failure on his own.

THERAPIST: But I'm wondering now, could you take a chance right now and look at your mom and tell her that deep inside "I feel like a failure."

JACK TO HIS MOTHER: Deep down, when you praise me, I still feel like a failure. (*turning to grandfather*) And same with you Grandpa. You all try to boost me and that feels good sometimes but mostly I just feel like a failure. After all those positives, I still feel like a failure ...

THERAPIST: And that is really hard, that's the last thing you want to do, to let them down, yes? (*therapist reflects intention informing Jack's action tendency of withdrawal*)

JACK: And it is hard for me because I do let you down, I don't want to hurt you, don't want to hurt you guys, I don't want to hurt you guys.... It's the last thing ... I would rather jump in front of a truck than let you down.

THERAPIST: Right, because that is what you are doing right now ... it's like you might let them down, even saying this right now?

JACK: That is what I am doing, I am holding back ... not jumping in front of that truck.

Processing the Encounter

The therapist shifts focus to Sonya and invites her to engage the risk Jack is taking in sharing his fear about being seen as a failure. Building on Jack's fear of letting them down and his own feeling like a failure primes his mother and grandfather's potential acceptance of Jack's emerging vulnerability. The therapist uses the enactment of Jack's fear as an opportunity for Sonya to engage an attuned caregiving response to her son. The mother's empathic presence works against Jack's failed confidence in his mother's reassurance and care.

THERAPIST: And Jack, right now, it is like you are jumping in front of that truck, you're taking a chance. (*turning to mother*) When he says this, right, he says that he feels like a failure inside, can you imagine what that feels like?

MOTHER: (*deep sigh*) Yeah probably, I can imagine what it might feel like. I am not good with failure either.

THERAPIST: Yes, because no matter how hard you tried your marriage hasn't worked, and with Jack's school, as a parent ...

MOTHER: (*interjecting*) That's right, that's right. I understand ... but I don't think I really understand, I want to understand Jack.

THERAPIST: You want to understand, you can't get all of it, obviously, you can only relate from your own experience, but you want to be able to understand what it's like for Jack

MOTHER: Yeah, I know, from grade one, Jack's always tried to get it right, to do things perfectly. Often feeling like his best is just not good enough.

THERAPIST: You have seen him struggle with that?

MOTHER: Yes, but when he says he's holding back emotionally, he's failing emotionally, that hurts to hear this. I know the academic thing is hard, but I don't want him to feel like a failure.

THERAPIST: It's like he is not even seeing himself truly.

MOTHER: I see him like my mother—she was the one that was so affectionate, she gave all the hugs in our family. She was always there for us. And Jack (*looking at him*) this one is like that, like: "Mom I need a hug." He's giving what he doesn't get. What he needs.

THERAPIST: Jack's so good at that. So, for him not to treasure or value that part of him and when it is so Jack and so needed in this family, it pulls you out.

MOTHER: (*now in tears*) He is teaching me that and he doesn't get credit for it.

THERAPIST: Yes, that is such a special part of him. (*mother nods*) The "Jackness" of that.

MOTHER: And the part of me that hurts, (*holding her heart*) is that hugs and anger are both valid and (*weeping*) and I don't think I ever realized that before. (*Jack now looking intently at her*)

THERAPIST: (*proxy voice*) I didn't know this. (*Jack hands his mother a tissue*)

MOTHER FACING JACK: I didn't know that. If you are so loving and expressive ... that you need to be expressive with everything. I didn't realize what you were holding back. (*Jack nods in response*)

THERAPIST: All parts of him.

MOTHER: All parts, the good and the bad. The strengths and the failures.

THERAPIST: It's almost like what you are saying is, (*shifts to proxy voice*) this hurts to see. It makes me sad that I didn't really see this, I didn't really see what Jack was going through. He so reminds you of your childhood and it is opening up something inside of you and to have this opening up inside of you, what's that like for you?

MOTHER: It's really, really, good, ... it feels like a gift.

THERAPIST: Yes, because you have been stuffing too and you have been walking on eggshells and losing with all you are managing on your own.

MOTHER: And it's so funny that when you have a baby. You just let those things out. You laugh. You cry and then somewhere along the way you start to edit, and I don't want to do that anymore.

JACK: I am tired of all of this, of pushing everything down.

GRANDFATHER TO THERAPIST: If Jack was ever able to let it all out—I know he is afraid, but I think it would be a freeing experience. This would seem better than living in this cramped space, where there is all this pressure. Just let it out and let the chips fall as they may.

JACK: But what if I ruin everything?

GRANDFATHER: That is impossible. That is not possible in this family, Jack.

THERAPIST: Yes, that's Jack's fear speaking. It is saying something so important. "If I am already feeling like a failure, if I am disappointing and hurting you, why would I let it all out?"

JACK: Why would I put that out there for someone to agree with me?

THERAPIST: Sure, if you end up seeing my disappointment in THEIR eyes.

JACK: Then you are a failure!

THERAPIST: So not saying it protects you and it protects others. And you have had to stuff yourself down or go away, so you don't rock the boat and keep the peace. Just like you did that with your dad.

JACK: And with my mom, until today. (*smiles*)

Integrating and Validating

The therapist summarizes the risks and shifts that family members made through engaging and processing Jack's fears. Meaning is made of these new experiences and the therapist validates the courage and risks family members take to confront and begin to work through their relational block and take more open positions honoring the emotions that were often masked by positive words and good intentions. This excerpt illustrates the fragility of the changes family members have taken, as the pull of the old pattern is significant in moments of uncertainty.

THERAPIST: And things are starting to shift and change where there is more space, and there will be a big change, and everyone will be affected, and you will be going through it all together. And what I just heard your mom say is that she doesn't want you to be in this locked down place. She knows something like this in her own life and now she reached for you and said "I am so tired of this."

JACK: I am so exhausted. (*starts to talk about him being the problem*)

THERAPIST: So, let me slow us down, when you see your mom and you see your grandfather and you have this amazing support team, that has your back and it is hard for you sometimes because inside you don't feel like you deserve it. (*therapist refocusing on present moment*)

JACK: It's really hard to accept help because you don't deserve it even if you need it, I don't want to waste your time.

THERAPIST: Right and then that's how you end up in your room and all alone. But today you came out of your room. And what you have done right here is break ground Jack. You took a big step and let your mom and grandfather know exactly how you feel inside, that when they say they are proud, it doesn't go inside because you feel like a failure. And that is hard to let them know how you feel because you don't want to disappoint them. Disappointing these two people is massive, and you let them know. Mom you said Jack is teaching you, he is teaching you about all emotions, that they are all ok and that is freeing, and grandfather you are saying: "Jack take a chance," it is impossible in this family for Jack to ruin anything. We love you no matter what. So, Jack you took another step that many adults don't get to, when you said that believing your failure kind of protects you, it keeps you from hearing it from them because you said it first. (*Jack starts to smile*)

THERAPIST: Can I ask, what your smile is?

JACK: I actually don't feel like a failure. (*mother laughs, cheers, and hugs Jack*)

Case Example—Working Through an Attachment Injury

Attachment injuries in EFT represent a fundamental breach of trust in a couple's relationship and interrupt the couple's ability to work through the vulnerability necessary for restructuring their mutual relationship bond (Johnson, Makinen, & Millikin, 2001; Makinen & Johnson, 2006). In EFFT attachment injuries between parents and children also represent a significant block to vulnerability. These injuries may significantly impact the ability of a child to risk their attachment needs without specifically addressing the injury itself. Further parental failures often trigger parental shame that distorts a parent's ability to be present emotionally to their child. The therapist must balance a focus on the injury without losing parental availability to the parent's own struggles to see beyond their failure or shame. The following case example illustrates the therapist working through an injury while promoting parental availability. The session example continues the work described in the previous chapter with Carl and his family.

Carl is a 16-year-old boy who described his family as "hostile and unwelcoming" and that all the pressure was on him because he was blamed for the majority of what went wrong in the family. Through Stage 1 sessions the therapist tracked the family pattern which singled out Carl as the family problem and shifted the focus of the distress in the family toward a predictable interactional pattern that included mother's over-responsive and controlling efforts to prevent Carl's isolation and withdrawal from the family. In the session example that follows, Carl's parents express regret over past escalations that resulted in physical abuse toward Carl. The impact of this injury resurfaced when Carl recalled how he had to "fight for his life."

Mirroring Present Process

This triggered his mother and she began to minimize his experience and focus instead on what she was dealing with at the time. Following the EFT tango (Johnson, 2019) the therapist redirected the process to the present moment and encouraged the family to slow down and make more space for Carl's experience and memories of these harsh moments in the family. The therapist validated the risk Carl was taking in speaking about something he had previously avoided. The therapist joins and supports the father's invitation to Carl to share more of his experience.

THERAPIST: You want him to know it is safe enough to say whatever. The good, the bad, even the ugly? (*father nods empathically*) And, the other thing is that Carl also ends up feeling like this is all his fault. (*father responds "Yes" with a tone of regret. Therapist turns to Carl who is looking away*) You get blamed sometimes and that stresses you out and the only way you can get away from this terrible feeling is to go to your room. (*Carl nods his head, still looking down, avoiding eye contact*) Because what happens in your room? (*softly*) Can you tell me?

CARL: I just watch the screen. I just sit there, sometimes for hours.

THERAPIST: How are you feeling in your room? Do you know?

CARL: I feel horrible.

Affect Assembly and Deepening

The session focus shifts to explore Carl's deeper emotions underlying his withdrawal. The therapist uses evocative interventions and validation to deepen Carl's felt experience that his avoidance so often hides.

THERAPIST: (*slowly using a soft tone*) That's so hard. (*pauses*) What's the horrible feeling?

CARL: (*silence*) I want to leave, (*more silence, therapist softly responding: "Yes, of course"*) and then never come back (*tears now running down Carl's face and father hands Carl a tissue*)

THERAPIST: Do you ever think that is what everybody really wants?

CARL: Yes. (*voice cracking with emotion*)

THERAPIST: Like if you weren't there, there wouldn't be any problems?

CARL: (*nodding*) I feel like everybody's life would be easier without me.

THERAPIST: That is so hard. (*pausing to acknowledge the pain in the room*) So when you see your parents' tears, and hear how much they love you, and how badly they feel for how they messed up because they hurt you. How do you make sense of all of that?

CARL: I don't know how to make sense of it? It's too much.

THERAPIST: It is a lot, and I want to try to help you hear because it is a lot. It is a lot and the way I understand their emotions, (Carl *now making eye contact with therapist*) is how important you are to them. (*softens tone and speaks with almost a whisper*) You are the most special person to them. (*pauses*) That is why your mom is in tears, and your dad is in tears. Okay? (*Carl nods in agreement*) But there are also these times when you were afraid, you were scared, you were alone. There was nobody there for you. (*Carl sighs, deeply*) And your parents really don't know about that time. They don't know you were scared and that you had to look after yourself. You said that earlier, today. What's it like for you that you said it out loud? *(therapist shifts chair alongside Carl)* What's it like for you right now? *(therapist focuses on Carl's fear in sharing his experience and inviting his parents into his loneliness and isolation around his pain. The therapist uses heightening, validation, and empathic responding to focus attention on his attachment-related fears and emerging needs)*

CARL: I feel bad about saying it.

MOTHER: *(softly reassuring Carl)* That's okay. That's the way you feel.

THERAPIST: *(to mother)* It's ok for him to feel that way?

MOTHER: It's ok for him to say how he feels. So, we can help. It's ok, Carl. We want to know.

THERAPIST: So, you are giving him this space to feel the way he feels?

MOTHER: *(distances, speaking dispassionately)* Whatever he feels, and it's my job is to reassure him.

THERAPIST: Yes, and let's give him space, now. *(turning attention back to Carl)* So you feel bad that you shared this?

CARL: Yeah, I feel bad and I don't want to make them sad.

THERAPIST: *(turning to parents)* Is Carl making you sad?

FATHER: *(looking at Carl)* My regrets are making me sad, not you. *(to therapist)* I feel sad because he is sad.

THERAPIST: That's the crazy thing about families. We all affect each other. Our emotions matter and what you are saying to your son is your regrets and your sadness is not his fault. *(therapist validates father and then redirects him to his son)*

FATHER: Not at all.

THERAPIST: *(to Carl)* Do you hear that? *(Carl nods in acknowledgment)* Yes, good. What's that like for you to hear that, right now?

CARL: It's a relief, but I still feel bad that I brought up all these regrets. *(still holding to his shame)*

MOTHER: *(turning to catch Carl's attention and speaking confidently)* But I need you to hear this, it helps me to hear this and to look at myself. I want to respond to you in a way that is more about you then me. *(spontaneous reach of reassurance from mother)*

THERAPIST: So, you are letting Carl know this is you, this is not him. And in the vicious cycle, that happens in your family. *(looking to Carl)* You get the opposite message, you get the message that you are the problem. It's all your fault, and when your mom is getting panicked she is saying these are her own issues and if your dad gets frustrated and disappears he is saying these are his own issues, but right now it doesn't feel that way for you. And this is all about giving you space to say how it is for you. You had the courage to say right off, I feel like it is all my fault. I feel like I had to stand up for myself. That's incredible that you said that, *(turning to parents)* that he could say that. This says a lot about this family. It says a lot about his emotional maturity. (*turning to Carl*) Do you think they really get it, though? (*therapist processes the encounter by reflecting and validating the family's emerging vulnerability and responsiveness*)

CARL: I don't know. (*looking at parents*) Do you get it?

MOTHER: (*urgently*) I try to help you, I say to you all the time that I don't think this is your fault ...

THERAPIST: (*interjecting*) I am going to slow you down. (*turning to Carl*) How would you know that your parents really got how this is for you? (*refocusing on Carl's attachment need*)

MOTHER: That's a good question.

THERAPIST: Carl, do you think your parents hear you when you say: "I feel like it is all my fault and I had to stick up for myself?" Do you think you could actually say it to them? Can you look at them and say it? (*therapist sets up enactment of Carl's emerging attachment fears*)

CARL TO THERAPIST: That I feel like that it is all my fault?

THERAPIST: That's the hard part, the part that makes you feel horrible, that makes you want to go away forever because you feel so bad and so alone. Your tears make me wonder if you are feeling that even now? Can you look at them? Right now?

CARL: (*turning to his parents*) I feel like it is all my fault. (*silence*)

MOTHER: (*reaching for Carl, holding his arm and softly speaking*) The only thing that is your fault is that you made us a family. Everything else is not your fault. We weren't a family until we had you.

Processing the Emotional Encounter

The therapist lends support to the family as they process this emotional encounter. The therapist reflects and validates his parents' different experiences as they directly encounter Carl's fears and shame. In processing the son's enactment, the therapist continues to expand this encounter shifting focus to Carl's relationship to his father.

THERAPIST: Oh, that is pretty special. Not only is this not your fault, but actually Carl you made this a family? How is that to hear?

CARL: It feels good.

THERAPIST: It feels good to hear your mother say: "This is not your fault." In fact, you are so important to this family, you have a special place here. Right?

MOTHER: And you were really wanted Carl, your dad and I really wanted you so bad.

THERAPIST: So, Dad, what is this like for you to hear your son say directly, to you, that he feels like this is all his fault.

FATHER: (*crying*) I feel so bad.

THERAPIST: Can you hear him? Can you hear your son?

FATHER: Yes, and what can I do, what can I do to fix it? (*therapist gestures for father to turn to son*)

FATHER: What do you need from me?

CARL: I don't know.

THERAPIST: That's a big question, a big question. So, when you say: "This is all my fault" and your mom says the only thing that is your fault is that you made them a family and that makes you feel good and the good part is what? (*therapist refocuses Carl on mother's words of reassurance and uses an evocative question to clarify Carl's experience*)

CARL: It makes me feel like I am wanted.

THERAPIST: Yes, it makes you feel wanted, like you are part of this family, this is where you belong, and what is that like to feel that?

CARL: Relieving and liberating.

THERAPIST: Relieving and liberating. Wow, do you feel that in your body, anywhere?

CARL: I feel like the tension I had in my chest is gone.

THERAPIST: So, some of that tension is relieved, knowing that you are wanted, that your parents want you, because that matters to you, right? It matters to you how they see you? That they choose you?

CARL: It does matter to me that they want me, that I belong.

THERAPIST: And what do you want them to see?

CARL: I want them to have hope in me, to not give up on me.

MOTHER: (*anxiously responding*) We do Carl, we see ...

THERAPIST: Ok, let's go slow here, to really see this because he is saying something really big. Carl is answering that question, he is answering that question of what he needs. (*to Carl*) So you said: "I want them to have hope in me, I want them to have hope in me." Let's figure that out, "I want them to have hope in me, that they look at me and they are hopeful."

MOTHER: (*calmly*) What do you think is hopeful Carl.

CARL: I want you to think I can be successful. That I want to be successful. I am trying my best as hard as I can, my best may not be what you want but I am working and I am trying to better myself, as hard as I can.

THERAPIST: You want them to believe in that, to trust that? To believe in you?

CARL: I am trying to be a good student, and I want to have a good future.

THERAPIST: You want those things, you want them to know that is inside you?

CARL: Right!

THERAPIST: Good for you, Carl. I feel that. Good for you!

CARL: Thank you.

Integrating and Validating

The therapist shifts to integrating and validating the family experience of Carl's vulnerability. In this final example the family makes sense of Carl's risk to share his inner experience including the responsibility he carried for the family's pain. The therapist continues to work through mother's tendency to overrespond to Carl's experience and through validating Carl's need and refocusing mother's attention to see her son, and his own desires and potential to have a positive future.

THERAPIST: (*turning to parents*) That's amazing, he is letting you see in, he's letting you see inside his room, he's letting you see inside himself. (*father nodding demonstratively in agreement*)

MOTHER: It's my instinct to tell him all the good things I see. I want him to know.

THERAPIST: (*to mother*) I hear you but right here, right now, you don't have to work so hard. Listen. He is telling you. He is teaching you about him. What he thinks and what he feels and what is happening on the inside. What's it like for you just to take that in? This is your son letting you in. This is what he feels, when you take that in, what does that do for you?

MOTHER: Its heartbreaking that I haven't done a good enough job.

THERAPIST: Ok, so can I help you here. (*mother nods in tears*) See your son is telling you, what he thinks inside. He is telling you what he needs from you. That he can do that, wow. I have kids, and I am not sure they could have done this so clearly.

MOTHER: I like it that he trusts me enough, he is very brave.

THERAPIST: Yes, and this says a lot about him and a lot about you guys.

MOTHER: I want to tell him all the shiny things I see.

THERAPIST: And Carl is saying to you: "I know that Mom, I feel that Mom and I want you to trust that Mom, I want you to trust that feeling is inside of me, you don't have to do it. You don't have to make this better. You just need to see me." (*therapist uses proxy voice and empathic conjecture*)

MOTHER: Ok.

THERAPIST: Ok? Are you sure?

MOTHER: Ok, I will try,

THERAPIST: You are going to hold on to this moment. This is so important, that is the piece you need to hold on to, that he has this already, on the inside. Do you hear that George?

FATHER: I do.

THERAPIST: And right here, right now, we are doing something very different than your cycle, your vicious cycle has prevented moments like this from happening and what we did was break out from that. (*to parents*) You both showed your son was underneath, what was coming from your side and you were able to say so clearly, that yes, you hurt him. (*turning to* Carl) and that was hard because there was so much emotion and it was like, oh, oh, is that all my fault too? And your mom said that only thing that is your fault is that you made us a family, which was a beautiful thing, right? That let you open up a bit more about you, and you were able to say to your parents: "I end up feeling like it is all my fault, that makes me want to disappear." Because this is painful, and it hurts. Your parents heard your hurt and they wanted to know how to help. Then you said: "I want them to hope, I want them to trust, I want them to see that I want to be successful and that I am doing the best that I can. I have that feeling inside of me." You want your parents to believe you, trust that this is true of you, that you have this strength in you. Right? (*Carl smiles and nods in agreement*)

In this segment, Carl was able to access and explore the shame that was triggered in his interactions with his parents. Carl's shame had roots in the physical abuse he suffered as a young boy, which led him to believe that he was bad and was responsible for all that was wrong in the family. Given the injury that had happened in the past, both parents were afraid that they had failed their son and their anxiety about their mistakes led them to overreact in their caregiving responses. Their over-reaction gave Carl the message that he was a problem that needed to be fixed. Carl's strategy to withdraw as a means to escape his parent's worry and concern exacerbated the negative cycle, and reinforced his sense that he was defective (model of self) and everyone would be better off without him (model of other).

In this session, Carl moved out of his withdrawn position to directly and clearly stating how overwhelmed he felt given his deep despair and sense of responsibility for all that went wrong in the family. When Sarah and George were able to hear and see their son's emotional pain, they were able to comfort and reassure him from a position of emotional balance. Carl was able to take in their reassurance and from the part of himself that felt good and lovable, ask his parents for their trust and belief in him. The injury of the physical abuse was worked through by all of the family members, beginning with the acknowledgment and expression of regret from the parents to Carl, and ending with Carl sharing in present time, the impact of the abuse on his own self-worth and sense of belonging and love in the family unit. The session ended with Carl physically shifting from sitting with his head down staring at the floor to sitting straight in his chair, shoulders back with a huge smile on his face.

Summary

Throughout the EFFT process the therapist alliance provides a secure base for family members to explore the emotional experiences blocked by patterns of distress. In Stage 2 the therapist works from this platform to elicit and expand a child's underlying emotions and needs typically identified in Stage 1. The therapist deepens the child's experience of vulnerability and supports the child, exploring and sharing the attachment-related emotions with the child's parent. Through Steps 5 and 6 the therapist directs parental attention to these attachment-related signals and prompts parental efforts to acknowledge and support the child's emerging experience. Through new levels of vulnerability parents and children are better able to review the negative expectancies they have held as a result of the relational blocks in the family. The case examples in this chapter illustrate how new steps of vulnerability can trigger parental blocks to acceptance and the therapist actions that facilitate a deeper awareness of a parent's own vulnerability. As the family takes new risks to share and respond to the emotions that signal attachment and caregiving responses, the parents and child move closer to restructuring their relationship around new positions that foster felt security and promote exploration.

EFFT Practice Points

The following process points highlight the EFT therapist's focus on deepening emotion and promoting acceptance of a child's attachment-related emotions and needs.

1. De-escalation of the family's negative interaction pattern and parental openness signal the therapist's shift toward deepening a child's vulnerability and promoting parental acceptance.
2. The therapist heightens parental openness and establishes parental readiness to seek a new response to their child's underlying emotions and attachment-related needs.
3. The therapist deepens access to and exploration of a child's attachment-related emotions and needs. These new experiences may prime new caregiving motivations and actions moving the parent to a greater expression of accessibility, responsiveness, and emotional engagement.
4. A child's deeper emotional experiences often trigger parental blocks to acceptance including parental shame and fear. The therapist guides parents toward working through these blocks (e.g., view of self and view of child) and shifting toward greater responsiveness and acceptance of a child's newly expressed vulnerability.
5. Steps 5 and 6 prepare the family for restructuring new positions of engagement organized by attachment and caregiving responses.

Working through the family's relational blocks at a deeper level of engagement fosters confidence in parental availability and a more attuned awareness of the child's needs for connection and support.

References

Allen, J. A. (2008). The attachment system in adolescence. In J. Cassidy & P. R. Shaver (Eds.), *Handbook of attachment theory: Research, and clinical applications*, 2nd Edn. (pp. 419–435). New York: Guilford Press.

Johnson, S. M. (2019). *Attachment theory in practice: Emotionally focused therapy with individuals, couples, and families.* New York: Guilford Press.

Johnson, S. M., Makinen, J. A., & Millikin, J. W. (2001). Attachment injuries in couple relationships: A new perspective on impasses in couples therapy. *Journal of Marital and Family Therapy, 27*, 145–155.

Kobak, R., & Mandelbaum, T. (2003). Caring for the caregiver: An attachment approach to assessment and treatment of child problems. In S. M. Johnson and V. E. Whiffen (Eds.), *Attachment Processes in Couple and Family Therapy* (pp. 144–164). New York: Guilford Press.

Kobak, R., Duemmler, S., Burland, A., & Youngstrom, E. (1998). Attachment and negative absorption states: Implications for treating distressed families. *Journal of Systemic Therapies, 17*, 80–92.

Kobak, R., Zajac, K., Herres, J., & Krauthamer Ewing, E. S. (2015). Attachment based treatments for adolescents: The secure cycle as a framework for assessment, treatment and evaluation. *Attachment & Human Development, 17*, 220–239.

Makinen, J. A., & Johnson, S. M. (2006). Resolving attachment injuries in couples using emotionally focused therapy: Steps toward forgiveness and reconciliation. *Journal of Consulting and Clinical Psychology, 74*, 1055–1064.

Moretti, M. M., & Craig, S. (2013). Maternal versus paternal physical and emotional abuse, affect regulation and risk for depression from adolescence to early adulthood. *Child Abuse and Neglect, 37*, 4–13.

Moretti, M. M., & Obsuth, I. (2009). Effectiveness of an attachment-focused manualized intervention for parents of teens at risk for aggressive behaviour: The Connect Program. *Journal of Adolescence, 32*, 1347–1357.

SEVEN

Restructuring Attachment and Caregiving Responses

Step 7. Restructuring family interactions focusing on sharing of attachment needs and caregiving responses.

The culmination of Stage 2 results in the restructuring of parent and child interactions where a child's attachment needs are expressed and a parent's availability is assured through accessible and responsive caregiving (Johnson & Lee, 2000). As such Step 7 is the pivotal change event in successful EFFT treatment. The enactment of caregiving for expressed attachment needs creates a corrective emotional experience that reorients the expectancies that inform parent–child relationships and these shifts also impact the family's emotional climate. Shifts in the family's level of positive affect and expressiveness increase the likelihood that other relationships in the family will be similarly impacted by the restructuring of a relational block.

In this chapter we describe the EFT therapist's role in guiding family members through a corrective emotional experience where a child's attachment needs are expressed to an available caregiver and the caregiver responds effectively to those needs. Building on this success the family is better able to face other relational blocks that have been less prominent through treatment and to explore the positive impact on reestablishing secure bonds within the family.

Case examples illustrate EFT interventions used in Stage 2 to facilitate the enacting of attachment needs and the processing of these new experiences throughout the family. These final steps are essential for effective resolution of the distress driving the family's negative pattern and broadening felt security across family relationships.

Goals

Four goals guide the therapist direction in Step 7. First, the child's attachment needs are clarified and shared to a responsive caregiver. The child's sharing often follows a direct statement of the parent's availability or a direct invitation. Second, the parent provides an attuned and effective response to the child's expressed need. The therapist supports the parent's engagement, processing, and sharing of the impact including a clear understanding of the child's attachment need. Third, the therapist works with the child to receive the parent's response and processes the impact of the parent's more attuned caregiving response. A fourth and final goal includes expanding the positive impact of the restructuring enactment with other family members.

Often an increase in felt security inspires the sharing of greater vulnerability in other family relationships. This ripple effect may also lead to the identification of additional insecure bonds in the family. Once identified the therapist will proceed with the same Stage 2 steps in working through additional relational blocks. Through processing the family's successes in working through these blocks and enacting new positions of vulnerability and availability, the therapist frames these new positive cycles as an antidote to the family's original negative interaction pattern. The therapist heightens the positive emotions resulting from new patterns of attachment communication and caregiving availability.

Access Points

In Step 7 the therapist is more directive in guiding the family into taking new positions in attachment and caregiving interactions. The therapist intervenes in the session following each of these key access points.

1. Coherent signaling of an unmet attachment need. Through Steps 5 and 6 the child's specific attachment is poignantly expressed. As a parent moves forward into a more engaged and accepting position the therapist directs the enactment of the child's attachment need. Broadly construed a child's attachment needs are associated with support (e.g., secure base) and safety (e.g., safe haven). These needs and how they are expressed may differ by developmental stage and therefore require a parent's sensitivity and responsiveness to discern the balance between support and safety, particularly for adolescents. For example, a youth might express anger as an expression of agency and need for autonomy and if the parent perceives the conflict as an unwanted or unacceptable response the parent and child will mis-attune and over time failed reparation will result in a relational block. The therapist uses evocative strategies to "tune into" the underlying experience of the child and to assist in making explicit the child's attachment need. This is often most clear in a heightened state of vulnerability where the question at hand is "what do you need from your father/mother in this moment?"

2.   Enactment of parental responsiveness and engagement. In Step 7 the therapist guides the child's reaching and the parent's caregiving responses using validation, evocative responding, and heightening to facilitate a deeper, more coherent response. Through pacing the enactment, the therapist slows and focuses parental attunement and responsiveness to the child's expressed need and thereby promotes clarity in the signals of response between parent and child. The therapist actively refocuses the interaction on the expression of the child's need and the specificity and sensitivity of the parent's response to these emotional cues.

3.   Child engages caregiving response. The therapist works through the child's acceptance of the parent's caregiving response. Initially children may immediately take in their parent's support or respond with mistrust and fear. The therapist amplifies the positive shift and deepens the child's engagement with the parent's caregiving. Conversely, when a child is uncertain or mistrustful the therapist returns to working through the child's relational block by focusing on their immediate feelings of distrust triggered by the parent's specific caring attempt. Through processing the impact of the parent's support and care the therapist explores ways these new moments of connection provide opportunities for the child to reconsider their view of self and view of their parent.

4.   Impact on the parent–child relationship. Following the enactment, the therapist explores the impact of the parent and child's emotional encounter. Specific experiences are identified particularly as they relate to the child's view of self and view of their parent, and similar attention is given to the parent's view of the child and view of themselves as a caregiver. When the session includes another parent or caregiver the therapist will also process the impact of the enactment on the caregiving alliance and support both caregivers' reflections regarding the child. The successful enactment provides the base for parents and children to begin to build greater confidence in the parental availability and deeper understanding of a child's needs.

5.   Expanding impact upon others. The effect of a reparative enactment spreads out into the family's own understanding of itself. The therapist explores the impact on family values, affirming ways in which through these new encounters the family is better able to achieve its goals of security and safety. Focusing on these new interactions, the therapist heightens the positive impact of restructured relationship pattern by focusing on new interactions that replaced the previous relationship block and including other family members in observing changes and experiences of the family. Emphasis is placed on the positive emotions (e.g., pride, joy, love) associated with more secure responses within the family and how positive cycles of interaction are the antidote to the family's initial negative interaction pattern.

6. Additional relational blocks. Processing the impact of change in the family may result in identification of additional relational blocks. Unmet family needs may surface as the most distressed family relationship is repaired and the therapist encounters other sources of family distress. Typically, the progress made in resolving the initial relational block prepares parents to be more responsive to these additional blocks. The therapist shifts her focus to the new relational block and follows the same steps used in Stage 2 to work through the remaining blocks.

Restructuring Interactions

This chapter explores the therapist's role in restructuring interactions organized around successful enactments of a child's attachment need and the parent's caregiving response. Special attention is given to EFT use of enactments and their role in facilitating parents and children taking new positions that lead to greater felt security in the family. EFT interventions are reviewed as they are used throughout the process of restructuring family members' positions. A case study demonstrates the process of restructuring focusing on the phases of an enactments and following the moves of the EFT tango.

Minuchin (1974) pioneered the use of enactments in family therapy using therapist directives to engage family members in conversations with a therapist's influence. The use of enactments in family therapy is more impactful when focused on specific impasses in family interactions (Friedlander, Heatherington, Johnson & Skowron, 1994). In EFFT as well as other attachment-based family treatments, injuries and empathic failures in families are repaired through directly engaging the underlying needs of children with actively responsive parents (Kobak, Grassetti, & Yarger, 2013).

Johnson (2019) suggests that this type of encounter is best understood as bonding events where the engagement of secure attachment behaviors with an attachment figure ultimately leads to transformative interactions.

> These kinds of events are coded as so significant by the human brain that their affect is disproportionately impactful on the quality of family relationships, just as family connection is disproportional important in healthy development. *This kind of on-target systematic sculpting or choreographing of core defining attachment interactions is a crucial advance in the practice of family therapy.*
>
> (pp. 193–194)

In EFFT the therapist elicits the underlying pain and fear found in a child's relational block with her caregiver. Through guiding and validating these experiences, the therapist highlights the poignant vulnerability of the child's attachment needs and then engages a parent's active response to these needs through a series of enactments. This then sets in motion a transformative process of security-instilling interactions that transform the expectancies children hold about their value and their parent's availability, and in tandem the parent's value of the child and their own sense of importance as a caregiver. Enacting positive cycles of vulnerability and secure responding broadens and builds the felt security in the family that supports the mutual and distinct needs for connection and exploration.

The goal of an EFT enactment is to promote the felt security experienced by family members through concrete experiences of emotional engagement and empathic responding. Enactments also provide interactions that reveal existing blocks to felt security. Similar to enactments used in EFCT, the sequence of an enactment includes three phases (Tilley & Palmer, 2013).

1. Setting the stage. Enactments in Step 7 focus on the child sharing their attachment needs from a position of vulnerability. Steps 5 and 6 create a context for sharing these needs to a parent who is responsive and accessible. The parent's caregiving intentions are made explicit and the therapist focuses on clarifying the parent's awareness and attunement to the child's experience, often as they work through any remaining blocks to the child's expressed needs. The therapist uses evocative interventions including heightening and empathic conjecture to make clear the felt need of the child along with their stated longing.

In the following example, the therapist choreographs an enactment by saying to Charissa who in tears shares that she often feels unwanted in her family and a disappointment to her father. The therapist conjectures to Charissa,

> It would be too hard to turn to your father right now with tears in your eyes and let him know what you need? Right too hard to tell him that you need his comfort and reassurance that you matter, you matter to him?

The therapist seeds Charissa's attachment longings in the presence of her father who has just shared his regret and deep remorse over his distance from his daughter and his desire to comfort her in the pain he so clearly sees in the session. The therapist sets the stage through framing and heightening the father's responsive position and seeding the daughter's attachment longings.

2. Directing the enactment. A critical step in the enactment process is the therapist's use of a directive to either the child or the parent. For some families the enactment takes place spontaneously as the parent or child follows the emotional cues present when the therapist frames the enactment. In spontaneous enactments, the therapist may still be needed to guide and refocus the parent and child on their efforts to reach and

respond. A therapist may ask the parent or child to repeat a caregiving response or an attachment bid to emphasize and heighten its impact, particularly if the enactment begins to lose its emotional salience. In the case of a spontaneous enactment, the therapist will seek future opportunities to enact a child's coherently shared attachment need and parent's clear caregiving response. The intentional sharing and responding of a child's attachment need is a clear marker of the shift toward secure attachment.

In other situations, the therapist may use a directive with a parent to invite the child to share his or her need. This is more likely when a parent has just worked through his or her blocks to caregiving and the child's attachment need has been clearly articulated. Alternatively, the therapist may ask a child to turn toward their parent in a moment of heightened vulnerability. This is more likely, when a child is processing his or her fear or lack of confidence in the presence of a fully accepting parent, after the parent's availability has been readily assured. In either situation, the therapist recognizes the risk that either parent or child is taking through their initiative and is prepared to respond in support if the child or parent struggles to respond to the enactment reach.

In Step 7 the enactment focuses on the engagement of the attachment and caregiving system where affective attunement and empathic presence are essential to establishing an emotional bond. Therefore, the therapist guides and refocuses the sharing between parent and child to maintain focal attention to the leading edge of each person's experience, particularly as they risk, reach, and respond with clear expressions of an attachment need and caregiving support.

3. Processing each person's experience. The final phase of an enactment involves exploring each person's experience of the encounter including a specific focus on the emotional impact of the enactment. The therapist will combine evocative questions and validation to support the exploration of the present experience, often noting the attachment-related themes (e.g., care, comfort, reassurance) and caregiving intentions (e.g., seeing, valuing, supporting) and how these themes reflect views of self and views of other. This reflexive communication instills the attachment meaning of the interaction and provides opportunities to review past expectancies associated with negative views of self (e.g., lacking worth) or negative views of other (e.g., uncaring, rejecting). The therapist may also contrast how this interaction is different from the relational blocks that interfered with the parent and child's ability to communicate at this more direct and impactful level.

In the example above, the therapist uses an evocative question to explore Charissa's father's experience of having his caregiving response received. "What was it like for you when Charissa took in your words and asked for a hug from you?" The father reflected on how he felt he was really able to be the father he wanted to her. "I want her to know that I am here for her, and that any time she needs my support, my hugs. I'm ready!" The therapist reflects the father's caregiving intention and heightens his statement of availability. In response, the father further qualifies his intention. "I now understand better. A hug is always waiting but it needs to be right for Charissa. It's about her needs and that is not always what she wants." Through processing his experience, the father more accurately attunes to his daughter's needs rather than relying on his intention alone. The therapist can use an enactment at this point to circle through the process again focusing now on the father's intention to support his daughter in the ways that she finds most needed.

In summary, Step 7 is pivotal in the EFFT process of change as it requires family members to face their relational blocks to attachment and caregiving and find security together through shared vulnerability. These moments of vulnerability lead to new relational patterns that stand in contrast to the negative cycles that reinforce self-protection and reactivity in family interactions. The corrective emotional experiences in Step 7 shift the family in directions of safety and security where deeper emotions are made explicit and used to inform the needs and resources families use as they regain their emotional balance. Broadly, these interactions initiate deeper emotional experiences through the contact that is made regarding themes of safety, security, and significance. Successful enactments that promote attachment communication and caregiving responses broaden and build a felt sense of security in the family. This strengthens the family's capacity to remain resilient under hardship as the following case example illustrates.

EFT Interventions in Step 7

Evocative and processing interventions are essential in EFT change events. Use of evocative responses, conjectures, and heightening promote emotional engagement, which is essential in the EFFT process of change. Following the tenets of attachment theory (Chapter 2), the EFT therapist uses emotion as the target and agent of change in relationships and as a language for connection. Emotion is pivotal in shifting and transforming relationships at an attachment level. Processing interventions focus on making shared meaning of new family experiences. The therapist balances evocative strategies with reflection and validation to consolidate new understanding of the changes taking place in Stage 2. Reframing interventions contrast the family's new corrective experiences with the previous negative patterns of distress which dominated family attempts at connection and correction. The therapist's use of enactments is critical to restructuring relationship positions in Stage 2 and additional focus is given to the process of restructuring enactments in the section below.

Evocative Interventions

Evocative strategies are important in Steps 7 and 8 to focus emotional experience in the present moment. Evocative questions are used to capture a family member's emerging experience particularly related to attachment and caregiving themes. For example, a therapist might ask an adolescent "What's happening right now as you see your mother's tears, hear her regret for not being there for you?" The therapist might intersperse heightening between evocative questions to intensify the focus on the underlying attachment emotion being expressed. For example, a therapist responding to a client who becomes tearful in response to a parent's availability. "This is so different for you. Right? To have your mother at your side, reaching for you, reassuring you how important you are to her, what happens inside of you as you finally feel her care in this moment?" Empathic conjectures also intensify focus on a present moment by tentatively asking a client to take one step further into his or her experience. A therapist's attunement and awareness of attachment and caregiving themes is effective in deepening experience through an empathic conjecture.

Often these conjectures in Step 7 are focused on attachment-related fears and the enactment. A therapist might conjecture to a youth faltering in expressing their needs to a parent,

> Right, you come to a point where you want your mom to understand, to see you, but it would be another thing entirely to actually go to her and share what this is really like. It's almost like part of you is saying don't turn, don't ask, don't share with her. That would be too much, but another part of you really longs for her comfort and her care, right? Help me understand what is happening right now as I say this?

These same interventions are used to deepen a parent's awareness to his or her caregiving intentions. A therapist may ask, for example, "What is it like for you right now, as her mother, to hear how afraid she is that she will fail others, that she will fail you?" The therapist places focal attention on the parent's caregiving response.

These same interventions are useful in promoting the positive impact of a bonding interaction in the family with other members. A therapist may use empathic conjecture to deepen a parent's awareness of the impact of a repair between her partner and their child.

> It's like a part of you is so relieved to see the two of them repair because of the divide that has grown in the family, and I wonder if another part of you can see your partner's concern, strength, and love in this moment. What's that like to see her care and compassion?

The conjecture invites the family to move toward more positive emotions and reflect upon ways they are now being more successfully secure together.

Processing Interventions

In Step 7, processing intervention promotes new understanding based on new experiences as relational blocks are replaced by bonding interactions. The therapist uses reflection and validation to slow the process and enable family members to make sense of their unfolding experience particularly as these new experiences provide reason to review the expectancies they may have held about parental care and availability or a child's need for support and vulnerability. A therapist may ask a child after a bonding interaction with his previously distant parent, "What words come to mind as your feel your mother's touch on your shoulder, her presence at your side right now?" The therapist helps the child to tune into his experience and to put words to the care that he is receiving in the moment.

Reframing is useful in setting a context for the struggles families may face in risking and reaching with vulnerability. The therapist reframes the present fears of taking new steps in light of the history of the family's negative cycle and consistent patterns of disappointment. A therapist uses a reframe to help a parent better attune to their child's fear that surfaces in an enactment.

> Right, it's so hard to understand why she doesn't trust the care you are offering right now. It's like the history of your family pattern, the distance and hurt, is speaking louder than your words or reassurance right now. Let's take our time here.

The ability to see the daughter's fear of reaching and risking an attachment need makes sense in light of the past pattern and reframing the struggle in terms of the past normalizes the fear, creating space for that fear to be acknowledged and understood.

Practical examples of these interventions are illustrated in the following case example emphasizing the EFT practices used in restructuring interactions. Specific attention is given to the role of enactments in shifting positions within a family's relational block.

Step 7—Case Example

The following case example illustrates a Step 7 change event where the daughter turns to her father with her need to know that she can turn to him for support. Previously she remained distant from him for fear he would disappear or delegate her concern to her mother which would further escalate the division in their estranged marriage and her place caught between her warring parents. This excerpt illustrates the therapist's use of EFFT to consolidate the father's engagement and support, clarify the daughter's attachment need, and conduct an enactment of the daughter's need and the father's caring response. This example also illustrates how the therapist continues to follow the EFT tango process through this change event.

Laura (16) sought treatment following the request of her father, Ray, who was concerned about the impact of his separation from Laura's mother Shelley. Laura reported being "caught between" both of her parents, particularly when her mother Shelley would confide after a recent fight with Ray. Ray was worried about the negative impact on Laura and while Laura expressed interest in treatment she did not want to involve her parents. As her confidence in the therapist grew, Laura agreed to conjoint sessions with her parents, however the parents refused to attend these sessions as a couple. Treatment proceeded focusing on each parent–child dyad and the following session excerpt follows Laura's sessions with her father, Ray.

The therapist identified the father and daughter's relational block which centered on Ray's efforts to manage his daughter through advice giving and intrusive monitoring of her behavior. Laura typically placated her father's concerns telling him what she believed he wanted to hear and otherwise remaining silent about her concerns. Through Stage 1 the therapist validated Ray's concern and care for his daughter, which prompted disclosure of Ray's fears about Laura's risk for substance abuse and dependence. Ray's concerns were rooted in his previous experience with Laura's older sister Jody, who continued to struggle with substance use problems having failed a recent rehabilitation program. Laura's guarded behavior and placating responses were especially triggering for Ray as these were the same behaviors he observed with Laura's older sister. The following example illustrates the therapist working through Ray's fears about Laura's future after Laura shared the negative impact of his pressure on her. The three phases of an enactment are highlighted as well as the therapist's use of the EFT tango process.

Setting the Stage

In this example we see the therapist mirroring the present process through her focus on the father's response to his daughter's desire to trust him more and to turn to him. The therapist uses the present moment to focus the father and daughter on a new level of engagement and uses their emotional experience as a resource and focus for this new possibility. In the excerpt below we see the therapist setting the stage for an enactment through affect assembly and deepening. The therapist focuses Ray's deeper emotions, organizing his fears by reflecting and validating his past struggles with Laura's older sister Jody. The therapist is aware that Ray can be overcome by his fear and lose contact with Laura in the process. Keeping his focus on Laura and his present concerns for her, the therapist uses Ray's deeper emotional response to underscore his care and clarify his intention. This sets the stage for Laura's enactment reach toward her father and as this emotional signal is clarified, Laura reacts to the father's vulnerable availability, expressing her fears about his health.

THERAPIST: She is your youngest daughter, and it makes sense that you would be worried about her. Especially when she sends signals that remind you of Jody. You get scared and try to take control. So, hearing Laura say, "I want you to trust me more," is really hard to hear because of your fears?

RAY: (*flippant*) yeah, but I am not sure that "trusting" her alone is enough. She is only 16!

THERAPIST: (*soft and slow*) And that is really hard. She is your youngest and you know first-hand what can happen, that maybe your worst fears will materialize, and something really bad could happen to her. (*Ray looks at the therapist, his eyes watering with tears*) This just cannot be, you are working too hard to make sure this doesn't happen, what if you do all this, and then you still lose her?

RAY: (*tearful*) I just couldn't take it, not again, not with Laura.

THERAPIST: Oh, so this is scary for you to see your dad upset, that scares you? You need to take care of him, yeah? What if you are too stressful for him and he gets sick?

LAURA: I don't want him to be stressed about me. I will do better, I was doing my homework just before we got here. (*reactive response intensifying her reassurance to her father*)

RAY: Yes, she did really well and when I spoke to the teachers they all said what a good student she is. (*father exits from his fears, following his daughter's attempt at reassurance*)

THERAPIST: (*refocusing*) Right, Laura, I see that you want to please your Dad, of course you do, but his tears, there a few minutes ago, they made you feel guilty?

RAY: She doesn't have to worry about me.

THERAPIST: Right, you don't want her to worry about your health, but she loves you, and cares about you, so it makes sense she would worry. (*therapist normalizes daughter's reaction*) But Laura, when your dad is scared, and he says he doesn't want anything bad to happen to you, he is saying that because he loves you, not that he is disappointed in you, but he is trying to take care of you. (*therapist reframes father's emotional response as an expression of his caregiving intent*)

RAY: And maybe not always in the best way, I can get carried away with my lectures.

THERAPIST: But when you are lecturing her, you are now telling her this is what you do when you are afraid for her, and this all matters so much because she is precious to you. She matters to you, that is what you want her to know? (*therapist reframes father's anxious lecturing in the context of his caregiving intent*)

RAY: Of course!!! (*shifting toward Laura, reaching for her hand*) You know that, right? You are my baby girl, I want to be there for you.

THERAPIST: So, you are saying pretty clearly to Laura right now that you want to be there for her, yes?

RAY: (*looking at Laura*) I am here for what you need. (*Laura squirms and looks away*)

The therapist assembles the father's care and concern for his daughter. Processing interventions are used to validate and reframe the father's anxious fears focusing on his underlying caregiving concern. The therapist deepens and clarifies his emotional experience which enables the father to send a clear and coherent message of his availability, support, and care. The therapist continues to set the stage by working through Laura's fear and focusing her explicit concern about her father's vulnerability.

Directing the Enactment

In this section the therapist employs the third EFT tango move, choreographing engaged encounters. The therapist actively guides, supports, and directs Laura in sharing her need for her father's attention, ultimately seeking his confidence and care.

THERAPIST: What's this like for you Laura? What is it like that your Dad wants to be there FOR you? That is new? You have been busy looking after yourself and you have had a LOT to look after here with so much going on, and it is you alone, Jody is not here, your brother is married with his own family, you are all alone here, dealing with all this stuff. Your parent's marriage, your dad's health, his worries ... (*Laura nods in agreement still avoiding eye contact*) And it is so hard to really open up like you did before ... letting your Dad know you need him to trust you, to believe in you. But that's hard because you also don't want him to worry, you don't want to be a burden. You see his stress and you back off. There's no way you can really talk to him about what you need?

LAURA: (*whispering*) I can't.

THERAPIST: (*leaning in*) You can't? That is too hard? What's going to happen, can you help me? What would happen if you talk to him? (*heightening the block Laura is experiencing, seeding her attachment longings*)

LAURA: (*still looking down*) He will be gone.

THERAPIST: Oh, if you open up, your dad will leave? He would be disappointed in you and then he would leave? Then you really would be all alone

LAURA: That is what he has done before. (*looking up angrily with a challenging tone*) Isn't that right Dad? You don't like a situation and then you just leave.

RAY: (*abruptly*) That was another situation, that was your mother and I, and your sister, you know that she needs to hit rock bottom.

THERAPIST: (*redirecting*) Hold on Ray. Can we take it slow here? I just want to make sure you are hearing Laura here because I know you want to be able to hear her. You want to be there for her, maybe there is a new way here. Where she can talk and you can hear her? Right now, Laura is talking to you. She is saying she can't talk to you because she is afraid you will leave. She's afraid too. (*therapist holding eye contact with Ray*) You see if she really opens up, maybe you won't like what you see, she is taking a chance right now, can you see that she is afraid, afraid she will be all alone? (*therapist refocuses father to daughter's attachment-related emotions, evident in the present moment*)

RAY: (*softens*) Yeah, I can see that, (*to Laura*) I am so sorry, love.

THERAPIST: You are hearing her. You can see how hard it has been for her?

RAY: She has been through a lot. It shouldn't have been that way.

THERAPIST: Can you tell her?

RAY: I do want you to be able to come to me. I get why you would be afraid. But it is you and me now. We are together, we are family. (*clarifying caregiving intention and invitation*)

THERAPIST: And a family sticks together, right? (*empathic conjecture to which Ray responds "Absolutely!"*) What's that like Laura to hear your dad say "We are together, we are family."

LAURA: (*smiling*) It's good.

THERAPIST: Yeah, it feels good to know where you belong, that you are family together. And you are 14, with a lot of growing up to do, and along the way, there are going to be ups and downs, right?

RAY: (*to Laura*) I want you to know you can call me, no matter what.

LAURA: I would be afraid to call you.

THERAPIST: It would be hard to call your dad? What if stuff is happening? What if something has gone wrong?

LAURA: Yeah, I don't want to cause a fight.

THERAPIST: Between your parents? That is a tough place because maybe stuff would be happening at your mom's that might be a problem and that would be hard for you, yes? You don't want your parents fighting? So, you are stuck in the middle here. This is hard. How can your dad help you? He is here now, and he wants to be there for you.

LAURA: He needs to listen to me. I need to know he won't go all ballistic about mom.

THERAPIST: Right, things are complicated with your mom and your dad. You need to have a safe place to go. You are being really brave here saying this out loud to your dad. Do you think you could tell him what you really need from him?

LAURA: (*softly smiling, tentative*) I need to be able to talk to you without you talking about mom.

THERAPIST: You want your dad to hear you? Hear what is important for you?

LAURA: (*to father*) You know I can't count on mom, she has too many problems of her own.

RAY: But I want to know how I can be there for you, how I can help you.

LAURA: Just listen to me. Think about me and not mom. I need you to hear me to take me seriously. I need to know you care about me. (*coherent statement of attachment need*)

Processing the Encounter

Following the successful shifts Laura and her father make to reach and respond in new positions of vulnerability and support, the therapist explores this new experience focusing on the actions and responses that the daughter and father took to test the vulnerability and needs expressed through facing the fears which blocked attachment needs and caregiving responses. The therapist replays the experience highlighting view of self and view of other themes present in their experience.

THERAPIST: Laura you take this big chance, like you are right now, and talk to your dad. It's so important that he hears you, what you need, and how he can help. That is what feels like being a family, yes? (*therapist primes parental availability and heightens attachment-related need. Ray reaches over and hugs his daughter*)

THERAPIST: Ray, what are you are saying to your daughter right now with that hug. (*therapist makes explicit father's caregiving response, symbolizing his action's importance*)

RAY: (*smiling*) That I am proud of her, that she spoke up, she reached to me.

THERAPIST: And for you Laura? What is it like for you? You told your dad what you need. Do you think he is listening to you right now? (*Laura nods, softly saying "yes"*) And what's it like to feel your dad close with his arm around you, telling you he is proud of you?

LAURA: ummmm ... good?

THERAPIST: Good. It's so hard to really believe this, after all it is brand new, yeah? Usually it is you Ray talking and you Laura listening. But you did something big here Laura. You told your dad that you were afraid that he would leave if maybe you did something he would be disappointed in and dad, you told Laura, that you wanted to be there for her, through thick and thin. (*therapist reflects the attachment and caregiving actions and related emotions*)

RAY: Absolutely.

THERAPIST: And then Laura you took another big step and told your dad you didn't want to hear him talking about your mom but to listen to you, to what was happening for you. You really trusted your dad for what you really needed. You took what he was offering you. He wanted to know what you needed. Good for you, you were really brave today. (*therapist highlights daughter's view of her father*)

LAURA: (*smiling*) I didn't think I could do it.

THERAPIST: Right, I hear you. I guessed that, eh? (*Laura smiles in agreement*) So, this is really big for you both. You both did something really important for you and your family. Ray, you let Laura know you are scared, when you lecture her and get stern with her, that it is all about being afraid something bad will happen to her. And for you Laura, the last thing you want to do is stress your dad, but there is stuff happening for you, and you let your dad know that you are afraid to open up for fear he will leave or if you talk maybe it will just start another fight. So of course, you stay quiet, but you did something really different here. You didn't stay quiet. You told your dad you needed him to listen to you. And he did! (*smiling*) I'm so happy for you two.

DAD: (*smiling back*) Thank you, I'm so proud of Laura.

THERAPIST: Yes, Laura really showed courage and spoke from her heart. Not something she felt she could do. Can you tell her right now how proud you are? What you see her in this moment. (*therapist invites father to enact positive emotion, highlighting father's view of his daughter*)

DAD: Sure. (*reaching over to take her hand*) Laura, you are amazing, I'm so proud of you. I need to hear these things from you because you, you are important to me.

LAURA: (*jokingly*) That's better than feeling like a disappointment!

THERAPIST: Right, so different than what you can also feel. It's funny because this is so different than you feared and it's a relief and it's so good to know that your dad heard you, and he was here just for YOU in this moment.

Through processing these reflections, the therapist promotes opportunities for Laura and her father to make greater meaning of their experience and further integrate the enactment into their relationship as a father and daughter at a time of significant need. The therapist uses the success of their enactment to engage the positive emotions both experience through the impact of the repair.

Promoting Positive Impact

The shifts in working through relational blocks have a positive impact on the family climate as new pathways to security and safety are realized in the relationships causing the greatest distress for the family. The therapist harnesses the positive emotions that result from new moments of trust and confidence found specifically in re-engaging actions of safety and security, processing the effect of these changes in the relationship of parent to child. These positive emotions and congruent responses about self and other show the therapist that the process is on track toward repair and renewal of attachment bonds.

The use of EFT evocative interventions to promote contact and sharing of positive emotions enhances the satisfaction the family members derive from these changes but also enhances the likelihood that they will feel loved and cared about. Similar to the principle of capitalization found in couples, the sharing of positive emotions and experiences amplifies the positive impact of those emotions and their meaning at a relational level (Gable, Gonzaga, & Strachman, 2006).

Through sharing these positive experiences together, family members are more likely to experience greater satisfaction with these changes but also with their relationships in general. More than the benefits of positive affect alone (e.g., Frederickson, 2001), the positive emotions associated with a repair are likely to also lead to an increase in the positive expectations of another's reliability and responsiveness and greater feelings of personal confidence and effectiveness (Fosha, 2000). In this way the power of relational reparations is experienced through the positive emotions that are directly experienced and enhanced through sharing these experiences in the family.

The positive affect generated through corrective emotional experiences encourages exploration including new expectations for care and support. These shifts promote a "broaden and build" cycle of security that is fueled by positive emotions associated with feelings of pride, love, relief, and confidence (Mikulincer & Shaver, 2016). These positive cycles increase emotional engagement, support growth activities, and reinforce positive views of self and other. These resources strengthen the family's ability to support personal and social development and through the family's felt security engage a "growth enhancing psychological catalyst" (p. 67).

Expanding Impact to the Family

Following the integration and validation of restructuring events that define Step 7, the therapist expands the focus from a specific relational block to the family as a whole by involving other family members. The impact of one corrective experience may ripple through the relationships of the family and open new opportunities for others to review and renew the bonds that define the family. Shifts in specific family relationships may unbalance other relationships, revealing additional relational blocks. The family as a network of attachment relationship can be influenced by shifts in one relationship triggering further distress in another relationship. Through Step 7 the therapist promotes the positive impact of the specific corrective experiences and at the same time monitors family responses to assess for emergence of additional relational blocks.

In Miguel's case, his parents had threatened residential treatment or boarding school if he did not correct his truancy and fighting at school. His parents felt distraught and defeated by Miguel's obstinance and destructive behavior. The family was embarrassed by the public nature of his conflicts particularly given his parents were both employed by the school district. Through the assessment and Stage 1 sessions the five family members were present, and the family's negative pattern was identified focusing on the relational block between Miguel and his father. The father's critical and demanding stance toward Miguel had resulted in his son's shut down withdrawal. He sought to avoid conflict but was failing at school and was occasionally bullied by other students. Prior to a Stage 2 session, Miguel asked that further sessions be with his parents exclusively. He found it hard to discuss his fears and worries in front of his older brothers because they would tease him about any weakness he showed. After Miguel shared his need for support from his father and both of his parents responded with greater confidence in the family's ability to face Miguel's school challenges as a team. As Miguel risked letting his parents, especially his dad, into his fears, both parents began to see his vulnerabilities underneath what they previously interpreted as disrespect. Miguel's courage to face his fears inspired his father and motivated the father's efforts to support his son more directly.

The therapist convened a family session including Miguel's older brothers, to expand the impact of the changes made by Miguel and his parents. Miguel's mother shared the progress she saw in the family as a whole and particularly between her husband and Miguel. Miguel's older brothers began to tease Miguel for being "such a baby." Instead of avoiding any confrontation, Miguel stood up to them saying, "I am not a baby. I just didn't know what to do. I'm done hiding and backing away. It is ok, to be scared." Joining his son, the father replied to Miguel's brothers,

> Miguel is right. I haven't done a great job showing you boys the courage Miguel is showing. I taught you how to hide your feelings. (*choking back emotion*) Miguel reminded me that real courage is confronting fear not running from it. I'm proud of you Miguel.

Both brothers looked surprised and confused while Miguel tried to hide his smile. The therapist helped Miguel put words to feelings of joy and satisfaction at hearing his father's affirmation instead of disappointment. As dad reached over to hug Miguel, both brothers started to smile, and the therapist shifted to engage the brothers' responses to their father's words and their brother's courage.

The therapist invited the family to name the differences that they saw in the family as a whole as a result of the changes that Miguel and his father were making. Evocative interventions focused on eliciting and expanding the positive emotions that his parents and brothers showed to Miguel and his efforts to improve at school. The therapist used the family's experience in session to contrast to the negative cycle that was so prevalent in the early family sessions. The therapist asked of the family, "What do you notice most about our conversation today compared to the past, when you got caught in your pattern? What's different for you, right now?" Similar to the initial assessment, the therapist was intentional in inviting each family member to reflect on their experience of the family and what it meant to them that their family made these changes. Finally, the therapist used reflective questions to highlight how the father and son saw themselves differently as a result of working through and changing the difficult patterns that had taken hold of their relationship. In EFFT the therapist actively engages positive emotions associated with shifts the family has made toward security, and promotes reflective conversations focusing on individuals' view of self and other.

Working Through Additional Blocks

The therapist expands the exploration of the resolution of a relational block in the context of the broader family system. Typically, the therapist with parental support will reconvene the family members who participated in previous sessions and use the session to review the new experiences and changes that have occurred in working through a block. Expanding the focus of change and impact enables other family members to share their experience which may reinforce change and also point to other relational blocks not yet resolved. The therapist uses the session to explore the impact of vulnerability on other family members. This may result in uncovering other relational blocks in the family.

Alissa (24) sought individual treatment for mood-related symptoms and a loss of self-confidence following the recent end of a long-term relationship. She returned to live with her family after moving away from her former partner. The therapist suggested family sessions after recent conflicts with her parents. The family sessions focused on working through Alissa's defensive response to her mother's anxious over-involvement. Her mother was worried about Alissa's wellbeing following her most recent depressive episode, and fear she held from her sister's suicide that occurred in her 20s. The EFFT sessions included the father and a younger brother Sean (14). Alissa found the initial course of individual therapy helpful in addressing her loss and feelings of hopelessness yet she was not able to assuage her mother's fears. Through Stage 1 the therapist focused on strengthening the caregiving alliance between the parents and promoting the father's support as he had previously remained distant to the mother-daughter struggle, often away on business related travel. The mother and daughter's relational block was exacerbated by the father's rational approach to both women and his implicit criticism of what he perceived as his wife's over-reaction to Alissa's "growing pains."

In Stage 2, Alissa expressed her fears about succeeding in the adult world and the loss of confidence she experienced from the recent loss of her long-term relationship. Together her mother and father responded with understanding and affirmation of their confidence in Alissa. The therapist led Alissa through the enactment of her need for support and confidence from her parents in this time and less involvement in her personal affairs. Alissa asked that as she prepared to move out on her own that the family make time to connect around positive occasions and allow her room to struggle if she needed with her own independence. In processing the impact of these shifts in the family, Alissa's younger brother, Sean, withdrew in the session.

Sean's silent protest was met with pressure to comply with the family's success, which only intensified Sean's withdrawal. The therapist processed the escalating tension with Sean and his parents. Following the tender moments that were expressed with Alissa, the parents were responsive and open to Sean's concerns. In this case, Sean's concern over his father's absence from the family was obscured by the attention Alissa's "problems" had brought into the family. The therapist returned to the steps of Stage 2 and began to illicit Sean's underlying emotions and attachment needs. Sean's angry protest first appeared as a direct challenge to the father, who dismissed his concern as a need for attention. Working through this block the therapist refocused on Sean's pain at his father's absence from sport-related events. The therapist provided support to Sean, inviting him to enact the pain he experienced when his father had missed a recent student awards banquet where Sean was honored. Sean expressed how bad he felt that his father missed this moment and other times important to the family. He expressed his need to see "his dad show up" and the fears that his father's work was more important than the family. Sean's father apologized and hugged him, providing reassurance that he had heard his son's need and the family's broader concern about his availability. The family then discussed how they might be more intentional in creating family experiences now that their family was changing. The father expressed his commitment to monthly family outings and coordinating his work commitments with events important to the family and Sean specifically.

This family has demonstrated success in working through their most problematic relational block. Their success in enacting vulnerability and attachment/caregiving responses promotes greater flexibility and increased access to attachment-related emotions. In this example, the therapist is able to move quickly through a second relational block because of the progress the family has already made. The therapist's attention and awareness in processing the impact of the initial enactment, provided the family with a second opportunity to re-attune to other relational blocks and address unmet attachment needs in the family.

Summary

In the final steps of Stage 2 the therapist guides the family through restructuring reactive positions rooted in the relational blocks that disrupt attachment communication and effective caregiving responses. Relational blocks are resolved through corrective emotional experiences that are enacted through a process guided by the therapist where a child's attachment needs are clarified, shared, and empathically engaged by a responsive parent. The EFFT process accesses deeper emotion in a context of shared vulnerability that enables family members a new basis for reviewing attachment and caregiving assumptions (view of self and other) previously organized by the family's negative interaction pattern and specific relational blocks. The therapist uses these corrective emotional experiences to process the shifts in security that occur in a specific relationship to the broader network of family relationships, strengthening affectional ties in the family, and instilling new meaning through positive emotional experiences. Engaging the positive impact of security can also uncover other relational blocks that can be then revisited following the Stage 2 process. Families who repair ruptures and correct empathic failures are better able to address practical parenting decisions and practices that were previously complicated by the reactive patterns of negative affect. Working through these relational blocks and engaging vulnerability fosters a secure family system that broadens and builds resources for healthy development in families.

EFFT Practice Points

The following process points highlight the essential therapist practices in guiding the primary EFFT Stage 2 change event. Parent and child positions are restructured inviting children to reach to parents with a coherent and clear statement of his or her attachment need.

1.   The therapist choreographs the restructuring change event enabling parents and children to overcome the relational blocks in caregiving and attachment responses.

2. The therapist leads the enactment through setting the stage for the child's vulnerable reach through prompting and heightening parental availability.
3. The therapist plays an active role in directing the enactment and refocusing parental and child response to attachment and caregiving emotions and themes.
4. The therapist processes the attachment-related impact of the enactment on the parent and child's relationship, view of other and view of self. The therapist promotes increased child confidence in parental availability and greater value in parent's experience of his or her child and their self-understanding as a parent.
5. The therapist explores the positive impact of the resolved relational block with other family members. The impact may be shared in ways that promote new steps toward family security and parental availability or may also uncover additional relational blocks. The therapist returns to Steps 5 and 6 with these new blocks as security in the family system is strengthened through resolving these additional blocks.

References

Fosha, D. (2000). *The transforming power of affect*. New York: Basic Books.

Frederickson, B. L. (2001). The role of positive emotions in positive psychology: The broaden and build theory of positive emotions. *American Psychologist*, 56, 218–226.

Friedlander, M. L., Heatherington, L., Johnson, B., & Skowron, E. A. (1994). Sustaining engagement: A change event in family therapy. *Journal of Counseling, 41*, 438–448.

Gable, S. L., Gonzaga, G., & Strachman, A. (2006). Will you be there for me when things go right? Social Support for Positive Events. *Journal of Personality and Social Psychology, 91*, 904–917.

Johnson, S. M. (2019). *Attachment theory in practice: Emotionally focused therapy with individuals, couples, and families*. New York: Guilford Press.

Johnson, S., & Lee, A. C. (2000). Emotionally focused family therapy: Restructuring attachment. In C. E. Bailey (ed.) *Children in therapy: Using the family as a resource*, pp. 112–136. New York: Norton Press.

Kobak, R., Grassetti, S. N., & Yarger, H. A. (2013). Attachment based treatment for adolescents: Repairing attachment injuries and empathic failures. In K. H. Birsch (Ed.) *Attachment and Adolescence* (pp. 93–111). Stuttgart, Germany: Klett-Cotta Verlag.

Mikulincer, M., & Shaver, P. R. (2016) *Attachment in adulthood*, 2nd Ed. New York: Guilford Press.

Minuchin, S. (1974). *Families and family therapy*. Cambridge, MA: Harvard University Press.

Tilley, D., & Palmer, G. (2013). Enactments in emotionally focused couple therapy: Shaping moments of contact and change. *Journal of Marital and Family Therapy, 39*, 299–313.

EIGHT

Consolidating Security in the Family System

Step 8. Exploring new solutions to past problems from more secure positions.

Step 9. Consolidating new positions and strengthening positive patterns.

The final EFFT stage is focused on consolidating and integrating the key changes made by the family in two important ways. First, the family is now better able to face past problems with new relational resources. Through EFFT the family's relationship to the presenting problem or symptoms has changed, whereas past demands often divided family members and negative patterns escalated these divides, new shifts toward more secure ways of relating strengthen the family's ability to face old problems in new ways, together. Second, the therapist leads the family in consolidation of the changes made and promotes opportunities for the family to form new understanding of their experience as a family. This occurs as a family is able to make meaning through an active construal of the changes each person has made to shift the family from its past patterns of negativity to present patterns of trust, safety, and security. As the family transitions from treatment, the therapist's ultimate objective is to support a new trajectory of exploration and growth, where new patterns of availability and safety promote greater resilience.

In this chapter we focus on the unique ways the EFT therapist instills greater confidence in the felt security a family has attained. Specific goals and intervention markers are identified that promote consolidation through this final EFFT. Brief case descriptions illustrate the work of the EFT therapist in helping families revisit remaining problematic issues promoting efforts for the family to work together in new ways against these problems or stressors. As treatment concludes the therapist guides the family toward deepening the meaning and importance of the changes they have made including ways these new experiences reflect a new family identity. The use of attachment rituals and educational resources are also proposed.

Goals in Stage 3

In the final stage of EFFT treatment, sessions are organized around two primary goals. The first goal is helping the family address past problems that remain a current concern. The therapist invites the family to use the new relational resources gained through treatment to face problems that in the past triggered their negative interaction pattern. At this stage the therapist guides the family toward more vulnerable and responsive discussions of these specific concerns. This may require the therapist to redirect family members to more responsive, accessible, and emotionally engaged positions as they work to resolve longstanding issues. The process of working in and through past problems instills greater confidence in the family's felt security as the family faces these challenges together.

A second goal centers on consolidating the gains the family has made in treatment through their new understanding of their relationships and family identity. The EFT therapist focuses on helping the family articulate new confidence in attachment relationships and take steps to increase this felt security. This final goal marks the shifts the family has made toward more secure patterns of engagement. Family members are invited to make meaning of these changes and the difference they have made in how family members see themselves, their family, and their future together.

Access Points

In Stage 3 the therapist guides the family in using their new relational resources to address concrete problems that remain in the family and to use these new experiences to shape new understanding of what it means to be in this family. Through these final sessions the therapist follows specific access points to intervene and support the family's ability to engage, reflect, and invest in the growth they have achieved.

1. Return to a prevailing or past concern. The therapist follows the family conversation as they redress a past concern or initiate discussion of a specific related problem. The therapist guides the family toward the more secure patterns they established in working through past relational blocks. The therapist tracks the family interaction and uses evocative and process interventions to keep the family on track with accessibility, responsiveness, and shared vulnerability.

2. Family interactions demonstrating more secure positions. The therapist highlights positive cycles of security where family members demonstrate accessibility, responsiveness and emotional engagement. Key moments of connection are emphasized and reflected

202 Following the Stages and Steps

upon as a family unit. The therapist aids the family in co-constructing a new narrative that emphasizes the family as a safe haven and secure base (Byng-Hall, 1995; Dallos, 2008). Family members are able to recount a coherent narrative that elaborates the growth that has occurred in the family's ability to support and care for one another.

3. Family transition to termination. When family members express reservations about discontinuing treatment or express concerns related to maintaining treatment gains, the therapist acknowledges and validates these issues, making space to reframe these concerns in light of the value they have found in new patterns of security.

Step 8—Finding New Solutions

Following restructuring of family positions and resolution of the family's relational blocks that disrupt caregiving and attachment communication, families more readily solve problems and adjust discipline practices that are no longer influenced by the negative emotional states and patterns of distress. Parents who have re-established positive cycles of security are better able to balance the varied needs for connection and support through more accurate and attuned communication. Parents of adolescent, for example may experience greater negative emotions from youth who are frustrated in response to ineffective attachment responses and unmet needs.. Parents in turn are more likely to respond by misreading their child's emotional signals either over- or under-responding to their child's signals for support (Kobak, Grassetti, & Yarger, 2013). In more secure family relationships, emotional engagement involving conflict is less threatening and family members are better able to balance the competing emotional tensions in navigating limit setting, parental monitoring, and personal responsibility and choice. In fact, for families with adolescent children the process of working through goal differences related to autonomy is pivotal to the parent and youth retaining a secure bond (Allen, 2008).

In Step 8 the therapist guides the family through addressing problems or areas of concern that in the past they were unable to resolve because of the insecure patterns and blocks defining the family process. Attention is given to normalizing missteps and triggers that have cued the self-protective responses of the past, especially in the context of fear and uncertainty. The therapist guides the family through these situations by experientially identifying the relational blocks and new resources the family has in working through these blocks together. Family role play or enactments may be used in anticipation of a past relational block as the therapist engages the family in working through their fears together. Finally, the therapist may frame the family's commitment to growth and normalizes the probability that past triggers may occur and the family's capacity to see these moments of mis-attunement will better enable them to find their emotional balance and join together against their previous pattern. Parenting practices are more flexible and the family's ability to navigate needs for care and support are strengthened through the family's greater emotional balance. Co-parental alliances are strengthened and family efforts to invest in maintaining and deepening their family commitment to greater security are encouraged.

In the case example of Laura and her father Ray (Chapter 7), as the therapist continued treatment building on the father and daughter renewed bond of trust, Laura found greater confidence in her father's availability. In session she confided to her father about her recent experimentation with marijuana. Laura shared how she was facing significant peer pressure to fit in with her friends and their expectations. She then explained how she had tried cannabis at her mother's apartment, knowing that this was permitted in her home. Laura feared this was a step too far, as it reminded her of her sister's ongoing struggles with drug use. She felt guilty and concerned that her mother might share this with Ray in a future conflict. Father and daughter then discussed how Laura might find ways to avoid this situation and Ray offered to pick her up from her mother's apartment at any time that she wanted. They agreed on a plan to check in with each other about the pressure she was under. Laura also agreed to exploring a few after-school programs to broaden her network of friends. Ray felt relieved by Laura's honesty and acknowledged courage and trust in seeking his help. Laura felt reassured that she could talk to her dad without him going away or reacting in an intrusive and judgmental manner.

Family adjustment to parental discipline and guidance often result after families move away from the negative emotional climate of rigid patterns and blocked interactions. New family interactions focused on accessibility, responsiveness, and emotional engagement may require parents to revisit how they respond to specific situations and the strategies they use in these parenting situations. For example, James and Camille had adopted fixed positions in parenting their daughters with James taking a laissez-faire and distant approach. When conflicts erupted between Camille and their daughters James would intervene with harsh and demanding criticism of those involved in the conflict and then retreat. Angela (13) bore the brunt of his criticism and developed mood-related symptoms that disrupted her social and school activities. Through Stage 1 of EFFT the family identified the negative cycle that generated an unsafe and unpredictable environment. The relational blocks between Angela and James and the couple were identified and dyadic sessions focusing on the caregiving alliance enabled Camille and James to focus on being more responsive to Angela. Through Stage 2 Angela explored the hurt and fear that had accumulated with her father and her need for support from both parents, particularly James, as she had no longer felt safe turning to him for comfort or help. The therapist guided James and Angela to move from their shared under-responsive/minimizing block to a new pattern of Angela sharing her fears and James responding with comfort and reassurance. Through strengthening the caregiving alliance and resolving the block between James and Angela the family regained their emotional balance.

Still James preference for a laissez faire parental approach was stressful for Camille and often resulted in chaos or excessive parenting demands for Camille. Parenting issues took focus as Angela's symptoms resolved and the family agreed that the chaos was difficult particularly as family schedules became more complex. The girls often took advantage of their father's "nice guy" approach. James recognized the need to bring a firmer presence but feared he would trigger his daughter's fear. Camille offered her reassurance and support in those moments knowing that James felt he needed to protect others from his controlling side. In a family session, Camille and James discussed with their daughters how the parents were now working as a team and that dad was going to be saying "no" more and being more stringent on the rules to help manage the chaos and that the family needed to talk together when there were concerns rather than assuming that it was just a "mother's job" to manage the family. The daughters joked in the session whether the "new dad" would ever be as tough as mom and James laughed as he said "that sounds like a challenge, you better watch out, there's a new sheriff in town!"

Step 9—Consolidating Secure Cycles

Through EFFT families regain their emotional balance and find new resources at an emotional level. Family interactions characterized by more secure relating will demonstrate greater emotional engagement, increased parental availability, and child vulnerability. Families who navigate this process are more likely to report a change in the emotional climate of their family, shifting from chronic defensiveness or distance to new levels of positive engagement and warmth. Families are less likely to be triggered by negative interactions and when these experiences occur the family is less likely to be organized by these events. Instead, the family is more likely to organize around positive interactions and these new levels of security promote greater exploration and more effective problem solving. In Step 9 the therapist draws attention to new meaning in the family through changes in the family's emotional climate, changes in the family's identity, and intentional practices that promote attachment behavior.

Change in Family Climate

The shift toward security in the family promotes a more positive emotional family climate. The therapist reinforces cycles of positive affect that promote greater emotional balance and connection (Johnson, 2019). For example, caregivers who share support for one another and are themselves more secure are more likely to care for their children in sensitive and responsive ways (Cowan, Cohn, Cowan, & Pearson, 1992). Parental support and warmth are a resource to children's regulation of emotion and children who experience closeness and warmth are more likely to express their emotion which in turn promotes children's socio-emotional development (Morris, Silk, Steinberg, Myers, & Robinson, 2007). Through EFFT, the therapist targets emotional experience as a resource to promote change and contribute to the ultimate wellbeing of the family. In Step 9 the therapist elicits and expands positive affect associated with change and the security the family has now realized.

Change in Family Identity

As John Byng-Hall (1995) noted, the greater the felt security experienced by family members the greater the family environment is perceived as secure. Attachment-based treatments used in family intervention emphasize the ways in which attachment narratives provide prognostic indicators of attachment security (Kobak et al., 2013). For example, when an adolescent is able to rely on parents in a time of need and receive support in a way that results in the youth feeling supported and secure, one can say the young person has an attachment narrative of security. Through the EFFT stage of consolidation the therapist is leading the family in narrating a new "secure script" for the family.

In EFT (Johnson, 2004) the therapist assists the couple in forming a coherent narrative that encompasses the experience of treatment and the new-found understanding of their relationship. The ability to share a coherent story about one's attachment experience is a sign of security and a likely indicator of the ability to attune well to others' experience (Hesse, 1999). Dickstein (2004) found that among married parents the quality of their attachment relationship provided a proximal indicator for overall family functioning. Specifically, the author noted that couples with strong attachment told attachment narratives that were coherent stories of their relationship's growth and development over time. Secure couples also reflected on how individual growth occurred in the context of their relationships, and their interactions while not without negative experience were seldom if ever organized by these negative experiences.

These findings point to the EFT therapist's work in guiding a family toward narrating their new experiences of security as a family. The therapist frames the family's growth in terms of its success overcoming a rigid negative pattern that blocked family members from what they needed most. Positive cycles are highlighted and framed in contrast to past negative patterns to further instill a secure script focused on accessibility, responsiveness, and emotional engagement. Finally, the therapist works with couples and families to identify shifts and growth that has occurred as the family works through emotional blocks that shift how parents, partners, and child see themselves and others in the family. The fundamental EFT question "Will you be there for me when I need you most?" is asked and answered through the family's own growth.

Attachment Rituals

Rituals in relationships are a source of enacted meaning that provide a sense of belonging and value. In EFT attachment rituals are used to help couples to symbolize their investment in maintaining and deepening the felt security of their relationship (Johnson 2004; Johnson, Bradley, Furrow, Lee, Palmer, Tilley, & Wooley, 2005). As a ritual these practices provide predictable activities that commemorate the value of the security a couple shares. The meaning of a ritual determines its value more than the nature of the activities or timing that constitute its practice. The practice of these rituals provides families an intentional means to sustain and invest in their attachment bonds.

Family rituals provide resources that promote healthy development across the life span. Wolin and Bennett (1984) described the significant role rituals play in defining family identity through clarifying boundaries, informing roles, and articulating family rules. Rituals play a pivotal role in providing a sense of belonging and shared identity and support a means to maintain bonds over time (Crespo, Davide, Costa, & Fletcher, 2008; Eakers & Walters, 2002; Fiese, 1992, 2006; Fiese, Tomcho, Douglas, Josephs, Poltrock, & Baker, 2002). Among adolescents, Crespo and colleagues found that family rituals promoted self-esteem, belonging, and wellbeing (Crespo, Kielpikowski, Pryor, & Jose, 2011). Family rituals then provide active means for carrying out meaning that is intrinsic to a family's own story (Crespo, 2012). Rituals provide a rich resource in EFFT for symbolizing in practice the value found in attachment relationships.

In EFFT the therapist works with the family to identify activities related to connection. These may include times of transition (e.g., greeting, leaving), recognition and honor, or support and care. The purpose or meaning of the ritual should be made explicit as this differentiates a ritual from a routine activity (Fiese et al., 2002). The power of a ritual is a function of its unique meaning to a family and helping a family navigate a discussion of a shared activity requires family members to identify values and acknowledge differences within the family (Johnson et al., 2005). The EFT therapist's focus on symbolizing attachment-related meaning is an important component in the EFT tango in shaping understandings of inherent impact of self and system (Johnson, 2019).

EFT Interventions and Consolidation

EFT interventions used in the consolidation stage focus primarily on processing client experience and guiding family conversations in the treatment session. The therapist promotes opportunities for family members to explore growth as they face past problems and to engage new meaning through the new experiences they have as a family. Evocative interventions are necessary to highlight present experience and to focus family awareness on the positive emotions including the meaning they carry. Often these are the focus in positive patterns of engagement as family members find strength and value in more secure positions.

Evocative Interventions

Evocative interventions are used less often as the therapist's role is focused on processing and making meaning of the family's new inter-action patterns. The therapist uses evocative responding to highlight new experiences and expand the positive emotions that result from more secure interactions. For example, the therapist may slow a family conversation to focus on a child's more vulnerable response.

THERAPIST: What was it like when your daughter shared her fear with you? Something she has in the past, felt she had to hide from you.
FATHER: To be honest, it felt right. Natural, almost like I didn't notice until you said something.
THERAPIST: So, when she turns to you in this vulnerable moment. She is seeking your reassurance. What happens, when you see her doing this, especially as her father?
FATHER: I feel proud. Like I am her dad and I love that feeling. I can make a difference in her life—at least in this moment. I feel proud of her and proud to be her dad.

The therapist explores the impact of the daughter's attachment bid and contrasts this new response with the daughter's former self-protective response. The use of evocative responding helps to deepen the father's awareness of his own experience including his view of self and view of his daughter. The therapist might further consolidate the moment by having the father engage an enactment, inviting him to share this experience with his daughter furthering the father's ability to see his daughter, and also instilling greater confidence in the daughter's experience of her father's availability. These new experiences enable the therapist to heighten the positive emotions associated with these interactions and increase opportunities for more reflexive conversations that speak to both view of self and view of other.

Processing Interventions

A primary focus of consolidation is promoting a meta-perspective on the changes the family has achieved. Processing interventions invite family members to identify differences in the family's experience of trust, caregiving, and relevant support. The therapist uses reflection and validation to promote attention to new experiences and emphasize their importance to the family. For example, the therapist might reflect a family's sense of pride in seeing the growth they have accomplished. "It is so important that you can see what you have done, it took courage and commitment to fight for something better in your relationship together and now to be proud of what you have accomplished." The therapist instills positive emotion through reflection and validation of the family's success. Similarly, the therapist uses reframing interventions to highlight changes the family has made in facing attachment-related emotions and needs.

THERAPIST: So, in the past there was no conversation, just yelling and then silence, but today what you are describing is so very different. I mean the trigger was right there, but the cycle never started.

MOTHER: Yes, I could see it coming and I could feel her defensiveness. Then I remembered it may be fear. She may be afraid. Just see her fear ... is what I said to myself. So, I was quiet, and I listened, and her anger turned to tears.

THERAPIST: Right. This is so different because the old pattern would have you challenging her demand, calling her disrespect. But you saw something different this time. This is what is new. You could see her fear even if it was angry fear. The old pattern did not take over, you were there for her. You were strong in a different way, in a way she needed.

Through framing the mother's new response and contrasting her availability against her more defensive position in the cycle the therapist highlights the mother's new position and its impact. The therapist could invite the mother into further reflection by conjecturing about how the mother sees herself in her caregiving at that moment.

It's almost like, a part of you knew how to be strong against her anger, but you found another part of being a mom, that could be strong with her anger, and even more with her fear. What's does this say about you as a mom?

The therapist could also shift the frame to a relationship question, asking the daughter and mother: "What does this now say about both of you that you can face this fear together?"

In this example, the therapist acknowledges that triggers may return and that self-protective responses are typical. However, when a family has a way of seeing these triggering moments in less threatening ways and when they have more resources for acknowledging what may actually be happening at a deeper level in these moments, they are less likely to lose their emotional balance. The following case example illustrates the EFT therapist's focus on meaning and the active engagement of family members using evocative and processing intervention to bring closure to the treatment process and new views of the family.

Step 9—Case Example

The Park family sought family therapy after discovering their eldest daughter Emily (16) was struggling with self-harming behaviors, hopelessness, and aggressive behaviors at home. The family participated in seven sessions of EFFT treatment including sessions with the parents, Emily, and her three other siblings (Kevin [13], Alice [11], and David [7]). The parents initially sought individual treatment for Emily but after discussing the home-related distress the family agreed to conjoint treatment. The family was highly structured in their actions and appeared to rely on rules to foster order and loyalty as a family.

The EFFT assessment session highlighted the negative interaction which centered on episodes of Emily's anger often directed toward her mother's intrusive or controlling actions followed by intervention by the father to restore peace and order. Tensions in the family related to changes in stressors associated with changes in schooling for the two oldest children who coped with these changes in equal and opposite directions. Emily would protest and challenge her parent's decisions and attitudes, where Kevin preferred a more rational approach focused on non-emotional logical arguments. Consequently, neither child clearly expressed their fears or vulnerability directly, and the resulting negative interactional patterns created family discord and a chronically tense family environment.

Treatment progressed quickly for the moderately distressed family. Emily's mother expressed her fear to approach Emily and trust her judgment. Mother also shared her sadness of not being effective in responding to Emily's needs, which was her ultimate intention. Emily responded asserting her need for her mother's trust and her confidence that she would ask for help when she needed it. In turn, the parents' attention shifted to Peter's isolation in the family and failed efforts to reach him after support for his upcoming school transition faltered. Through sessions with the son, both parents were responsive to the fears he expressed regarding his social difficulties and transition to a new school. For example, his father shared from his own challenges at a similar time in his life which promoted a more vulnerable bond between the father and son, who while interacting often, seldom connected at a deeper level. Through the treatment the couple met for a conjoint session to discuss their own struggles as parents and the ways in which they often were divided by the challenges of the family. In these sessions, the couple's personal challenges from the spill-over demands of parenting, schooling, and work left each partner feeling distant and uncertain, which neither had acknowledged. Following the couple through the EFT tango the couple reconnected around their shared commitment to each other and their children.

The final session included both parents and Emily and Kevin. The tension that defined the initial family meeting was strikingly absent as the parents joined one another on the couch with Emily and Kevin at their side. The atmosphere was playful between the siblings as mother and father settled into the session, trying to offer a few serious observations about the changes they saw taking place in the family. Emily shared that she "trusted her mother more" and that she also felt like she could be more vulnerable. In her words, the "family had gotten much better" at which her brother Kevin teased her for giving the answer the therapist was expecting to hear. Interrupting, mother shared how she saw Emily opening up more and that the conversations they shared helped her understand her daughter better, which was a source of relief.

The therapist highlighted these changes and focused on the ways mother and daughter were finding greater trust together and Emily was finding mother's interest and support something she could rely on. She teasingly tapped her mother's shoulder saying: "I feel like I have somewhere to go to ... I have my sidekick." After further evoking the mother's response to the daughter's reassurance, the therapist invited her to share this with her daughter. "I love you, Emily. And I accept you and I hope even when you don't feel this way you will count on my love for you." The therapist framed the mother's support in contrast to the times Emily felt unwanted and unworthy in her mother's eyes. The father then interjected, voicing his appreciation for Kevin's help in understanding what Kevin needed from the family. The therapist framed the father's appreciation as an invitation for more vulnerable conversations going forward, which the therapist contrasted with the more "business like" manner with which the family had dealt with the son's school transition.

As the session moved to conclusion, the mother tearfully shared what she felt was the lesson her family was teaching her.

> We have to relearn how to be a family ... we can no longer travel as a pack. We need to start to move in separate ways ... and that is hard for me, because I loved when we were able to all just be together.

The mother's sadness over the transitions that middle adolescence was bringing to the family were framed as an expression of love and connection. She expressed her fear that somehow through all the changes they would lose what it meant to be a close family. Her husband in response comforted her with reassurance and a hug reminding her that as parents they would find a way together to be close even as their children began their own journeys. The therapist concluded treatment by focusing on the shifts the family had made toward greater vulnerability and stronger availability, and as a result a secure base for their future.

Termination

EFFT is typically a short-term treatment process concluding in fewer than 10 session. Termination processes are less complex as a result. Still families show concern for leaving the support and structure of the EFFT process. The therapist invites the family to discuss their transition from treatment. Evocative strategies are useful in naming the family members' fears and making space for the family to process these questions together. The therapist encourages the family to hold their fears together, and to be explicit about circumstances that would require more support.

Termination of a family process may transition to couple therapy when issues in the couple's relationship extend beyond the resolution of family distress. It is important for the therapist to clarify the treatment contract and future process when transitioning to couple therapy independent of family treatment as in many ways EFFT may provide a logical transition to EFCT for devitalized couples. Through EFFT parents are working through blocks to attachment responses that also influence their romantic relationships. In this way, the process of EFFT can move couples more quickly to the restructuring stage of the EFCT process.

Parents may look for ongoing resources to continue to strengthen and invest in the progress they have made in building more secure bonds. The therapist may refer parents to additional resources that focus on attachment-related parenting resources (e.g., Neufeld & Mate, 2004; Siegel, 2014; Siegel & Hartzell, 2003).

EFT-Related Enrichment Programs

Couples and families may also benefit from EFT-related enrichment programs designed to strengthen attachment bonds in couples and families. *Hold me tight* (Johnson 2008) was developed as a practical educational resource for couples that includes practical conversations and exercises that mirror the EFT process. Hold me tight (HMT) group workshops were developed to offer community-based psychoeducational programs that have demonstrated efficacy in improving couple relationship satisfaction (Conradi, Dingemanse, Noordhof, Finkenauer, & Kamphuis, 2017; Wong, Greenman, & Beaudoin, 2018).

Hold me tight: Let me go (HMT/LMG; Aiken & Aiken, 2017), based on Johnson's HMT program, offers families of adolescent children a structured program that guides families through a series of lessons, discussions, and conversation exercises that mirrors the aims of EFFT. The program goals of HMT/LMG include fostering a deeper understanding of the overarching role of attachment as an organizing principle in family relationships. A second goal focuses on increasing family members' understanding of each other's emotional responses and family experiences. The third program goal highlights the negative interaction patterns in the family. A final goal involves actively engaging parent and youth in experiences that promote security through accessibility, responsiveness, and emotional engagement. The following case example was provided by Paul and Nancy Aiken.

HMT/LMG Case Example

Jessica's mother, Claire, suggested they attend an HMT/LMG workshop after finding that recent conversations about Jessica's academic work and priorities were resulting in unresolved conflicts. Jessica (18) routinely concluded that her mother did not understand her life and had unrealistic demands and expectations compared to her peers. Overall, Jessica enjoyed success in academics and athletics, until a series of poor school marks. Jessica's father Drew, joined Claire and Jessica at the workshop.

The program began with a parent session focused on parental caregiving and partners' caregiving alliance. Claire recognized through discussion and exercises that she and Jessica were caught in a negative pattern, which she explained to Drew using a recent example.

CLAIRE: I got an email from school and there was a concern about a drop in Jess's grades in several classes. I panicked and when Jess got home from school I confronted her about it and I offended her. She locked herself in her room for hours. I felt like I was a horrible mom, so I kept trying to fix it but Jess is keeping me at a distance.

Through the parent session Claire and Drew discussed how they wanted to be more responsive and supportive of Jessica and how Drew could be a resource to Claire when she was plagued with self-doubt in her parenting. Claire and Drew practiced having a conversation focused on mutual support in their caregiving. As a parenting team they identified a common pattern that was occurring with Claire and Jessica. Claire saw clearly how her fear fueled her reactive response to Jessica and how her anger turned to criticism when Jessica withdrew, and Claire's self-doubts and shame kept her engaged with Jessica when she wanted to be left alone.

The following session included parents with youth and following a series of joining exercises the youth were invited to initiate a conversation focused on a recent family conflict. Jessica independently brought up "mom's drama moment" about her grades. Through structured discussion Jessica identified her trigger and why she went away.

JESSICA: I could see you were upset when I walked in the house and before I could say a word you were like: "what's happening," "why did the school have to call," "you should have told us," "what else are you hiding."

Together Jessica and her parents walked through the experience making sense of the actions, perceptions, and emotions that played out between them. Jessica said she knew that her mother cared but in that moment the criticism and judgment made Jessica feel diminished, like a child, and then she withdrew. Jessica explained: "Please consult with me, ask me, talk to me about what I think is going on. I'm 18, can we have a more adult to adult-like conversation?" Claire listened carefully and acknowledged that she had over-reacted and rushed to judge Jessica. Claire apologized and shared her wish for a different kind of conversation. Drew expressed his appreciation for their taking time to talk through this rough spot and all three were relieved and feeling more connected after talking through the conflict.

In HMT/LMG a final exercise is used to invite family members to revisit the previous conversation from a position of greater vulnerability. In this exercise, Jessica is asked to revisit that moment where she felt fear or hurt, and in that moment she said: "My mom doesn't care about me." Following a guided exercise Jessica identified the painful feeling she felt when her mother did not see her and was invited to share the deeper impact of that moment. She then followed with a specific, clear, attachment-related statement of her need.

JESSICA: (softly but confidently) Next time please do not make assumptions about what is going on with me—do not criticize or judge me—just be curious—please ask me what I am aware of—ask me directly what is going on with me and trust that I will be honest with you.

Claire acknowledged her request and expressed regret for hurting Jessica with her judgmental words and fears. Jessica reached toward both parents in reassurance of the connection they shared made now more explicit through vulnerably facing a relationship rupture.

HMT/LMG provides families an opportunity to revisit relational challenges that are common in parent and adolescent relationships where the goals of autonomy and safety need to be navigated, relationally. Following the EFFT model, the program enables families to identity the negative patterns and relational blocks that distort attachment communication, then focuses on the caregiving resources and attachment-related emotions to revisit blocked opportunities for care, connection, and support. Focusing on the caregiving and attachment resources, families are guided toward repair and a more secure pattern of relationship.

Summary

The consolidation stage of EFFT enables families an opportunity to intentionally focus on the growth they have achieved in strengthening the connections they share. The therapist actively facilitates the processing of positive experiences to further articulate the impact and importance of the new patterns of security the family has achieved. Family members share in this process together as they make sense of how their family has changed and steps they may make to invest more purposefully in sustaining and deepening their felt security. The EFFT process ultimately focuses on the resolution of relational blocks and negative family patterns to redirect the trajectory of the family toward its future, particularly at a developmental level. As such the EFFT process sets the family on a new course and in the consolidation stage the EFT therapist works with this family to recognize both how far they have come but also where they are set to go into their future, together.

EFFT Practice Points

The following process points highlight the final steps in the EFFT process of change. The therapist strengthens the bonds that the family have made through addressing past problems from new positions of greater security and consolidating the changes made to attain the safety and security the family now shares.

1. The therapist invites the family to address problems that persist through working through blocks that may occur as these past problems are confronted.
2. The therapist uses new awareness and renewed confidence in child vulnerability to parental confidence to explore new solutions.
3. The therapist promotes family activities that further invest and explore in new levels of safety and security. The therapist uses enactments and attachment rituals to promote family efforts to further strengthen the attachment bonds strengthened through EFFT.
4. The therapist guides the family through making meaning of the changes the family have achieved through contrasting how the

family has changed through treatment, gaining greater flexibility
and deeper felt understanding of family needs and resources.
5. The therapist may recommend psychoeducational resources to
promote family efforts to continue to strengthen the family's bonds
of connection and resources for growth.

References

Aiken, N., & Aiken, P. (2017). *Hold me Tight/Let me Go program: Facilitators'
guide.* Ottawa: International Centre for Excellence in Emotionally Focused
Therapy.

Allen, J. P. (2008). The attachment system in adolescence. In J. Cassidy & P. R.
Shaver (Eds.), *Handbook of attachment: Theory, research, and clinical
applications* (pp. 419–435). New York: Guilford Press.

Byng-Hall, J. (1995). Creating a secure family base: Some implications of attachment theory for family therapy. *Family Process, 34,* 45–58.

Conradi, H. J., Dingemanse, P., Noordhof, A., Finkenauer, C., & Kamphuis,
J. H. (2017). Effectiveness of the "Hold me Tight" relationship enhancement
program in a self-referred and a clinician-referred sample: An emotionally
focused couples therapy-based approach. *Family Process, 57,* 613–628.

Cowan, P. A., Cohn, D. A., Cowan, C. P., & Pearson, J. L. (1996). Parents'
attachment histories and children's externalizing and internalizing behaviors:
Exploring family systems models of linkage. *Journal of Consulting and Clinical Psychology, 64,* 53–63.

Crespo, C. (2012). Families as contexts for attachment: Reflections on theory,
research, and the role of family rituals. *Journal of Family Theory Review, 4,*
290–298.

Crespo, C., Davide, I. N., Costa, M. E., & Fletcher, J. O. (2008). Family rituals
in married couples: Links with attachment, relationship quality, and closeness. *Journal of Personal Relationships, 15,* 191–203.

Crespo, C., Kielpikowski, M., Pryor, J., & Jose, P. E. (2011). Family rituals in
New Zealand families: Links to family cohesion and adolescents' well-being.
Journal of Family Psychology, 25, 184–193.

Dallos, R. (2006). *Attachment narrative therapy.* Maidenhead: McGraw-Hill
Education.

Dickstein, S. (2004). Marital attachment and family functioning: Use of narrative methodology. In M. Pratt and B. Fiese (Eds.) *Family Stories and the
Life Course.* (pp. 213–234). Mahwah, NJ: Lawrence Erlbaum.

Eakers, D. G., & Walters, L. H. (2002). Adolescent satisfaction in family rituals
and psychosocial development: A developmental systems theory perspective.
Journal of Family Psychology, 16, 406–414.

Fiese, B. H. (1992). Dimensions of family rituals across two generations: Relation to adolescent identity. *Family Process, 31,* 151–162.

Fiese, B. H., Tomcho, T. J., Douglas, M., Josephs, K., Poltrock, S., & Baker, T.
(2002). A review of 50 years of research on naturally occurring family routines
and rituals: Cause for celebration? *Journal of Family Psychology, 16,* 381–390.

Fiese, B. H. (2006). *Family routines and rituals.* New Haven, CT: Yale University Press.

Hesse, E. (1999). The adult attachment interview. In J. Cassidy & P. R. Shaver (Eds.), *Handbook of attachment* (pp. 395–433). New York: Guilford Press.

Johnson, S. M. (2004). *The practice of emotionally focused therapy: Creating connection*, 2nd Ed. New York: Brunner/Routledge.

Johnson, S. M., Bradley, B., Furrow, J., Lee, A., Palmer, G., Tilley, D., & Wooley, S. (2005). *Becoming an emotionally focused couple therapist: The workbook*. New York: Brunner-Routledge.

Johnson, S. (2008). *Hold me tight: Seven conversations for a lifetime of love*. London: Hachette.

Kobak, R., Grassetti, S. N., & Yarger, H. A. (2013). Attachment based treatment for adolescents: Repairing attachment injuries and empathic failures. In K. H. Birsch (Ed.) *Attachment and adolescence* (pp. 93–111). Stuttgart: Klett-Cotta Verlag.

Morris, A. S., Silk, J. S., Steinberg, L., Myers, S. S., & Robinson, L. R. (2007). The role of the family context in the development of emotion regulation. *Social Development, 16*, 361–388.

Neufeld, G., & Mate, G. (2004). *Hold on to your kids: Why parents need to matter more than peers*. New York: Ballentine Books.

Siegel, D. J. (2014). *Brainstorm: The power and purpose of the teenage brain*. New York: Penguin.

Siegel, D. J., & Hartzell, M. (2003). *Parenting from the inside out: How a deeper self-understanding can help you raise children who thrive*. New York: Penguin Books.

Wolin, S. J., & Bennett, L. A. (1984). Family rituals. *Family Process, 23*, 401–420.

Wong, T. Y., Greenman, P. S., & Beaudoin, V. (2018) "Hold Me Tight": The generalizability of an attachment-based group intervention to Chinese Canadian couples. *Journal of Couple & Relationship Therapy, 17*, 42–60.

PART III

EXPLORING
CLINICAL REALITIES

NINE

Case Example—EFFT and Treating an Internalizing Disorder

Internalizing problems with children and adolescents represent a serious mental health problem given the dire consequences that can unfold with untreated anxiety and depressive disorders. These problems may be invisible to others, but a suffering child or adolescent is facing exaggerated feelings of guilt and negative core beliefs about self, often leaving the child believing that he or she is a failure or unlovable (Reinecke, Dattilo, & Freeman, 2003). When unacknowledged these experiences of anxiety and depression become fixed internal perceptions of self that are codified in negativity. This negativity generalizes to relationships with others and a youth's ability to function and succeed in school and work, and at the most severe level, impacting a child's will to live.

A child's family relationships are integral to an understanding of the role of negative emotion and a child's ability to cope. Internalizing problems are defined as "problems of emotion or mood caused by difficulties regulating negative emotions" (Graber, 2004). Family relations provide an essential resource in a child's development of emotional regulation. As emotional regulation develops primarily in the context of the child's relationship with his or her parents, it makes sense to include the family in the treatment of these problems (Southam-Gerow, 2007). Treatment approaches to date have had uneven results with Cartwright-Hatton and Murray (2008) reporting that "even in well-resourced treatment trials, barely half of all cases remit." Typically, treatment protocols have involved cognitive-behavioural interventions with children and adolescents, without any direct participation of parents (Compton et al., 2014). EFFT focuses on the most vital resource to children, their family, and helps make visible and audible the problems these children face with the people that matter the most. By strengthening the attachment bonds and opening up the caregiving system, the child is less isolated, the family conflict that may be contributing to the symptoms is reduced and the child is resourced through the love and care of his/her parents.

The map of EFFT suggests that the more secure an adolescent's relationship with his family members, specifically his caretakers, the more independent and confident this individual is in exploring her environment

(Johnson, Maddeaux, & Blouin, 1998; Johnson, 2004). Research has shown that insecure attachment, by itself, will not invariably lead to anxiety or depression, but impacting an adolescent's relationship environment is a moderating factor that a relationship-focused treatment like EFFT could influence (Brumariu & Kerns, 2010; Siegel, 2013). The EFT therapist works to create a therapeutic environment that is safe and scaffolds emotional conversations that are transparent, clear, and regulated. By processing the relational blocks that exist in distressed interactions between parents and children, the EFT therapist opens up the caregiving system, and provides key healing opportunities for troubled adolescents. The following case example was provided by Gail Palmer.

The Case of Tina and the Baxter Family

"We're Not On The Same Page"

Tina, age 17, came to therapy at the request of her parents, Mike and Deb Baxter, following a serious suicide attempt. Mike and Deb have been married for over 25 years. Mike and Deb sought treatment for Tina, who was attending college and living at home. Their eldest child, Josh, had completed post-secondary education but had been unable to find employment and was not involved with the family. Tina's career choice in her college program was in the same profession as her father and she had just transitioned from high school to college.

Assessment

The parents were seen alone for the initial session as they wanted to ensure that the therapist was aware of Tina's early history and were also needing to debrief the trauma surrounding Tina's suicide attempt. Both Mike and Deb were terrified that they had almost lost their daughter to a drug overdose. Following an overnight stay at the hospital, Tina refused to discuss the event and wanted her parents to "move on." The therapist supported the parents in the retelling of the story, validating their courage and ability to support each other with their fear and guilt related to this crisis. Both Deb and Mike were feeling inadequate in their parenting roles and felt they had failed both Tina and her older brother, Josh.

After Tina's release from the hospital, Mike and Deb were distraught and traumatized by these events and concerned that Tina refused individual treatment following the overdose. The parents also reported that Tina was sexually molested when she was eight years old by an extended family member. Both Mike and Deb were unclear about the details of what had happened although formal charges were filed at the time. In their words, "Tina changed after this. She became distant from her father because she hated all men." Tina, at age 12, was hospitalized for the treatment of a serious eating disorder.

Deb was currently receiving individual psychotherapy and her therapist made the referral for family therapy. Both Mike and Deb were open to family intervention and to help around learning how to talk to their adolescent children. They were uncertain whether Josh would attend family treatment as he had participated in family therapy when his sister was recovering from her eating disorder and stated that he would not "do that again." The caregiving alliance was strained between Mike and Deb and the couple stated they were on separate pages since Tina was eight. At that time, Mike supported his family members rather than his daughter. Deb was left alone in trying to help her daughter. She tried to engage Mike in this crisis, but he refused to talk about it with her. Many fights ensued between the couple at that time and Deb reported that she would "scream and yell" at Mike, attacking him and his character. Mike would remain stoic and would stonewall his wife. Deb stated she was no longer angry with Mike and felt guilty for the fights that had ensued between them at the time of Tina's sexual assault. Mike was also regretful for the actions he had taken at the time and was open to finding a way to talk to Tina about the past.

Josh refused to attend the sibling session and consequently Tina was seen alone in the assessment session. In this session, Tina stated that she did not want to talk about herself and that she was attending the session because her parents had asked her to come. She said she was finished with mental health professionals and that she was focused on moving on with her life. She reported that she felt better since the suicide attempt and thought that perhaps the seizures had helped to clear her mind. She stated that she hadn't intended to kill herself, that her action was impulsive, driven by a desperate need for her parents to listen to her. She stated that her parents did not hear her, and that they did what they needed to do despite what she wanted them to do. Tina talked the whole session in a self-contained, cool kind of way, stating that she didn't want to get angry anymore and that she really needed to concentrate on herself.

The therapist focused on accepting and making sense of Tina's external world, emphasizing her strengths and acknowledging her relationship with her parents, including her willingness to attend therapy even though this was not her own idea. The therapist gently invited Tina to explore more about what was happening in the family that was creating problems and an inability to communicate. Tina agreed to a family session which we scheduled for the following week. Given the gravity of Tina's suicide attempt, her refusal to engage in individual treatment, and the distress of the parents, family therapy was thought to be the optimal treatment plan.

Initial Family Session

The EFT therapist began this session by inviting the family to talk together, about how things are going, stating that they had shared the past events and the history, separately, but now was their chance to talk together. The mother, Deb, needed help from the therapist to focus on talking directly about her family. By validating the mother's need to "be on the same page" with her husband and daughter, the therapist was able to highlight how this is not always the case, reflecting her physical position of being in the middle between Mike and Tina. Deb was then able to say: "I am hoping that Tina begins to see that we are not terrible parents." Mike professed that his daughter was well aware that they were there for her and talking about his relationship with Tina stated: "We have a distant relationship, that we understand, even though I don't like it, but that I have established a relationship with Tina without speaking." The therapist emphasized that his "heart's desire" and hope was that Tina would know that they are there for her, eliciting and reinforcing his parental intent to caretake his child. The therapist then made room for Tina to speak and she began by saying "this family word, is pretty well non-existent."

The therapist sought to understand each person's perspective on the family while tracking the unfolding interactional patterns keeping the family in distress. There was an entrenched cycle between Mike, Deb, and Tina that had existed for several years. There had been little direct contact between Mike and Tina as she would walk out of the room if her father came near her. Tina avoided her father's gaze and addressed all of her concerns directly to her mother. Deb was both mediator and translator for Tina and Mike. If Mike wanted to say something to his daughter, he would ask his wife to transmit the message. Deb would keep Mike informed of what was happening to his daughter but there were times that Mike did not want to hear. Deb insisted that Tina had problems that she needed to work on and that she resented being in the middle between her husband and her daughter. Mike felt that Deb was overprotective of Tina and would interfere between him and the children. Both parents presented as overwhelmed and distressed, Mike talking rapidly and profusely and Deb being quieter yet visibly saddened by the telling of her family story. Tina's position in the cycle was explored more using the first two moves of the EFT tango (Johnson, 2019):

THERAPIST: So, it's like they have a game plan, or I don't know, how you would describe it? They are talking together about how to approach you and you are saying, "if you have something to say then say it" because if they can't say it direct, then what does that say to you? (*first move of EFT tango, mirroring present process; father attempts to interrupt and therapist blocks father's interruption*) I need you to hold on (*to Tina*) what does that say to you?

TINA: Yeah, I don't want to deal with all the drama, if you have something to say to me, say it to me, so we can move on.

THERAPIST: (*slowly, gently*) Yeah, it's like you are saying I don't want the drama because when there is drama about me, I don't know about you, but I might be feeling like there is something wrong with me? (*Tina visibly sad, head down*) Yeah. You help me Tina, is that what you end up feeling? (*raises her head to meet the therapist's gaze*) Yeah that's true. (*2nd move of EFT tango, affect assembly and deepening*)

THERAPIST: (*more animated*) Is it that my parents can't talk to me? Is there something wrong with me? (*heightening primary affect*)

TINA: I am sometimes told that I have major issues, that I need to grow up. I hear sometimes some pretty mean things, but I don't say anything.

THERAPIST: (*focusing on present moment, empathic conjecture*) Right, but right now you are saying that impacts you, to hear those things.

TINA: Yes, but at the same time because I am growing up and because of the field I am going into, I don't let it bug me, I don't react anymore the way I used to.

THERAPIST: Sure, you have a way to cope, yes, you move on, but underneath all of that is this hurt to hear some mean things about you, of course you need to move on.

TINA: I don't get mad.

THERAPIST: Yeah like you don't get mad anymore because you don't want to have the big drama, you don't want to get mad but usually when we get mad there is hurt underneath but now you just don't say anything.

The blocks to the parental responsiveness were identified and touched on in this session. The therapist invited Deb to talk about her own emotional experience in her family, apart from her role as peace keeper for Mike and Tina. As she moved away from talking from either her husband's or her daughter's perspective, she began to touch her grief.

MOTHER: (*in tears*) Yeah, like the relationships are broken, Mike doesn't talk to Tina, Tina and Josh don't talk, and I don't know how it all happened, we weren't that kind of family, we were always together. (*Deb's grief was acknowledged by the therapist and connected to how she protected herself from feeling that grief through her role as mediator and translator*)

THERAPIST: So that makes so much sense then, it is so much better to focus on trying to fix things in the family between your husband and daughter, than to feel this kind of loss? This loss of togetherness that you guys once had?

Mike's position in the family was either to blow-up or withdraw when he was unhappy. He would get frustrated with his kids and his wife and try to fix all the problems in an effort to avoid the "horrible" guilt and shame he was feeling. The therapist explored Mike's more vulnerable feelings of shame and guilt in an effort to help him identify the block that stood in the way of his ability to communicate with his daughter following the moves of the EFT tango.

FATHER: I think every morning about my kids and how to fix it. It's with me every moment of the day.

THERAPIST: The horrible feeling, is not having a talking relationship, the loss of Daddy's girl, you can't talk to her because you have this horrible feeling that stands in the way.

FATHER: Yeah that is the worst of it that we don't talk.

THERAPIST: Yeah, and then this has happened. It hasn't happened out of nowhere and I am wondering if you are also wondering what it has been like from Tina's side. (*promoting parental accessibility*)

FATHER: I think about it all the time.

THERAPIST: Yeah but because of the cycle you guys are caught in, you don't talk, you don't tell her you think about her all the time and that you miss your relationship with her? Yes? You try to fix it, make it better because maybe if you could do that, what would that do? (*mirror present process*)

FATHER: She would be happier.

THERAPIST: And if she was happier, what would happen to that horrible feeling? Maybe you would feel better as dad too? (*empathic conjecture, affect assembly and deepening*)

FATHER: (*eyes fill with tears*) I am here for her, I want to be there for her.

THERAPIST: Yeah that moves you, how much you want to be there for her. Can you tell her now how that feels? (*engaging encounter through an enactment*)

FATHER: (*to Tina*) You know I think about you, I try to be there for you, you know that. (*Tina rolls her eyes and looks away*)

THERAPIST: I can see, Tina, this is hard, to talk directly, (*processing impact of enenactment*) I just asked you to do something that you haven't done in years, and I am sure there are very good reasons for why this has happened, and that its why we are here, we need to figure this out together. I see the pain you are all in, and of course you would be. Mom, you feel the loss of your family and how it was and dad you have this "horrible feeling" and loss of a talking relationship with your daughter and for you Tina, talking is hard because there is drama or you hear mean things about you, so of course, you want to stay away from that. (*fifth move of EFT tango integrating and validating*)

Further exploration of the family dynamic and how it evolved, revealed that Tina's sexual abuse constituted an attachment injury for the family as it was a watershed moment when the security in the family was redefined. Mike and Deb were alienated from each other as to who they supported, Mike's first family or their family. The couple's conflict left Tina alone and she was given mixed messages by her parents about her abuse. They questioned her, took her to doctors, and did little to help their little girl make sense of what happened and give a clear message that it was wrong. Today they were still not able to talk together about this event. Tina insisted she had talked to her parents in the past about what had happened, yet they had not listened to her and the parents stated that they had never been told either by Tina or the doctors who treated her. This dynamic kept the family stuck, disconnected, and unable to progress. The parents were locked into their own shame and guilt and Tina felt isolated, alone, and defective.

Parent Session

The next session, the EFT therapist worked with parents alone to help them deal directly with what had happened to Tina as a little girl and begin to face their own blocks to accepting what had happened. In this session, Mike tearfully revealed that he had been abused as a child and had never spoken about this experience until recently with Deb, who was supportive of her husband and understood how he had been paralyzed in his own caregiving of his daughter due to his own denial of his abuse. The therapist validated the strength and courage the couple were demonstrating in opening up the past and facing the trauma together. They were encouraged to rely on their new-found security as a couple to face directly what had happened to their daughter. The parents' defensive reactions had been to minimize, deny, and confuse the trauma. The therapist validated how these defenses protected them from facing the harsh reality of the daughter's abuse and identified that their protection isolated Tina. They were helped to see that Tina desperately needed to be seen and validated by them without questions, or investigation. The parents were encouraged to put aside their defensive responses and empathically respond to Tina through acceptance and understanding. By the end of this session, Mike and Deb showed openness to approaching Tina in a new way with the therapist's support and the plan for the next session was that they would take the initiative to have a different conversation with their daughter.

Second Family Session

The next family session the therapist began the session summarizing the stuck feeling of the family's interactional pattern and leaned into the positive caregiving intent that the parents had expressed in their separate session. Tina was congratulated in her courage and strength to attend this session, given how difficult the last session had been and the parents were invited to talk directly to Tina about the past. The therapist introduced the topic by referring to attachment injuries that can happen in families and that keep them stuck and unable to feel secure and connected to one another.

FATHER: Yeah there were a lot of things that happened and Tina says she doesn't want to go back but there are a lot of things we have tried to move forward on and one of those things is the situation with our outside family, with things that happened when she was young, I don't think that I addressed it properly, I never addressed it with Tina, that she was hurt and I wish I was more in tune, I didn't realize how much damage I was doing to Tina, ... (*looking at Tina, speaking softly*) I am sorry about what happened. It wasn't right. I wasn't thinking right.

THERAPIST: And you feel that sorry now for not letting her know that it was wrong and that you did not support her.

FATHER: I think about it more now than I did then. I have had a lot of time to think about all of those things that happened. I can't go back but I wish I had been there more for her. But I can't see pain, unless it is bleeding, I couldn't see.

THERAPIST: At that time, you didn't see clearly, you didn't see what was happening to Tina.

FATHER: I wasn't aware of myself and my own abuse.

THERAPIST: Not being able to look at yourself blinded you from seeing Tina. And you were trying to stay away from pain of the abuse that you experienced.

FATHER: And pretending it wasn't there, trying to move on, just keep moving on, hope it would go away, and it didn't. It didn't go away.

THERAPIST: Right, your way of protecting yourself from the pain of your abuse kept you from seeing your daughter's pain. The more you didn't look at yourself, the more you couldn't see your daughter.

FATHER: And it wasn't right. I should have been there.

THERAPIST: I hear you. Right now, you are sharing with your daughter what happened to you and how that blinded you from seeing her. Can you tell her?

FATHER: (*tearfully, looking at Tina*) I just wish I was more there for you, and I am trying to make it up because I know that you must have gone through hell, and I just wasn't there for you. You were a complete victim and I am proud of who you are.

THERAPIST: (*leans toward Tina*) You can't look at him right now?

TINA: (*shakes her head no*)

THERAPIST: (*softly*) This is too hard, but he is saying some important things, he is saying he wasn't there for you. And the sadness and sorrow you're feeling (*looking at father*) is all about how precious she is and the sorrow you feel for letting your little girl down, (*to Tina*) and for you Tina to see your father's sadness, if you were going to look at his face, you would see his tears, that's what you would see, because he cares about you. (*framing caregiving intent and priming underlying emotion*)

FATHER: (*crying*) I am so sorry. (*Tina smiles and looks away*)

THERAPIST: And for you to feel this is about you, this is about your pain.

TINA: (*looks at Mother*) Why is everybody crying? I don't like this ... ugh (*holding herself*).

The therapist accepted Tina's block and helped her make sense of how she wasn't able to take in her father's sadness right now and supported Mike working through his shame. Instead of withdrawing or trying to fix the situation, Mike acknowledged his failure to be with his daughter when she needed him most. Mike's sadness regarding not seeing Tina's pain was voiced and he was then able to initiate a repair directly with Tina, by expressing his sorrow and regret directly.

MOTHER: I just feel his sadness.

TINA: It feels like it is on me.

THERAPIST: All this emotion is not your fault. It's not your fault. Your father is feeling this because he cares about you and when we care, we feel sadness when we hurt the people we love. I know you care too. It's hard to see your father in pain. But he is strong enough to shed these tears.

MOTHER: That was very hard for him—I know he has been wanting to say it.

THERAPIST: (*to Tina*) and you didn't feel any of this at the time, you went through this by yourself, you had to be strong all by yourself. (*validating and making sense of Tina's block*)

Although, Tina was confused and disturbed by her father's sorrow, Deb was able to support her husband by acknowledging his pain and she affirmed his desire to openly share his more vulnerable experience with Tina. In the parents' session, the parents' divide over what happened when Tina was eight was fully processed. Mike was able to share more directly with his wife what had stood in the way of his not seeing his daughter's pain, including his own abuse as a child. Deb could then soften in her own anger of being deserted by Mike at this time and shared how her own anger created more conflict and divide for the family. Mike and Deb came to this family session, with their parental alliance repaired and strengthened. The therapist then moved to work with Tina more directly with her block to receiving her father's message.

THERAPIST: So, having your father reach for you like this, it's like really? really? I don't know where to put this?

TINA: Yeah.

THERAPIST: I don't know how to understand it, because you went through that by yourself and you had to develop your own way of dealing with it. Don't feel, just put one foot ahead of the other and be strong, which is what you did, right? You wouldn't have made it in any other way, because you had to go on. Do you see, I know it is hard to look at your father, but you hear his sorrow, can you help me, what's that like to see his caring.

TINA: (*silence*) I want to say it's a bit late.

THERAPIST: Sure, that is perfectly legitimate that you would feel this way and (*using proxy voice*) maybe "I don't want to say that because I don't want to hurt him."

TINA: I mean like it is nice to see that things are being acknowledged now but it's something I have resolved.

THERAPIST: Right, right, so it's kind of like you have moved on, and like where were you dad? Is that it?

TINA: Yeah, yeah.

THERAPIST: And for you to say that right now, Yes, I can see dad how you feel but do you realize what I went through? For you to say that, you would feel that your father couldn't hear that?

TINA: (*shaking her head*) No, it doesn't make sense. It's too late.

THERAPIST: Because he said that he is sorry that he wasn't there, and for your dad to feel his sorrow also opens the door for you to feel it. But that's not going to solve it, right? You have your own experience with this and because you were alone and went through a lot of it alone. It's kind of like you are saying: How can you be there today when I was all alone. And keeping your door shut you are saying "I don't want to go back." (*therapist uses proxy voice and organizes and makes sense of Tina's block*)

TINA: I do need to move on.

At this juncture, the therapist works to help process Tina's block to receiving her father's caregiving response. The therapist legitimizes Tina's self-reliant defense as this was her experience growing up and validating her emotional response in the moment. It is also an effort to help father understand where his daughter is emotionally at this point in time. It is important that the focus remain attuned to Tina's emotional world, otherwise the disclosure becomes about father and again misses daughter and she remains unheard and invisible.

THERAPIST: (*to father*) And what's that like for you that she is saying that she wants to move on?

FATHER: I am getting it. I understand her.

THERAPIST: You understand what it is like to just move on to protect yourself or she wants to protect you?

FATHER: No, no, she wants to move on, she is very committed to her own growth. Right but I hear that she hears me. I have had this monkey on my back for too long.

THERAPIST: Yeah and that monkey had a strangle hold on you, it didn't let you see Tina and what she needed. And right now, you took charge and you let Tina know that you were sorry, but you don't expect her to be a certain way.

FATHER: Well in a perfect world I would love for us to be able to have a big hug. The reality is she is the kind of person that needs to think this through and take it away and process her experience.

THERAPIST: She is self-reliant and needs to rely on how she has learned to look after herself.

FATHER: Totally.

THERAPIST: And that is how she survived, and you understand that?

FATHER: As long as you know and that you can take away from today that I am really sincere and that you know I am there for you I would cross a million miles to be there for you to get to you.

THERAPIST: (to Tina) What's happening?

TINA: I don't know why this is just about us. She wasn't there for me either. She was in the exact same spot.

The therapist then focused on the mother who needed to work through her defensiveness and explanations before she could acknowledge her remorse and regret. Through this process she was able with great sadness to apologize to her daughter for not being there for her. The triad had moved away from their usual pattern of parents' caregiving being blocked by their shame, and Tina feeling unheard and not seen by her parents, which kept them stuck and unable to process together what had happened to Tina and acknowledge their hurt and regret. Mike's admission of failure to be there for Tina, his expression of regret and also his acceptance of Tina's need to rely on herself, allowed Tina to take the next step of asserting herself with her mother directly. The therapist then turned to Tina exploring her response to her parents' efforts to acknowledge and share their sorrow.

TINA: I used to be sad about it but now I am not, because if I didn't go through that I wouldn't be where I am. I am everything that happened to me. It was terrible, and no one should ever go through it, but at the same time I don't regret it and I don't see my life going any other way.

THERAPIST: It's part of who you are and how you have developed and the person that has this strength is because of what you have been through.

TINA: Yeah, that's true.

THERAPIST: Right, right, yeah, absolutely, that is very mature, and the other part that will be able to get comfort and not have to do it alone because when we are alone everything is worse, everything is harder, that's when it is the darkest.

MOTHER: And that's where we are because dealing with the past has been dragging us down and we do need you to hear us. We want to hear you.

THERAPIST: But it has been dragging you guys down, (*to Tina*) it's been a burden you have been carrying, you have been surviving because you had to, you were on your own. You have grown through it and gotten strength, but you are also witnessing parts of your parents that you didn't see before. Now you are seeing them being honest and acknowledging and saying I am sorry. They are saying that they weren't there, and they are seeing you not as that 8-year-old kid, or the 12-year-old. They are seeing that you are way past that, you are a young woman and that is part of your strength and your resilient 17-year-old self.

The therapist explores both past and present with Tina as she needs her parents to recognize her growth and who she has become. Tina's question to her parents remains the same, "Do you see me?" Today she is asking: "Do you see I have grown—I am strong—will you be there for me today the way I need you—not just with sadness and regret over the past?" As both parents are able to hear and see Tina in the past and in the present, they are truly expressing accessibility, responsiveness, and emotional engagement.

Mother and father's acknowledgment of their role in Tina's abuse was an important first step in helping this family heal. The parents' opening up around their guilt, rather than relying on their strategies of over-activation (mother) and under-activation (father) allowed them to begin to attune to Tina in present time and give space to Tina to talk about her own experience as a 17-year-old young woman. The end of this session marks the end of Stage 1 as the parents are now emotionally accessible and responsive and the blocks to the caregiving system have been identified and processed. Tina's relational block with her parents were also processed by helping her to make sense of what was happening with her parents and giving voice to her own emotional response in the present moment. Tina's typical strategy would be to ignore her parents and rely more on self. The therapist acknowledged and validated her strategy which helped Tina give voice to what she needed as a young woman from her parents.

Stage 2—Restructuring Relationships

Engaging Attachment Needs and Caregiving Responses

The Stage 2 work focused on the attachment bonds between mother and Tina and father and Tina in order to work deeper with each one of these relationships and to help Tina feel heard and seen by her mother and her father. Deb engaged in overzealous attempts to correct Tina's childhood experiences through anxiously attending to Tina in an over-protective way. Father tended to avoid contact with Tina, talking to his daughter through his wife and attempting to please her through doing tasks for her. The couple's estranged relationship had made it difficult for them to create a supportive parenting coalition with each other. The therapist structured the next treatment steps as dyadic sessions in order for Tina to have her needs heard by each parent. The dyadic sessions interrupted the usual pattern of Tina avoiding direct contact with Mike and Deb mediating the conversation between Tina and her husband. The following excerpt is from the session between mother and Tina.

THERAPIST: (*interrupting*) Let's go slow. You are talking about your own reactions here and Tina talking about hers, so let's go slow so you can hear each other. Because you want to be able to hear her? And you are doing a great job, Deb, and I want you to know I can see that.

MOTHER: (*shaky*) Yeah, I have a thing with my worry.

THERAPIST: It's hard. Sometimes our kids teach us, how to be with them. They grow up and we are trying to adjust ourselves and know how to react. And sometimes the only way we can be there is to listen and hear what they are needing because as they get older and more mature, they are able to do that.

MOTHER: She's my first.

THERAPIST: Yeah, it's like an experiment, we're learning, right? And you are saying you can see how much Tina has grown. And yes, there has been bad stuff that has happened to her, but you are also saying I see her strength.

MOTHER: Definitely. She is a stronger person. I know that. (*the therapist is helping Deb to stay open to Tina and organize her responses to her around her caregiving instincts and to mitigate her reactivity to guilt about past failures. The therapist helps Deb stay attuned to her daughter in the present moment by normalizing parenting as a learning process that is more about staying open to the changes chil-dren go through than being a perfect parent*)

THERAPIST: Coming out of the things she has gone through, like you said Tina: "I wouldn't be the kind of person I am today without going through the stuff I went through, even with the problems." And that is amazing that you can turn something that was so bad into a strength. You are not the victim. You are a survivor. You are able to say "Hey I am here where I am, given where I have been. And every time I hear you worry and try to save me from some-thing" that affects you, right? (*Tina nods in response*) Because she doesn't see what you want her to see?

TINA: Basically, that I can handle it on my own.

THERAPIST: I can handle things on my own, right? (*Tina nods again in agreement*) You want her to have some confidence in you?

TINA: Yeah.

THERAPIST: Because if you need her, you know you can go to her. Am I assuming something? You can go to your mother? (*Tina nods in agreement*) So, it's not that you can't speak up for yourself, you can do that.

TINA: Yeah, because when there is a problem, I will go to her, but I don't think she needs to talk to me.

THERAPIST: Ok, I don't think you need to come to me because I want you to believe in me and see me. I am not the 8-year-old kid or the 12-year-girl anymore, is that it? When I say that, does that hit home for you? (*Tina nodding in agreement*) What would that be like if she could see you and listen to you and see? (*first move of EFT tango, mirroring present process*)

TINA: It would be a lot easier. I wouldn't be carrying something on my back.

THERAPIST: You would feel a little lighter? You wouldn't have so much weight on your back? That's a lot of responsibility that you are carrying? (*Tina nodding*) Is that what it feels like?

TINA: ... Yeah, I mean, (*rubbing her back shoulder*) I feel like I am carrying everyone's worries.

THERAPIST: You feel you are carrying everyone's worries. And it's kind of like they can't see all of you because the worry is blocking, because they see their worry, if you are always worried and want to protect me, you are not seeing the strong side of me. (*Tina is silent*) (*with proxy voice*) And if I am carrying all those worries what does that do to you? (*second move of EFT tango, assembling affect and deepening*)

TINA: (*more silence*) Sometimes I doubt myself because personally. I think I am doing really well in life right now (*with sadness*), but the only things that people seem to see are the bad things.

THERAPIST: Oh, yeah, that hurts, when the only things your mother sees are the bad things about you?

TINA: Right and she makes me feel a little bit lower about where my life is going when I should be super happy. (*tearing up*)

THERAPIST: (*softly*) Sure it is sad—(*proxy voice*) It's like you are saying: "I get those worries on my back, it starts to penetrate, even though I am strong, it starts to weigh me down and then I start to doubt myself and feel bad about myself and I get scared." Is that it?

TINA: Yeah.

THERAPIST: Do you think you could tell her? Turn and tell her, this feels very important, and I am blown out of the water about how able you are to articulate this, and this feels very important for you to share directly with your mother (*third move of EFT tango, engaging encounter.*

TINA: I could but I just said it, and in the past, I have said the exact same things before.

(Tina's block is evident here and is revealing that there is vulnerability for Tina that has not been processed)

THERAPIST: And your mother hasn't listened. *(Tina nods in agreement)*

THERAPIST: So, it's hard and what's the point because if I actually open up like this and the same things happen. *(therapist validates Tina's block)*

TINA: Sometimes when we get into an argument. I have said something and then she says nobody says these things to me. I am going to watch TV alone.

THERAPIST: This is where things get painful *(validating the pain of her mother's rejection)*. So, it's kind of like, if I speak up and I may hurt my mother and then she's going to say, "I don't want to be with you."

TINA: I don't talk, and she just keeps talking.

THERAPIST: So, you are not getting angry, you trying not to talk at all, and that is not working, but you are trying to do a new dance step with her, and when your mother is saying at the start of the session that she is trying to take a step back, you're saying, hey I don't know, this part doesn't feel like it is changing. Do you really understand what it is about for me? And it would be too hard to say anything directly to your mother because it has happened so many times, you would talk and then your mother would leave, and you would be alone again. Sure, this makes sense to me Tina. That would be really hard to take that chance with your mother, to open up, tell her about your hurt, and then she would be hurt, and you would be alone. *(to Deb)* What's that like for you to be listening to Tina? *(fourth step of EFT tango, processing the enactment)*

The therapist works here to make sense of Tina's block though summarizing and normalizing her protective strategies in order that Tina feels seen by the therapist rather than pushed to do something different. Tina's past efforts to talk to her mother are acknowledged and connected to her fear that her mother will be hurt by what she is saying and ultimately reject her. The therapist is also helping Deb understand her daughter's emotional responses so that she is able to attune to her.

MOTHER: I feel bad. I am hearing her.

THERAPIST: What is it that you are hearing?

MOTHER: Well as she is saying this I am envisioning sitting on the couch and her tone triggers me sometimes.

THERAPIST: So, you can see the dance and how it gets going between the two of you, but the way Tina is talking right now, and she is not pushing you away or just not responding she is actually opening up to you.

MOTHER: I guess that's why it is hitting me more. She is not yelling at me. I am actually sitting here, and I do see that I try and figure it out but all I can really do is to try and take baby steps.

THERAPIST: Ok but before you try and fix yourself, let's just try and listen to her. And you are saying: "I am actually hearing her in a different way, because you are just talking together, and I am not getting defensive."

MOTHER: Yes, and that is rare for me.

THERAPIST: Well it is hard right, because you are very committed and like mothers and guilt. They go together, like two peas in a pod, but your daughter can open up in a way that is really amazing and she can describe her response to you, she is really mature, very mature.

MOTHER: I did hear her and I am still kicking myself, I look back and go "oh God." (Mother's anxious block)

THERAPIST: You are being driven by a worry inside of you, and that's driven by this need to protect this daughter you love.

MOTHER: I did it on the way here, so ...

THERAPIST: (priming mother's attunement) Let's focus on what Tina is saying here, I see you trying to get after yourself and what I am hearing is that Tina is just opening up and she is letting you know what it is like for her, when she gets this weight on her back and she feels she is carrying the load, not just from you but everybody and that weight starts to pull her down and she starts to doubt herself (Mother: yeah) and you are saying this worry comes and it takes over me, and it is hard for you to relax and say: "She's ok. Tina is ok. You're ok."

MOTHER: I do try to be positive.

THERAPIST: (softly) Deb, can you try and stay with me? So, when I say you are ok and Tina is ok your daughter is actually thriving, what's that like for you?

MOTHER: I am proud of her and know I have had something to do with her success.

THERAPIST: Yes, you do believe in her, encourage her, and support her.

MOTHER: Absolutely.

THERAPIST: So, this other part that gets triggered, this worry. Worry has a grip on you, you need to protect her, and this mother bear gets going and charges in and protects her. Your protection is on over-drive, and when Tina says she's moved on and actually she is stronger for some of things that she has gone through, you're saying it is hard for me, I keep getting dragged back I still need to be fierce about how I protect her.

MOTHER: This happens all the time. She is a beautiful young woman.

THERAPIST: Then it's like what you were saying last time that some of this is fueled by guilt when you didn't protect her and compensating for a time when you weren't there and what Tina is saying that when you do that now mom you are not seeing the 17-year-old girl I have become, you are back in time and for you to be released by that, that would be a big step. You are talking about it to find a way to find your balance today, for Tina as a 17-year-old and for you as a mother of a 17-year-old, and you have had stuff that has been hard but you have lived through and what I am seeing is that you guys don't have a distant relationship, you actually have a close relationship. You are trying to figure out how not to over step and Tina is saying yeah mom, there are times you do overstep and you say things that actually undermine me and what I am needing from you is for you to actually believe in me and have confidence in me and see where I am today. (*therapist reframes Deb's anxious efforts and Tina's feedback as part of a new dance together, where the mother/daughter dyad are engaged in an attachment/caregiving pattern: Tina cues Deb and Deb responds to her daughter's needs*)

THERAPIST: (*to Tina*) That is what I am hearing? Is that a fair summary? (*Tina nods*)

THERAPIST: (*to mother*) And she can't turn and ask for that because she is afraid you won't hear her and what she is really needing is for you to see her as she is today.

THERAPIST: What would it be like for you to see her as capable?

MOTHER: I do see her, I think that is on me ... it's very hard for me to say that to her.

THERAPIST: My worry is about me not Tina. (*mother responds in agreement*) Do you want to tell her that?

MOTHER: (*turns*) I do believe that you don't need me mixing in your social media and I do know that I do that, and I guess I am in protection mode, I call myself mother bear. I don't want anyone to hurt you, but I go too far (*Deb can now see herself more clearly and acknowledges how her overprotection impacts her daughter. Deb's openness and transparency helps Tina see her mother, and that her anxious behaviours are about her mother rather than herself*)

THERAPIST: And you are saying this is you not her.

MOTHER: And I can say that I will honestly try even harder, I will step back and not get crazy in my head. I am very proud of you. I will step back.

THERAPIST: And you are saying I am proud of you and when I get worried it's not about you Tina. It's me and I need to find a way to calm myself and not put that on you. (*therapist refocuses on mother, and helping her to be clearer about her own emotional responses*)

MOTHER: And not be the nosy parent, I never had that. I used to feel invisible.

THERAPIST: You had no one to worry about you, no one who had you on their mind?

MOTHER: (*voice breaking*) I had no one to show up at my track meets, I could be gone for three days and no one would notice, and when I left home at 16, I had nobody.

THERAPIST: So that's what you are saying to her, this is not you, it's me, it's me giving to you what I never got. (*Deb cries*)

TINA: I feel bad.

THERAPIST: It's ok, we all need to be able to talk about what we didn't get and what we need and the sad parts that don't get seen. And for you to feel for yourself. I think is really good, it's really good. (*therapist helps Tina keep her emotional balance, to see this her mother's pain that is not connected to her. Tina looks at mother, smiling with love*)

THERAPIST: And what's it like for you to hear your mother?

TINA: Now I can see it more.

THERAPIST: You can understand it more? That your mother's worry isn't about something being missing in you but more about her own fear and her own need to give you what she didn't get.

TINA: Yeah. (*smiling at her mother*)

THERAPIST: Good for you guys, you have a special relationship.

In this part of the session, the therapist is working with mother to help her navigate through her anxious block by making sense of her over-protection as tied to the past and her own negative feelings about having failed Tina when she needed her. Deb is hyper-vigilant to danger cues regarding her daughter, which communicate to Tina that she is not capable of looking after herself and that the world is a dangerous place. By helping mother see what her daughter needs, mother is able to recognize that her reaction is more about herself than Tina. She acknowledges that she is motivated by a desire to give Tina what she never received as a child from her own parents. When Tina can see the overprotection as more about her mother than herself, she is more resilient and she can understand her mother, be more open and loving to her and see the caregiving intent behind her mother's behavior. By Deb having the strength to be vulnerable with her daughter, Tina can see her mother more clearly and can feel more secure that her own vulnerability can be accepted by her mother.

The next session included Tina and Mike and focused on an exploring of Mike's attachment history. Mike was the caretaker in his family of origin, attempting to fix everyone's problems, and ignore his own pain. Within his family today, he would sacrifice his own needs for others and when his self-sacrifice would not work, he would become angry and depressed and would eventually withdraw from the family for days. Within the first family session, Mike had begun to talk about his outside position in the family, how he felt his wife protected Tina against him, and how no one saw the efforts he was making. The more Mike was able to give voice to his own experiences, the better able he was to begin to see his daughter and her needs. The following is an excerpt from the dyadic work with Tina and her father. In this session, Tina moves out of her position of ignoring and avoiding her father to expressing directly to him how his criticism of her hurts her. The therapist holds father so that he can see and feel Tina's hurt that is behind her anger by focusing on her tears. Mike feels regret and apologizes for his anger, asking Tina for her help in how he can help her and is now more open to being there in the way that she needs him. As a father and daughter, they have begun a new interactional pattern where each is working out their way of being father and daughter together.

TINA: I just hear the same thing over and over again.

THERAPIST: The same message and do you know how your father actually feels about you?

TINA: Oh yeah! I hear it all the time, every day, over and over again, all the time. I am going to go nowhere. (*father looks surprised*) So, I have to listen to him or I can't benefit.

THERAPIST: So, what you hear is not that your father is there for you but it's more that you are not going to succeed in anything unless you do what he says.

TINA: I am sure that's not his intent, but it comes across that way. (*Tina sees her father's effort but she experiences his frustration as a rejection of her*)

THERAPIST: Yes, because you don't want the message about not succeeding especially when you are trying so hard to get ahead in life.

TINA: I have to get ahead by myself, my schoolwork is by myself. It's my life.

FATHER: (*angry*) And how do you get there?

THERAPIST: Right. That's what a parent wonders or worries, but it is her journey. It is her journey, if Tina makes or breaks it, and obviously having your encouragement and support makes a huge difference. There is no doubt about it, you would do just about anything for your daughter. (*therapist helps Mike cope with his daughter's dismissal by reinforcing his intent to be there for her*)

FATHER: She never asks me ... and there is no question how much I care.

THERAPIST: So in your heart you want Tina to feel free to be able to talk to you and for you there is nothing standing in the way of that, nothing standing between you.

FATHER: Absolutely, I never say no. I want to be there to help her.

THERAPIST: And can you hear Tina what she is saying, right here, right now that she ends up getting the message that she is not going to make it, (*to Tina*) and that that is what upsets you? (*Tina nods*) Right, after all I would imagine that there are times that you get a little bit scared. (*Tina starts to cry as she nods in agreement*) and hearing your father say you are not going to make it, makes it even harder, yeah? You do want to succeed, you want your father to be proud of you, confident in you, because if he doesn't believe in you, who will?

TINA: (*starts to shake, crying*) I try so hard. He doesn't see that.

THERAPIST: Right, it hurts when you get the message sometimes that your father doesn't believe in you.

FATHER: (*looks at Tina and softens his voice*) You are right Tina, I did come on too strong. I did too much, too much, I am sorry about that.

THERAPIST: So, let's slow down here, because Tina is just showing you the more tender parts of her. This is really, really important, and she is tired and worn down.

FATHER: (*softer and comforting*) Yes, yes.

THERAPIST: (*to Tina*) And for you to let your father know how you feel is really, really good, because we are as strong as the people who are around us, you can't do it alone, nobody can, right? (*Tina nods in agreement*) But you need to feel like that he can hear you, he can see you, get you, understand you, otherwise you don't feel like you have the support that you need and some of that has to do with his anxiousness, he is so eager to help, that it kind of takes over, and then there is no space for Tina to just say what she needs, even if it's "I can't talk about it right now, I'm pooped."

FATHER: It was bad timing.

THERAPIST: So, what's it like for you Tina to just speak up, do you think he is hearing you, what happens for you?

TINA: In this moment probably but if we hadn't come here, I would have just gone home, and I would have been harassed, I would just hear: "It's going to be ruined." I can just hear it, that's what happens.

THERAPIST: (*validating, refocusing on present moment*) Yes, that's what ends up happening, and what you are saying to your father right now is that when I am upset and angry there is something else going on here, right? I get scared that you think I am not going to make it, or that somehow, I am going to screw up, is that it?

TINA: I don't believe it, I have heard it so much.

THERAPIST: So, you developed a hard shell, you have heard it so much you don't believe what he is saying, of course you need to do that. But can you tell me about the hurt part, the part that does get hurt?

TINA: (*silence*) I don't get that.

THERAPIST: Right because when we were talking, and I said that you got scared that maybe he thought you weren't going to make it, that's when the tears came. (*Tina nods with acceptance*) Then I wonder if you end up feeling like he is not understanding you and not really seeing the Tina you really are, its more about him and your dad wanting you to succeed.

TINA: Yeah when he says those things like "maybe you are not going to make it," I maybe get a little scared, but he cannot hurt me. I just wish it didn't HAVE to be that way! It makes me upset that he thinks this way, but it's not going to stop me.

THERAPIST: It is so good you can let him know how you feel, that it angers you not to have his support. Of course, that makes total sense because you need his support and it scares you when he doesn't believe in you. We all want our parents to believe in us. (*heightening the attachment-related affect, normalizing the caregiving need*) You have had to believe in yourself but there is a part of you that wishes it didn't have to be this way. (*therapist validates Tina's need for exploration while also reflecting her longing for a different response*) And to imagine that you wouldn't always have to look after yourself, that you wouldn't have to lock everything up just to keep going, that maybe, just maybe your father could believe you for once (*Tina begins to cry*). What's it like to see Tina's tears?

FATHER: (*softly looking at Tina*) It hurts.

THERAPIST: Right, and to see her hurt, hurts you?

FATHER: (*leaning in, tentatively and softly reaching for his daughter*) Right, I just want her to ask how can I help?

THERAPIST: She is letting you see her pain, and she wishes it wasn't this way.

FATHER: (*looking at her*) Well, I do want to learn from you Tina, I want to change and all that I really want is to make sure you are safe, to know that you are happy, and for you to know that I am there for you.

THERAPIST: When you see her tears, you feel?

FATHER: I feel sad too (*voice lowers with a softer tone*) I feel good that she can let me see. That takes a lot of courage, I could never let anyone help me. It took me a very long time to learn what she knows now.

Tina was calmed by her father's reach for her and was able to let him know that it made a difference to her to hear that he believed in her. The therapist highlighted the difference in Tina's nonverbal presentation (her body relaxed, she started to smile) and noticed how quickly and openly Mike responded to his daughter when she let him know how his words affected her. The session ended with a summary of how this conversation was dramatically different from the negative pattern Mike and Tina had been stuck in for years. Tina was exhausted by the huge emotional step she had taken in this session, and the therapist validated and made sense of how her body was responding, given the risk she had taken to let her father know directly how she was feeling and congratulated her on her courage. Mike was helped to see his impact in his daughter's life and how important and crucial his role was in Tina's life. The therapist made note of how the conversation shifted for them when

Mike could really see and feel Tina's hurt. When he felt her pain and let her know that, Tina felt seen and heard by him, which meant she was not alone with her pain, and that she could share and receive compassion. This was a major step for this father and daughter, as they had not spoken directly in years and in this session, with the therapist's help, were able to talk about the past hurt, and acknowledge Tina's continuing need for her father, her anger for the past, and her longing for support going forward in the future.

This session was pivotal for both Mike and Tina and for the family as a whole as this relationship was the most distressed relationship in the family. Mike had felt for years that he needed to stay away from Tina, because he was a toxic influence, and that he could best parent Tina by staying on the sidelines and leaving the parenting to Deb. Mike however resented his position as he was frustrated in not being able to have influence on his daughter and this frustration would leak out in critical comments, which again would reinforce his need to withdraw and stay distant. Hearing that his words mattered, and that Tina needed his support and encouragement, began to shift Mike's view of self. When he saw that his emotional presence had a positive impact on Tina, he began to feel that he was a good father and that his daughter needed him. Tina was able to open up and acknowledge that she was hurt and saddened by her father's disappointment in her and instead of her father denying or dismissing her feelings, she saw her pain on his face. Tina began to feel that she mattered having experienced her father's remorse and empathy without his shame. She began to trust her parent's emotional accessibility and responsiveness.

A final session was conducted with Deb and Mike and Tina revealed that the negative pattern of Mike and Tina avoiding contact and Deb meditating between the two of them had been de-escalated and all family members were feeling the release of tension surrounding that dynamic. Mike was able to talk directly to Tina and Tina was able to be open with him about her own needs. Deb had given Tina more space and was actively looking after her own needs instead of hovering over her daughter. The couple were able to devote more time to their relationship and Tina reported that she felt freer to explore her world and reach for her parents when she needed them. Tina talked about her anxiety regarding her school work and how she was afraid that she might fail.

Mike and Deb were able to keep their emotional balance, hearing Tina's fears without dismissing or rushing to solutions and asked her how they might help. Tina reported relief in being able to talk about her anxiety and was reassured that her parents would respond in the way that she needed. Although Josh was never seen in therapy, the parents reported that he had emerged from the basement where he had withdrawn, was engaging directly in family life and was actively looking for a job. Finally, the family was able to come together and support one another when Deb's mother became ill as their resources as a family were now mobilized. The new positive cycles were highlighted and celebrated by the therapist and the contrast between the negative cycle and their new way of interacting was summarized. The family now had a new narrative of family life that was focused on the present not the past, and they were enabled to creatively find solutions to problems together and repair conflicts as they emerged.

Conclusion

Follow-up contact with the family one year later revealed that Tina continues to thrive and grow and is continuing her education, while living at home. Both parents returned to work and are committed to improving their marital relationship. The family courageously faced the dragon of the abuse together and in doing so the negative interactional cycle in the family was restructured. The caregiving blocks of guilt and shame were acknowledged, processed, and shared which allowed Tina to break her own isolation of not being seen or accepted. Both parents were able to acknowledge their regret directly with Tina and become more aware of their own emotional world. As they became more self-aware they could see how their own fears and shame prevented them from truly seeing their daughter. In session, the therapist supported the parents to express directly their sorrow and regret to their daughter, rather than try to anxiously overprotect (mother) or fix and avoid (father). As the parents modelled vulnerability for Tina, Tina could more clearly see the caregiving intent behind her parent's behavior. The therapist validated and made sense of Tina's self-reliant behavior and give voice to her need to be seen and heard for who she was in present time. The parent's acceptance of her in the present moment, helped Tina to speak more openly about her own hurt and pain. This process then began a learning process for Tina to express her emotions directly, without internalizing her fears and engaging in self-destructive behaviors.

Through the EFFT process, the family experienced how to speak about the unspeakable, the abuse, the suicide attempt, together. This new emotional experience provided them with the opportunity to face the pain and sorrow together, and breaking the isolation of not speaking, not hearing, and not feeling. By facing their ultimate fears, the fears of not protecting their child and having failed as parents, Deb and Mike were able to provide a safe haven for Tina to express her catastrophic fears of being defective and being abandoned. As these new pathways to secure connection were constructed, Tina was able to see more about her parents that then allowed her to see more about herself. Her own negative self-perceptions left unexpressed, undermined her ability to grow and thrive and left her susceptible to anxiety and depression. The EFT therapist provides the family with an experience of being seen and felt that fosters empathic responsiveness and emotionally attuned communication between all family members. By working with the most salient resource in Tina's life, her family, the EFT therapist was able to effectively and positively intervene in her internalizing problems of depression and traumatic stress.

References

Brumariu L. E., & Kerns K. A. (2010). Parent–child attachment and internalizing symptoms in childhood and adolescence: A review of empirical findings and future directions. *Developmental Psychopathology, 22,* 177–203.

Cartwright-Hatton, S., & Murray, J. (2008). Cognitive therapy with children and families: Treating internalizing disorders. *Behavioural and Cognitive Psychotherapy, 36,* 749–756. Compton, S. N., Peris, T. S., Almirall, D., Birmaher, B., Sherrill, J., Kendall, P. C., . . . Albano, A. M. (2014). Predictors and moderators of treatment response in childhood anxiety disorders: Results from the CAMS trial. *Journal of Consulting and Clinical Psychology, 82,* 212–224.

Graber, J. A. (2004). Internalizing problems during adolescence. In R. M. Lerner & L. Steinberg (Eds.), *Handbook of adolescent psychology* (pp. 587–619). New York: John Wiley.

Johnson, S. M. (2004). *The practice of emotionally focused couple therapy: Creating Connection,* 2nd Ed. New York: Brunner-Routledge.

Johnson, S. M. (2019). *Attachment theory in practice: Emotionally focused therapy with individuals, couples, and families.* New York: Guilford Press.

Johnson, S. M. Maddeaux, C., & Blouin, J. (1998). Emotionally focused family therapy for bulimia: Changing attachment patterns. *Psychotherapy, 35,* 238–247.

Reinecke, M. A., Dattilo, F. M., & Freeman, A. (Ed.). (2003). *Cognitive therapy with children and adolescents: A casebook for clinical practice* (2nd ed.). New York: Guilford Press.

Siegel, D. J. (2013). *Brainstorm: The power and purpose of the teenage brain.* New York: Penguin.

Southam-Gerow, M. A., & Kendall, P. C. (1997). Parent-focused and cognitive-behavorial treatments of anti-social youth. In D. Stoff, J. Breiling, & J. D. Maser (Eds). *Handbook of antisocial behavior* (pp. 384–394). New York: Wiley.

TEN

Case Example—EFFT and Treating an Externalizing Disorder

Behavior problems in childhood and adolescence are a source of stress and strain for families and challenge their ability to address these problems effectively. Externalizing disorders in childhood, also referred to as disruptive behavior disorders, are maladaptive behaviors directed toward others or one's environment that also negatively impact the offender's own wellbeing (Reef, Diamantopoulou, van Meurs, Verhulst, & van der Ende, 2011). These behavior problems include a range of negative actions including: Not listening, disobeying rules, disrespectful attitudes, lying, bullying, physical aggression, stealing, and property destruction. Children diagnosed with externalized disorders find it difficult to control their emotions and impulsivity. Externalizing disorders are fairly common, accounting for more than half of all children referred for mental health services (De Los Reyes & Lee, 2017). The mental health disorders frequently referred to as externalizing disorders include: Attention-deficit/hyperactivity disorder (ADHD), oppositional defiant disorder (ODD), conduct disorder (CD), antisocial personality disorder (ASPD), pyromania, kleptomania, intermittent explosive disorder (IED), and substance-related disorders.

Tragically, far too many families discover that the negative impact of externalizing behaviors during childhood persist into adulthood. Externalized disorders in childhood predict low levels of success in school and employment (Hann, 2002) and increase risk of adult psychopathology including mood-related disorders and substance abuse (Scott, Knapp, Henderson, & Maughan, 2001). Research suggests that as children, diagnosed with an externalized disorder, transition toward adulthood the resources required to help them increases exponentially (Edwards, Ceilleachair, Bywater, Hughes, & Hutchings, 2007). For children diagnosed with a disruptive behavior disorder and the families raising them the trajectory toward wellbeing is trending in the wrong direction.

Families mutually impact and are impacted by the symptoms of externalizing disorders and their personal and social consequences. Carr (2013) reported that family-based interventions show promise in treating externalized problem behaviors. Studies on insecure attachment illustrate how family relationships provide a resource for understanding and influencing the impact of family intervention on externalizing disorders (e.g., Allen, Porter, McFarland, McElhaney, & Marsh, 2007; Kielly, 2002). In Bowlby's earliest work, he questioned the role of maternal separation and its effect on the characteristic absence of affection and warmth found among juvenile delinquents (Bowlby, 1946). He reasoned that the youth's lack of compassion and empathy appeared to generalize to their broader social world based on a deeper hostility and distrust rooted in their parental relationships.

Researchers consistently provide continued support for the assumption that attachment insecurity and externalizing behaviors in childhood and youth are linked (Burke, Loeber, & Birmaher, 2002; Greenberg, Speltz, DeKlyen, & Jones, 2001; Rosenstein & Horowitz, 1996; Tomasic, 2006; Van Ijzendoorn, Schuengel, & Bakermans-Kranengurg, 1999). Theule and colleagues (Theule, Germain, Cheung, Hurl, & Markel, 2016) identified a strong relationship between externalizing behaviors and insecure attachment styles, specifically when the child is determined to have a disorganized attachment.

The growing evidence suggests that insecure attachment contributes to the development of externalizing behavior through deficits in affective functioning and emotion regulation (DeKlyen, & Speltz, 2001). The presence of insecurity in family relationships holds promise as a marker and entry point for treatment of externalizing disorders found among children and youth. We believe EFFT's family-based interventions and affect regulation strategies provide a sound theoretical framework for understanding and promoting positive changes where externalizing behavior problems are disrupting the family system.

EFFT

In EFFT, the therapist recognizes the key to working with "acting-out" adolescents is helping them find the developmental balance of establishing autonomy while maintaining a sense of relatedness with their parents. Unfortunately, the negative child behaviors associated with externalizing disorders make it difficult for these children to relate well to others, including their parents. As the isolation increases so does the child's need to protect themselves from the pain of losing relatedness. It is discouraging to hear messages every day that you are a "bad child" and to make sense of the relentless negativity, most children with externalizing disorders develop high degrees of shame and a negative view of self. This shame is so pernicious because it leaves the child feeling isolated and cut off from others, but also disconnected from a sense of their own experience. Shame blocks self-compassion and reinforces a message of being unlovable. In this darkness it is hard for a child to imagine sharing their fears and risking someone confirming they are unlovable, so they choose further isolation which can never heal the pain of disconnection.

Anger at others and avoidance are two effective, short-term protective strategies for shifting the focus away from shame and the pain of disconnection while concealing the underlying vulnerable, attachment needs. Parents see their child's anger or "not caring attitude" which seems to suggest they want separation when beneath the surface these children actually need their parents' comfort and understanding to deal with the isolation. As parents and disruptive children fail to read each other's emotional signals clearly both are compromised in communicating their needs and effective responses. Over time these negative interactions dominate the relationship and insecurity takes hold.

As a result of this weakened bond, a troubled child may look more toward peers to meet their needs, but research suggests peer relationships, although essential for normal social development, cannot effectively care for the child's attachment-related needs (Ainsworth, 1989). Peers may provide mutual support, but they do not possess a parents' same attachment role, which is typically oriented to the best interest of their child's more vulnerable attachment needs. The more a child turns toward their friends and away from their parents for comfort, the more defensiveness and reactivity intensifies within the family. As cycles of mis-attunement mount and the distance between increases, both parents and children are easily frustrated because they do not expect to be heard or understood. Tragically, the constant, unresolved negativity results in these children getting stuck in the chronic activation of their attachment system needing help but having nowhere to turn for reliable comfort. In their moments of greatest attachment need they find themselves alone and not wanting their parents to make it worse. These desperate children are lost in disconnection and the only viable option to survive seems to be to either fight for any response or try to turn off their attachment needs. Both strategies of escaping the pain of disconnection come with compounding consequences and more messages of being labeled the "problem child."

A family's ability to effectively respond to disruptive behaviors particularly when they are rooted in insecurity requires restoring a sense of relatedness between child and parents. Research is increasingly showing that adolescent autonomy is more readily established not at the expense of attachment relationships with parents, but through a backdrop of secure relationships that are likely to endure well beyond adolescence (Allen & Land, 1999). Expanding awareness underneath the animosity toward more vulnerable attachment needs helps make the implicit attachment and caregiving systems more explicit. Relatedness is the antidote to isolation and "acting out" behaviors. Empowered with a sharper attachment focus, families can establish the security necessary to help adolescents develop the emotion regulation capabilities to both pursue autonomy and maintain a sense of relatedness (Allen, Porter, McFarland, McElhaney, & Marsh, 2007).

A critical step in facilitating a change in the family's emotional climate involves a focus on the function and meaning of problematic behaviors. A basic tenet of EFFT is all behaviors, including negative responses, are understandable in an attachment context (Chapter 2). By validating negative experiences and the positive intentions embedded in protective behaviors, family members are encouraged to find healthier ways of meeting their needs. In tracking the present process, the therapist supports the family to see these predictable patterns of distress and protection. Anger and withdrawal offer temporary strategies of self-protection from the pain of disconnection. Recognition of these defensive strategies is important but for family members to let go of their defensive responses they must be able to replace them with more effective strategies.

If children cannot express their vulnerable fears and hurts resulting from a rupture in their connection with a parent, a child needs their self-protective strategies. Accessing and deepening the focus on the primary emotions accompanying these protective strategies provides the raw material and vulnerable information necessary for new conversations to replace old ones. We want to exchange disconnecting conversations with connecting ones. In facilitating family members turning toward each other instead of reactively defending it is imperative for the therapist to be ready to encounter real-time blocks of mistrust related to caregiving and care-seeking. The overarching goal of EFFT is to invite parents and children to explore these blocks by engaging and sharing attachment-related emotions as they work through these blocks to recover the inherent resources found in their loving responses. The following case example was provided by George Faller.

The Case of Sal

"Everyone Is Angry"

Joey (45) and Angela (44) sought family therapy to better manage the disruptive behaviors of their oldest son Sal (16). Sal was diagnosed by a school psychologist with oppositional defiant disorder (ODD). Sal met all eight criteria including: Losing his temper; arguing with adults; actively defying adult rules and requests; deliberately annoying others; touchy and easily annoyed; blaming others for behavior and mistakes; angry and resentful; and spiteful and vindictive.

Joey and Angela feared that Sal's escalating anger was contaminating the family by adversely affecting his younger brother James (14) and sister Mary (11). They complained that Sal lacked empathy and caring. Despite their best parental efforts, Sal never takes responsibility for how his bad behavior negatively impacts the entire family. Given his talent to upset everyone through his constant chaos and discord, the rest of his family flippantly calls him "Super Sal." Family therapy was sought by his parents who were desperate for help in correcting Sal's destructive behaviors.

Stage 1—Stabilization and De-escalation

Assessment and Working with Family Patterns

At the onset of the first family session, the therapist is specifically focusing on gaining awareness and insight into the dynamic patterns of attachment success and distress in the family's relationships. The easiest way to access the family's strengths and limitations is by tracking real-time moments of connection, disconnection, and repair that show up in the therapy room. By tapping into the live family process, the therapist takes the lead in starting to organize and make explicit the patterns of distress dominating the family's interactions. This transcript is an example of an initial family assessment in which the tension between family members gives the therapist a window into the patterns of distress and begins to pinpoint where the distress is located in specific relationships.

THERAPIST: How can I help your family today?

FATHER: (*starting off with a laugh*) Well it seems that we are all good at fighting and poor at communicating. We are hoping to reduce the fighting and tension in the house.

MOTHER: (*shaking her head with a stern look on her face*) Let's be more specific. Most of us get along well, it is really only Sal who finds it difficult to get along with everyone. He has the problem …

SAL: (*interrupts and harshly raises his voice*) As usual you don't know what you are talking about. I'm not the problem but you are. Why do you even bother speaking? No one ever listens to what you say. I don't know why you decided to become a mother because you suck at it!

MOTHER: (*clenching her fists*) Right. You are an expert at deflection and blaming others. Well the good news "Super Sal" is we are bringing you here to talk to an expert, so you can hopefully see the monster you are becoming. If you don't change your ways, something drastic is going to happen.

SAL: (*rolling his eyes and laughing sarcastically*) Where do you think I learned deflection? From the master. You are the true monster in this family. I cannot wait to get away from this train wreck of a family and I hope something bad happens to you. (*pointing at mother*)

FATHER: (*interrupts Sal and throws hands in the air*) Okay. Let's calm down and stop being so disrespectful. You know mother isn't a monster. We're here to learn to stop passing along this hot potato of anger and hate.

SAL: Here we go again, pointing the finger at me. She calls me a monster first and then I get in trouble. Whatever I don't really care anyway. Everyone in this family has anger problems. Screw everyone.

MOTHER: (*starts to cry*) I don't know where it all went wrong. You need help Sal, but you push away all attempts to help you. And your father makes it worse by allowing you to be so rude.

As the tension in the room increases, Mary takes hold of her mother's hand while James turns away grabbing his phone and ignoring what is happening in the room, while the father looks down at the floor in bewilderment. One minute into the session and the therapist is already flooded with information and the experience of the family's distress.

THERAPIST: (*raising his voice to match the intensity of the situation*) Wow, I can see how fast the hot potato gets passed around. Holy cow, there's a lot of anger and hurt happening in your family. I can see how quickly everyone turns to protect themselves. Can I jump in for a moment and see if I can help make some sense of what is happening?

The therapist starts with the most alive emotion in the room, Sal's anger. By repeating the initial trigger, mother saying that "only Sal finds it difficult to get along with everyone else" the therapist attempts to slow down the rapidly overwhelming responses by tracking the moves and helping each member organize their experience by validating the intent of their protection.

By reflecting the function of Sal's anger in pushing away negative messages and providing a sense of resolve against his perceived unfairness of his mother's criticism, the therapist begins to help the family members understand and experience his anger in a new way. Validating the function of mother's anger to push for change and correct the bad behaviors, the therapist again helps to reframe how everyone understands anger. After normalizing their anger, the therapist then encouraged both Sal and his mother to see how their actions also led to an impact on others. The therapist highlights how the mother's attempt to motivate change causes Sal to attack back in order to back her off and the more mother feels disrespected, the more she criticizes. The more she complains the more Sal retaliates with anger. They are stuck in a negative cycle of anger feeding anger. The family starts to see that Sal's disruptive behaviors are more than just something wrong inside of him, they are behaviors embedded in patterns of relationship insecurity.

Next the therapist attempts to enlarge the focus by helping everyone in the family begin to track their moves around conflict. Witnessing defensiveness in action allows the therapist to clearly identify the real-time blocks to engagement and connection. Watching both parents interact reveals the negative cycle of mother pushing while father tries to keep the peace. These different parental styles clearly add more tension to the family environment and reinforce the chaos. As long as the family dynamics make it unsafe for Sal to share his vulnerable attachment needs underneath his anger, it is unlikely his protective strategies of disruptive behaviors will change.

Not every pattern in the family needs to be explicitly identified in the first session, rather the therapist attempts to get the family to see that although each family member's responses are different what they share in common is their actions represent attempts to survive the stress of disconnection. Regardless of the move, each family member is trying to deal with the negativity in a way they think works best but when the smoke settles after a fight it seems the interaction only seems to make things worse. Every fight not repaired leads to more distrust and distance in relationships. Patterns of self-protection driven by reactive responses of insecurity create and sustain negative reinforcing patters. Identifying the moves that don't work is the first step to the most important next step of replacing them with moves that do work.

Parents' Session

The parental session is crucial for building an alliance with both parents and getting their "buy in" to become agents of change in their family. After the family session, Joey and Angela entered the parent session feeling defeated and desperate for change. Before parents can see their children's unmet, vulnerable needs hiding behind the destructive behaviors, therapists need to join parents where they are; incredibly frustrated with the child's bad behavior. Leaning into the parents' perspective allows the therapist to honor their parental care and family concern and their willingness to seek help and confront their family's escalating reactivity.

Validating Joey and Angela's good intentions, commitment, sacrifice, and willingness to engage in parenting is crucial to avoid being blamed for the family's problems. In their weary state, they need encouragement that offers hope for finding new responses, rather than criticism for the moves that don't work. Joining the parents in their frustration at working so hard following the rules they were taught as children by their parents only to futilely spin their wheels with Sal, highlights their loving attempts to hang in there and face the challenge. Instead of giving up they are continuing to fight for their son. The good news is Joey and Angela can play the major role in changing the family's dynamics and becoming a big part in the solution to helping the whole family communicate differently.

Parents need help to improve their emotional responsiveness not judgment about what they did wrong or could do differently. Helping both parents see how each family member is dealing with stress in consistent ways provides a platform to organize the family dynamics. The therapist supports the parents to track the predictable actions associated with a family's negative pattern; Sal's anger triggers mother's anger triggering father, James and Mary's withdrawal. As the parents' awareness of the negative patterns grows so does their understanding that regardless of any family member's particular move, protection in one family member breeds protection in another. Focusing on the in-moment experience the therapist actively explores whatever is getting in the way of the parents responding with empathy and understanding to their children's needs.

It was apparent right from the first parent session that Joey and Angela put a lot of pressure on themselves to be great parents. They experienced Sal's disrespect as proof of their failure. The therapist is a resource for managing the parents' fears about their child-rearing responsibilities by normalizing their expectations and providing an attachment frame about good enough parenting. As both parents became less reactive and defensive their capacity increased to focus more on Sal and to get curious about the function of Sal's acting out behaviors. They assumed Sal felt bad about himself underneath the anger, but neither parent experienced Sal's pain.

The therapist affirmed their assumptions as part of their attuned caregiving system and discussed the importance of helping Sal put words to these negative feelings underneath his acting-out behaviors. Joey and Angela were relieved to hear that although Sal seemed not bothered by his defiant role in the family, the idea that underneath the anger there could be hidden pain at constantly being seen as the "problem child" made sense to them as parents. This shift in awareness at seeing Sal's disruptive disorder more as a product of insecure attachment and less as a function of some deficiency in Sal was empowering to the parents and resulted in less pressure to Sal's bad behavior and more attention on caring for the pain Sal couldn't share. Angela and Joey expressed a desire to take the lead in handling Sal's bad behavior in a different way and they shared responsibility for not being able to get to what mattered most in their relationship with Sal.

The EFT therapist is constantly assessing the strengths and limitations of parental caregiving. The parents' willingness to enter treatment demonstrates an awareness of needing help and understanding there is a problem in the family dynamics. Exploring how each parent positions themselves around the presenting issue reveals much about the status of the caregiving system. Typical blocks to an open and responsive caregiving are different combinations of negative views of child, negative views of partner or negative views of self. Parents need to provide emotional accessibility, responsiveness, and safety to develop and maintain a secure bond with their children. The therapist explained the necessary parental balancing act of providing both discipline/structure and comfort/support. Often parents over-identify with one responsibility and come up short on the other.

Identifying if a parent's actions are over or under responsive reveals the direction in which change needs to occur. Through replaying her last fight with Sal, the therapist helped Angela to experience the caring intent behind her consistent discipline. Angela saw her effort to motivate Sal's positive behavior through discipline eventually became counter-productive because it only reinforced Sal's negative view of himself as the problem child and his need to protect himself with reactive anger. Sadly, Sal's angry push back only strengthened Angela's negative view of Sal and her need for additional discipline. Explicitly identifying this pattern including the parent's intentions and the results of their efforts increases parents' motivation to find new ways of reaching their goals.

Angela's open stance to exploring her contribution to the negative cycle encourages Joey to do the same. The therapist stressed the importance of a strong parental alliance and how their uniting together to deal with Sal truly increases the likelihood of success. Joey shared how his intermediary role between Angela and Sal left him feeling helpless and unfairly blamed by both of them for failing to help. His growing resentment and attempts to not escalate an already tenuous environment, left him wanting to remove himself from the equation more and more. As Joey started to understand the function of Angela and Sal's anger to demand attention and create change, he realized how his lack of engagement was leaving them both feeling abandoned. Like Angela, Joey expressed a desire to change his response to the situation.

Expressing desire for change doesn't necessarily translate into knowing how to change this pattern. Assessing the couple's general comfort level with vulnerability helps the therapist focus on potential strengths or blocks to more secure engagement. Parents who are blocked in connecting to their own vulnerability need help through their partner and/or the therapist to experience the resources of these underlying emotions to promote connection. In this case, the therapist asked Angela and Joey: "How often do you both share vulnerable conversations?"

ANGELA: Never. We talk a lot about logistics, but we never really talk about deeper fears and insecurities. Neither of us grew up in families where anyone talked about feelings.

JOEY: (*nodding in agreement*) Right, we love each other and support each other and talk about the challenges of parenting Sal together but we tend to do our best to remain optimistic.

THERAPIST: Ok, I think I'm getting it. No one really knows how to talk about deeper fears and insecurities. I never met someone who didn't do vulnerability who didn't have good reasons. Especially when we are young if we don't get help talking about our inner world then we learn to keep it to ourselves. People who do vulnerability well do so because the people around them have responded well to their risks. We all need success in sharing vulnerability if we are going to do more of it. Both of you haven't had much success and as a result your children also don't know how to share vulnerability. The good news again is if we create enough safety then we can learn the language of vulnerability that pulls those we love closer, rather than the anger that pushes away.

JOEY: We want that for our family. (*Angela nodding*)

The therapist then prepped the parents for the next family session where the focus would shift to their children and especially Sal. The therapist explained the goal of the family session is not taking anyone's side, only opening up space so the family can begin to understand and explore their protective moves and explore the vulnerabilities underneath. The therapist underscores Joey and Angela's desire for a different conversation and makes explicit the goal of the next session is to gather the information and raw material (vulnerabilities) needed for a new conversation.

The therapist forecasts the likely upcoming challenges of getting to Sal's vulnerability. Like everyone else in the family, Sal doesn't know how to talk about his more vulnerable feelings, so he used anger and avoidance to manage his pain. The therapist normalized the probability that the parents often get emotionally triggered when witnessing their child's version of reality, which may interfere with their ability to empathize. This is framed as an opportunity to externalize a real-time block to attunement and a chance to work through the mistrust that is preventing Sal from shedding his "Super Sal," villain persona.

By providing safety for the parents to explore their own experiences in the midst of their interactions with Sal, the therapist is reinforcing the theory of change in EFFT, which is doing it differently rather than just teaching them new concepts. Understanding their reactive patterns and new ways the family can engage without them provides a target to aim for in treatment. The therapist ends the parent session by providing the parents with a vision of what it looks like hitting the target and their family engaging in a very different, positive conversation. This vision replaces the discouragement of the negative cycle with the hope of the positive cycle of responsiveness.

Sibling Session

The goal of the sibling session is to develop an alliance and empower the kids to see their own agency in changing family patterns. Free of their parent's evaluation in the session, children tend to provide a more accurate picture of the family's reactivity and its impact. The therapist attempts to strengthen the alliance by validating their reluctance to engage in treatment while giving attention to their concerns and exploring what they want out of treatment. The siblings recognize the family is stuck in defensiveness and not doing well. It doesn't take long for them to surmise their only real choice is between maintaining the ineffective status quo of protection or risk new moves. Stressing the importance of their active participation in the process of healthy change is vital to empowering their engagement. The session example that follows illustrates how the therapist uses an attachment frame to promote siblings' investment in the treatment process.

THERAPIST: I never worked with a family that replaced negative moves with positive ones where everyone didn't do it together. Parents can't change it on their own. Kids can't change it on their own. The key to working together is changing the level of communication from defensiveness that pushes family members further apart to connecting conversations that pull people together. In my experience you know who is best at starting new, softer, connecting conversations, parents or children?

SAL: (*irritated and sarcastic*) Obviously parents because they have so much worldly experience.

THERAPIST: Good guess but actually it's the kids. Kids tend to be better at initiating vulnerable conversations. In general, parents spend so much time giving advice and knowing the right thing to do that they don't like talking about what it feels like when they are unsure or make mistakes. (*therapist is explicit about the treatment goals of having vulnerable conversations*)

JAMES: (*surprised and now paying more attention, interjects*) That is interesting. Are you just messing with us?

THERAPIST: (*smiling*) No, I'm serious, although there will be times I mess with you! Kids often need to take the lead in showing their parents how to talk about uncomfortable stuff. When kids are hanging out with other kids and one starts talking about something in their life that is difficult, the other friends don't feel a pressure to fix the problem they just try to understand and support each other.

SAL: I never thought of that, but you are right. I never really get into arguments with my friends and we are all good at listening to the crazy stories of our families.

MARY: (*laughing*) I can't wait to see Mom go nuts when she hears this information.

THERAPIST: Thanks for sharing your concerns Mary. You are very observant of what goes on in your family. Your mom is quick to give advice, so her hearing you all might at times be better at knowing how to respond to someone else's struggles may come as a shocker. The good news is I already explained some of this to your parents. They were a little surprised, but I think they are starting to understand. Actually, both of your parents expressed to me their desire to find new ways of communicating. They want to learn how to do these difficult conversations better.

SAL: (*laughing*) Yeah right. My mom is good at saying what people want to hear. Believe me she is only into one-way conversations.

MARY: (*sighing*) Stop being so negative Sal.

THERAPIST: (*putting his hands up to stop*) Hold on a second. Mary, I appreciate how you believe your parents are capable of change and Sal you certainly have good reasons for your doubts, given all the fights you have been through.

The therapist intervenes to highlight the reactive moment where Sal's negative response triggers Mary's criticism. The therapist tracks their responses and reflects back to each sibling the negative patterns of self-protection. Both express anger and do not share their underlying fears and hurts. The therapist points out how this negative feedback loop happens so quick that neither of them really has a choice and it has been running unchecked and rampant throughout this family for years. Once they see it and experience the therapist's support, they have a chance to begin to change it. The therapist ended the session expressing his hope that the kids could set the stage for change by authentically engaging, just like they are doing now.

The therapist makes clear that it is not one person's job to create change in the family, instead each person must take responsibility for their own actions. Ultimately, however the therapist underscores that it is their parents' responsibility to create a safe environment necessary to risk. The EFT therapist provides support to the parents in this regard specifically and provides a secure base for them as they work through their negative pattern.

Stage One Second Family Session

Following the assessment sessions, the family returned to conjoint sessions with everyone present. Attempting to build momentum on the parents' willingness to initiate more vulnerable conversations, the therapist encourages the parents to express to their children their desire to change the family environment by replacing reactive conversations with more vulnerable ones.

MOTHER: We acknowledge that despite our best efforts we have not been great at role modeling talking about feelings besides anger. We want to do it differently.

SAL: (*looking skeptical he shakes his head*) It's too late. I'll be off to college in two years, try it then.

MOTHER: (*frustrated, raises her voice*) I knew you would say something negative, you can't help yourself.

FATHER: (*sighs*) Hey Sal. Stop giving mom a hard time, she is trying. How about you try ...

THERAPIST: (*interrupting keeping the focus on Sal's reactive response*) Hey mom and dad, let's try to stay curious about what might be blocking Sal from wanting to try. Help me out here Sal, if you are going off to college in two years then it makes no sense to do things differently now? You have figured out how to take care of yourself and you are just counting the days when you can be free of this house?

SAL: Exactly. I don't want to be here. Things will never change. My mom is a good actor but deep down I know she doesn't like me. *(there is a hint of hurt mixed with anger in his voice)*

THERAPIST: Wow. You don't think things can change and deep down in your heart you believe your own mother doesn't like you. I'd imagine that must be annoying and hard for any kid to think their parent doesn't like them?

SAL: It's not a big deal, I accepted it a long time ago.

THERAPIST: *(nodding in agreement and using sadness in his voice)* Right. To think your mom doesn't love you is painful for any kid on this planet. To survive the hurt you learned to not care. To deal with it you learned to depend on yourself. You are a strong kid Sal, I'm impressed with your resiliency. *(therapist reflects underlying emotion and notices resilience)*

FATHER: *(reaches from his chair to put his hand on Sal, while his mother sits stiffly in the chair)* I'm sorry pal, I didn't know you felt that way.

SAL: *(pushes away father's hand)* It's no big deal, I'm fine.

The therapist summarized this interaction by putting emphasis on the parents' efforts and Sal's emotional experience. He thanked mom and his father for initiating a different, more vulnerably focused conversation and gave Sal permission for learning to rely on his protection of "not caring." The therapist then checked in with James and Mary and helped them process their reactions to the new vulnerable conversation attempt. They were both unsure what was happening. Validating the normal mistrust that prevents new responses, the therapist acknowledges both the risks taken and the good reasons there is so much doubt, given the years of negative cycles in the family. The therapist holds an attachment frame for the family in the face of distress and disconnection while reassuring them that if they keep reaching toward each other, the distance will shrink as the trust grows.

The therapist also observed that despite the mother's intentions for more vulnerable conversations, she was defensive and rigid throughout the session all the while father stuck to his familiar in-between role. The parents' curiosity and empathy for Sal's world was blocked and their defensiveness was triggered as Sal's anger seemed to take charge. As a result, the therapist decides to postpone the next family session and continue with a second parent session to explore the block to mother's caregiving.

Follow-up Parent Session

The following parent session focused on the couple's caregiving alliance and mother's defensive responses throughout the previous session. Replaying a moment in the last session the therapist focuses the parents on a moment when Sal said "my Mom doesn't like me," the therapist said "Angela, I saw you go stiff, what happens when you hear Sal say, 'You don't like me?'"

ANGELA: It is just proof that his diagnosis is correct! (*contemptuously*) Despite all I do for him, he always reverts back to being negative. It's exhausting, and I don't know why I bother.

THERAPIST: Right. His negativity breeds your negativity. Of course, it's exhausting to keep running into the negativity every day. Yet, despite the exhaustion you keep trying. I saw some tension in your face when Sal said you don't like him? What happens right now as I repeat Sal's words that you don't like him? (*therapist validates her exhaustion and invites her to explore this further*)

ANGELA: I get all tense because he is right. I want to be a better mother and I promise myself I'm going to do better but when he tells me something bad about myself then I just freeze.

THERAPIST: So, there is a lot going on for you. If you are freezing then that is your body saying you are stuck with no good options. Tell me more.

ANGELA: (*raises hands in futility*) Exactly. I either fight with him which never works, or I agree with him and sink into a dark hole of despair and sadness. (*revealing negative view of self instead of negative view of Sal*)

THERAPIST: No wonder why you freeze, moving in either direction makes things worse. Does anyone ever see that inner struggle you have choosing between two bad options? Do you ever share this with Joey? (*therapist shifts focus to caregiving alliance and follows the mother's emotional cue*)

ANGELA: (*starting to cry*) No I keep it to myself. There is no point making Joey feel bad with this crap. I just try to handle it on my own. (*with a far off look in her tearful eyes*) It's like I'm a lonely, little girl again with nowhere to turn for support. No one in my family cares to listen to me. (*sobs more deeply*) I don't want to show anyone my tears. I'm sorry. The past is the past.

THERAPIST: How sad and tragic. A scared little girl with nowhere to turn for help learns to be strong and fend for herself. You don't need to be sorry, your tears make so much sense. For years they have been hidden away. Your story sounds so similar to Sal's, resigning yourself to handle fear and pain on your own. Like Sal, that scared little girl inside you has never had someone come find you and shine a light in the darkness. To survive you learned to be hard on yourself and push yourself to be strong. No wonder why you do the same to Sal. It's your way of dealing with fear and hurt. Being strong is how you know how to love.

ANGELA: (*wraps her arms around herself and starts rocking*) I'm a terrible person who deserves to be left alone. Sal is right, I'm the real cold, monster.

JOEY: (*reaches over and pulls his wife into a hug*) I never knew you felt this way. I thought you were angry and wanted to be left alone. I'm so sorry. (*Joey starts to tear up*)

THERAPIST: Right. You never knew. In this moment you see her pain and immediately it moves your heart to come to the rescue. Beautiful job. Joey, can you tell Angela you see her in the dark hole and you want to be there with her because she deserves love in the darkness, not isolation and shame?

JOEY: Certainly. I'm here babe and I can sit with you as long as you want. Now that I know that you are scared underneath the toughness, I'll never leave you alone. (*Joey strokes her hair as she rests with her head leaning on his chest*)

ANGELA: (*smiles at Joey*) It is kind of weird, but this feels good to not be alone, thank you Joey.

Angela experiences the power of Joey's responsiveness and support enable her to more freely explore her relationship with Sal. This newly discovered security found in the couple's relationship primes and promotes more parental availability, particularly in Angela's increasing willingness to face fear and pain within the family. Joey's comfort strengthens their caregiving alliance by building trust with Angela that he will respond to her pain in a way no one ever has before. This experience of successfully engaging around more vulnerable emotions offers Angela a sense of what she never provides to Sal. Feeling a new experience of calmness with her own fears, Angela uncovers a deeper motivation to try again to reach with more responsiveness to her son. Given the shift in mother's defensiveness and father's readiness to support, the therapist along with the parents develop a plan for the next session focusing on the mother to apologise for being defensive and demanding including her understanding of her own high expectations.

Family Session

In the whole family session, Angela starts off sharing with her kids some of her childhood experiences that shaped her tough exterior. As father held mother's hand, she apologized for not knowing how to do vulnerability with them and expressed a desire to change. James and Mary were very receptive and forgiving. They were very interested, asked a lot of questions and showed empathy when their mother spoke about her childhood struggles. Sal, however, sat back and looked disengaged. At one point when mom expressed genuine sadness, Sal closed his eyes like he was bored and was going to sleep. The therapist noticing Sal's indifference and recognizing the emergence of his relational block also saw an opportunity for mother to engage a different response: "Does Sal's disinterest of your revelations make sense?"

ANGELA: Absolutely. When you get used to being alone, you don't want people to see your weakness. You also don't want to see other people's weakness. I totally get why Sal doesn't want to bother seeing someone else's pain.

THERAPIST: That's what it looks like being tough. When you are left alone to handle things. No one is there for you. Right?

ANGELA: Right. Tough but alone.

THERAPIST: This is huge, Angela, can you tell Sal he is not doing anything wrong or bad but actually his lack of responding makes sense? He is being tough.

ANGELA: (*turning to him with a soft smile*) Definitely. I totally get why you don't trust what I am saying. You are not doing anything wrong. I'm sorry I've waited this long to tell you it's not your fault but mine. You are a tough kid.

SAL: (*looking a little confused and nodding*) I wasn't ready for you to blame yourself, I figured you would blame me. That is definitely different. Thank you. (*smiling but awkward*)

Angela's acknowledgment and acceptance of Sal's apparent disinterest shows an openness toward him and less defensiveness in response to what she previously interpreted as disrespect. This new move by mother provides a marker to measure her progress working through some of the blocks to her caregiving system. As Angela's expectations of Sal are made clearer through seeing her own experiences and how she also coped by hiding her needs, her negative view of Sal and herself diminishes and through these experiences Angela is better able to see Sal and his needs. It is easier for a parent to value their child's needs when they are able to see their own.

Father, James, and Mary all cautiously witnessed this new interaction between Sal and mom. They supportively nodded and showed appreciation on their faces. The therapist reflected the new responses and applauded their success in accomplishing a vulnerable conversation. Building upon a more secure foundation of parental openness the therapist decides the next session was good timing to go deeper and explore Sal's vulnerabilities and insecurities lurking underneath his disruptive behaviors.

In the next whole family session, the therapist attempted to expose the attachment needs underneath Sal's reactive behaviors. Unfortunately, Sal became reluctant to engage in the family session as he felt there was too much focus on him as the problem. As his frustration mounted, Sal surprisingly stood up and walked out of the session saying: "This therapy stuff is bullshit!" The therapist used the rest of the session to highlight the negative cycles with the family and show each family member how their protective moves in handling the threat of disconnection creates further reactivity in others. Sal's angry exit was framed to the family as his adaptive "tough guy" strategy of avoiding feeling bad about himself in the immediate moment but which unfortunately continues to keep him stuck in the role of the "acting out child." After the family session, the therapist talked to Sal in the waiting area and apologized for pushing him in front of his siblings. They both agreed next session to do an individual session where Sal would have time to discuss how he thought the treatment was going.

Individual Session with Sal

Although Sal's parents were ready for a new conversation, it was premature for Sal to risk explicitly sharing his vulnerabilities, especially in front of his siblings. In the individual session with Sal, the therapist repairs the alliance with Sal by promoting safety through specifically focusing on their attachment-related conversation. The therapist meets Sal in his defensive block and helps him to be present with his emotional experience, instead of avoiding his feelings. Together, Sal and the therapist honor the good reasons he doesn't want to let his guard down and they also explore the costs of his protection; increased isolation.

Sal begrudgingly acknowledged how difficult it is to "get the message all the time that you are a problem." The therapist validated Sal's negative view of self as adaptive and supports Sal to pay attention to what he felt when as he says "I'm a problem." With tears in his eyes Sal describes feeling all alone and not liking himself. If the root of Sal's problem is isolation, then the therapist must ensure that in the moment of his risking showing his vulnerability Sal experiences connection in his loneliness. Sal needs to experience success if he is going to risk sharing his vulnerability and if there is no success then it makes sense why he covers it up with anger. The therapist responds to Sal saying, "I'm touched Sal that you let me in to see your isolation and I want to help you get the comfort we all need to handle sadness effectively." Sal nodded in appreciation.

The therapist reminded Sal that it was the therapist's responsibility to make it safe for Sal to risk sharing his hurts and if Sal didn't feel safe then it is perfectly ok for him to stop at any time. The therapist reiterated that he believed Sal's parents are ready and willing to change their responses and now there is a great opportunity for Sal to access his courage to face hard stuff together and to be honest about what he wants and what he needs. Sal agreed to give it a shot. Getting Sal's buy-in to vulnerably engage in conversations was necessary in transitioning to the Stage 2 process of EFFT.

Stage 2—Restructuring Relationship Positions

Engaging Attachment Needs and Caregiving Responses

The therapist assessing the family as being less reactive, Sal agreeing to explore what is underneath his "acting out" behaviors and witnessing both parent's openness, accessibility, and responsiveness to their child's emerging vulnerability, are all clear makers of de-escalation and a sign the family is ready for the deeper work of Stage 2. The primary goal focuses on engaging new relationship encounters that redefine the felt security in specific family relationships. The therapist seeks to engage child vulnerability and promote parental availability.

Following Sal's individual session and his expressed need to feel safe addressing his concerns with his parents alone the therapist invites the parents and Sal to a session focused specifically on understanding Sal's experience of relating to his parents.

The therapist sets the tone of this session by intentionally explaining the rational for this separate session to explore the dynamics of their particular relationship without worrying about the interference of the other children. Guided by the EFFT decision model, the therapist focuses on experientially working through relationship blocks to foster responsiveness. Both parents show their agreement as the therapist reiterates a desire to understand what happens to Sal when there is an argument. Then the therapist asks about their most recent fight and by revisiting a recent escalated argument, the therapist recounts the specific events of the argument to trigger the relationship block making it the focus in session.

Bonding Session—Parents and Sal

Focusing on Sal's annoyed expression at the mere mention of the fight, the therapist reflects Sal's irritation. The therapist focuses on mirroring the present process, highlighting the emotion emerging in the discussion of a family conflict.

THERAPIST: I can see right now that this fight brings up so much frustration. As we discussed last session, it seems your anger is trying to protect you from the constant negativity you feel in your family. When she (*mother*) highlights you doing something wrong immediately the anger is there and it's strong. I guess I'm curious what would happen if you didn't get angry and couldn't push away her criticism. What would happen if the negative messages started to stick and accumulate?

SAL: (*looking confused*) I can't let that happen. It's not an option (*anger in his voice*). There is a lot of negativity coming my way. (*looking perplexed*) If I don't block the criticism, all the negative would destroy me and (*looking down at floor and pausing for moment*) I'd be giving in and agreeing with everyone else that says I am bad, a bad kid.

THERAPIST: Oh my, no wonder you push back so hard. (*with sadness in his voice*) If the negativity gets in it is proof that you are bad, and it would destroy you? No wonder you are so good at deflecting the criticism away. I guess if I had to choose between being angry or destruction, I'd choose anger all the time too. (*therapist focuses on assembling affect and deepening. Therapist tone shifts from mirroring his need to stand strong but also the sadness of him fighting alone for his own value, worth, and respect—to not giving into being seen as bad*)

SAL: (*nodding in agreement and now looking sad*) I guess I never looked at it like that, but you are right. It's tough. I don't know how to not be angry.

THERAPIST: Of course, it's tough. You are stuck with either anger or getting eaten up by all this negativity. Having to push away the idea that you are bad, a problem, unwanted ... right? Does anyone see this constant struggle? (*Angela reaches out to put her hand on Sal's shoulder with tears in her eyes*)

ANGELA: (*tearfully*) I'm sorry Sal, I never knew you were hurting so much. I thought you always just mad at us and hated me.

SAL: (*pushing her hand away*) You were never there for me. (*looking away*) I remember when I was 6 years old, and I was running outside by the pool and fell. I broke my arm. (*rubbing his arm with tears in his eyes*) It hurt so bad and I came running to the house and you yelled at me for being so stupid because you warned me not to run by the pool. (*Sal pauses, wiping away his tears*)

SAL: (*angrily*) I hate you and I don't need your pity now. I know I'm on my own so just leave me alone. (*Angela pulls away wrapping her arms around herself and starts to rock back and forth*)

ANGELA: You are right. I have been a bad mother. I don't blame you for hating me. I hate that I did that to you. I hate me too. (*Sal looks at his mother with surprise and Joey reaches over to hug Angela*)

JOEY: (*to Angela*) It's ok you didn't know any better. No one was there for you. No one saw your pain. I love you for doing your best. Don't say you hate yourself. (*Joey hugs Angela but she resists and stiffens in response*)

THERAPIST: Joey, I so appreciate your efforts to reassure Angela. She never shows her tears because no one ever comforts her and that is finally changing.

THERAPIST: Angela, you did a great job in surviving and to keep the hurt away you learned to be hard on yourself and everyone else. You had to find strength when you are crumbling inside, alone. Yet you are finally realizing that the shame and hiding drives you away from what you need most. Right? (*Angela looks up and nods*)

THERAPIST: Is this making sense Angela? Why in this moment it's hard to take in Joey's hug because you feel like you are failing as a mom and what you are trying to do is show up for Sal? The shame is a shield that pushes away the love we need. Sal has learned the same thing. So much of his ODD behaviors are attempts to manage his shame. Everyone sees his anger, but nobody sees his hurt and shame inside. It's like everyone deep down is alone and is desperately trying to defend themselves from feelings like they don't matter ... or they are bad. The good news (*therapist opens his arms and smiles*) is the cure for shame is empathy and connection instead of isolation. Right now, I can see you Angela making eye contact with me which shows me how you are trying to show up for Sal in a new way. Do you want to be there, right now so Sal doesn't have to deal with all this hurt and anger alone? (*therapist choreographs an engaged encounter*)

ANGELA: (*nodding assertively*) I do.

THERAPIST: Excellent! I believe you can. Can you turn to Sal and tell him you understand his protection and you don't want him to be alone in his pain?

ANGELA: (*reaching over to grab Joey's hand*) Sal, me and dad never knew how much pain you are in underneath the anger. We don't know what to do but we definitely don't want you to be alone in the pain. Now that we know about your struggle we promise to do a much better job trying to help. (*Joey reaches over and rubs his son's shoulder*)

SAL: (*not knowing what to say just nods but he doesn't push away his father's hand*)

This session really captures the importance of the therapist being ready for and working with multiple relational blocks. Predictably as Sal's vulnerability emerges so does his block to sharing his sadness. He learned early on to not trust his mother to comfort him (*negative view of mother*), as his story falling at the pool is good evidence that she will not see him. This mistrust and his rejection of her attempt to comfort him then triggers Angela's shame (*negative view of self*) and fear she is failing at something that really matters. When rebuffed, Angela sinks into her shame and in the process shifts the focus to herself instead of being present to Sal's hurt. Shame causes her to move away confirming to Sal that she will not be there for him (*reinforcing Sal's negative view of mother and himself*). Caught up in shame Angela cannot see the protest in Sal's anger, that it is about what he needed or needs. The therapist normalizes the function of Sal's anger and Angela's shame as protection from the pain of their disconnection. Angela receiving support in her shame from Joey and the therapist (*reducing her negative view of self*) provides support for her to refocus her attention on Sal's anger and pain. Angela giving Sal permission for his anger starts to add the missing ingredient, her responsiveness and reduces his negative view of his mother. The therapist focuses on working through relational blocks by making explicit these blocks to caregiving and care-seeking that fuel the family's negative cycle and reactive responses as they emerge in real time.

The next session the therapist decides to again see Sal alone with his parents. Focusing on continuing to make progress working through Sal's fear of reaching for his parent's comfort and his parents' ability to respond to Sal's vulnerability without their own stuff getting in the way, the therapist starts off encouraging Angela and Joey to again give Sal permission for his frustration when he is uncertain because it is his way of trying to stand up for what matters. The heart of their relational block is how they all meet in their shame that fuels defensive anger to keep others away and leaves everyone alone. Instead of playing their part and allowing Sal's defensiveness to trigger their shame which in turn reinforces Sal's shame, this is an opportunity for Angela and Joey to connect with Sal by validating his anger and mistrust and seeing this protection as a means to ward off the pain of being seen as the problem child.

The therapist promotes acceptance and helps process the parents' ability to show up in a new, engaged way. Rather than seeing Sal as bad they start to see what he is going through is bad and he needs others to see that with him. They are finally seeing some of his hidden vulnerability and they want more. They jump at the chance to stop the "shame hot potato" game and share how they are understanding Sal's anger in a new, less blaming way. Both parents apologize for their protection dumping negativity on Sal and they ask Sal for another chance to earn back trust. Sal shrugs his shoulders at his parent's apology and invitation to try and understand him again.

THERAPIST: Sal, I notice you shrugging your shoulders, what happens when your parents say they are sorry and want to do it differently? (*mirroring present process*)

SAL: I don't know. It feels good that they are starting to understand better. They seem sincere, but it also feels like if I trust them something bad might happen.

THERAPIST: (*nodding*) Sal this is great how you are putting words to your mixed feelings. Part of you feels good to be understood and another part of you doesn't trust what they are offering. Help me understand what bad thing do you think might happen? (*shifting focus to affect assembly*)

SAL: (*clinches his fists*) If I let my guard down, I'm going to get criticized.

THERAPIST: (*leaning toward Sal*) Wow. So, if you start to believe in the good stuff then you are going to be blindsided by the negativity. You are so used to the negative that you always need to be on guard, bracing for an attack.... It must be pretty exhausting to always protect yourself against the bad messages. (*Sal looks away and then shakes his head in agreement saying quietly*)

SAL: It is. (*takes a deep breath, sighs, and pensively looks down at the floor*)

THERAPIST: (*softly*) It must be so tiring. I wonder, do sometimes the negative messages get past your defenses? Do you sometimes fear that the negative messages are actually true, that you are bad and that you are unwanted? (*therapist exploring negative view of self*)

SAL: (*reacts with frustration*) It's hard not to just give in to being bad. I'm always in trouble. No one in my family likes me. I am the problem child. They all just put up with me.

JOEY: (*father interrupts, trying to reassure*) No! You are not the problem child. We think you are smart and terrific and ...

THERAPIST: (*interrupting Joey*) Thank you dad for responding to Sal. You want to help him and reassure him when he feels bad about himself. If it's ok, I'd like to know more about the dark place inside Sal that he never talks about and no one sees. He is finally letting us inside of the struggle underneath his angry behaviors. (*therapist turns to Sal*) It must be so hard to keep finding yourself alone in a place where everyone thinks you're bad and you don't like you either.

SAL: It sucks. Deep down I hate myself. No one really loves me. I deserve all the bad things that happen to me. (*Sal puts his hands over his face and starts to cry and then his voice shifts to an angry tone*) I'm a loser who lets everyone down, so please just leave me alone.

THERAPIST: (*seeing tears in Angela's eyes*) What is happening Angela as you see your son's tears?

ANGELA: It breaks my heart. I know that place of hating myself and I just want to help him.

THERAPIST: Right, his sadness touches your heart. Can you look at Sal and tell him you feel sad for him?

ANGELA: (*looking at Sal and trying to find Sal's eyes*) I feel so sad for you. You deserve love not isolation. I just want to give you a hug. (*she leans toward Sal but hesitates*) Can I give you a hug? (*Sal doesn't answer but continues to cry and Angela embraces Sal with a big hug and rubs his shoulders. She then reaches out to pull Joey toward them. Joey kneels alongside Angela and reaches out to Sal*)

JOEY: (*speaking softly*) I am so sorry for always leaving you alone in this horrible place. Thank you for telling us about all of this. (*Sal allows the embrace and doesn't push away his parents' efforts to respond. As his body sinks into their loving embrace, he begins to sob deeply. His tears pull forth his parents' empathy and their gentle, persistent touch reminds Sal he is no longer alone*)

For the first time, Sal receives comfort in his dark place of shame and pain. Over the previous sessions, mother and father earned trust by owning their own struggles to responding to Sal and by validating instead of reacting to Sal's defensiveness. As both Sal and Angela worked through the blocks of their negative views of self (shame) and other (blame), it freed up Angela to do something different than what she knew as a child. In the pivotal moment of Sal showing his vulnerability, not only did Angela feel empathy and respond but she also helped Joey reach toward Sal.

Typically, because Joey is stuck in the middle of their fighting, he freezes up to not alienate either side and effectively leaves Sal alone. Joey's caution chronically delegates him to the sidelines. However, Angela's perfectly timed nudge frees Joey from his bind and allows his heart to move unhindered to Sal's side. Joey too experiences the power of meeting someone in their vulnerability instead of trying to rescue or reassure away their pain. Instead of leaving Angela and Joey alone in their shame he learned to join them in it. Both parents responding to Sal's underlying pain and accepting his anger as both a protection from his fears and a need to be seen on his own terms, shifts their relationship toward security. This corrective emotional experience adds the missing ingredient of safe, attuned responsiveness to Sal's vulnerability and starts to lift the negative stigma of Sal being seen as a "problem child", replacing this prescription with a more accurate view of a "hurting child."

Sal Asking for What He Needs

The therapist decides another session for the parents and Sal is necessary to make explicit Sal's needs and to give the parents a clear opportunity to respond to them. Their responsiveness in the last session was an important step toward building trust but Sal directly asking for what he needs and taking in his parents comforting response is critical to restoring confidence in the trusting bond of felt security. Both Sal and his parents reported a much calmer week with less anger and fighting. Every time there was some emerging anger, one of the three would say "remember there is some vulnerability underneath anger." The family was amazed at how quickly anger can dissipate when replaced with vulnerability. Building on this theme of how vulnerability empowers the whole family with a clearer map of what repair and responsiveness looks like, the therapist reframed Sal's ODD behaviors as a desperate kid's attempt to survive an untenable situation. With the mention of ODD the therapist notices Sal's face flinch in pain. The therapist reflects the pain and uses it as a doorway to revisit Sal's shame. This time with his parents engaged the therapist tries to help Sal put words to his longings in the shame. It is important for the therapist to adopt a patient approach and to be ready for a lot of ambiguity and not knowing what is needed in places of shame, because up till now asking for help wasn't an option. To help Sal express his needs and longings the therapist first needs to open up a space for the pain and shame causing the needs to emerge. As Sal shares how lonely he often feels and his parents sitting on both sides of him reach out to hold his hand, Sal's shame triggers:

SAL: OK. Well ... (*pausing*) I guess ... I guess what is so hopeless is I don't believe it will really change. Deep down I believe I'm broken and not fixable. (*pulling away from his parents touch and wrapping himself in his arms, starting to cry*)

Both parents reach out to rub his back as they too also become tearful in response.

THERAPIST: Wow, this is really different. (*with tears in his eyes*) You are not alone Sal. Your parents are in the darkness bringing their love to shine a light. Deep down you are afraid you are broken and things will not change? I want you to listen to your heart right now, how can your parents help you with this pain and fear that things will not change? (*therapist is encouraging Sal to feel and put words to his longings for comfort that accompany his fears*)

SAL: (*still looking at the floor*) I guess I want them to tell me I can change, and I will be OK someday.

THERAPIST: Exactly. You need their hope when your hope is so low. Can you turn to them and ask them "do you believe I can change because I sometimes don't think I can?" (*therapist setting up enactment*)

SAL: (*looking up toward his mother and then toward his father with tears streaming down his face. Sal makes a bid for reassurance*) Do you really think I can change?

MOTHER: (*reaches over to hug Sal simultaneously as father also embraces him*) Absolutely. We can do this together. (*crying*) I'm so proud of you. You are helping us all to change.

FATHER: (*kissing his son's head*) I'm so sorry I didn't know how to help you with these fears. You are so brave to lead the way. Now that I know about your darkness, I promise to bring light. And if I don't know how to help I can always just sit with you in the darkness so that you are not alone. You are not broken, you are so strong to endure this pain for so long. I love you Sal. (*father rubs his hair*)

SAL: (*takes a deep breath and relaxes into their embrace. After a few moments of being held, Sal looks up with a smile on his face*) That sure beats being alone. Thank you, dad and mom, for being there for me and believing I can do it. I definitely feel calmer and more hopeful. It is kind of weird. (*laughing*) (*father and mother smile together as they join Sal in laughing as they reach out to grab one another's hand*)

The therapist helps process what it was like for all three of them to experience Sal going to the heart of his fears and asking his parents for help and then trusting and receiving their loving response. Understanding why the new vulnerable responses work better empowers family members to replicate these new ways of being together. The therapist explicitly promotes positive emotions as markers of transformation (e.g., joy, calmness, relief, peacefulness) after bonding moments allow the therapist to know the therapeutic process and the family's secure bond is growing. If the root of Sal's problems is isolation with fear and pain then the solution is connection. The therapist highlighting and celebrating the emerging physical signs of connection enables the family to do the same, and in the process this makes overt the positive cycle of connection that is replacing the negative cycle of self-protection and isolation.

Family Session

After the bonding event between Sal and his parents, the three of them decided they wanted to share with James and Mary the changes they were making and invite them into their success in having deeper, more vulnerable conversations. It is not enough to change the family's climate of defensiveness by solely focusing on the parent's relationship to Sal. Instead the therapist helps the parents use the corrective emotional experience with Sal as a springboard for extending the parents' availability to their other children and by making space for the change others see in Sal and his relationship to the family, the parents attempt to share their shift toward engagement and positive interaction to the other children. The therapist joins the other siblings in facing their blocks to sharing their attachment needs and the parents' blocks to seeing and responding to these needs, leading to a new level of trust in the family.

Over the next few sessions, with some encouragement from Sal and their parents, James and Mary share their struggles with not getting attention and sometimes feeling invisible. Stuck for so long in the family's negative climate focusing on Sal's bad behavior with Sal and mom's anger so intimidating, James and Mary both felt it was best to stay quiet and not make things worse. The therapist helped father and mother give permission for James and Mary's withdrawal and the costs of their protection in hiding their fears and needs. Like Sal before them, James and Mary experienced comfort to their vulnerable attachment needs, which they typically hid. Sal joined in and shared how proud he is of his siblings. Just like every negative, defensive interaction strengthens the negative cycle, so too, positive cycles of responsiveness build momentum for secure cycles. The family grows stronger and safer after every responsive interaction in which attachment needs are met.

Conclusion

The family continued in treatment for a couple more sessions during which they practiced repairing inevitable misses, celebrated feeling closer through continuing to engage in vulnerable conversations and intentionally building into their everyday routines practical ways of staying mindful of the importance of their attachment needs. The family decided Saturday afternoons are the perfect time to check in on how every member is emotionally doing while going on a family hike. They called it going on a "vulnerability vacation."

After the last session, the children were ready for a break, but Joey and Angela wanted to go deeper in their work, so they entered couple therapy. Although Sal's ODD behaviors of angry outburst and disrespectful behaviors didn't magically disappear, his symptoms dramatically improved as evidenced by Sal no longer meeting the criteria for an official ODD disorder. Prior to family therapy Sal met all eight factors for an ODD diagnosis and now because his angry, protective strategies are no longer chronic he doesn't meet any. Sal proudly testifies that it is certainly easier to be less angry when you have more effective tools to get your needs met.

Sal was so engaged in the therapeutic process that he didn't want therapy to end and therefore he decided to do individual therapy with another therapist. As Sal continued making progress processing his fears and pain underneath his anger, he grew in compassion, empathy, and calmness. With his parents' help, Sal learned that empathy is the antidote to shame. Instead of chronically avoiding his feelings, Sal curiously leaned into his emotions and discovered he was actually very adept at doing vulnerability. Underneath the armor there resides quite a sensitive kid. "Super Sal" the impressive steadily replaced "Super Sal" the annoying. With his sense of relatedness strengthened by his parents, Sal found it much safer to pursue autonomy in a more secure world.

The therapist helped this family speak the language of vulnerability together. Although there were many impediments to learning this new language, the therapist trusted that deep down, vulnerability is every human's native language. As both parents took ownership for their blocks to their caregiving system and risked working through their blocks, it unleashed their empathy to lovingly shine a light into the dark, hidden vulnerabilities of their children. Feeling seen and touching their longings for help in their isolation, the children headed toward their parents instead of pushing them away. United this family changed their defensive family slogan "everyone is angry" into the simple underlying message of "we all need help." A secure attachment doesn't fix all of life's problems, but it does give families the best place to find love and comfort in the midst of the adversity.

References

Ainsworth, M. D. S. (1989). Attachments beyond infancy. *American Psychologist, 44,* 709–716.

Allen, J. P., & Land, D. (1999). Attachment in adolescence. In J. Cassidy & P. R. Shaver (Eds.), *Handbook of attachment: Theory, research, and clinical applications* (pp. 319–335). New York: Guilford Press.

Allen, J. P., Porter, M., McFarland, C., McElhaney, K. B., & Marsh, P. (2007). The relation of attachment security to adolescents' paternal and peer relationships, depression, and externalizing behavior. *Child Development, 78,* 1222–1239.

Bowlby, J. (1946). *Forty-four juvenile thieves: Their characters and home-life.* London: Baillière, Tindall & Cox.

Burke, J. D., Loeber, R., & Birmaher, B. (2002). Oppositional defiant and conduct disorder: A review of the past 10 years, part II. *Journal of the American Academy of Child and Adolescent Psychiatry, 41,* 1275–1293.

Carr, A. (2013). Thematic review of family therapy journals 2012. *Journal of Family Therapy, 35,* 407–426.

DeKlyen, M., & Speltz, M. L. (2001). Attachment and conduct disorder. In J. Hill & B. Maughan (Eds.), *Conduct disorders in childhood and adolescence* (pp. 320–345). New York: Cambridge University Press.

De Los Reyes, A., & Lee, S. (2017). The high cost of childhood disruptive behavior disorders. June 1, www.statnews.com/2017/06/01/disruptive-behavior-disorders-children/

Edwards, R. T., Ceilleachair, A., Bywater, T., Hughes, D. A., & Hutchings, J. (2007). Parenting programme for parents of children at risk for developing conduct disorder: Cost effectiveness analysis. *British Medical Journal, 334,* 682–685.

Greenberg, M. T., Speltz, M. L., DeKlyen, M., & Jones, K. (2001). Correlates of clinic referral for early conduct problems: Variable- and person-oriented approaches. *Development and Psychopathology, 13,* 255–276.

Hann, D. M. (2002). *Taking stock of risk factors for child/youth externalizing behavior problems.* Bethesda, MD: National Institute of Mental Health

Keiley, M. K. (2002). Attachment and affect regulation: A framework for family treatment of conduct disorder. *Family Process, 41,* 477–493.

Reef, J., Diamantopoulou, S., van Meurs, I., Verhulst, F. C., & van der Ende, J. (2011). Developmental trajectories of child to adolescent externalizing behavior and adult DSM-IV disorder: Results of a 24-year longitudinal study. *Social Psychiatry and Psychiatric Epidemiology, 46,* 1233–1241.

Rosenstein, D. S., & Horowitz, H. A. (1996). Adolescent attachment and psychopathology. *Journal of Consulting and Clinical Psychology, 64,* 244–253.

Scott, S., Knapp, M., Henderson, J., & Maughan, B. (2001). Financial cost of social exclusion: Follow up study of antisocial children into adulthood. *British Medical Journal, 323*(7306), 191–194.

Tomasic, M. A. (2006). Childhood depression and conduct disorders as related to patterns of attachment (Doctoral dissertation). Retrieved from Dissertations and Theses database. (UMI No. 3252742).

Theule, J., Germain, S. M., Cheung, K., Hurl, K. E., & Markel, C. (2016). Conduct disorder/oppositional defiant disorder and attachment: A meta-analysis. *Journal of Developmental and Life-Course Criminology, 2,* 232–255.

Van Ijzendoorn, M. H., Schuengel, C., & Bakermans-Kranengurg, M. J. (1999). Disorganized in early childhood: Meta-analysis of precursors, concomitants, and sequelae. *Development and Psychopathology, 11,* 225–249.

ELEVEN

Case Example—EFFT and Working with Stepfamilies

"We're Not Blended, We're Lumpy"

Sharon moved with her teenage daughter, Becky, into the home of her new husband Frank and his children Sarah and Josh, exchanging the bustling city of Toronto for a quiet small town in rural Quebec. For Sharon, the joining of the two families signaled a new beginning in her life: A fresh break from loneliness and isolation in the big city, and relief from the painful fallout of a bitter divorce. Frank saw the prospect of sharing his home and his life with Sharon as a chance for companionship and practical support in parenting his two children. Both Sharon and Frank were certain they had found their life partner! All of their children shared their optimism about this adventure of a new life together.

One year later the grand adventure looked entirely different than they had anticipated. The combined weight of their stepchildren's demands felt overwhelming and unreasonable, particularly with regard to the two 13-year-olds, Becky and Sarah. Becky and Sarah attended different schools and with separate circles of friends they seemed to inhabit separate worlds. These differences left them and the family feeling like they did not belong with each other. The girls' separateness somehow symbolized the alienation and distance that defined the entire family: Two separate camps who seldom shared time together. Each day began and ended with Sharon and Frank needing to give separate time to each of their children. They were so disappointed that their dream of a warm and close family group seemed unattainable that they decided to seek family therapy. Sharon summed up their situation when she told the therapist: "We're not blended, we're lumpy."

Working with Stepfamilies

In the United States of America 16 percent of all children live in stepfamilies (Pew Research Center, 2015) and one in ten children in Canada are part of a stepfamily (Statistics Canada, 2017). Stepfamilies are defined as two partners living in a committed relationship along with a child from a previous relationship. Typically, stepfamilies form following the disruption of a previous family through divorce or death. Other stepfamilies are created from original single parent households. Straight, gay, married, or cohabiting, the variations in stepfamily life are many, yet the majority of these families share the common complexity involved in joining two partners, while at the same time joining two family units. Many stepfamilies feel very vulnerable in the early stages of their life together when their hopes for family cohesion fail, in the absence of guidance or direction regarding what to expect as they develop their new family group (Papernow, 2013).

The vulnerability stepfamilies experience is inherent in the complexity of holding hopes and dreams along with the relational risks and rewards as they deal with unforeseen demands, competing developmental needs, and mixed relationship backgrounds. Second marriages appear to be more susceptible to dissolution with 60 percent of remarriages ending in divorce (US Bureau of Statistics; Coleman, Ganong, & Fine, 2000). More than one in five of Canadians who remarry leave their second spouse within an average of 7.6 years (Statistics Canada, 2012). Children of stepfamilies are twice as likely to struggle academically, emotionally, and psychologically, compared to those from intact original families (Wallerstein, Lewis, & Blakeslee, 2000). Many of the newly formed couples end up in couple therapy, and stepchildren are overrepresented in North American mental health clinics (Dunn, 2002). Stepchildren can suffer from behavioural or symptomatic disorders resulting from the pain of the transition from divorce to remarriage (Hetherington & Jodl, 1994), and the conflict and turmoil characteristic of the first two years following remarriage lead many stepfamilies to seek therapeutic help (Visher & Visher, 1996). These challenges often lead to the impression that stepfamily life is inherently problematic, rather than a recognition of the resilience of family relationships when they are able find ways to stand together through the trials of stepfamily life.

Research has focused on the negative impact of divorce on the lives of children with less understanding regarding what helps children who, after divorce, are now living in stepfamilies (Marquardt, 2005; Wallerstein et al., 2000). What are the factors that contribute to success in stepfamilies, and how can these families provide stability and promote resilience for children? Stepfamilies provide children with the opportunity to view multiple adult roles, the experience of seeing parents happier in intimate relationships, and the chance to learn how to adapt to change and be flexible. Successful treatment approaches that have been identified by clients include validation and normalization of the stepfamily experience, psycho-education about stepfamily life, support of the newly formed couple, and the reduction of feelings of helplessness (Visher & Visher, 1996).

Common Challenges

The major hurdles facing a stepfamily include parenting differences between the residential parent and the stepparent, the children's losses and loyalty binds, conflict and demands from the children's non-residential parent, and the consequent pressures on the newly created romantic partnership. Although these obstacles are a normative part of stepfamily development, the process of navigating these demands may take years to resolve. Ultimately it is how the family faces these challenges together and not simply how to confront each difficulty that determines the success of the stepfamily. A family's unrealistic expectations, judgmental attitudes, isolation, and lack of effective support can destabilize and demoralize, which may in turn interrupt the regular process of stepfamily development. For the family therapist, understanding the unique and complex stepfamily dynamics and the challenges they face, provides important direction in promoting effective treatment (Katz & Stein, 2005).

Complex Structure

Stepfamilies may look the same as any family from the outside, but on the inside, their experience of family life is unique. This can be seen most clearly in the differences in parenting relationships found between a parent and biological or adopted child compared with a stepparent's relationship to the stepchild. It is rarely automatic or even necessary that the stepparent become a parent to their stepchildren, especially if the children are older (Emery, 2011). Children in stepfamilies often belong to two homes with polar opposite values and every occasion or life event, is divided between two separate households (Marquardt, 2005). Ahrons and Rodgers (1987) originally coined the term "binuclear" family to underscore the typical ways in that children moving between more than one household is expected in divorced and remarried families. Stepfamilies must navigate these multiple family units and at the same time retain a constancy of belonging for each of its members. Stepfamilies with stronger identities are better able to facilitate the flow children often make between two households by maintaining recognition of the unique value of each household and the different roles that parents and stepparents may serve in a child's life (Papernow, 2013).

In Sharon's case, she felt that her family was "lumpy not blended" as Sharon's divorce had left her feeling like a failure as a mother because she had not given Becky an "unbroken" family experience. She longed for unity and cohesion, and the distance between Becky and Sarah scared her: "Will this marriage ever provide the 'intact family' experience that I so badly want to provide for Becky?" Further, Sharon's ex-husband had remarried and he was only marginally involved with

Becky. This increased Sharon's feelings of failure, and she desperately hoped that Frank's gentle and open nature would fill this paternal void. She had trusted that remarriage would restore her family to an ideal state, and so when she saw "lumpiness" after a year of trying so hard to blend, she began to lose hope in the challenge of achieving the goal she longed for.

Stepfamilies and Loss

Children in stepfamilies experience the transition from their original family as a significant loss. Alongside grieving this loss, children face the additional challenge of working through loyalty binds that may emerge with their biological or adoptive parents. They also need to adjust to a new family life which may have different values and an unfamiliar culture. The introduction of the step parent can be threatening and frightening to children as it signals that their other parent is now being "replaced" and they are forced to share their residential parent with a new adult. For many children, rejecting the stepparent is the only way they know to express feelings of loss and loyalty to their now-absent mother or father. Too often children become caught in the challenge of adapting to a new family life they did not choose and simultaneously become drawn into an ongoing battle between their parents, who are now divorced but not emotionally disentangled.

Becky was thrust into life in the country, far from her familiar home, her friends, and her old neighbourhood in the city. She had lost the position as her mother's only co-habitant, and this new home came with different rules and different expectations. Becky lost her exclusive relationship with her mother, a dramatic change as she now had to share not only with her mother's new partner but also with two other children, one of which was her same age.

Stepparent and Stepchild Relationship

When a stepparent is introduced into an existing family group the challenge is to develop new relationships in a family culture that is already established. Stepparents do not have shared history or shared parenting ties to help them feel a sense of belonging with their new stepchildren, and they may have their own children who need particular attention and care. Meanwhile the stepchildren frequently feel guilty about caring for a stepparent as this may signify disloyalty to their non-residential parent. In fact, this new stepparent may signal the end of any possibility of reunification of their original parental unit. The couple also face a challenge as, unlike first-time families, they do not share the joy of a shared attachment to the offspring. They too can feel conflicted and guilty about sharing their attention and resources with their stepchildren as their biological children are needing their parental care. Conversely, many stepparents struggle with feelings of invisibility, loneliness, and alienation as they experience exclusion from the biological parent–child bond (Papernow, 2013).

As newly formed stepcouples begin to live together, they face the challenges of parenting with someone they are still only developing a relationship with. They have vastly different connections with children in the new family. Added to that, the children they now need to parent may be grieving the loss of their first family. A strong bond between stepparents and stepchildren does not instantly happen and while love and affection can grow, there is an inside/outside dynamic that is naturally part of stepfamily life, especially in the beginning stages.

Sharon found herself feeling irritated and frustrated with Sarah whose personality was so different from Becky's. Frank on the other hand was surprised and confused that Becky immediately began to withdraw from him when she moved into his home. Frank ended up feeling invisible, alone, and alienated from Sharon and Becky, and Sharon felt caught in the middle between the man she loved and the child she cherished. Such feelings can become a challenge or threat to the developing couple bond and can negatively influence how they develop a parenting coalition. As stepfamilies do not share in mutual attachment to the offspring, the resulting asymmetry can create a difference in the way they relate to the children. This in turn can lead to opposing parenting styles, which polarizes and divides the couple, and impacts how the children are parented.

Frequently, stepparents react to feeling on the outside by asserting their authority through discipline before a relationship with the stepchildren has been established. Others like Frank withdraw from family life causing Sharon to feel she had to choose between him and Becky. Sharon began to feel guilty about the changes Becky had experienced and, wanting to compensate for this pain, began to align with Becky and even considered moving out in order to have separate and dedicated time with her. Other residential parents try to please both partner and children, ultimately becoming unavailable to both. Finally, some avoid the struggle altogether and relinquish their parental role to the spouse.

Forming New Parental Coalitions

Research has shown that the biggest challenge facing newly formed stepfamilies is ongoing parental conflict from the first marriage (Hetherington, 2003). The co-parenting arrangements established following the divorce may become disrupted with the introduction of a new partner. Ex-spouses can feel threatened by the new partner, especially if they did not want the divorce and when there is early re-partnering or they see the new partner as a threat to the children's affection for them (Ganong & Coleman, 2004).

Frank's children, Sarah and Josh, spent half of their time with their mother, who was openly hostile and critical of both Frank and Sharon.

Sarah and Josh felt required to choose sides between their mother and their father. This is a bind that causes immense stress for children, causing the most harmful impact of divorce (Emery, 2012). It has been well established that children are more negatively affected by conflict than by the actual divorce or the creation of a stepfamily (Afifi, 2003). The dilemma for the new stepfamily is that the relationship between the divorced parents, although transformed, does not end (Emery, 2012). The newly re-partnered couple are challenged to find a mutually agreed upon vision as to how to respond to the past while also developing and creating their own secure bond and new family life.

Strengthening the Couple Bond

The relationship between the stepparent couple becomes the foundation of the new family unit, but this bond is tested time and time again as the couple negotiate the complex challenge of forming a stepfamily. It can be tricky as the parent–child relationship long pre-dates this new couple relationship. The struggle is: "How do we maintain our close bond when I feel so excluded or conflicted?" "How do we find time for us when the children need so much?" Sharon and Frank had begun to place all of their attention and time with their own children, devoting little energy toward their own relationship. Some couples put their relationship first, but this is harder on the children. As Papernow (2013) notes, "prioritizing the adult step couple relationship over parent–child relationships pulls parents away from their kids, resulting in an extremely difficult transition for kids" (p. 52). The direction for effective treatment is to support both subsystems rather choosing one over the other. Stepcouples dedicated to fostering resilience in their children and improving their relationship with one another are the most equipped to meet these challenges.

EFFT and Stepfamilies

In emotionally focused family therapy the therapist sees, hears, and understands the distress in stepfamilies through the attachment lens, viewing the drama and the steps to the complex dance in terms of each member's best attempt to preserve and maintain vital attachment bonds in the face of loss and uncertainty. This approach can explain and predict steps to the dance of distress and can significantly enhance and fortify stepfamily life. This attachment-based perspective brings clarity to understanding stepfamily distress and works to resource the stepfamily unit, by providing a joint sense of purpose for the stepcouple and a sense of belonging for the children.

Attachment theory provides an important bridge from understanding the complexity of stepfamily life to helping mitigate the challenges faced by stepfamilies. The theory accounts for differences in relationships between the adult couple, between biological or adoptive parent and child and between stepparent and stepchild. Attachment theory states that the attachment bond developed in early childhood between caregiver and child is a survival mechanism in human evolution. According to John Bowlby, the first author of attachment theory, the attachment figure becomes a secure base from which the child is able to explore the world (Bowlby, 1988). Disruption of the significant caregiver–child bond can result in severe negative consequences for the child.

Visher, Visher, and Paisley (2003) described stepfamilies as being "born of loss" and point out that although every member in the new stepfamily is experiencing loss, they may have difficulty with or be resistant to acknowledging and grieving this loss. Suppression or avoidance of the grieving process that is inherent in stepfamily life keeps families stuck and unable to help and support one another in this normative process. Remarried couples do not share the experiences of being each other's first and only love. They are also not jointly the attachment figures for all offspring. Children have lost their original family and have lost time with the non-residential parent. Their sense of loyalty to the non-residential parent (also an attachment figure) can result in behaviours and attitudes that block support and love from the residential parent and or stepparent. The strong sense of identity and belonging that comes with first family membership is missing. This can set the stage for competing attachments within the stepfamily unit as members vie for security, love, and attention (Furrow & Palmer, 2007). The difficult and conflictual thoughts, feelings, and behaviours present in new stepfamilies can be understood and explained in terms of attachment distress rooted in the loss of first family life and symptomatic of the transition from the first family to the developing stepfamily unit.

The EFT therapist uses attachment theory as a lens, a way to see and make sense of the multiple realities and dilemmas that exist in stepfamily formation (Furrow & Palmer, 2007, 2011). It was critical for Sharon and Frank's family that their EFT therapist viewed their problems from an attachment perspective and, as such, considered them to be normative and understandable. Their challenges were validated and normalized, and the therapist helped them to see their struggles as part of a normal course of development and not indicative of a defect in themselves, or each other. The therapist attunes to each family member, hearing and understanding the various attachment strategies used by members to cope with feelings of loss, sadness, and fear. These vulnerable feelings may be expressed instead as hostility or withdrawal, and this can lead to negative interactions between stepfamily members. The attachment lens helps the therapist to understand the distress and know that competing attachments are characteristic of stepfamily life.

Becky withdrew from her new stepfamily, refusing to eat dinner with the other family members and rejecting her mother's efforts to reach out to her. Becky's refusal to eat with the family was an expression of her own sadness and grief and a fear that she had lost her mom forever and as a result was now alone in the world. The more Sharon tried to talk to Becky, the more silent Becky became, the more frustrated and helpless Sharon felt. This negative interaction pattern further exacerbated the insecurity in the attachment bond between Sharon and Becky, and reverberated in other family constellations, including Sharon and Frank and the sibling relationships. Attachment problems arise from an inability to identify and confide the pain of multiples losses; when family members focus instead on negative behaviours and perceptions of others as hostile and different or dangerous. The challenge for the EFT therapist is to help all members identify the family problems as not only the result of the bumpiness of new stepfamily development but also as expression of fears of abandonment and rejection from those others that are most meaningful and significant (Furrow & Palmer, 2007).

Yet another layer of complexity involves fostering attachment security among stepfamilies' competing attachments between the new couple's relationship and the caretaking attachment between parent and biological or adopted child. The couple can find themselves in the position of needing to choose between the couple relationship and the parent–child relationship. It is essential to the stability and growth of the stepfamily unit that balance is found between these competing needs. By the end of their first year, Sharon and Frank were virtually ignoring their own relationship to focus on their respective children. This left the family vulnerable to dissolution. Another couple might ignore or dismiss the children's bids for attention to shore up their own relationship, resulting in the child responding through protest or despair (Furrow & Palmer, 2011).

The EFT therapist uses a strength-based and growth-oriented approach. This involves acknowledging and honoring the various attachment relationships in the new family helping to lift members out of disillusion and despair to find a new family niche, uniquely their own.

Sharon and Frank were helped by their therapist to accept their own ambivalent feelings toward their stepchildren and also to begin to empathize with each other around the challenges each faced in blending their separate units. Both partners were able to give each other space in spending time with their own children separate from the whole family and Sharon created mother and daughter outings for herself and Becky. Frank and Sharon also began to focus more on their own relationship and their therapist orchestrated bonding moments in their sessions where they could share authentically and vulnerably ask for what they needed. This helped them to rekindle the closeness and connection they had cherished in the early days of their relationship.

The EFT therapist mobilizes family members toward change by accessing, distilling, and deepening attachment-related emotion and then moving this new emotional experience to new bonding conversations with one another. Emotion is the music of the attachment dance, and when the therapist focuses on emotion, family members are moved to discover and explore new experiences in present time that promote healing and integration. In order to repair and resolve attachment injuries that may have occurred within the parent–child dyad, the EFT therapist works to facilitate and structure emotional conversations. Likewise, the new stepcouple need to have safe, emotionally vulnerable conversations with one another to meet one another's needs and build intimacy and strength as a united couple. In the beginning sessions, the EFT therapist reframes more reactive surface emotion, as part of the way this family member protects themselves in the stepfamily unit, and honors and makes sense of this emotion through the attachment lens.

For Becky, her dismissal and rejection of her mother's efforts provided a form of protection. Her actions were reframed as a needed shield in this new family that was foreign and unknown. The EFT therapist explores this emotion further by inquiring with curiosity and compassion how Becky now experiences her mother, a mother who chose this foreign and strange family. The EFT therapist sees secondary emotion as a window into the more primary, vulnerable affect, which in this case, with Becky, is related to themes of loss and fears of abandonment. By following the emotion in the room, that is expressed both verbally and non-verbally by all family members, the EFT therapist is harnessing the most powerful agent of change. In this way, the stepfamily is not only validated and educated about their new life together, they are eased into conversations that reshape, repair, and restore their relationships with one another and bring a new definition and meaning to their life together.

EFFT Process of Change and Stepfamilies

The treatment of stepfamilies follows three stages, stabilization and de-escalation, restructuring interaction, and consolidation. Within these three stages, there are nine steps in the model of change. Within each session, the EFT therapist uses the EFT tango as a guide for how to lead the session and utilizes the five moves of the tango to facilitate the therapy process. In the first step of Stage 1, assessment and alliance, the EFT therapist begins seeing the whole stepfamily together in order to build an alliance with each family member, and to hear each member's perspective on the problem. Observing the dynamic as it unfolds in session between the parent, children, and stepparent allows the EFT therapist to begin to track and reflect the present patterns of interaction between the family members. The interactional patterns are made explicit and are normalized by placing them in the context of the newly forming stepfamily unit. The reactive positions in key problematic cycles of interaction are identified and reframed as attachment protest or protection and the negative interactional cycle is externalized as the problem. The family begins to see that their struggles are not the result of individual problems or a defective family structure but that they are in a normative process that has become stuck (Furrow & Palmer, 2007).

Following this initial assessment period, which would typically include whole family session, parent and stepparent session, and sibling sessions, the future sessions would be structured along the attachment boundaries. The continuation of Stage 1, cycle de-escalation and Stage 2, restructuring interaction, would occur in a two-prong process. Parents and children would be seen in separate sessions for treatment in conjunction with separate couple sessions for the parent and the stepparent to strengthen the parenting coalition by also strengthening the couple bond. Restructuring the negative interaction within each subsystem would have the overall goal of increased attachment security between parent and child and parent and stepparent. The parent–child sessions would focus on bringing the parental care-taking system back online, through promoting parental emotional accessibility and responsiveness and helping this unit to grieve together and specifically for children to express directly their feelings of sadness, grief, hurt, and fear. The goal is for loss to be acknowledged, validated, and shared, so that children may receive comfort, reassurance, and support from their biological or adoptive parent (Furrow & Palmer, 2007).

The couple sessions would be focused on helping the new couple express directly with each other their needs in fulfilling their parenting and stepparenting roles, specifically the stepparent receiving reassurance, support, and empathy from their partner in their outside role, and for residential parents to receive assistance, support, and encouragement from their partners in their parenting tasks (e.g., Braithwaite & Baxter, 2006; Cartwright, 2012). In both treatment streams, the EFT therapist moves the process through the EFT tango, using skills of tracking and reflecting cycles of interaction, accessing, exploring, and enacting primary emotional experiences, and restructuring positive interactions to build and broaden attachment security. Stage 3, consolidation, of the EFFT treatment would end with a whole family session, helping all family members consolidate new positive cycles of interaction and to begin to construct a new narrative of their stepfamily life. The following case example was provided by Gail Palmer.

Case Example—The Temple Family

"We've Changed Enough"

The Temple family was referred for family therapy as a requisite step in the couple's application to adopt a child. Lionel and Tracy, both in their late thirties, had been married for one year, this being a second marriage for Lionel. He had two teenagers, Kieran (16) and Liam (13) who lived with the couple the majority of the time. The children's mother had remarried and moved out of province and had sporadic and limited contact with the boys. Both partners described their desire to adopt as a natural evolution, as they felt moved to share their new-found love with a child who needed love. They also hoped through parenting a child together, that they would further strengthen their marriage and solidify and unify their new family. Their application to adopt had been placed on hold by the adoption agency in the middle of their home study and the couple were motivated to secure family therapy in order to be able to achieve their goal to adopt.

Assessment

In the initial family session, Tracy described how anxious she was in being able to "complete her family" and recounted how hard she had been working to fit into Lionel's family and get close to the boys. She stated she had been very conscious of not wanting to be critical or authoritarian with them and had generally taken a "hands-off" approach as she stated it was not her role to be their parent. It was very important to her that she not repeat what she had experienced with her own stepfather who had come into her life as a teenager and with whom she had a contentious and hostile relationship. Tracy resisted the notion of becoming the "wicked stepmother" to Lionel's sons and sought ways to avoid this becoming her role.

Lionel acknowledged the changes Tracy made coming into the family and stated he was often distracted with work after spending many long hours at two jobs in an effort to overcome the financial debt he had incurred from his first marriage. In Lionel's view, the boys had adjusted well and showed good progress at school and at home. Kieran agreed with his father, saying that he was fine with the family changes as he was away at school or with his friends and that he "really didn't care" what his father and Tracy did because he would be leaving home in a year. Liam, on the other hand, was very quiet and kept silent for much of the conversation. When the conversation focused on his experience of the family, Liam shared that he was happy, but his face saddened in response as he turned away and avoided eye contact with everyone in the room. When the therapist reflected Liam's sadness, Tracy responded by describing Liam as a quiet boy and that she felt closer to him when she accepted his quiet nature as part of his personality. Liam nodded silently when asked how this was for him and Lionel explained how his son was a "good boy" who never was in any trouble and seemed content to spend time alone in his room often playing video games.

Kieran's nonplussed demeanor changed to irritation and impatience as the session continued, stating angrily that he had homework to complete. Lionel acknowledged Kieran's concern and attempted to pacify his protest. All the while, he also explained to the therapist how he wanted his sons to be happy and how hard he was working to try and make that happen. In this moment, a flash of sadness crossed Lionel's face as he took a breath. The therapist commented on this sad look, and Lionel denied feeling sad, shifting the focus back to Tracy's comment that the boys were happy and that the family was doing well. Lionel explained that his style was to focus on solving problems rather than dwelling on feelings and emotion. In his words, "that's really not what our family is like...."

Case Conceptualization

The initial family session revealed the Temple's family dance and how the family was responding to the attachment themes of loss and belonging that organized this stepfamily structure. The therapist moved through the EFT tango, accessing the differing levels of emotional expression and noted moments where negative emotions appeared to block the parents' openness and engagement. This informed the overarching pattern for this family where emotional contact was avoided. Preference was given to more superficial descriptions of the family including a flat narrative that seemed to be motivated by a desire, particularly by Tracy and Lionel, to be viewed positively.

The family's expressions of sadness or frustration evident throughout the session were rationalized, placated, or minimized by family members. Both children withdrew and avoided their emotions when interacting with their father and stepmother. Kieran appeared sullen, impatient, and irritated, often reluctant to participate. Liam avoided eye contact, remaining quiet and accepting the family's description of him being shy. Tracy took the lead in the discussion as the spokesperson for the family, offering her view of the children seen almost exclusively from her point of view. Lionel, on the other hand, fluctuated between trying to please his new wife and placating and pacifying his children. Adoption provided a joint venture for the new couple and Lionel and Tracy united around meeting the requirements of the adoption process, including attending seminars and completing a home study interview process. The boys, while resigned to this process and the session, clearly were impacted in ways the family had yet to acknowledge.

Stage 1—Stabilization and De-escalation

The therapist's goals in the initial sessions were to establish a strong working alliance with each family member and to explore each individual's emotional experience. An initial session with the couple provides the therapist with an assessment of the parenting alliance, and how available they were to the children's attachment needs for safety, security, and an understanding. Also, the couple's relationship would be explored and attachment histories for each person taken. Tracy and Lionel were open and receptive to therapy, and their strengths included their strong love for each other and their joint desire to build a strong family unit. As a family, however, their mutual efforts at parenting were blocked by their different roles as biological father and stepmother. Tracy's fears of rejection and not belonging and not being accepted by the biological family unit led her to focus on obtaining another child rather than seeking her own unique relationships with Lionel's boys. Conversely, Lionel's position of being in the middle between his wife and his children, led him to feel responsible for everyone's happiness and the success of this new family. His focus on pleasing others kept him unknown and distant from his sons. The initial couple session revealed that the couple required ongoing couple sessions alongside the family work to help them work though their differences in their co-parental alliance. The couple's inter-actional dance as father and stepmother blocked their accessibility to the boys and their ability to effectively support each other. Tracy's over-extension in her parenting response was met with the boys' rejection of her efforts followed by Lionel's passive response to Tracy's pleas for support and expressions of concern. The couple's differences in co-parenting had resulted in tension between the couple and their romantic bond. Lionel needed to find his own voice around how he wanted his children to be parented while also being able to listen and attune to Tracy's concerns. Tracy needed support from Lionel in her own feelings of being on the outside and her loss of Lionel through his avoiding strategies.

The following excerpt is from a Stage 1 session with Tracy and Lionel, in which the focus was mainly on each partner's experience and behavior in the couple's negative cycle. The couple were caught in a classic pursue/withdraw pattern, with Tracy actively protesting the loss of connection with her new husband and blaming Lionel for paying attention to his children and his work. Lionel would either defend himself by justifying his actions when confronted or avoiding contact with his wife. The more anxious Tracy would become, the more she would double her efforts to create connection, the more overwhelmed Lionel would become and withdraw. The therapist in this section is beginning to track the moves in the cycle between them, in order to make the pattern explicit and begin to frame this dynamic as the problem. The therapist is also using the five moves of the EFT tango to create a soft bonding moment in session that reconnects the couple with their love for one another in order to build hope between the couple and foster resilience around their parenting alliance.

THERAPIST: (to Tracy) So help me understand what has been happening when it comes to being a family together for the two of you? What happens between you when it comes to the boys. (tracking question focusing on the couple's interaction)

TRACY: (*energetically*) Well I don't really know. (*turning to look toward Lionel*) Lionel keeps everything to himself about the boys, when I ask him, he says everything is fine and the boys really don't talk to me. They only talk when he is around. He keeps me separate, he keeps me out and it's like I don't really exist.

THERAPIST: That sounds hard, not knowing what is going on with your husband. (*empathic reflection, attachment frame*)

TRACY: (*exasperated*) Oh! but I know something is up. I know something is bugging him. It is obvious! (*frowning*) He sits around and there is this heaviness but when I prod him, probe for what it is, I get nothing.

THERAPIST: Sure, that makes sense. Sounds like that would be very frustrating. (*validation of surface emotion*)

TRACY: (*crossing her arms, turning away from Lionel*) I just don't understand him. Maybe it is the difference between men and women. I am the only woman in the house. All I get is grunts and everything is fine.

THERAPIST: (*leaning in toward Tracy*) Well I can see how hard this would be not to know where things are at with Lionel and to feel on the outside with the boys. The only way in for you is through your husband and when you are in tune with him, you know something is up. So, you prod, you poke, and I wonder, being the only woman in the house, what that feels like for you? (*validation, attachment frame, evocative question*)

TRACY: (*face looks sad*) Like I don't belong. (*pauses*) And when Lionel gets like this, we don't have any time together, there is no fun, no date nights, no joy for us.

THERAPIST: Sure, it sounds like you miss him, you miss his company. (*therapist extends an empathic conjecture regarding her underlying sadness about being alone*)

TRACY: (*frustrated tone*) Lionel is either at work or driving the kids. (*speaking directly to Lionel and with agitation*) They are not little, you know, they could take the bus.

LIONEL: (*looking at Tracy, defending himself*) They need me. You know their mother is not around. I told you right from the start. I have two kids that pretty much depend on me and they have been through a lot.

THERAPIST: (*therapist turns to Lionel*) So Lionel, I can see that you are trying to help Tracy see how you need to be there as a father and how important it is to you as their father, but I am also wondering what is like to hear that she misses you? (*therapist reflection of present process, evocative question*)

LIONEL: I do want to be there for her too. I guess I don't always do a good job. (*face is still*) I need to look after a lot of different things, there is the financial fallout from the first marriage, my two jobs ... it's all too much sometimes.

THERAPIST: I can see that you are carrying a lot around with you and that has to be difficult. What's it like when Tracy wants to talk to you about what is happening for you in these moments? (*validation, tracking question*)

LIONEL: (*flat tone*) I am not really used to it. I pretty much look after things myself. I always have.

THERAPIST: And to share with Tracy, with your new partner, maybe for the first time in your life, to experience having a partner there beside you, someone you can share your problems with. (*heightening, attachment frame*)

LIONEL: (*More animated*) Well, I think it is my job not to burden her. These aren't her problems. I am not too sure she wants to hear all about my kids. Then it is more of the same. We don't spend enough time together. I figure it is up to me to figure it out. (*his voice trails away*)

THERAPIST: So, you go silent and say everything is fine, in an effort to fix it yourself and not to burden Tracy, as her happiness is very important to you. But then you, Tracy feel shut out and like you don't belong because you see it is not fine and you not be able to talk about it. It is very hard for the two of you, that despite your best intentions, you get stuck. In this cycle, you are not able to talk to each other about what you need, and it is this pattern that is stopping you from really being close and being a team together. (*formulating the cycle, reframing the problem*)

TRACY: (*looking at Lionel, frustrated*) Well I didn't wait all this time just to be alone.

LIONEL: (*looking at Tracy, pleading*) And I do want to be with you. This is all about wanting to be with you.

THERAPIST: This is so important, your relationship with one another. Tracy you do not want to be alone and (*leaning in and looking at Lionel*) Lionel, you are staring right at Tracy right now, with softness in your eyes, and you are saying "I do want to be with her" (*first move of EFT tango, mirroring the present process between the couple*)

LIONEL: (*reaches for Tracy's hand*)

THERAPIST: And what's that like to look at your wife, and let her know what is in your heart? (*evocative question*)

LIONEL: Well, I don't do it enough.

THERAPIST: But you are doing it right now. You are looking at her, you are holding her hand and you are declaring "I do want to be with you." And when you say those words, and you hold her hand, what's happening for you? (*second move of EFT tango, accessing underlying emotion*)

LIONEL: I feel good.

THERAPIST: Yeah, I can see that. Can you tell me about good? (*exploring positive affect*)

LIONEL: It's a relief. We did get together for a reason.

THERAPIST: So, your body feels relief, you remember what drew you to this woman, yeah? (*heightening*) (*Lionel nods*)

THERAPIST: Can you tell her? (*third move of the EFT tango, set up enactment*)

LIONEL: I do love you babe. I am so sorry I got you into all this.

THERAPIST: Yeah, you feel love and sorrow, both of these feelings, because she is so important to you.... And for you, Tracy, right now, to have Lionel here with you, right here, right now, he is here with you. (*fourth move of EFT tango, processing enactment*)

TRACY: (*eyes soften*) Mmmmm ... it gets hard to remember that.

THERAPIST: Sure, your love for one another is so evident right now, and you both feel it strongly right now. You took this big leap to be together. It isn't easy to do what you are doing. All couples in your situation find it hard. And when it gets hard, all of us find ways to cope. For you Tracy, when you can't find Lionel, you work harder, get more active, trying to make a connection with Lionel, and for you, Lionel, you are caught, you want to make it good for both Tracy and the kids, and when you can't do that, it's hard, and you stay away, and then both of you, lose contact with the love that brought you together in the first place. The love you are feeling right now. (*fifth move of the EFT tango, summarizing*)

By the end of the session, the couple agreed with the therapist's formulation of their problem as being their cycle which exasperated their ability to be close as a couple and to function well together as a parenting team. The family treatment plan included couple sessions interspersed with family sessions with the goal to strengthen the couple relationship in order to provide a stronger foundation for the family unit.

Stage 2—Restructuring Interactions

In Stage 2 of EFFT the therapist focused on the blocks that interrupted Tracy and Lionel's best efforts to respond in an emotionally accessibly way to Kieran and Liam. Working through these parental blocks begins with a focus on the child's attachment-related emotions and needs. In the Temple family, it was critical to help Lionel, the biological parent, focus on his children and to separate out the marriage relationship from the parenting relationship due to the conflicting and competing nature of the attachment needs of the two sub-systems. Kieran and Liam needed their father's undivided attention and Lionel needed the opportunity to be entirely present for his children. The EFT therapist now actively restructures the family's in-session interactions in order that the boys can openly express their attachment emotions to their father and to help Lionel to become more accessible and responsive to his sons.

Session three was scheduled for Kieran and his father alone as this dyad appeared to be the most distressed relationship. Kieran had remained withdrawn and sullen in the first two sessions but did agree to a separate session with his father. The therapist playfully joked with Kieran for coming into the session and spent time inquiring about his football games. (*building alliance*) The therapist begins the session focusing on tracking the interaction between Lionel and Keiran.

THERAPIST: So, guys this is our chance to talk about how it goes now between the two of you, at home, in your relationships with each other. I recognize there have been lots of changes in your family and I am wondering if you could give me a picture of what that is like now between you? (*focusing on possible interaction pattern*)

LIONEL: Well, there isn't a lot of time, between work, school, and football but we like to spend time together when we get a chance. Kieran is pretty busy these days with his friends which is what I would expect. He is getting older and doesn't want to spend all his time with his old man and he has his video games which I can totally understand, I like playing those games too. But we like football, and I coach the games. So, we spend a lot of time at the field.

THERAPIST: I can see you guys have a lot in common and it is great that you enjoy football together, but I am wondering, Kieran, your father says that you are busy with your friends and don't have much time to spend with him. I am wondering if that is how you see it? (*therapist shifts focus to relationships and emotional connections*)

KEIRAN: Pretty much.

THERAPIST: Yeah and you guys have football in common, yes, your father coaches you? He has been doing that for a long time, yes? Is that the way it is? And then off the field, you are off with your friends, yes? (*reflection*)

KEIRAN: (*irritated*) I really don't have much choice. They're not welcome at our house.

LIONEL: (*abruptly*) Sure they are. You can bring your friends over anytime.

KEIRAN: (*voice rising*) You say that now but if Tracy were here it would be a whole different story. I ask you if I can have friends over and you say yes, but then you go upstairs and talk to the boss and the whole story changes.

LIONEL: (*now defensive*) I really don't think that is the case.

THERAPIST: Can we slow down here a bit. This sounds really important. Kieran, this is really frustrating for you and I think it is really important that we try and understand what this is like for you. And this sounds like this is brand new for you Lionel, you didn't know that Kieran was so upset? (*reflecting present process, focusing on Kieran's protest, an attachment-significant emotion*)

LIONEL: No, I thought he wanted to be with his friends.

KEIRAN: (*incredulous, voice rising*) I do!! But I also want to occasionally be able to relax in my own home with my friends too and not have to always be over at their house. There was a time when they could come over anytime. (*sarcastically*) But not now! We have new rules! Everything has to be quiet by 9 o'clock and, oh no, there could never be a sleep-over!!

THERAPIST: (*soothing voice*) This sounds really hard Kieran, and it sounds like there has been a lot of changes. A lot of changes and changes you didn't have any control about and you sound really unhappy about all of this, yes? (*empathic conjecture, heightening*)

KEIRAN: The queen runs the show. (*glaring at his father*) You never stand up to her. Its Tracy's rules and Tracy's house!! What we want doesn't matter!

LIONEL: (*tersely*) That is not true. You really don't know what happens between Tracy and myself.

THERAPIST: Ok, guys, let's go slow. Let's try and understand this. Lionel, this seems to be news to you that Kieran is so unhappy, and I am thinking that it is a really good thing, Kieran, that you are trying to let your father know how you are feeling about these changes. (*first move of EFT tango, reflect present process*) Lionel, what would it be like for you to know more about how it is for Kieran? Do you want to know how your son feels about things in this family? (*evocative question, shoring up father's engagement*)

LIONEL: Yes, of course.

KEIRAN: (*sarcastically*) Sure thing dad. Are you sure the boss will let you?

THERAPIST: A lot has changed in this family and it sounds like now Kieran you are not too sure where things stand between you with your dad. (*empathic conjecture*)

LIONEL: Well I think Kieran is not understanding Tracy. After all, she really is trying very hard and really likes the boys....

THERAPIST: (*interjects*) Can I interrupt you Lionel? I can see it's important to explain Tracy's side of this, but I think it's important what Kieran is trying to say to you right now about how things are for him. Can we just stay right here? (*evocative response, refocusing on father/son dyad, supporting Father's engagement*)

LIONEL: (*to Kieran*) Sure.

THERAPIST: Yes, that is really important, you do want to be there for your son, you want him to feel like he can open up to you so that you can really understand. (*reinforcing parental intent*) (*slowly and softly*) Kieran, this is so frustrating for you, I can see that. This is big and hard for you. There is a whole lot going on for you that maybe your father does not know anything about. (*second move of EFT tango, evoking Kieran's deeper emotion*)

KEIRAN: (*tearful, voice breaking*) I am so sick of all the changes, that is my whole life, changes. I can't take any more changes.

THERAPIST: It is so important to let your father in and it takes a lot of courage to show him how sad you feel. (*third move of EFT tango, reinforcing enactment from son to father, validation of Kieran's sadness, an attachment significant emotion*)

KEIRAN: (*crying*) I hate feeling this way, I can't stand it, this really sucks. (*father reaches out to touch son's shoulder, Kieran shakes him off*).

THERAPIST: (*softly*) This is really painful Kieran, you miss how it used to be, of course, things were different when your mom and father were together. Of course, you feel sad. and when your father reaches for you, it's too hard to trust that, yeah? It's like you don't know if you matter anymore to your father? Tracy is more important? (*fourth move of EFT tango, processing enactment from son's side, validation, tracking process, empathic conjecture*)

KEIRAN: (*nodding in agreement*)

THERAPIST: And that has to be very hard? Sure, you are growing up, you are almost ready to move away from home, but that doesn't mean that you don't still need your father, yes? I can see Lionel that you want to be there for your son right now. (*reflection of father's non-verbal attachment response*) What's it like for you when you see his sadness? (*fourth move of EFT tango, processing enactment*)

LIONEL: (*talking to Kieran*) This sucks for me too. To see you so hurt. I didn't know (*voice drops*) I am so sorry. (*eyes fill with tears*)

THERAPIST: You feel for Kieran and his hurt. That was the last thing you wanted was your boy to be hurt, it brings you to tears. (*heightening father's remorse and sadness*) You both are feeling really sad about the changes, there has been a lot of changes. (*reinforcing the attachment bond between father and son*)

LIONEL: (*spontaneous enactment from father to Kieran*) I want you to know I am here. I am your father.

THERAPIST: Yes, you want Kieran to know you are here, you haven't gone away. And Kieran letting you know how he feels about all this lets you be able to lend him a hand and let him know he is not alone. You guys are in this together. (*fifth move of EFT tango, summary, validation of attachment-significant emotion*)

LIONEL: You will never lose me. You got me for life.

KEIRAN: (*lifts his head, looking at his father, laughing*) I wouldn't go that far!

The therapist has helped Lionel move past his block of defending his new wife to listening to his son and Kieran is encouraged to express the pain under his frustration. When Kieran was able to access his sadness around the losses he has endured, he is able to send a clear emotional message to his father about his vulnerability, which pulls for a caregiving response from his father. Lionel is demonstrating emotional accessibility and responsiveness to Kieran's vulnerability, offering his son his unconditional and never-ending support.

The therapist circled back to Kieran, asking what it was like for him to share his sadness underneath his anger, "exhausting," to which Lionel let Kieran know how proud he was that Kieran was able to take this step to open up and share his emotions with him. Lionel shared that he was trying to figure out how to be the best father, and to do that he needed to know how his son was feeling. He admitted that he was learning himself how to talk about feelings, that this was a new process for him too and that he wanted to work on this together. Kieran smiled at his father's praise and then talked about how much he enjoyed their time together on the football field. Kieran moved from withdrawn and avoiding eye contact at the beginning of the session, to becoming more involved as the session progressed. When the therapist inquired about how this session was for him, he acknowledged it was "good." The playful interchange between Lionel and Kieran increased as the session ended, and the therapist noted the positive affect that was evident. Kieran stated that he wanted to bring in his little brother for the next session as "he really needs it."

The next family session focused more on Liam and his concerns regarding his place in the family. Liam was the quieter of the two sons and Kieran began the session saying that Liam has needs too that had been overlooked with the family changes. The therapist validated Kieran for supporting his brother while also making space for Liam and Lionel to work on their relationship directly. The therapist made explicit that their father wanted to know how each of his sons were feeling and structured an enactment between Lionel and Liam to ensure that Liam felt his father's emotional presence. Kieran again interjected and offered that his younger brother felt closest to their mother. The therapist again validated Kieran for his support but quickly refocused the interaction between Liam and his father. The therapist validated how hard it must be for Liam to be away from his mother and conjectured that it might also be hard for him to talk about what he was feeling because he didn't want to hurt his father's feelings.

The therapist invited Lionel to respond to his son's dilemma and Lionel made it perfectly clear to Liam that he wanted to hear how he felt, that he didn't have to protect him as he "could take it" and it was his job to take care of him. With his father's reach, Liam dropped into his sadness but quickly denied it, saying "I'm ok." With the therapist's validation and support, and offering a conjecture that Liam really needed to know that it was safe to talk about his mother and how much he missed her. The therapist highlighted Liam's loyalty bind between his love for his mother and the presence of his stepmother in his life and made sense of his withdrawal and avoidance as a way to protect himself from the pain of his loss and the bind he was in. When Lionel understood that his son's quietness was coming from his son's internal conflict, he was able to see Liam more clearly and reach to him with openness and reassurance. With this signal of his father's availability,

Liam deepened further into his sadness, confiding that he thought his mom had gone away because she didn't love him and maybe he had done something wrong. Liam offered reassurance, and an explanation for the mother's absence, reassuring Liam that his mother's absence had nothing to do with her not loving the boys. Lionel offered to help Liam contact his mother and supported both boys in their relationship with her. The session ended with the boys smiling and being relaxed with their father. Lionel thanked his sons for this conversation as he learnt more about how to be the father he wanted to be and the father his boys needed.

Lionel took what he had learned from his sons back to Tracy and the couple integrated their new insights about the boys into their plans for adoption which they decided to forestall. The couple continued to focus on strengthening their marriage so that they could build a stronger foundation for the family and increase support for one another.

In a final couple session, the therapist focused entirely on the couple's bond with each other with the goal to deepen their connection through the sharing of their own attachment fears and needs. Tracy's sadness and loss about not having a child of her own and a child with Lionel was the entry way into a deeper emotional conversation between the couple. As Tracy shared her sadness with Lionel, Lionel was able to comfort and be present with her pain and responded that he too had longed to have the shared experience of having a child with Tracy. As the couple were able to connect and be present with each other around their mutual sadness and loss, the therapist reflected the present moment and heightened their felt sense of closeness and connection. Expanding on what it felt like to be close to his partner, Lionel stated how much he needed Tracy in his life. In an enactment, Lionel, visibly moved and emotionally vulnerable, shared how much he needed Tracy's support and when he had that he was a "better man." Lionel's reach for Tracy moved her to tears and when the therapist explored her emotion, she shared how afraid she was that if they didn't have a child together that maybe she would lose him and how afraid she was if she wasn't a mother, and if they weren't parents together, that maybe she wouldn't be "good enough" for Lionel, that he would be "disappointed" in her and in their life together. The therapist supported Tracy to share directly with Lionel, and she expressed that knowing how much he really needed her, reassured her and helped her feel loved and that she belonged. Lionel's full emotional engagement enabled Tracy to dig deeper and disclose that what she really needed was to know that she was important and special to Lionel and that he wanted to be with her regardless of what the future would hold. Lionel reached back and moved closer to her physically calling her "my beauty queen" and holding her close.

These new exchanges were summarized and contrasted with their negative cycle, emphasizing how the couple had a new strength to rely on when they felt divided about the children. By focusing on their mutual need for one another and expressing their longing for support and reassurance from one another, they were able to feel secure. This new felt sense of security resourced them, not only as a newly married couple but as father and stepmother, to face the challenges of stepfamily life together.

Stage 3—Consolidation

A final session with the family focused on the changes made within the family and the new experiences and meaning the family had gained through facing these challenges. A session was held with the whole family unit to track and reflect how the family was functioning currently and help to solidify and consolidate the changes they had made. In general, the family continued to have issues associated with stepfamilies but the family climate had shifted. There was an open flow of conversation between all the family members and the emotional tone was light and easy, reflecting a recovery from the withdrawn, avoidant pattern that was characteristic of the family in the beginning of treatment. Lionel said that he never realized he could actually learn to talk about his feelings as feelings were not talked about in his family growing up and how proud he was of both of his sons that they had skills as teenagers that he didn't have and was just acquiring as a 50-year-old man. He expressed appreciation of Tracy and how she had helped him to grow emotionally. The boys responded positively to their father's praise and Kieran stated that he liked how much Tracy supported his father and that he could see that his father was happier now. Liam joked and said that he even was letting Tracy come to some of his football games that his father coached. The therapist reinforced and celebrated with the family their wins and reinforced how courageous all of them had been to face these challenges together. As the family talked about Kieran's plans to attend college out of the city, and how they felt about this new transition all of the family agreed that they had moved from "we have changed enough" to "we can change together."

Conclusion

Stepfamily life is a natural evolution following divorce yet is complex and challenging due to the competing attachments between the new couple who is encountering their second chance at love and children who have now been assigned a new family. EFFT provides a clear and comprehensive map to intervention with distressed stepfamilies, honoring the needs of both subsystems while repairing and strengthening the caregiving attachment system. Sharon and Frank navigated the lumpiness in their blending by understanding and accepting the losses encountered by their children, and strengthening their bond to support them in their fears and insecurities. The Temple family was helped to give the children a voice in expressing their pain with the changes in their family, engaging their father to be present and available to help them with these losses. The couple were strengthened in their co-parenting alliance by processing their fears around their relationship and their need for support and reassurance from one another. By helping parents reconnect with their kids and couples support each other in building a realistic parenting coalition, EFFT helps give children back their childhood and resources new family formations in their efforts to grow and find their new family identity.

References

Afifi, T. (2003). "Feeling caught" in stepfamilies: Managing boundary turbulence through appropriate communication privacy rules. *Journal of Social and Personal Relationships, 20*, 729–755.

Bowlby, J. (1988). *A secure base: Parent–child attachment and healthy human development.* New York: Basic Books.

Braithwaite, D., & Baxter, L. (2006). You're my parent but you're not: Dialectical tensions in stepchildren's perceptions about communicating with the non-residential parent. *Journal of Applied Communication Research, 34*, 30–48.

Cartwright, C. (2012). The effects of co-parenting relationships with ex-spouses on couples in step-families. *Family Matters, 92*, 18–26.

Coleman, M., Ganong, L. H., & Fine, M. A. (2000). Reinvestigating remarriage: Another decade of progress. *Journal of Marriage and the Family, 62*, 1288–1307.

Dunn, J. (2002). The adjustment of children in stepfamilies: Lessons for community studies. *Child and Adolescent Mental Health, 7*, 154–161.

Emery, R. E. (2011). *Renegotiating family relationships: Divorce, child custody, and mediation.* New York: Guilford Press.

Furrow, J. L., & Palmer, G. (2007). EFFT and blended families: Building bonds from the inside out. *Journal of Systemic Therapies, 26*, 44–58.

Furrow, J. L., & Palmer, G. (2011). Emotionally focused therapy for remarried couples: Making new connections and facing competing attachments. In J. Furrow, S. Johnson, & B. Bradley (Eds.), *The emotionally focused casebook: New directions in treating couples* (pp. 3–30). New York: Routledge.

Ganong, L. H. and Coleman, M. (2004). *Stepfamily relationships: Development, dynamics, and intervention.* New York: Kluwer.

Hetherington, E. M., & Jodl, K. M. (1994). Stepfamilies as settings for child development. In A. Booth & J. Dunn (Eds.), *Stepfamilies: Who benefits? Who does not?* (pp. 55–79). Hillsdale, NJ: Lawrence Erlbaum.

Hetherington, E. M. (2003). Social support and the adjustment of children in divorced and re-married families. *Childhood, 10*, 217–236.

Katz, L., & Stein, S. (2012). Treating stepfamilies. In S. A. Shueman & B. B. Wolman (Eds.), *Handbook of family and marital therapy* (pp. 387–420). Berlin: Springer Science & Business Media.

Marquardt, E. (2005). *Between two worlds: The inner lives of children of divorce.* New York: Three Rivers Press.

Papernow, P. (2013). *Surviving and thriving in stepfamily relationships: What works and what doesn't.* New York: Routledge.

Pew Research Center (2015). The American Family Today (Report No. XXX). Retrieved from Pew Research Center: www.pewsocialtrends.org/2015/12/17/1-the-American-family-today/

Statistics Canada. (2017, August 2). Portrait of children's family life in 2016. Retrieved from www12.statscan.gc.ca

Visher, J., & Visher, E. (1996). *Therapy with stepfamilies.* New York: Brunner/Mazel.

Visher, E. B., Visher, J. S., & Pasley, K. (2003). *Remarriage families and step-parenting. Normal family processes: Growing diversity and complexity,* 2nd Ed. (pp. 153–175). New York: Guildford Press.

Wallerstein, J., Lewis, J., Blakeslee, S., & McIntire, K. (2000). *The unexpected legacy of divorce: A 25 year landmark study.* New York: Hachette Books.

Websites

Statistics Canada www.statcan.gc.ca.
US Bureau of Statistics www.census.gov.

TWELVE

Case Example—EFFT and Traumatic Loss

Watching the ambulance drive away with her dead brother, Layla (16) felt the sheer terror of facing her fear and pain utterly alone. Hours earlier she found her younger brother David's body in his bedroom, dead following a self-inflicted gunshot wound. Instantly, Layla's world turned upside down and her family was ripped apart through the impact of this loss and her parents' intense grief and marital discord. The intense pattern of emotional disconnection organized the family's shared response to this traumatic loss leaving Layla to carry the fear and pain about her brother's suicide alone. The family's silent suffering embedded the unresolved loss and its visceral impact on family member relationships for years to come.

Although the family's corporate avoidance provided a level of homeostasis, it could not contain the curiosity of Layla's children's interest in the mysterious death of their uncle. Layla found herself divided between the needs of her own children's understanding and her mother's attempts to silence the conversation about this death. In this moment, Layla attempted to guide her young boys through the harrowing story and found she was re-experiencing the impact of this devastating loss. Her mother withdrew in a way that felt identical to Layla's experience of her mother's avoidance at the time of her brother's death. Layla was attempting a conversation that she had never had with her own mother and now her mother's withdrawal seemed to replay the family's history of silence, echoing the loneliness and isolation that resulted. She fought to keep this pattern from replaying in her own relationship with her children.

This chapter illustrates the promise of EFFT in the treatment of relational distress related to unresolved traumatic loss within a family system. The principles and practices of EFFT are explored when the therapist is working with family members impacted by traumatic loss. The case example of Layla's family demonstrates the successful treatment of a family as they revisit a traumatic loss whose grief has now spread over generations. The case provides key insights to engaging the family in addressing this loss and promoting greater resilience for the family as a whole. This case example was provided by Lisa Palmer-Olsen and George Faller.

Trauma and Family Relationships

The symptoms of trauma exposure and not uncommon to the families seeking treatment for relationship disorder. Following some estimates, almost 50 percent of children in the United States (approximately 35,000,000) have experienced at least one type of serious childhood trauma, according to a survey on adverse childhood experiences by the National Survey of Children's Health (NSCH, 2013). In addition, other findings suggest that 10 percent of adolescents have experienced more than 15 types of victimization (Hanson, Moreland, & Orengo-Aguayo, 2018). The prevalence of traumatic exposure is widely reported in adulthood as a study of 3,000 American adults showed that 89.7 percent were exposed to multiple traumatic events in their lifetime (Kilpatrick, Resnick, Milanak, Miller, Keyes, & Friedman, 2013). Although the majority of children and adolescents who are securely connected often manifest resilience in the aftermath of a traumatic event, yet children who have been exposed to multiple traumas and have experienced their caregiver(s) as emotionally unavailable and/or unsafe are more likely to face greater risk for developing significant long-term mental health symptoms (Goff & Schwerdtfeger, 2013).

The absence of responsive caregiving in the advent of traumatic exposure places children at risk for maladaptive responses to traumatic loss and adversity. In a complex and distressing environment without any resource for emotional safety and security, the child's world remains largely unpredictable and leaving them at greater risk of further traumatization and psychological distress (Johnson, 2002). Children face greater risks for isolation and further trauma exposure when parental availability is uncertain (Crittenden & Heller, 2017). A child who has been left to face their feelings alone as a result of trauma, may turn to anxious pursuit style strategies such as clinging, hyperactivity, and lashing out or withdrawal type strategies such as inattention, disassociation, or numbing. The function of secondary attachment strategies provides children and adults with self-protective responses to the lack of support and emotional availability through important others (Ainsworth, 1964; Mikulincer, Shaver, & Solomon, 2015). For example, a perceived lack of partner support before and after a traumatic event is one of the most important factors determining vulnerability to post traumatic stress disorder (PTSD) (Charuvastra & Cloitre, 2008). The importance of the relational resources in coping with trauma has led some authors to conclude that PTSD is itself a crisis of social connection (Figley & Figley, 2009; James & MacKinnon, 2012).

Although some will seek to numb their experience and withdraw from others to cope with overwhelming negative affect, reaching toward supportive others has shown adaptive and beneficial outcomes related to trauma exposure (Olff, 2012). Stress is qualitatively experienced differently whether we face it alone or share it with another person (Johnson, 2002). Individuals who experience vital connection with others, have a diverse social network, and the more they perceive they have social support after a traumatic event, the less they are at risk for developing PTSD (Dworkin, Ojoalehto, Dedard-Gilligan, Cadigan, & Kaysen, 2018; Ozer, Best, Lipsey, & Weiss, 2003; Platt, Keyes, & Koenen, 2014). Therefore, the process of healing should help survivors to "establish safe emotional connections to significant others" (Greenman & Johnson, 2012, p. 2) to buffer the potential damage of this trauma exposure.

EFT Treatment and Traumatic Events

Emotionally focused therapy provides an important relational resource to address the trauma-related symptom and improve the overall quality of relational support. Research findings highlight the potential impact of EFT on trauma-related experiences and related interpersonal difficulties associated with exposure. For example, two studies demonstrate the positive effects of EFT on relationship outcomes for couples where one partner has been diagnosed with PTSD (MacIntosh and Johnson, 2008; Weissman et al., 2017). Other studies have examined the positive effects of EFT treatment on relationship adjustment for couples facing depression (Denton, Wittenborn, & Golden; 2012; Dessaulles, Johnson, & Denton, 2003) and promoting partner support when facing life-threatening health conditions (Couture-Lalande, Greenman, Naaman, & Johnson, 2007). Other findings demonstrate EFT effectiveness in addressing relationship adjustment for parents raising chronically ill children (Clothier, Manion, Gordon-Walker, & Johnson, 2002; Gordon-Walker, Manion, & Clothier, 1998). Though none of these studies examine the effect of EFT treatment on family relationships these studies point to the role of EFT as a resource for relationship adjustment when confronted with psychological distress and other relational stressors commonly associated with trauma exposure.

In EFT, negative interactional patterns reflect the negative emotions associated with separation distress in relationships of importance. In the presence of traumatic events the EFT therapist factors these events into an understanding of these relational patterns. Family members caught in patterns of insecurity in their family relationships cope with the related distress in predictable ways (e.g., avoidance, anxious responding) and traumatic exposure may influence these existing strategies through reinforcing or reversing these relational strategies. Differences in family responses may reflect the nature of the trauma and degree of exposure and these differences impact patterns of alienation and isolation in the family (Saltzman, Babayon, Lester, Beardslee, & Pynoos, 2008). In EFFT, the therapist is focused on repairing these negative patterns that block a family's ability to resource and support one another particularly in the face of emotional impact of traumatic events and restoring security as a resource for resilience in the family.

EFFT Process of Change and Traumatic Experience

In Stage 1 of EFFT with trauma, the therapeutic goal is to help the family to understand how the trauma impacts each member's positions in the negative patterns and to identify and process the blocks to attachment and caregiving. The therapist respects the resources available in the family to support those impacted by traumatic exposure and prioritizes the development of safety and stability through Stage 1. The impact of traumatic experiences is acknowledged, and secondary attachment strategies are identified within the context of the family's negative interactional pattern. The EFT therapist may educate family members regarding the psychological impact of trauma and its influence on relationships (Johnson & Faller, 2011). As the family reactivity de-escalates over the first few sessions by uniting against the negative pattern, the increased responsiveness creates the safety needed to confront and work through the trauma in Stage 2 of EFFT. The therapist identifies and initiates a process for working through the relational blocks that exacerbate the trauma symptoms while Stage 2 focuses on replacing the negative patterns created by the relational blocks with positive patterns that promote healing.

It is in Stage 2, the restructuring phase, that the vulnerable emotions for the child are accessed and expressed and in response to clear emotional signals, parents are able to provide comfort and care. As part of the change processes in this stage of therapy, the child's working models of self and others are positively revised as they experience the availability and responsiveness of a previously disengaged caregiver. The impacts of trauma that have blocked caregiving and care receiving are thereby similarly attenuated.

The goal of Stage 2 in EFFT is to restructure attachment and caregiving processes in the family. The focus of Stage 2 shifts to the unexpressed attachment-related emotions and unmet attachment needs and promoting the active acceptance and engaged response of these needs. Typically, the focus in Stage 2 begins with a deepening focus on a child's attachment-related emotions and longings. This process is led by the therapist expanding the child's emotional experience, in a family environment that is safe and responsive enough for the child to risk emotionally and potentially have a corrective, healing experience. The process balances emotional exploration and processing of the empathic failures and relational ruptures experienced often in the context of traumatic experiences. Additional attention is given to trauma-related responses (e.g., dissociation, shame, etc.) that can become disorienting.

The EFT therapist provides support and reassurance to reorganize and reorient the individual to the safety resources present in the moment (Johnson, 2002). Through contacting disowned emotions and aspects of self, the EFT therapist expands the child's sense of self and integrates this into a new conversation with the parents. As the parent listens and responds to a child's coherent story with clearer emotional signal, the therapist supports the parent's ability to respond from a caregiving position that is actively attuned and provides comfort and support. The EFT therapist follows the five moves of the EFT tango, processing on a deeper level the attachment fears and longings and in real time, choreographing a redefining enactment between child and parent. The final stage of EFFT focuses on consolidating the changes made by the family through the steps they have taken toward a more secure connection. The family may revisit past problems with new relational resources where the focus is on maintaining the positive cycles informed by family connections defined by accessibility, responsiveness, and emotional engagement (Johnson, 2019).

Stabilization—Promoting Safety and Predictability

The EFT therapist's main goal when working with a family following a traumatic experience begins with establishing a level of safety and predictability in engaging family members in treatment. As the therapist fosters an alliance with each family member, special attention is given to the predictable patterns organizing distress in the family and the role that the traumatic event plays in these patterns. Through this initial phase of alliance building and assessment family members are invited to share their individual perspective and experience of the specific traumatic event and how each understands this impacting the family. The therapist tracks the ways in which family members have coped with the traumatic event and the degree to which they have been able to turn to one another for support in moments of distress. Successful and unsuccessful attempts at responding to distress are explored and related to the patterns of coping that define the family's overall response to the traumatic event.

Often the focus for a family is on the traumatic event as a primary impediment to family cohesion and flexibility. The EFT therapist seeks to expand the family's perspective, fostering an understanding and awareness of the family's crisis of connection in the here now of relationships rather than an exclusive focus on the traumatic past. Special attention is given to the strengths of the family and the ways in which each member has been coping with this specific event. Support is provided for each family member in their own experiences of the event and related response, recognizing that differences in perception and experience can prove threatening to family stability and disruptive to current efforts to cope as a family unit. Highlighting the family's resilience in the midst of a challenging environment, the therapist makes explicit the positive intentions motivating each family members' protective responses.

Additionally, the EFT therapist maintains a particular focus on the role that trauma events have played in the family cycle of insecurity. Greater attention is given to monitoring and promoting safety in the context of the exploring and engaging relational experience that are impacted by traumatic experiences. The EFT therapist provides stability and predictability in the treatment process to promote the processing and sharing of more vulnerable emotional experiences. This trauma sensitive focus is described below, and a case example is used to illustrate the use of EFFT with family working through the impact of a traumatic loss on their relationships and personal wellbeing.

Assessing Safety and Trauma History

Creating safety is crucial to any trauma work. Therefore, a lack of safety is a contraindication in working with trauma and especially when working within the EFT model for family therapy. At the onset of EFFT and during the assessment phase, the EFFT therapist needs to assess for substance abuse and violence immediately. Abuse of any kind, including severe neglect and verbal abuse, robs families of the safety needed to confront and heal the trauma as a family system. If the therapist determines a child is in danger, then steps must be taken to protect the child. If the therapist cannot help the family create a minimum level of emotional and physical safety necessary to openly engage in the process, then it is unsafe to risk exploring the trauma. In this case, increasing vulnerability among family members would be counterproductive and to continue to engage in therapy would worsen the impact of trauma.

Another factor to incorporate early in treatment is developing a comprehensive global assessment of each family member's trauma history and each individual's readiness for conjoint treatment. Variables such as the number of times exposed to trauma (Adverse Childhood Experiences Score) (Dube, Anda, Felitti, Chapman, Williamson, & Giles, 2001), duration of the event, age of onset, proximity to event, and possible resiliency factors are all relevant in guiding treatment and understanding each family member's experience (Johnson & Rheem, 2012). Taking the time to thoroughly evaluate potential strengths and limitations resulting from the present and past traumatic events increases the likelihood of the therapist attuning to client's experiences.

Processing Experience and Promoting Predictability

The therapist actively monitors and maintains their alliance with family members including the pacing of EFT interventions. Trauma responses can often feel like a rollercoaster of emotions. Interventions such as reflection, validation, and normalization help family members with affect regulation including the ability to stay engaged with their experiences and meaning making. Careful attunement and tracking helps the therapist gage the family member's ability to tolerate sharing their traumatic experience. The therapist is continually looking for signs of flooding (hyperarousal) or avoidance (dissociation) in session, which indicates the client may needs help to safely ground and return to the present moment. This focused attention on each family member's state of emotional regulation and "window of tolerance" (Siegel, 1999, p. 253), and quick action to assist in containment when family members fail to regulate, is essential to creating the safety necessary to increase their tolerance to address the trauma with supportive others rather than in isolation.

If there is too much defensiveness in the family that prevents the safe exploration of the trauma then separate individual therapy is encouraged for the trauma survivor. As interpersonal blocks are processed in the family sessions, it is helpful for the trauma survivor to have a separate space for processing their trauma-related experiences and communication of needs and feelings with the therapist. Ideally, the trauma survivor is able to name, feel, and speak from their emotions and experience related to the trauma in a regulated way before entering family sessions where they will be asked to do the same thing, but in the presence of family members. Both family and individual therapy can be coordinated to determine the best route to creating the necessary safety for treatment.

As trauma symptoms can appear unpredictable and dysregulating, the ability to help clients make sense of their experiences can be beneficial in the beginning stages and throughout trauma work (Allen, 2001). Therefore, providing education about traumatic stress and how it impacts relationships is another helpful tool in creating safety. In EFFT, education is never done in a purely didactic manner that is distant from the families' lived experience. Information about trauma symptoms and recovery is shared in the context of the family members' shared experience. Education given in this way becomes an intervention that helps ground the family members in the here and now and also enables them to integrate and make sense of their experience. When family members start to understand their behaviors are normal and predictable after a trauma, they start to gain some safe distance from the event and a greater stability to revisit the event when they are ready.

The EFT therapist reflects and summarizes family members' experiences as they work through emotionally laden experiences. These summaries support meaning making for the family and the narratives necessary for integrating traumatic experiences into their shared relational experience.

These statements help families move beyond a content focus on the problem and invite exploration into the process of *how* they are interacting with one another. Process summary statements also connect the *why* of the family interactions. Used effectively, clinical summarizations can be a useful tool for the therapist in service of externalizing the presenting problem. Following the EFT tango, the therapist moves between individual and family experience, each time assessing the emotional impact and meaning for family members as they witness the other's experience. These attachment-related reflections often help family members slow down their reactive negative interactions and create space to explore the vulnerable feelings hiding underneath the defensive pattern. Meaning making empowers trauma survivors to understand how they got to where they are and sets them up to take control over their traumatic experiences instead of remaining helpless victims to the negative family pattern.

Case Example—Simon

"No One Says His Name"

Layla, 34-year-old mother of two sons, sought family therapy with her family of origin for unresolved issues around her brother's death by suicide. She initially sought individual therapy for the distress she experienced when she was attempting to explain to her school-age children her brother's death by suicide. In recounting these events Layla began re-experiencing the loss through intrusive thoughts and panic episodes; this was complicated by her mother's attempts to quiet her grandson's questions and concerns, which Layla felt was a direct emotional rejection of her son's empathic concern and a replay of her mother's ongoing strategy for avoiding any discussion of this traumatic loss.

The impact of her mother's intervention triggered Layla's own experience of her family's emotional isolation during the time of her brother's suicide. Layla had discovered her brother's body, and her mother Alice followed shortly behind her. Alice began to scream hysterically and became unreachable the moment she saw her son. Alice was quickly transported to the hospital leaving Layla alone with the police and paramedics. Her father and brother were also unavailable, as they were out of town. Looking back on this moment Layla, as an adult, understands that she put her feelings aside to keep herself protected and emotionally stable. She had no one available to turn to and falling apart would not help her mom or herself. Layla had no idea that this emotional isolation and absence of support would become the family's way of dealing with this loss. Individuals in the family kept their emotions to themselves and the family avoided referring to the loss of her brother and were not allowed to speak his name. The family's pattern of avoidance suspended each in their pain and traumatic feelings for years. Layla did not want to pass this legacy on to her own sons. Following the recommendation of her individual therapist, Layla invited her family to join her for family therapy. Her parents, Kurt and Alice, now ten years divorced and estranged, along with her older brother Jacob, agreed to attend. After years of conflict, Layla was hopeful that therapy could break through their family's rigid pattern of disconnection.

Stage 1—Stabilization and De-escalation

In the initial family session, the therapist inquired about what brought each person to this session, seeking to provide a content of safety and understanding that each person might have different expectations of the session. The parents revealed that they were concerned about the health of their son Jacob, who was abusing alcohol, and his distant relationship with Layla. Both parents acknowledged that they had not spoken to each other for several years, but that their current worries for Layla and Jacob made coming together a priority. The EFT therapist highlighted the parents' explicit caregiving intent in overcoming their distance to come to the session on behalf of their adult children. The therapist invited the family to share their experience as a family around their relationship struggles and the death of their son and brother.

The therapist focused on mirroring the present process and tracking the family responses as they entered into a conversation that they typically avoided. Jacob summarized his experience of the family's approach to issues in general, stating: "We don't deal with anything! We assume that time will heal and then we bury it all deep under the sand." Layla nodded in agreement and added that this has left them cut off with hurts that never get addressed or resolved. Through the session, both parents remained closed and non-communicative, avoiding each other's gaze and direct conversation. Layla and Jacob physically mirrored their parents cut off by sitting on opposite sides of the room and the emotional climate was tense as each individually expressed their concerns about the family. As their sharing unfolded, the therapist focused on the emerging relational blocks becoming clear in the conversation and summarizes the family's dilemma by reflecting on the present moment and validating their experience.

THERAPIST: What I notice as we sit together, is just how quiet everyone is, and how hard it is for all of you to give voice to your feelings. I just heard you, Jacob, say this is what happens in our family everything gets buried. And you Layla, you continue to say there is a lot of pain underground in this family and it has always been that way. And I am noticing now, for both, mom and dad, there is a lot of silence and I am thinking there must be some very good reasons why not saying anything, feels like that is the safest thing to do? (*parents both look down and nod their heads*) Can you help me Kurt, what happens for you when you hear your children speak about their disconnection and loneliness in this family? (*evocative question*)

FATHER: I'm not sure what to say exactly. I am always alone now and really always have been.

THERAPIST: So, when your son says everything in this family gets buried, I am wondering what that is like for you to hear this as I know you said in the beginning that you were worried about him, and that you as his dad want to help your son (*evocative question, reflecting parental caring intention*)

FATHER: Absolutely, but I also know that I cannot control Jacob, he is so headstrong I can only control myself and when the two of them are fighting I am always getting caught in the middle, or if he is fighting with his mom I cannot help because we were not speaking until recently.

THERAPIST: Right, I hear you, and you have had to do that all alone, for some time now, right? You have had to take responsibility for yourself and ended up feeling helpless?

FATHER: I have been sober 10 years now, but it is still one day at a time. I have taken responsibility for my role in this family mess and I have apologized so many times to my ex-wife and my children for withdrawing from everyone after my son killed himself. I could not deal with the pain or the guilt and certainly could not face Alice knowing she still blames me for everything.

THERAPIST: That's a big step, to take that action as you have these last few weeks and face your family. To do something big like that, for your family. Is this also a message you are trying to send Jacob? To your family? A hope to make things better for your family by facing your biggest fears?(*validation, reinforcing parental intent*)

FATHER: Yeah, I guess so, but it is a bit late (*pauses, then weeping responds*) ten years too late, given that our son shot himself with MY gun. (*the room goes silent and Alice begins to cry along with Layla as Jacob moves closer to his father*)

THERAPIST: This is really hard to talk about your son, and his death. I can see your face just went still and you started to cry, and for you Alice the mention of your son and how he killed himself brings you immediately to tears.

MOTHER: (*crying*) Kurt and I have treated one another like the other did not exist for the last 10 years. It has just been too painful to interact with him after my David's death. To hear him trying to do the right thing for us, feels great but doesn't cover up the pain and horror of losing our son. I also feel tremendous guilt from that day and how everything has been handled since then, it kills me when my only two children are fighting or angry with me. I have only just begun to see how any conflict with either one of my children, sends me into complete terror. (*she begins to cry more and takes a deep breath, then looks up at Layla*) I fought with my son before I left to the store that day. I feel such tremendous guilt for not stopping and making things right before I left him in the house, and now when any fight starts it sends me over the edge. That is why I just stayed away from Kurt for ten years, I couldn't face another conflict, so I let him disappear.

THERAPIST: Alice, what I am hearing from you is that the pain doesn't go away, the guilt stays right there too, and no amount of time really makes the pain of losing your son in such a tragic way go away. That is something you and Kurt will share forever, and right now, that pain is alive in this room. (*validation, heightening, focus on present moment*) It feels like this is still not a conversation you and Kurt had, until recently during our time together in treatment. And before this last week, actually, no one has ever felt safe enough to talk about what happened to your son. You have all been so alone in this loss. It was so extremely overwhelming to lose your son to suicide, but what I am hearing is that you also lost each other during this trauma in your family. No one was talking or sharing with one another during the aftermath of David's death. It was like David's death fractured all the relationships in the family, no one could rely on anyone anymore because everyone was falling apart.

MOTHER: (*taking a big breath*) Well, their father and I have dealt with this best way we could and we ended up divorced. Now, we need to focus on Jacob and Layla because if they are not ok, Kurt and I will not make it another year. I cannot handle the stress of anyone fighting, it may be a little easier now that Kurt is getting more involved, but I am still afraid. (*tears rolling down her face with struggling to catch her breath*)

THERAPIST: As their mother you don't want to forget them and their feelings. You want to make sure you and Kurt are there for them now in ways you could not be there for each other or them, after David died. I can see in your eyes how important this is to you, there is a big part of you in pain knowing that Layla and Jacob felt so alone during the aftermath of David's suicide. That's why you are here today right? (*reflecting parental intent*) You have taken an important step here, to show a lot of courage in talking about what previously no one spoke about. Can I ask you, Jacob and Layla, what's it like for you to hear your parents talk about the time in the family after David died?

LAYLA: (*sarcastically and contemptuously*) No one says his name! Not one of you has uttered his name in ten years! So it feels a little strange to sit in this conversation and hear them both use his name period not to mention it is already extremely new for them to even be acknowledging one another. My parents literally have not seen one another or talked since the divorce and I would even say since David died. It is bad enough we lost our brother and I am sure we all feel guilty about that, but to lose everyone all at once made it even worse. It is so painfully obvious we have not put his death to rest. We are all so raw and yet when we do have the opportunity to talk, or hear one another, we just shut them out. No one wants to open up that box.

"No one says his name" symbolized the impact this traumatic loss had on the family and their subsequent solitary efforts to cope with unspeakable loss and grief. That day's shock fractured the family and the way they had interacted with each other for the last 20 years. Each family member sought emotional stability through self-protective strategies that buffered them from the pain of an incomprehensible loss, the suicide and feelings of helplessness and horror that have continued to echo in silence through the family. As Johnson noted, the aftermath of trauma can be like, "an absorbing inner state and a corresponding way of engaging the world, whereby, after a while, everything leads into a sense of darkness, helplessness and hopelessness and nothing leads out" (p. 21). This session highlighted the relational blocks in the family's avoidant pattern. The numbing effect of their avoidance became maladaptive as it blocked new information and growth and stunted this family's emotional engagement.

In the following session the therapist framed their negative pattern using the phrase "code of silence" to externalize the pattern of avoidance that had taken hold of the family in many ways. First, Layla's heightened awareness of her own pain led her to bring her family to therapy. Her position was framed as asking the family to wade into the emotional waters that they had all previously resisted. Jacob's drinking was reframed as a way of numbing out the things that felt terrifying and intolerable for him to know, which also left him riddled with anxiety and forced to drink to mediate his distress. The therapist described Kurt and Alice's avoidance of each other as a way to mitigate their personal pain as when they came in contact they saw their own pain reflected in each other's eyes.

Psychoeducation about the impact of trauma, and specifically suicide was also offered as a way to help normalize and validate the family's current functioning and to provide an antidote to the shame they were feeling. Finally, hope was offered to this family, their courage and strength was recognized as well as their openness and willingness to speak together. The therapist ended the session by painting an image of this family becoming a safe harbor for all and that the therapist's intention was that their future conversations together would lead them into that refuge.

Following the initial family sessions, a parent session and sibling session with Layla and Jacob were arranged. Typically, in EFFT, the whole family session is followed by these assessment meetings to develop a coherent story about the parenting alliance, the traumatic experience, and the connection between the two. A similar process occurs with the sibling subsystem. The separation of parents and children allows both groups to have conversations in a context that allows greater freedom to speak about difficult issues and for the therapist to explore with each group their attachment fears and longings. The more concentrated time also helps deepen the therapeutic alliance, create more opportunity to assess for safety and build on existing strengths and to set the stage for future family sessions.

The parent sessions were extremely difficult for both Kurt and Alice as they had not spoken directly for over ten years. The first session the therapist listened to their concerns regarding their children, especially Jacob. They described their sense of helplessness regarding his drinking and at one point in the session Alice snarled "it runs in the family," to which Kurt went silent and turned away. The therapist reflected this moment in the session, and asked how it was for them to be sitting together right now. Alice became annoyed with the therapist and stated she was not in session to talk about their past relationship "because that was dead long ago" but to talk about how they could help Jacob and Layla. Alice blamed herself for being so weak and staying in a bad marriage too long. The therapist apologized for the misstep and reinforced the strength of both parents to put aside their differences to be there for their children. It was important in this session, to build an alliance with Alice and Kurt and be sensitive to the shame they were feeling about their divorce and the impact of their relationship on their children. The therapist offered some concrete help for Jacob in terms of a referral and both individuals expressed gratitude that the therapist was offering help. The EFFT therapist reinforced that their involvement with Jacob and Layla was crucial and that they were irreplaceable as their parents. Even as adults, Jacob and Layla still needed their parents and the therapist wanted to help them be able to talk together and break the "code of silence." Alice and Kurt agreed to this treatment plan and another session was scheduled.

Alice began the next session focusing on Kurt and his "alcoholism and emotional abandonment" of both Jacob and Layla. The therapist supported Alice in her concern for her children and reflected her frustration, wondering if her loss of Kurt as a co-parent was a particularly difficult for her. Alice opened up more about her experience following David's death, stating,

> When David killed himself with Kurt's gun, Kurt came home from a hunting trip and packed all his weapons up, including the one David used to shoot himself and never spoke to any of us again. He stayed outside gardening and getting drunk for ten years, until I divorced him.

The therapist continued to validate how alone Alice had been and how hard this must have been at a time when she would have been the most vulnerable and the most devastated. As Alice began to soften and her eyes filled with tears, she quietly said "He blames himself for the divorce and for David's death and so do I, we never got over that and we never even tried." Kurt remained silent as Alice spoke but his face flushed and he shifted uncomfortably in his chair. The therapist acknowledged how hard it must be for him to listen to Alice and her account of the years following David's death and invited him to talk about how this period had been for him. Kurt stated that he "didn't remember much" about that time but that Alice got what she always wanted with the divorce.

The EFFT therapist followed Kurt's emotion, validated his anger which led him to express more directly his anger at himself and "how not a day passes when I don't think of how I killed my son." The therapist accepted Kurt's horrific shame and guilt and acknowledged how incredible it was that given that level of pain, he could remain sober. Kurt broke down and sobbed which triggered Alice's tears, and she held her head and wept. The therapist held the space for the parents to grieve and offered her support to them, as they were unable to support each other. The therapist made sense of their pain and the help-lessness often experienced in the face of the enormity of their grief, which made many marriages vulnerable to dissolution. By making explicit Kurt's good intentions to use avoidance to manage his pain, the therapist helped Kurt see the cost of his avoidance, leaving the rest of his family alone in face their pain. Recognizing the negative pattern motivated Kurt to come up with a different response.

A follow-up session was set for Alice and Kurt to process further the expression of grief and shame that had been shared between them and to understand further how the impact of the trauma on the two of them reverberated with their children. Kurt was surprised and embarrassed by the vulnerability he had experienced and was confused as to the meaning of what had transpired between them. The therapist reflected Kurt's new definitions of himself as it related to his role as father. "You were able to show yourself so clearly, the grief that you carry about your son, David. You took that chance because this is something that you live with daily and that takes strength and tremendous courage." Alice supported Kurt in his disclosure, stating that it helped her under-stand him more and what had happened between them. She was able to talk about how she had "just got busy" after David died and that she needed to be strong and financially support the family. She revealed with sadness that she "has never been able to process deeply her true feelings with anyone" as she often attempted to "not go there."

As the therapist gently explored and held Alice, she revealed that she couldn't let her remaining children down like she had let David down, and that "really I didn't deserve to be sad." Again, the therapist vali-dated and made sense of Alice's regret, guilt, and shame and placed it in context of the way she interacted with her family, helping her to see that as she "over functioned and tried to make everything go away and be more positive," her strategy to be there for her children had inadvert-ently left Layla and Jacob alone emotionally. Both parents by the end of this session were able to see how their attempts to survive the enormous pain and guilt of this tragic loss, blocked their ability to be emotionally accessible and available to Layla and Jacob. They were encouraged by the therapist to take this opportunity now to be there for their children in different kind of way that was now possible given their demonstrated ability to break the "code of silence."

The sibling session was focused on strengthening the relationship between Jacob and Layla. They reported that they were "not close" as they had different values and lifestyles and according to Jacob "not much of a relationship." The therapist tracked their interactional pattern and was curious about how the distance between them began from each of their perspectives. Jacob stated, "When David killed himself, our entire family disappeared. We didn't just lose our brother, it was like everyone was murdered and no one was talking about any of it." Layla became visibly sad when her brother said this, and when the therapist explored her emotion, she stated she was "all alone" from the moment she entered their home on the day David died.

Both Jacob and Layla had similar negative experiences around the "disconnect of our parents and that when David died we lost everyone, not just him." As the therapist made sense of the disconnect between them as resulting from the trauma of David's death, Layla moved away from her role as family "case manager" to sharing with her brother the events of that day. Jacob was unaware what had transpired and apologized to his sister for never asking her if she was ok and never actually knowing the facts of that day. The therapist supported the bonding conversations that Layla and Jacob were having, summarizing the work they had done.

THERAPIST: You two really have so much in common, this shared grief, that you have carried alone, both coping in your different ways. But right here, right now, you are doing something so different and letting one another into this space that has always been closed off. When you lost David, you also lost each other and your parents, the whole family felt like it was demolished. It seems so important to name this as being the largest injury to the family, surviving the feelings about your brother's death alone. I think this is a good place for us to start as a family once we get everyone in the room. Layla, would you be willing to open this conversation up in a different way with your parents if we invited them into this session?

LAYLA: The idea terrifies me! We haven't talked in this way in so long. As long as my mom isn't shutting me down right away and Jacob stays next to me I feel like we could go there.

The therapist decided after these family and subsystem sessions that the family was de-escalated and ready for the deeper work of Stage 2. Both parents expressed a desire and demonstrated increased emotional accessibility and responsiveness toward their children while also acknowledging some of what blocks their engagement. All family members have a better understanding of their cycle of mutual avoidance, and how the impact of David's death is still driving the lack of safety and security within the family unit. For the first time, the family is united in wanting to change their patterns of disconnection.

Stage 2—Restructuring Interactions

The next family session included both parents and adult children and the therapist summarized the efforts the family had made in the parent, sibling, and previous family sessions. The therapist framed the struggle the family faced to overcome the "code of silence" that blocked family members' sharing the loss and loneliness they experienced in their grief. Layla responded bursting into tears over the family's inability to have a "real conversation" and the impact she saw this having on her young children who sought to understand the death of their uncle. Reacting to the intensity of Layla's response, Alice tried to redirect her attention to the good steps the family has taken and the ways she (Layla) has been a good mother to her children. The relational block between mother and daughter is evident in this interaction as mother tries to still her daughter's pain and protest rather than make space for her vulnerability. The EFT therapist shifts the focus to the present process and through reflection and validation of the parent's attempts and refocusing on the importance of his death.

THERAPIST: (to Alice) Alice, I see that you are trying to be a good mom to Layla right now, I see that in how you are reaching out her, but I am hearing something a little bit different. Can I help you with this? (to Layla) What I am hearing right now Layla, is that what you are really longing for is a chance to talk, about your experience, as a young girl who experienced the trauma of finding your brother and what that was like for you to carry this for so long, all alone?

Layla expressed her doubts that her mother really wanted to hear her, and her fear that what she had to say was too much for her to hear, and that she didn't want to cause anyone in her family pain. She was afraid that her mother might break down, her father might relapse, and she knew her brother was struggling too. The therapist reflected Layla's fear and reframed her experience as an invitation to engage the mother's caregiving intention and explore new opportunities for her mother and father to respond to Layla's concerns. Both parents responded to the daughter's fears with reassurance as the therapist reflected Layla's fears to the parents, and the therapist in turn invited the parents to share this directly with Layla. Alice responded by acknowledging her tendency shift to the positive but in this moment, she recognized how important it was for her to be present in a new way. One that she was not able to do in the past. Kurt spontaneously reinforced this message, stating that he knew he hadn't been available, and this was "horrible" for him to see how he had let his daughter down. Speaking directly to Layla, Kurt offered reassurance that as her parents they would be able handle what she had to share.

THERAPIST: (*to Layla*) So I hear your mom saying she wants to know, and I hear your dad saying he is also here, what's that like for you Layla to hear your parents wanting to be there for you in a way they haven't before? (*first step of EFT tango, mirror present process*)

LAYLA: Confusing and uncomfortable I am not sure I can rely on their words.

THERAPIST: I can see that. Is this a good thing or is this something that you don't know what to do with?

LAYLA: Yeah, for sure, I have never had this happen and my dad barely hugs me.

THERAPIST: (*softly, slowly*) Right, this wasn't your experience, this wasn't what happened 20 years ago, when you were all alone? (*Layla's face looks fearful, eyes open wide*)

THERAPIST: This is hard, this is scary, you are so brave, and your mom and dad are right here, do you see them? (*reminding Layla she is safe in the room as she looks at her parents and says quietly, "Yes"*)

THERAPIST: You see that you are not alone right now but there was something so awful and so terrible 20 years ago that happened when it was so overwhelming and so hard for you as a young girl to manage. You were only 14. (*second move of the EFT tango, assembling affect and deepening*)

LAYLA: I was so scared. I didn't know what to do. (*crying, covers her face with her hands, starts to tremble*)

THERAPIST: Yes, of course, it was way too hard to see, and right now, you are telling us just how scary it was. How overwhelmed you were, and of course anyone would be. You are being so brave to share this moment, this memory. How are you feeling right now?

LAYLA: I feel sick to my stomach. I can still see his body lying there, I was terrified when I walked through the door and saw the blood everywhere. I originally thought he was passed out. I really thought someone had just hurt my brother while robbing our house. That was my first thought and I so wish it had been true. (*sobbing*). When I rushed over to see him, I saw the gun in his hand and he was unrecognizable, clearly had used my dad's gun to shoot himself in the head. There was blood everywhere ... I tried to throw a bed sheet over him but got scared and I just started to scream for my mom. We had left him home alone while we went to the grocery store. We left annoyed at him for not coming to help us. (*Layla collapses into her seat and starts to sob more deeply*)

THERAPIST: (*reflecting sadness in her voice*) Yeah, I can see the pain and terror right now in your eyes, I know how hard this is to share this and what you saw, and what you went through. I want you to know I am right here with you. (*Layla looks up at the therapist and begins to mirror her breathing, as she had practiced with the therapist. Slowly Layla began to talk through what happened that day which she was not able to do previously*) You must have been so afraid and in so much horror when you saw your brother had shot himself. You were going to him expecting to see his face and then to see the trauma, the gunshot wound. This must have been just so awful? Facing this trauma first, and then also by yourself, is just too much. This is just too much for a 16-year-old to manage and to hold. This is what you have held alone for all these years, the images, and the pain of what you saw. Your mom never saw what you saw, the sheet was placed over him by the time she ran in. When David made the decision to kill himself it ripped apart your entire world and your safety in the world with others. You had to try all alone to make sense of this very traumatic scene and also why your brother killed himself and process your own feelings. Losing a brother is devastating enough, but to lose him in this way and feel all alone must have felt overwhelming, and incredibly scary. (*reflecting and validating her experience the therapist uses a summary statement to help organize the intense emotion*)

LAYLA: (*shaking her head to try to regain her composure and stop her tears*) My mom came in shortly thinking that I was screaming about the dog. So, when she came into his room, she saw the blood and sheet over his head. She fell to her knees screaming. Somehow, she knew what had happened when she saw the gun. I had to move toward her, she was losing it, I tried to talk to her, but she just kept saying "call 911, call 911," over and over again. The police came within minutes and she was taken away because they could not calm her down. I just kept telling myself "this isn't about me, I have to protect my Mom." It wasn't about me at all, it wasn't my fault and I was afraid, in shock, and … I was going to lose my mom too if I didn't keep it together, so I stayed quiet and started cleaning up my brother's room and putting the groceries away. Looking back now, I know I think I was in shock. (*Layla looks now up toward her family, as if to tell them she was in shock on that day and wanted them to know. She kept looking in her father's eyes as if to make sure he was with her. She noticed her mom wasn't making eye contact and looked quickly away back to her dad*)

THERAPIST: Right, that makes so much sense that you would be looking even now to see if they are with you, you put aside how you were feeling on that day, but today feels different. Back then when you walked in and saw what had happened ... all those feelings had to be shut down. There wasn't anyone there to help you and then when your mom came she was overwhelmed and losing it. You knew you needed to protect her and call for help. You had to call 911 and get some help for your brother and for your mom, you couldn't fall down and scream from fear and the pain of knowing your brother was dead just after you left him at home alive. There was no one to turn to in that moment.

LAYLA: (*making eye contact with her mother*) Yeah and that was the last time we ever talked about that day or my brother's suicide. It has been 20 years, since he died and today is the first day I even told them that I was the one who put the sheet over his head. I never told them this, they all thought he had done that to protect them, but it was me. It was me who did that. I protected you from the awfulness of how he looked mom, but I didn't mean to silence this trauma and myself for 20 years. (*Layla's voice elevates, and she becomes more upset as she recalls this detail*)

THERAPIST: Yes. Layla, you didn't mean to shut down everything you felt and saw for 20 years. You have had to hold this all by yourself, and that's been so painful to be alone in that memory of your brother's body. Yet, you are talking about it now and that is so incredibly brave of you. I am wondering if you could tell your mom right now, what actually happened for you that day? You were just a 16-year-old girl whose world turned upside down and you deserved to be cared for too, but you had to control your feelings and keep them away from your mom. She was so upset already, you couldn't tell her what you saw because she was already being taken away from you, in your mind you had to stay under control, no one was accessible to you emotionally in that moment. (*engaging encounter, third move of the EFT tango*)

LAYLA: (*looking at Alice*) I felt so bad for you. I knew your pain was bigger than mine. You had the fight with him before we left and you called him "annoying." I knew you would never be the same, and if you needed to believe he tried to protect you with the sheet, then I wasn't going to tell you if that was the only thing that helped.

THERAPIST: (*moving in close to Layla, touches her knee, speaking softly*) And what about your pain Layla can you say something about your pain on that day? It feels important that we share that today.

LAYLA: (*sobbing*) I felt so guilty too mom, he told me he was in trouble, but I didn't ever think he'd kill himself. I feel so awful, I wish I would have just been more available to him like I am to my boys. I am so panicked all the time to leave them, the terror of making one wrong move haunts me daily, walking in my house I constantly worry. It is like my body knows something is coming. I am in constant worry especially if something went wrong that morning before school.

As Layla turned to her mother both parents reached toward their daughter to comfort her. Alice spoke of her regret and guilt over not seeing the pain Layla was suffering. Reassuring her with their words and contact both parents acknowledged her strength and bravery in sharing this pain and reiterated their intention not to leave her facing this alone. Layla shared how different it was for the family to share their experiences together and to know now that she did not feel she had to hold the whole entire story alone. The therapist processed the experience of Layla enacting her need for comfort and reassurance and the impact that her parent's attuned response had on her fears and pain. Jacob joined his parents in reassuring his sister. He expressed his pride in his sister while reaching out to hold her hand. Through their contact and shared experience, the family began to experience the shroud of shame and guilt begin to lift as each family member spoke directly about their grief and how they struggle to endure such a horrific loss. Layla stated that it made a huge difference to her to know that everyone in the family felt the same way as she did and that now she didn't feel she had to hold the whole entire story alone. The therapist is following the EFT tango processing the enactment experience and expanding its impact.

As the session concluded the focused shifted to making meaning of what the family had done together in the session. The therapist reflected on the shifts family members made in relationship to the difficult emotions that had driven them apart including the shame-filled responses to David's death and the silence that evoked between them. Their isolation locked the family into patterns of distance and disconnection even though what each needed was contact and concern from the others in the family. This focus on integration and validation of the positive impact of their engagement is the fifth and final move in the EFT tango. As they moved the hugs around the room and with different dyads, Layla said she "believed the dam has been opened and she was worried if she had the strength to let it out slowly…. I do feel like we took a step forward and can possibly talk about some of this now." And finally, the haunting of her brother's death could be shared as a team instead of burdened by just her alone. Layla smiled softly as she as felt her father lean over and hugged her again after hearing what she said. The sheet had been lifted off her feelings and her experience, finally, and her parents were no longer blocked and were able to run toward her.

This family moved quickly to new healing conversations through additional family sessions where Layla was able to directly ask her parents for comfort and support. These sessions also focused on Jacob taking a similar initiative with his own needs. Jacob described his own pattern of coping that included using alcohol to drain away his hurt and his fear of sharing his pain with his already devastated parents. His pattern of avoidance led to abuse, dependency, and feelings that he was a disappointment to his parents. In these sessions, Jacob shared his belief that everyone in the family saw him as "a loser" including himself.

Jacob's vulnerability provided new opportunity for his parents and his sister to respond with reassurance about their love for him. Jacob was able to process more of his fears and negative view of self within the family that was now accessible and safe to him.

Stage 3—Consolidation

The third stage of therapy, consolidation, is generally marked by a shift in the family climate and families are now able to integrate a new narrative of themselves and their family unit. It also allows families to revisit old problems with new solutions and more specifically to face the dragon of the trauma together. The goal of EFFT is to replace negative patterns of interaction leading to disconnection with vulnerable experiences of connection in order to strengthen the family's emotional bonds and promote healthy affect regulation and family resilience. In the beginning of the therapy, the EFFT therapist is assessing the echoes of trauma and its influence on the relationship distress between family members and each individual's ability to process information clearly and regulate their own emotional experience. In Stage 2 the family confronts the trauma together and discovers in the process that the echoes of trauma don't have to drive them apart but can actually bring them together. Now in Stage 3 the family wants to implement these new responses and changes into everyday life.

A final follow-up session was conducted with the family, a couple of months later. The family recounted how they had come together to share the twentieth anniversary of David's death and Layla recounted that while the pain and trauma of David's death had become less, the memories of him and who he was in their family never fully recedes and "at least now I am not hiding myself or my feelings." Layla described talking to her sons about David in front of her parents and proudly witnessing how easily her sons trusted and received comfort in their fears. The family emotional climate had shifted as there was an ease and openness between all family members and a flexibility between Alice and Kurt that allowed them to mutually enjoy their children.

The therapist helped the family integrate how they were now in a different place, with open and positive interactions between them. The family was also reporting that as conflicts came forward between them, they were more likely to work it through than blast out at each other and not speak for months. Together they began stepping into the emotional memories and feelings around David's death. They navigated the part of the story they have never shared with one another and found a more centered understanding and felt sense of what happened in their family after David's death. These new-found interactions became life giving and comforting and created a new empowering narrative about their family. This family was now facing fears together and honoring the legacy of David's life, working hard toward a mission to prevent teen suicide by telling their stories and the danger of emotional isolation. Layla was able to feel a sense of agency over the familiar surges of emotion when she tells the part of the story where she was left alone right after her brother's death. The family was finally working together, holding the pain of their son and brother's death as a team left all of them feeling more connected in the world and more able to reach deeper levels of connection with one another.

Conclusion

As this case and the growing literature on attachment theory suggest, EFFT appears to be a promising option in the treatment of trauma. The ill effects of trauma such as hyperarousal, irritability, flashbacks, trouble concentrating, avoidance, dissociation, and isolation all share a common trait of difficulties with affect regulation. Trauma survivors find themselves stuck fluctuating between the hyperarousal of the sympathetic nervous system or the numbness of the parasympathetic nervous system. Helping survivors learn to quiet their physiological arousal and modulate their emotional state is essential to healing and growth.

The social support of family bonds provides assurance of a natural environment for healthy affect regulation. Close connections to significant others play a significant role in making individuals trauma resilient, meaning they are more protected from the impact of a trauma before an event happens and quicker to recover after exposure to a traumatic event. Family members whose caregivers are emotionally responsive are well positioned to confront the fears, suffering, and helplessness of trauma and in the process, discover greater authenticity, meaning, and connection.

References

2011/12 National Survey of Children's Health. Child and Adolescent Health Measurement Initiative (CAHMI), "2011–2012 NSCH: Child Health Indicator and Subgroups SAS Codebook, Version 1.0" 2013, Data Resource Center for Child and Adolescent Health, sponsored by the Maternal and Child Health Bureau. www.childhealthdata.org.

Ainsworth, M. D. (1964). Patterns of attachment behavior shown by the infant in interaction with his mother. *Merrill-Palmer Quarterly, 10,* 51–58.

Allen, J. (2001). *Traumatic relationships and serious mental disorders.* Chichester, England: John Wiley.

Charuvastra, A., & Cloitre, M. (2008). Social bonds and posttraumatic stress disorder. *Annual Review of Psychology, 59,* 301–328.

Clothier, P., Manion, I., Gordon-Walker, J., & Johnson, S. M. (2002). Emotionally focused interventions for couples with chronically ill children: A two year follow-up. *Journal of Marital and Family Therapy, 28,* 391–398.

Couture-Lalande, M. E., Greenman, P. S., Naaman, S., & Johnson, S. M. (2007). Emotionally focused therapy (EFT) for couples with a female partner who suffers from breast cancer: an exploratory study. *Psycho-Oncologie, 1,* 257–264.

Crittenden, P. M. K., & Heller, M. B. (2017). The roots of chronic posttraumatic stress disorder: Childhood trauma, information processing, and self-protective strategies. *Chronic Stress, 1.* https://doi.org/10.1177/247054 7016682965.

Denton, W. H., Wittenborn, A. K., & Golden, R. N. (2012). Augmenting antidepressant medication treatment of depressed women with emotionally focused therapy for couples: A randomized pilot study. *Journal of Marital and Family Therapy, 38,* 23–38.

Dessaulles, A., Johnson, S. M., & Denton, W. H. (2003). Emotion-focused therapy for couples in the treatment of depression: A pilot study. *The American Journal of Family Therapy, 31,* 345–353.

Dube, S. R., Anda, R. F., Felitti, V. J., Chapman, D. P., Williamson, D. F., & Giles, W. H. (2001). Childhood abuse, household dysfunction, and the risk of attempted suicide throughout the life span: Findings from the Adverse Childhood Experiences Study. *Journal of the American Medical Association, 286,* 3089–3096.

Dworkin, E. R., Ojalehto, H., Bedard-Gilligan, M. A., Cadigan, J. M., & Kaysen, D. (2018). Social support predicts reductions in PTSD symptoms when substances are not used to cope: A longitudinal study of sexual assault survivors. *Journal of Affective Disorders, 229,* 135–140.

Figley, C. R., & Figley, K. R. (2009). Stemming the tide of trauma systemically: The role of family therapy. *Australian & New Zealand Journal of Family Therapy, 30,* 173–183.

Goff, B. N., & Schwerdtfeger, K. L. (2013). The systemic impact of traumatized children. In D. R. Catherall (Ed.), *Handbook of stress, trauma, and the family* (pp. 179–202). New York, NY: Routledge.

Gordon-Walker, J., Manion, I., & Clothier, P. (1998). Emotionally focused intervention for couples with chronically ill children. A two-year follow-up. *Journal of Marital and Family Therapy, 28,* 391–399.

Greenman, P. S., & Johnson, S. M. (2012). United we stand: Emotionally focused therapy for couples in the treatment of posttraumatic stress disorder. *Journal of Clinical Psychology, 68,* 5, 561–569.

Hanson, R. F., Moreland, A. D., & Orengo-Aguayo, R. E. (2018). Treatment of trauma in children and adolescents. In *APA handbook of psychopathology: Child and adolescent psychopathology,* Vol. 2 (pp. 511–534). Washington, DC: American Psychological Association.

James, K., & MacKinnon, L. (2012). Integrating a trauma lens into a family therapy framework: Ten principles for family therapists. *Australian & New Zealand Journal of Family Therapy, 33,* 189–209.

Johnson, S. M. (2002). *Emotionally focused couple therapy with trauma survivors: Strengthening attachment bonds.* New York: Guilford Press.

Johnson, S. M. (2019). *Attachment theory in practice: Emotionally focused therapy with individuals, couples, and families.* New York: Guilford Press.

Johnson, S. M., & Faller, G. (2011). Dancing with the dragon of trauma: EFT with couples who stand in harm's way. *The emotionally focused casebook: New directions in treating couples* (pp. 165–192). New York: Routledge.

Johnson, S. M. & Rheem, K. (2012). Surviving trauma: Strengthening couples through Emotionally Focused Therapy. In P. Noller & G. Karantzas (Eds.), *The Wiley-Blackwell handbook of couple and family relationships: A Guide to contemporary research, theory, practice and policy* (pp. 333–343). Chichester: Blackwell.

Kilpatrick, D. G., Resnick, H. S., Milanak, M. E., Miller, M. W., Keyes, K. M., & Friedman, M. J. (2013). National estimates of exposure to traumatic events and PTSD prevalence using DSM-IV and DSM-5 criteria. *Journal of Traumatic Stress*, 26, 537–547.

MacIntosh, H. B., & Johnson, S. (2008). Emotionally focused therapy for couples and childhood sexual abuse survivors. *Journal of Marital and Family Therapy*, 34, 3, 298–315.

Mikulincer, M., Shaver, P. R., & Solomon, Z. (2015). An attachment perspective on traumatic and posttraumatic reactions. In M. P. Safir, H. S. Wallach, & A. "S." Rizzo (Eds.), *Future directions in post-traumatic stress disorder: Prevention, diagnosis, and treatment* (pp. 79–96). New York: Springer.

Olff, M. (2012). Bonding after trauma: On the role of social support and the oxytocin system in traumatic stress. *European Journal of Psychotraumatology*, 3, DOI: 10.3402/ejpt.v3i0.18597

Ozer, E. J., Best, S. R., Lipsey, T. L., & Weiss, D. S. (2003). Predictors of posttraumatic stress disorder and symptoms in adults: A meta-analysis. *Psychological Bulletin*, 129, 52–73.

Platt, J., Keyes, K., & Koenen, K. (2014). Size of the social network versus quality of social support: Which is more protective against PTSD? *Social Psychiatry & Psychiatric Epidemiology*, 49, 1279–1286.

Saltzman, W. R., Babayan, T., Lester, P., Beardslee, W. R., & Pynoos, R. (2008). Family-based treatment for child traumatic stress. In D. Brom, R. Pat-Horenczyk, & J. D. Ford (Eds.), *Treating traumatized children* (pp. 240–254). New York: Routledge.

Siegel, D. (1999). *The developing mind*. New York: Guilford Press.

Weissman, N., Batten, S. V., Rheem, K. D., Wiebe, S. A., Pasillas, R. M., Potts, W., ... & Dixon, L. B. (2018). The effectiveness of emotionally focused couples therapy with veterans with PTSD: A pilot study. *Journal of Couple & Relationship Therapy*, 17, 25–41.

Epilogue

Our combined efforts over the past two decades have generally focused on answering a simple question. What does EFT look like in family therapy? An important question, if one assumes that the practices and process of emotionally focused therapy as an empirically established intervention shown successful in promoting improvement and recovery from relationship distress in couples might also have similar benefits for family relationships. All the more important if one recognizes the principle role of attachment theory in parent and child relationships.

Throughout this period numerous authors have explored application of EFT to family therapy beginning with Susan Johnson's initial formulations (e.g., Johnson, 1996, 2004; Johnson, Maddeaux, & Blouin, 1998; Johnson & Lee, 2000). Our goal was not to set forth another model of family therapy or a different version of emotionally focused therapy. Instead we have sought to systematically describe the lessons learned from years of practice applying EFT to families. As such our observations in this text are derived largely from clinical practice and build upon the theoretical and empirical foundation that has been a driving force of innovation in EFT. This text offers therapists and researchers more explicit direction in the practice of EFT with families. This work then provides next step in the development of EFT's application to family therapy and an invitation to its ongoing development.

Lessons Learned

In summarizing our efforts, we conclude with the following lessons learned in our own practice of EFT with families.

1. EFFT Assumes Three Levels of Intervention Requiring Different Skills in Working with Emotion

Family Level. The EFT therapist joins the family through tracking negative interaction patterns and their disruptive influence on attachment and caregiving processes. The EFFT process engages the emotional

climate of the family and through accessing and processing the emotional realities driving insecurity in that system. These emotional experiences are made explicit and then engaged relationally. The power of
negative emotion to saturate family experience can shift the emotional
balance of the family to rigid inflexible patterns that connote a consistent negative family identity. The therapist must be able to track interactions and engage emotional experience across the family system. EFFT
requires establishing an alliance with each member and the family as a
whole.

Interpersonal Level. As in EFCT the EFT therapist's focus is primarily
on dyadic interactions where attachment significance and separation distress provide insight into the rigid positions that individuals take in
response to critical moments of need. In EFFT the therapist explores the
relational blocks that interrupt family members' ability to seek care and
connection from attachment figures or distort caregiving responses to
these needs. Whether with couples or families the therapist is remains
focused on these relational blocks and their power to organize an individual's insecure experience of the couple or the family as a whole. Working
through these blocks requires engaging attachment-related emotion and
meaning as the basis for engaging new relational patterns. The EFT
therapist uses evocative and processing interventions to engage these relational blocks in the session. These relational blocks are live in session and
the therapist must be able to engage these moments as opportunities
rather than obstacles to new experiences. The therapist choreographing
and engaging encounters through affect-rich enactments promotes a
deeper awareness of these opportunities for relational repair.

Intrapersonal Level. EFT explores the expectancies that parents and
children hold of the availability and support of others in the family
systems. Individuals' view of other or view of self in the family inform
the responses family members have to threats, difficulty, or challenges
experienced in the family. In families defined by distress or disengagement individual responses are informed by specific attachment-related
strategies (e.g., avoidance, anxious) that shape interactions that often
reinforce the felt insecurity within the couple or family system. These
relational blocks in families are transformed through corrective emotional experience where individual models of self and other are reviewed
through the experience of greater felt security. As families gain greater
security their interactions are characterised by increased coherence and
clearer communication of attachment needs and caregiving responses.
The EFT therapist's ability to work deeply with emotion provides family
members new experiences of themselves and others that inform the
assumptions families hold about security and availability in the family.
The therapist's use of affect assembly and deepening attachment-related
emotion is essential in promoting the motivation, engagement, and integration of more relationally secure family interactions.

2. EFFT Requires the Therapist to be Flexible in Engaging Different Levels of the Family System

One of the challenges in providing a systematic description of EFFT practice is accounting for the flexibility needed in treating families who vary as much in their composition as they do in their presenting problem. In EFFT the therapist attends to family process at a system and subsystem level privileging a focus on interactional blocks in caregiving that are typically understood as a key source of family distress. The EFFT therapist privileges the most distressed dyadic relationship to organize treatment.

The therapist may encounter more than one relational block in the family, and these may occur within different subsystems (e.g., parent–child; couple), regardless the therapist focus is on the most distressed dyadic interaction in the family. This does not however necessitate splitting up the family into a series of dyads, rather this focus guides the therapist's work within a family session. For example, in two-parent families the therapist may increase parental availability through the support of a partner while at the same time focusing on the specific parent–child relationship where this availability has been blocked. The EFFT Decision Framework provides a direction through anticipating the choices that a therapist must make in organizing treatment. EFFT requires flexibility from the therapist in organizing treatment that can shift and change depending on the dynamics and composition of a family and its presenting problem.

3. EFFT Requires Parental Openness to Change as a Function of De-escalation

De-escalation is the primary change event defining the completion of the first stage of the EFT process. In EFFT de-escalation is realized through the lessening reactivity of the negative interaction pattern typically associated with the presenting problem. In making this pattern explicit to family members the therapist is also acknowledging the negative impact the pattern has on the family using relational reframes to shift the focus from the presenting problem to the negative pattern that is amplifying distress in the family. In EFFT, we recognize that the pattern is experienced differently across the family and most acutely in the relational blocks that commonly contribute to the negative affect and separation distress that fuels the pattern. The EFT therapist identifies these blocks and rigid positions that family members hold in response, accessing and expanding their experience to acknowledge disowned or underlying attachment and caregiving related responses. Through this work the therapist highlights the separation distress in the family and highlights the child's struggle to risk reaching with these poignant needs.

Parental openness is essential in moving forward into Stage 2 of the EFFT model where accessing, expanding, and engaging a child's vulnerability is necessary for promoting the enactment of new positions. The therapist's focus on parental openness begins in aligning with parents regarding the goals of treatment. We euphemistically refer to this aspect of alliance building as gaining parental "buy in." Many a parent has felt blame implicitly in relation to the suggestion of family treatment for a child-specific problem. Parental shame is often a side effect of confronting behavior or emotional difficulties with children and the recommendation of family treatment can compound this sensitivity.

The EFT therapist in the family and parent sessions makes space for the different experiences and "realities" of the family. Paradoxically, honoring a child's pain or vulnerability can also trigger parental blame particularly when a parent's response to their child's pain is parental shame. Therefore, the therapist joins the parent's intention to expeditiously address the child problem and at the same time address the relational distress that accompanies this specific issue. Through the steps of Stage 1, parental caregiving intentions are accessed and deepened through identifying and validating the parents own negative experiences of the relational block. Exploring these blocks and parental intentions often opens attention to the parent's caregiving history and their own family of origin experiences. Parents may enhance empathy in caregiving through accessing these intergenerational experiences and their association with the parents' own childhood experience of caregiving.

4. Relational Blocks are Evidence of a Breakdown in a Foundational Family Resource

The breakdown of effective attachment and caregiving responses fuels negativity in the family as essential needs in the family go unmet and attempts to correct the failing system feed distortion of caregiving responses and attachment communication. Caregiving in parent and child and partner relationship is essential for exploration and growth. In EFFT the goals of parent and child relationships are different than the mutual intimacy goals of a romantic adult attachment. The EFFT therapist honors the unique responsibility that a parent has in responding to their child's needs for safety and security.

The EFFT process privileges this parental caregiving responsibility by assuring a parent's openness to exploring the relational block before shifting focus to deepening the child's attachment-related emotions and needs. As is common in other attachment-related family therapy treatment, blocks to parental caregiving are addressed prior to enactments of a child's attachment needs. The parent is the architect of security in the family system. This unique responsibility takes precedent over the mutual repair of an attachment relationship as is done in EFT with couples. Although accessing and repairing a couple's attachment and caregiving responses are essential to effective EFT treatment, in EFFT the focus for parents is on caregiving primarily and may include more mutual concerns when the therapist is focused on the parent's caregiving alliance.

Parental blocks to caregiving often reflect relational and intergenerational experiences. As noted above, a parent's availability is informed by that parent's attachment history. A father or mother's expectations, values, and awareness of their child may share influences with their earlier experiences of being parented. Alternatively, the negative behavior of a child and related consequences may also contribute to a parent's loss of empathy toward their child, particularly when their child's actions threaten others, violate moral values, or threaten control or domination (Norris & Cacioppo, 2007). In EFT, relational patterns are mutually determined with two partners often using different strategies to cope with a common dilemma, insecurity. In EFFT we recognize there are mutual effects of parent and child interactions that fuel insecurity and negative emotion, yet there are also other sources of insecurity that inform blocks to caregiving. In working through these blocks, the therapist recognizes the essential role of adult support as a resource for caregiving. As Kobak and Mandelbaum (2003) suggest: "change in families is most likely to occur with the caregiver when the caregiver establishes greater confidence in the availability of another adult" (p. 158). The EFT model provides a number of resources to strengthen the resources of a parent's partner through greater accessibility, responsiveness, and emotional engagement (Johnson, 2019). Strengthening support through the caregiving alliances promotes openness and exploration through greater security in the couple's relationships. The therapist also provides an important resource for parents, particularly in the absence either physically or emotionally of another caregiver. In EFFT, we also recognize that a caregiving alliance is a kinship connection and for some families this caregiving bond is not limited exclusively to two parent families.

5. The Enactment is the Repair

This is perhaps the most obvious lesson in EFFT but also its most profound. The enactment of a child's attachment-related emotions and needs from a position of vulnerability and the available presence of a parent's attuned and effective response is the correction of the relational block. The shift that occurs in families where caregiving and attachment communication is in sync generates the felt security and confidence that parents and children need to maintain an ongoing cycle of security (Kobak, Zajac, Herres, & Krauthamer Ewing, 2015). EFFT keeps family relationships in focus throughout treatment and promotes reparative enactments with family members to strengthen bonds across the family. The therapist fosters further exploration as the positive emotions associated with more secure connections invite new exploration and vulnerability within the family. The power of corrective experience in one relationship ripples across other relationships as the family regains its confidence and emotional balance. As the family shifts away from insecurity rather than facing the negative cascade of mutually reinforcing strategies of self-protection the family moves toward a positive cascade of experiences that reinforce felt security and promote exploration so that families are better able to launch their young and remain connected with flexibility and resilience in the face of life's adversities. Developmental outcomes are optimized within families where there is a dynamic balance of connection and growth (Johnson, Maddeaux, & Blouin, 1998).

Conclusion

For the EFT therapist, the restructuring of attachment and caregiving responses requires more than a communication exercise—and more than a parent's emotional awareness and acceptance of a child's needs. These are important resources to effective parenting, however each lack the necessary glue that an affectional bond provides to relationship repair. The EFFT therapist guides a family toward the deeper emotional resources found in attachment and caregiving interactions. As an attachment-based approach, EFT focuses on the reciprocal influences of intrapersonal experience and social interaction (Bowlby, 1977). The EFT therapist not only improves parent and child communication but enables families to deepen their shared engagement in the adaptive resources of attachment-related emotion. It is through reaching into and through these more vulnerable experiences that a family is able to find a deeper emotional channel of connection, trust, and confidence. How we meet in vulnerability ultimately matters to our life together. Jack Kornfield summarizes this essential question:

> The poet Rilke said, "Ultimately, it's upon our vulnerability that we depend." We depend on others when we're infants. We depend on others to stop at the red light so we can go through the green. In so many ways, we're interwoven with one another, and we're vulnerable. The question is, how do we hold our vulnerability? How do we navigate the ocean of tears and the unbearable beauty that make up life? How do we hold praise and blame, gain and loss, birth and death, joy and sorrow?
>
> (Kornfield, 2018)

The affectional ties that define family life provide a safe and sound connection that are a resource for safety in times of uncertainty and a sound foundation leading to growth and development. Paradoxically our ability to depend effectively on others not only secures our wellbeing but promotes our autonomy and optimal functioning (Feeney, 2007). Through EFFT the therapist leads families through corrective experiences that transform vulnerability into a strength, fear into reassurance, and isolation into connection. Following the process and practices of EFT, the therapist guides families through their blocks to find new resources, repairing relationships that ultimately matter. Those we prize most in being family, are those that offer belonging and invite becoming.

References

Feeney, B. C. (2007). The dependency paradox in close relationships: Accepting dependence promotes independence. *Journal of Personality and Social Psychology, 92,* 268–285.

Johnson, S. M. (1996). The practice of emotionally focused therapy: Creating connection. New York: Brunner/Routledge.

Johnson, S. M. (2004). *The practice of emotionally focused therapy: Creating connection,* 2nd Ed. New York: Brunner/Routledge.

Johnson, S. M. (2009). Attachment theory and emotionally focused therapy for individuals and couples: Perfect partners. In J. H. Obegi & E. Berant (Eds.), *Attachment theory and research in clinical work with adults* (pp. 410–433). New York: Guilford Press.

Johnson, S. M. (2019). *Attachment theory in practice: Emotionally focused therapy with individuals, couples, and families.* New York: Guilford Press.

Johnson, S. M., & Lee, A. (2000). Emotionally focused family therapy: Restructuring attachment. In C. E. Bailey (Ed.), *Children in therapy: Using the family as resource* (pp. 112–136). New York: Guilford Press.

Johnson, S. M., Maddeaux, C. Blouin, J. (1998). Emotionally focused family therapy for bulimia: Changing attachment patterns. *Psychotherapy, 25,* 238–247.

Kobak, R., & Mandelbaum, T. (2003). Caring for the caregiver: An attachment approach to assessment and treatment of child problems. In S. M. Johnson and V. E. Whiffen (Eds.), *Attachment processes in couple and family therapy* (pp. 144–164). New York: Guilford Press.

Kobak, R., Zajac, K., Herres, J., & Krauthamer Ewing, E. S. (2015). Attachment based treatments for adolescents: The secure cycle as a framework for assessment, treatment and evaluation. *Attachment & Human Development, 17,* 220–239.

Kornfield, J. (2018). What really heals and awakens. *Psychotherapy Networker, May/June.*

Norris, C. J., & Cacioppo, J. T. (2007). I know how you feel: Social and emotional information processing in the brain. *Social neuroscience: Integrating biological and psychological explanations of social behavior,* 84–105.

APPENDIX 1

Applying EFT Stages and Steps to Family Treatment

Stage 1. De-escalation and Parental Engagement

Stage 1 in EFFT is focused on providing families a safe and secure context for exploring the presenting problem and its relationship to negative interactional patterns that reinforce and restrict the family's relational resources. Family distress and reactive responses are de-escalated through accessing and processing the underlying emotions associated with the negative pattern and interactional positions. De-escalation is also evident in a parent's openness and flexibility in caregiving responses.

Step 1. Forming an Alliance and Family Assessment

In this initial step the therapist establishes an alliance with the family through acknowledging and validating individual family experiences, giving family members a voice into the treatment. The alliance focus also includes identifying and prioritizing parental initiative and goals for treatment. An assessment of family functioning is conducted, including the relevant family sub-systems (e.g., parental, couple, sibling, identified patient). The treatment process is defined based on safety and the priority of family members' relationship to the problem.

Step 2. Identifying the Negative Interaction Patterns that Maintain Insecure Attachment

The therapist explores the presenting problem and related family distress by tracking the interactional patterns that accompany the family's experience of the problem. Tracking focuses on identifying the actions, perceptions, and experiences of different family members in response to the direct impact of the problem-oriented pattern. Specific relationship blocks are identified and the level of problem-related distress for specific dyads is delineated.

Step 3. Accessing Underlying Emotions Informing Family Interactional Positions/Relational Blocks

Relational blocks to parental availability and child vulnerability are identified and the emotional experiences related to these blocks are accessed and expanded. The therapist focuses on processing parental blocks to accessibility, responsiveness, and emotional engagement and eliciting underlying emotions associated with the parent's caregiving role. Concurrently, the therapist elicits and expands the child's experience of the relational block accessing the underlying emotions associated with the relational block. Attention is focused on the impact of failed attachment bids and the child's reluctance to seek comfort or support from their attachment figures. Parent sessions focus on accessing blocks in the caregiving alliance and the impact of couple distress on parental availability.

Step 4. Redefining the Problem in Light of Relational Blocks and Negative Pattern

Following the accessing and processing of underlying emotions the family problem is reframed in terms of the negative interactional pattern. The rigid positions associated with the pattern are understood in light of the underlying emotions and relational blocks are framed as obstacles to effective communication of attachment needs and caregiving responses.

Stage 2. Restructuring Family Patterns and Positions

Stage 2 in EFFT is focused on active engagement of secure patterns of engagement of attachment needs and effective caregiving responses. The therapist heightens awareness to disowned aspects of self and other that inform attachment needs and caregiving responses. The therapist promotes acceptance of these experiences and clear support for their significance in promoting a more secure response in the family. The therapist facilitates new positions of secure responding through the sharing of attachment needs with attuned caregiving responses.

Step 5. Accessing and Deepening Child's Disowned Aspects of Self and Attachment Needs

The focus shifts to accessing and expanding a child's disowned attachment needs and negative views that block the child turning toward their parent. Deepening child vulnerability promotes access and identification with the child's attachment-related emotions, typically resulting from failed caregiving responses or relational injuries. The therapist's focus is on expanding these emotions and making opportunity for attachment needs to be identified and expressed.

Step 6. Fostering Acceptance of Child's New Experience and Attachment-Related Needs

In this step the therapist promotes the parent's accessibility, responsiveness, and emotional engagement with the child's vulnerability. The therapist provides support to parents in working through blocks to availability and promotes confidence in a parent's availability through engaging caregiving intentions and when appropriate enlisting the support of the caregiving alliance. Through processing a parent's reactions, the therapist provides support in organizing that parent's response to their child's attachment emotions and needs.

Step 7. Restructuring Family Interactions Focusing on Sharing of Attachment Needs and Caregiving Responses

Following on the identification of the child's underlying attachment needs and the parent's acceptance the therapist moves the parent and child to enact act these needs and caregiving responses. The therapist guides the new interaction maintaining a focus on the affective experiences of vulnerability shared in enacting and responding to the child's needs. The impact of the enactment is processed with the child and parent placing emphasis on the new experience and meaning that arise in these moments. The therapist explores the impact of these changes on the family and re-engages the steps of Stage 2 with other relational blocks that may remain.

Stage 3. Consolidation

In Stage 3 of EFFT the therapist's focus shifts to strengthening the new patterns of security in the family. This includes helping the family address past problems with new solutions found through exploring these issues in a new context of safety and security. Families are able to express new narratives of growth and connection that incorporate the changes they have made and steps they will take to invest in these new patterns of connection and care.

Step 8. Exploring New Solutions to Past Problems from More Secure Positions

The therapist uses positive experiences of the restructured relational patterns to enhance the family's confidence in felt security. Through this foundation the therapist leads the family in exploring past problems that remain from a new position of security. The therapist engages the flexibility and emotional balance that the family has a gained to address practical problems related to parenting and family functioning.

Step 9. Consolidating New Positions and Strengthening Positive Patterns

The final step in EFFT is focused on making meaning and investing in the new patterns of security that the family has found together. The therapist highlights ways the family is able to engage new patterns of security especially when triggered by past problems and negative experiences. Sessions focus on helping the family contrast past patterns with new interactions and experiences. Through this the family forms new stories about their family as a secure foundation for their future growth and challenges that await.

Index

Page numbers in *italics* denote figures.

Made in the USA
Las Vegas, NV
29 December 2023

83701576R00193